Business Enterprise in American History

Second Edition

MANSEL G. BLACKFORD
K. AUSTIN KERR
Ohio State University

HOUGHTON MIFFLIN COMPANY   BOSTON
Dallas   Geneva, Illinois   Palo Alto   Princeton, New Jersey

To Our Parents and Families

Cover credit: Charles Sheeler. *Steam Turbine*. 1938. Oil on canvas. The Butler Institute of American Art, Youngstown, Ohio.

Printed in the U.S.A.

Library of Congress Catalog Card Number: 89-80918

ISBN: 0-395-43300-2

ABCDEFGHIJ-MP-9543210/89

Contents

Contents

Contents

7 ■ Business in a Democratic Society: The Progressive Era

Contents

Contents

Contents

Contents

Preface

The second edition of *Business Enterprise in American History* again focuses on two themes: the history of the business firm and the history of government-business relations. Business history, in our view, is something more than the study of the firm. The firm is of course central to business history, but it is most broadly understood in the context of the society and the political system in which it operates and which the firm, in turn, influences. And in the democratic society that exists in the United States, the larger political setting in which the firm has evolved provides an added dimension to its story.

The text examines the evolution of the firm over three centuries of American business history. From colonial times to the present, the book explores the ways in which Americans channeled their entrepreneurial ambitions and entrepreneurship into the firms that did so much to transform and enrich America.

The history of government and business are inseparable in the United States. Thus, the text also probes the political and legal settings in which business has operated. Firms have developed and changed over the years because entrepreneurial opportunities have changed and because government policies have influenced what Americans could and could not accomplish in their business activities. Moreover, for much of U.S. history, business leaders have exercised considerable power in forming government policies. *Business Enterprise* examines these interrelationships: how the different aspects of business management, institutions, and entrepreneurship in American society fit together; how business and government interact in vitally important ways; and how public concerns in this democratic society have affected business.

Our book serves two types of students: history students who are particularly interested in learning more about American business and students enrolled in a business school curriculum who want a better understanding of the workings of the American business system. In many respects, this book presents students with a traditional treatment of American business enterprise. Two of the most important traditional features are the straightforward chronological format and the attention given to rapid changes experienced by the business firm during the nineteenth century. A less traditional approach is our emphasis on the twentieth century. Half of the book is devoted to the twentieth century and special attention is given to developments in American business during the decades following World War II.

CHANGES IN THE SECOND EDITION

This revised edition is substantially different from the first. The coverage of colonial America is enlarged. We have added significantly more material on the impact of the Industrial Revolution on society and highlighted farming as an important business endeavor. In addition, there is more coverage of the roles that women and minorities have played in shaping the nation's business traditions. Examples, especially in the last three chapters, have been updated, and the text incorporates the best recent scholarship.

A new feature is a list of important events at the beginning of each chapter. These timelines show developments in both business and history and will help the reader's comprehension of the period covered. Also, we have included more tables, maps, and figures to present important data clearly.

ACKNOWLEDGMENTS

We have been fortunate to enjoy the support of scholars across the country whose remarks, along with the comments of our students, have guided and encouraged us in the preparation of this revised edition:

Stanley Buder, *Baruch College, City University of New York*
Peter A. Coclanis, *University of North Carolina*
Lisa M. Fine, *Michigan State University*
Joseph M. Gowaskie, *Rider College*
Harry C. McDean, *San Diego State University*
Michael V. Namorato, *University of Mississippi*
Patrick D. Reagan, *Tennessee Technological University*
Morton Rothstein, *University of California, Davis*
Alex J. Sajo, *Kansas State University*
Larry E. Schweikart, *University of Dayton*

We offer special thanks to our colleague William R. Childs. On our own campus we are blessed with an administration, led by President Edward Jennings, who is supportive of our efforts to continue learning ourselves so that we might help others to learn and widen their horizons. We thank Professor Ronald Racster, the Associate Dean of our Business School, who has also supported our business history program. We appreciate Larry Harbaugh's help in digging out information to update this volume. And our thanks go to Lynn Fauss and Rick Cooper for guiding us past the stage of "computer wimp," and to Mike Szczepanik for answering arcane questions about Nota Bene, the word processing and text filing program that has done so much to ease our chores as writers and researchers; you have facilitated our work in immeasurable ways. Our colleagues G. Micheal Riley, Dean of the College of Humanities, Associate Dean Marvin Zahniser, and Warren R. Van Tine, Chair of our department, have been patient with our needs and problems, and we appreciate their fellowship.

K. Austin Kerr
Mansel G. Blackford

Introduction

> Business is the very soul of an American; he pursues it, not as a means of procuring for himself and his family the necessary comforts of life, but as the fountain of all human felicity. . . . It is as if all America were but one gigantic workshop, over the entrance of which there is the blazing inscription, "No admission here except on business."
>
> —FRANCIS J. GRUND
> *The Americans in Their Moral, Social
> and Political Relations (1837)*

Business, the name commonly given to the organization of the production, distribution, and exchange of valued material goods and services, permeates American civilization, and our book focuses on business as a central topic of American history. The central position of business in the history of America, as the quotation above suggests, has long been recognized by citizens and scholars alike. In examining American business history we will explore some of the institutions, practices, attitudes, and values that have evolved over more than three hundred years.

In our exploration we shall focus on two main topics in American business history: the development of the business firm and the development of government-business relations.

The first major topic of the history of business in the United States is *the development of the firm*. Business firms are institutions, and, like other human institutions, have changed over the centuries; thus, this book is in part about alterations in the American

1

business firm—the conditions that cause them and, in turn, their effect on American life. Firms, moreover, are built and run by people—entrepreneurs and managers. Entrepreneurs hold a position of central importance in the history of the firm, for they are the individuals who transform businesses in some important way. Entrepreneurs are innovators. They may observe and seize profitable opportunities, taking risks in doing so, or they may observe some new way of creating or organizing a firm and thereby alter the practice of business. The entrepreneur and the firm are thus inextricably linked, but not all firms, or all persons engaged in business, necessarily create new practices or new institutions. Throughout American history some individuals have operated established enterprises in routine ways, and naturally it would always be correct to refer to such individuals simply as businessmen or businesswomen. In modern times, such individuals are usually called managers or executives.

In the study of the firm, business history is closely related to economic history. Economic historians concern themselves with the larger forces—such as economic expansions and depressions—that shape the formation of material wealth. Those forces are the settings in which business firms arise, mature, and decline. Because business activities are economic activities, distinctions between business history and economic history are easily blurred. But business historians examine institutions, not larger economic forces. They study individual firms and the patterns of their development. Those patterns and the ways in which firms relate to one another comprise the business system. Business historians understand business firms as components, in modern times, of larger industries—steel or autos for example. Those industries, in turn, are parts of the whole economy.

The larger forces that economic historians study are of course important for an understanding of business history. Not only do the activities of business firms help create those forces, but the economic setting influences opportunities available to business entrepreneurs and managers. Business historians are concerned with individuals and firms seizing opportunities created by larger economic forces; so understanding those opportunities, having an awareness of the setting—the economic history—in which Americans have engaged in business provides a necessary dimension for understanding business history. Our book will briefly describe the economic contexts in which Americans engaged in business.

The second main topic of business history is the *development of government-business relations.* All business firms operate in environments framed by law and politics, among other things. Business entrepreneurs and business managers have always sought to influence government policy in this country. In addition, people affected by business firms—consumers and workers, for instance—have often tried to influence the legal and political framework in which business activities occur. The importance of government and politics to business, and the efforts of business owners to influence government policy are inescapable realities of American life.

In its second main topic, *government-business relations*—what is traditionally known as the political economy—the discipline of business history is closely related to political history. Business historians share a concern with political historians in seeking to understand how the political system of the United States has interacted with the business system of the nation throughout its history. Government policy and the framework of the law have helped shape the opportunities available for entrepreneurs, along with the evolving economic setting. Politics, broadly conceived, has always affected the strategies of American entrepreneurs and the structure of the American firm. In American society, furthermore, neither business leaders nor political leaders have ever been autonomous groups. Some business executives have been politicians and vice versa. Politicians have often defended or promoted some form of business practice. In brief, the two subjects of politics and business have always been closely intertwined throughout American history.

The student of business history should have two principal objectives: first, to learn about particular aspects of the history of the American firm and the American political economy; and second, to gain insights into the larger framework, the big picture, of the American business system. This book, in approaching the first objective, examines the appearance of new aspects of business at various times in American history. We will note, for instance, the appearance of cost accounting in business, and explain the reasons for its development as some entrepreneurs encountered unprecedented problems in the middle of the nineteenth century. Such matters as production management and marketing strategies were, at one time, a result of entrepreneurial innovation. So too were political policies, such as developing the nation's interior resources and regulating firm size and competition.

An understanding of these and other aspects of American business history will lead the student to the second objective, comprehending the larger framework of the American business system, which of course is vastly different now from the business system first established in North America by the British in the seventeenth century. When Francis Grund observed in 1837 that America was a "gigantic workshop," Americans had not yet witnessed the rise of "big business." We will tell the story of the growth of the giant firm and of how giant U.S. firms themselves changed as the nation matured. By looking at differences in business firms and government policies historically and by exploring how business and the political economy developed over many generations, the student will gain a better appreciation of how changes in the business world of the nineteenth century laid the foundations for the business world of the late twentieth century.

STAGES AND THEMES OF AMERICAN BUSINESS HISTORY

To help the student understand the main topics of American business history, we will identify and briefly describe significant parts of the larger story. Americans have bought and sold goods and services, used natural resources, developed and exploited technologies, and worked through government to shape their economy and society in ways that have exhibited both continuity and change over nearly four centuries. The overriding theme of American business history is the story of entrepreneurs who seized changing opportunities and who, in doing so, fashioned and refashioned the institution of the firm and the conduct of business.

The firm lies at the heart of business history, and the history of the American firm has been one of overlapping stages. At the first stage in colonial times, the most visible firm was *the general merchant and planter* who both led economic activity and dominated the colonies' social and political affairs. The general merchant and planter, sometimes referred to as "all-purpose" business firms, enjoyed wealth that could not be invested profitably in just one main economic activity, so investments went in a variety of, or "general," directions. For instance, the general merchant or planter might have concurrently engaged in the production, shipping, wholesaling, and retailing of goods.

In the British colonies in America, the general merchant and planter operated alongside of and in conjunction with small firms that specialized in just one activity. In the second stage, which began shortly after the conclusion of the American Revolution in

1781, those small, specialized firms proliferated in a national economy of expanding economic opportunities. In this second stage of *specialized businesses,* which characterized business history during Grund's time, opportunities enlarged so that even the general merchant and planter focused sizeable capital investments on one particular business activity, and the old colonial "all-purpose" firm disappeared.

The second stage in the history of the business firm lasted until about 1850, when new kinds of business institutions began to appear: these fundamentally differed from the firms of Grund's generation in size and complexity. Thus, in the third stage in the history of the American firm, some businesses grew large and became known as *big business.* After the midcentury, entrepreneurs saw advantages to investing very large sums of capital to construct complex human organizations termed "bureaucracies." A bureaucracy, quite simply, is an institution with a life of its own, which is independent from the lives of the persons who work for it and which applies expertise to the problems at hand on a continuing basis. A key to bureaucracies is the idea that they are "ongoing" institutions. The business bureaucracies that began to appear on the American scene in the middle of the nineteenth century did indeed last a long time, and some still exist today.

These new big businesses invested very large sums of capital in complex human organizations in order to apply their expertise toward integrating various processes concerned with either producing goods or providing services. Big businesses developed first in the railroad industry during the 1840s and 1850s to coordinate train services and make them more profitable. Big businesses developed in some forms of manufacturing later, after 1870, when using experts working in bureaucracies enabled firms to produce and distribute goods more profitably than small independent businesses could.

This third stage, big business, did not mean that small independent businesses disappeared as an institutional form in the way that general merchants and planters had earlier. Small business firms have existed side by side with big business firms in the United States since 1850. But because big business firms came to dominate transportation, communication, and many forms (but certainly not all) of manufacturing during the third stage, Americans emerged with a dual business system, one composed of "center" and "peripheral" firms. Center firms were (and are) big businesses. Since their beginnings in the railroad industry in the midnineteenth century and their spread into other lines of economic activity, center firms have tended to accumulate greater and greater sums of wealth and to have concentrated those assets into the hands of fewer and fewer institutions. In other words, big business as a type of enterprise did not replace small business. With fewer assets and less access to capital, small business firms tended to revolve around the periphery of the business world created by big business during the second half of the nineteenth century—so they are commonly referred to as peripheral firms.

Just as big business firms in the third stage brought institutional innovations that did not replace the specialized small firms of the second stage, so too in the fourth stage diversification and decentralization of most big business firms supplemented but did not replace older institutional forms. The fourth stage in the history of the American firm began to unfold in the 1920s and continues today. In the fourth stage of *diversification and decentralization,* big businesses started using their assets to enter more than one field of production, or more than one area of service. That diversification posed enormous administrative problems for the bureaucracies involved. The resolution of those administrative problems brought decentralization of authority within the firm.

The shaping and reshaping of the institution of the business firm over the centuries of American history occurred as responses by men and women to evolving opportunities. The availability of some opportunities, notably the abundant natural resources that European settlers found on the North American continent, were beyond human control. After the American Revolution, Americans shaped opportunities for business activity through government in a political process that after 1920 fully included women, and after 1965, blacks. A central theme of American business history thus has been cooperation between private business leaders and public officials to foster entrepreneurial opportunities. The resulting relationship between the governmental and business systems, or "political economy," is the second main subject of this book. Like the story of the business firm, government-business relations evolved in stages.

There have been three stages in the history of government-business relations in the United States. (In the colonial period, British subjects lived under a system known as mercantilism, which involved government direction of business activity in order to enlarge the power of the British Crown.) After the American Revolution began in 1776, the first stage in government-business relations was *developmental.* Quite simply expressed, Americans used the governments they controlled—local, state, and federal—to develop business opportunities. The first meeting of Congress in 1789 resulted in a tariff law designed both to raise revenue and to protect American manufacturers from competitors abroad, thus providing private individuals with enlarged opportunities to invest their resources in manufacturing firms. That developmental tradition expanded in the nineteenth century, and continues today.

The second stage of government-business relations, *regulation,* supplemented the developmental tradition established in the earliest days of the Republic. Regulation began in a modern form at the federal level with the establishment of the Interstate Commerce Commission in 1887. The development of regulation was usually a response of business executives, allied with political leaders, to develop a conscious policy of directing business activities in some desired direction. In 1887, regulation of railroads by a federal commission began because of a variety of impulses that can be summed up in the belief that governmental intervention was necessary to ensure the prosperity of carriers and the chances for shippers and passengers to use railroad services at a fair price. Federal regulation spread to other industries after 1900.

The third stage of government-business relations—*the new regulation*—is a more recent phenomenon, which began in the 1960s. It did not replace traditional developmental or regulatory policies. The new regulation was innovative in that the spirit guiding it was less involved in providing business opportunities for the producers of goods and services than the traditional forms of regulation have been. The new regulation aimed at protecting consumers, the rights of employees, and especially the chances of all citizens to live and work in a healthful environment. With the success of the maturing business system in producing unprecedented economic wealth, Americans, through the new regulation, expressed concerns that weighed issues of justice, fairness, and health against traditional practices of both government regulators and business executives.

CAPITALISM AND AMERICAN BUSINESS

Capitalism is the social and economic system within which the American business firm has developed, and it is central to the story of American business. *Capitalism* defies precise definition, but in general it can be characterized as the private ownership and control of the means of production. Under capitalism, people invest in factories and stores, and the expectation is that businesses will generate profits and that the owners of the businesses will motivate, discipline, and control their work forces. Individuals have been investing capital in anticipation of profits since ancient times; yet historians usually reserve the term *capitalism* to describe a modern—as opposed to medieval or ancient—phenomenon. Whatever core meaning is given to capitalism, it must be inclusive enough to embrace a way of thinking and certain institutions (such as business firms) and practices that have emerged from that way of thinking.

Americans generally take the capitalistic way of thinking so much for granted that they are only vaguely aware that any alternative ways of thinking exist. If it was business that was at "the very soul of an American," as Grund observed in 1837, probably only a few individuals gave more than routine consideration to that aspect of their souls. But, in order to understand the development of business in America, more reflection is necessary. Grund quite rightly perceived capitalism as a way of thinking, for he viewed Americans engaging in commercial activities not simply to provide for life's necessities but also to secure personal happiness. He recognized what is often an unspoken assumption of capitalism: that by engaging in business as a rational, profit-seeking activity that people measure in monetary terms, individuals can enjoy fuller, more rewarding lives. In other words, Americans see themselves and others who live in capitalist societies as men and women who participate in the production of goods and services, who value those goods and services, and who profit from them not simply to provide themselves with food and shelter but to benefit the entire society and, indeed, human civilization.

Capitalism is not and never has been a static business system. Like the business firm through which it worked, capitalism has developed over time. In 1837, Grund assumed that he was observing a nation most of whose citizens were either business entrepreneurs or individuals hopeful of becoming business entrepreneurs. Clearly, his society was a society of capitalism. Today most Americans are neither business entrepreneurs nor individuals hoping or expecting to become business entrepreneurs. The business system has changed radically from Grund's time. In the late twentieth century, most Americans either work for large corporate or government agencies or are employees, not owners, of smaller firms. Yet, although business institutions and entrepreneurial expectations of people have changed, the United States is still a capitalistic society. The structure of capitalism in the 1990s of course differs from the structure of capitalism in the 1830s. What remains the same is the assumption that by engaging in business or in providing some service for which there is a monetary reward, Americans are adding not only to their personal benefit but to the benefit of the larger society. The unifying idea between the two periods is the belief that much of that benefit could be measured in monetary terms.

While business in its broadest sense—the making and distribution of goods and services—exists virtually everywhere on this planet, capitalism does not prevail in the world. Indeed, only a minority of the world's peoples live under the capitalist economic system. In most societies of the twentieth century, public agencies organize the production and distribution of goods and services according to social goals, not according to the individual goals of investors, whether they be small entrepreneurs or giant corporations. This method of organizing society is called socialism. Narrowly speaking, *socialism* means the public ownership of the basic means of production and distribution in a society; more broadly speaking, it means that public agencies, claiming to act on behalf of the larger good, direct and control economic activities. Business, in the American sense, does not exist under socialism. Karl Marx, the nineteenth-century German historian and philosopher who wrote *Capital* and co-authored the *Communist Manifesto,* was the most important theorist of socialism. The economies of the Soviet Union and the People's Republic of China (although their systems have their own dynamic history) for instance operate in traditions that stemmed from Marx's theories—these systems were, however, changing in the late 1980s. In these nations, state agencies, not the interaction of businesses, determine the quantities and prices of goods produced and distributed in their economies.

Sometime around the middle of the twentieth century, the U.S. economy became a "mixed" economy. The term *mixed economy* refers to a special sort of partnership between government and business that matured in the United States in this century. A business system in which private investment decisions do not always guide the economy is generally called a mixed economy. At different times in American history, government has invested funds in projects that were considered too expensive and long-term, too developmental, to attract private investors. In the late 1930s the federal government invested public capital to pursue social goals as part of the effort to end the Great Depression. During both world wars the federal government invested capital to meet war production goals, and following World War II the federal government has continued to provide large capital amounts for defense industries. Never, however, have the public investments that created the mixed economy challenged the basic underpinnings of the American business system—private ownership and control of business enterprises.

If capitalism is a limited construct in the contemporary world, so too has it been a limited construct in the larger stream of history in which Americans have participated. American civilization had its roots in the civilization of Western Europe, and prior to 1500, feudalism was the social and economic system of Europe. Like capitalism, feudalism existed in different forms in different times and places. In general, feudal society organized human relationships through custom, tradition, and the authority of a few local, militarily powerful figures who protected their neighbors. In feudal Europe, Christian doctrines were also instrumental in organizing human relationships. In a feudal society, human happiness was attained not through business activities or the creation of material abundance, but rather through the individual leading his or her life according to established custom, tradition, and church law. Europeans of the feudal period devoted their resources to great cathedrals that served spiritual, rather than worldly business, functions, unlike modern Americans, whose society has built great office skyscrapers or highly complex factories.

We begin our history of American business with an examination of the feudal origins of business activity in Western Europe. When Europeans first came to North America in the seventeenth and eighteenth centuries, they brought with them European business institutions and practices that had been developed in feudal times. Europeans started coming to North America, however, at a time when feudalism no longer was the prevailing system. Thus, American business had its origins in both the disintegration of feudalism and the rise of capitalism.

Part 1 describes the foundations of American business to 1790 as part of the growth of capitalism in the western world. This part examines the founding of the North American colonies as business enterprises, traces the development of the colonial American business system, and by focusing on the political economy explores changes that occurred in that business system during the years of the American Revolution and its immediate aftermath. Part 2 examines the growth of specialized businesses resulting from new opportunities opening up in the early and midnineteenth century and assesses the roles government played in creating those opportunities. The rise of big business between 1850 and 1920 and the ways in which the development of big business altered government-business relations are the principal topics of Part 3. Part 4 looks at the spread of diversified, decentralized corporations in America between 1920 and 1945 and the changes that this type of business brought to the political economy. Finally, new forms of governmental regulation and promotion of business, together with a consideration of the still evolving business firm, constitute Part 5.

Selected Readings

For those who would like to pursue additional work on their own, at the end of each chapter is a list of books and articles that deal with the topics discussed in that chapter. However, several books deserve particular mention at the outset. Alfred D. Chandler, Jr., *The Visible Hand: The Managerial Revolution in American Business* (Cambridge, Mass.: Harvard University Press, 1977), provides a masterly analysis of the rise of big business in America. Focusing on the firm and its management, *The Visible Hand* shows how the development of big business revolutionized management structures and methods in the United States. For a full introduction to Chandler's writings on the history of business see Thomas K. McCraw, ed., *The Essential Alfred Chandler* (Boston: Harvard Business School Press, 1988). Thomas C. Cochran, *Business in American Life: A History* (New York: McGraw-Hill, 1972), examines the evolution of business in the context of social and cultural change in the United States. We urge those who want to know more about the economic history of America to consult Glenn Porter, ed., *Encyclopedia of American Economic History* (New York: Charles Scribner's Sons, 1980), 2 vols. Finally, Harold C. Livesay, *American Made* (Boston: Little, Brown, 1978), and Robert Sobel, *The Entrepreneurs* (New York: Weybright and Talley, 1974), examine the lives of leading American businessmen. Our own work, written with Amos Loveday, *Local Businesses: Exploring Their History* (Nashville: American Association of State and Local History, forthcoming), will guide students in primary research of business history.

PART 1

The
Foundations
of American
Business

To 1790

IMPORTANT EVENTS, 1492–1775

1492   Columbus discovers the Bahamian Islands while searching for a trade route to the Orient.

1600   British merchants found the East India Company.

1607   The Virginia Company founds Jamestown.

1611   Colonists in Virginia start raising tobacco.

1624   The Dutch set up a trading post in New York.

1629   The Massachusetts Bay Company is founded.

1630   Some 1,000 Puritans migrate to the Boston area.

1640s   Black slavery becomes an established labor system in some of Britain's North American colonies.

1651–1673 The British Parliament passes the first Navigation Acts.

1681   Pennsylvania is founded, with Philadelphia as its leading city.

1690s   Rice cultivation begins in South Carolina.

1740s   Commercial indigo cultivation begins in South Carolina.

1757   Thomas Willing and Company becomes the first insurance company in colonial America.

1775   Colonial Americans produce 30,000 tons of iron, one-seventh of the world's total.

1

Business
in
Colonial
America

During the Middle Ages, Venetian merchants conducted business on wooden benches in the town square. When a merchant used up his capital, angry creditors broke his bench, putting him out of business. The English word "bankruptcy"—the Italian phrase *banca rotta* means "broken bench"—derives from this medieval practice. As this example suggests, the roots of American business lie deep in European soil.

The first American entrepreneurs were, in fact, Europeans whose firms had ties with the British business system, which itself was part of an emerging European capitalism. Until the American Revolution, most people living in the thirteen colonies that became the United States thought of themselves as British. Some of their ancestors had first come to North America from England in 1607, uprooting their families and risking their lives and fortunes to take advantage of business opportunities. Eventually, business activity flourished in North America as the population grew.

In the colonial American experience, several themes of business development stand out. The British government fostered commerce in America for the benefit of the British Empire under a theory of political economy known as *mercantilism*. Mercantilism embodied the view that the London government should regulate and promote business in order to increase the wealth and power of the British crown. Although overseas trade was the most dynamic arena of commercial opportunity throughout the seventeenth and eighteenth centuries, business opportunities also emerged from colonial Americans' ingenuity in exploiting the bountiful resources of North America. Business opportunities for Americans expanded as the colonial population increased and the colonial economy grew, especially after 1740. In seizing commercial opportunities, Americans followed European customs and business practices that changed very little in the colonial period. Business remained largely a family operation; a few families and firms amassed great wealth and invested in a range of business activities. But after 1740, more and more smaller, specialized opportunities for entrepreneurs evolved.

THE GROWTH OF BUSINESS IN EUROPE

The first permanent English settlers in North America, who arrived in 1607, were employees of the Virginia Company, which had been chartered by the crown and opened up to investors as a means of expanding England's imperial power. Such a company, and the policy of mercantilism itself, were relatively recent developments. In the early 1400s, much of Europe was still feudal, and business ventures of the sort represented by the Virginia Company were unknown. During the next two centuries, however, feudalism was essentially shattered, in large part by the business activities and practices of Venetian and other Italian merchants. By the seventeenth century, capitalism was fast emerging as the dominant European economic system.

Feudalism

During the thousand years between the end of the Roman Empire in the fifth century and the discovery of North America in the fifteenth, a social and economic system called feudalism prevailed in Europe. Feudalism differed from place to place, and some of its characteristics changed over the centuries. In general, however, feudalism can be defined by the personal bonds that characterized human relationships. In feudal Europe, central governments were weak, and powerful warrior-lords provided protection to inhabitants of smaller areas. Individuals swore allegiance to these local lords, and this bond became hereditary by custom. The warrior-lords dominated the agricultural lands around their manors, to which serfs, again from a tradition of hereditary allegiance, were bound. As the relationships between lords and their warriors and between lords and their serfs became embedded in custom and tradition, those bonds tied society together—not formal contracts, wages, or other monetary relationships.

There was, of course, economic activity within the agrarian world of European feudalism. There were barter relationships in local areas, and some regions produced surplus for trade. Towns emerged where handicraft manufacturing took place and where traders met to exchange goods. Europeans desired commodities, especially spices, from the Orient, and by the tenth and eleventh centuries, traders in northern Italian towns found themselves in a strategic geographical location for conducting business. Feudalism never gained the firm hold in Italy that it had in parts of northern Europe, and this, combined with the area's trading opportunities, nurtured the entrepreneurial activities and business advances that eventually led to the birth of capitalism. Belgian merchants began converting the surplus wool of northern Europe into cloth that Italian merchants traded in the Orient for spices. Such trade was the principal business opportunity that arose in medieval Europe, but there were others. For instance, Scandinavians exported furs, and German merchants beer.

While trading opportunities developed throughout Europe's feudal period, personal bonds continued to govern human relationships. The goals of Europeans influenced by the feudal mentality were not monetary or economic success in the modern sense but military security, loyalty to others according to the feudal traditions, and the worship of the Christian God. In feudal Europe, most savings went not into capital formation in the modern business sense but into maintenance of a clergy and the construction of cathedrals and other religious edifices, as well as castles of the secular nobility.

The Beginnings of Capitalism and New Business Practices

The personal bonds of feudalism were unsuited, however, for the demands of a trading economy operating over long distances through chains of many middlemen. In the satisfaction of these demands, then, were born the business relationships of capitalism that gradually promoted the breakdown of feudalism and the emergence of modern times in Europe. Those modern business relationships first appeared in the towns of northern Italy, and early American entrepreneurs used business practices that had been developed there as early as the twelfth century.

The more important Italian merchants became sedentary. Instead of moving about with their goods from place to place like peddlers, these merchants stayed in one city, where each had an office called a counting house. They relied upon foreign agents, who were usually trusted friends or relatives, to help buy and sell goods in distant lands. Merchants often worked in concert with each other through partnership agreements, which became standardized as time progressed. The business entrepreneurs who appeared to take advantage of the trading opportunities within Europe, and especially between Europe and the Near East, conducted their affairs and measured their success in monetary terms, not according to the bonds of personal loyalty that governed feudal relationships. Italian and other European entrepreneurs sought profits, and they saved their profits to provide capital for investments to secure still more profits. As trade expanded, the web of monetary activities inevitably spread to challenge, subtly but steadily, the traditional personal bonds of feudalism.

New business techniques enabled the Italian merchants to handle the growing volume of their trade. For example, they devised double-entry bookkeeping. Before this innovation, merchants had simply listed their transactions. In double-entry bookkeeping, they recorded every transaction in two parts—in one place as a debit to one account and in another place as a credit to another account. By periodically balancing their accounts, merchants could readily determine their current financial situation. Merchants also developed the bill of exchange as a financial instrument by which they could handle transactions with one another. Bills of exchange were written agreements between the buyers and sellers of goods. The seller drafted a bill for the goods telling when and how the goods would be paid for and sent the bill to the purchaser. The purchaser, in turn, wrote on the bill that he accepted its terms, thus endorsing it. If endorsed by a reputable merchant, the bill of exchange might pass as currency through the hands of many different people before finally being redeemed and paid off.

By the sixteenth century, the business techniques of the Italian merchants were established elsewhere in western Europe. Printed manuals taught entrepreneurs double-entry bookkeeping. Selling on credit grew in popularity and some merchants assumed important roles as bankers. The use of samples in commodity transactions, as in the sale of wheat, was an important merchandising advance.

Mercantilism and the Promotion of Business Enterprise

Along with the emergence of the new business practices and business relationships that fatally weakened feudalism, many other developments contributed to the growth of capitalism in western Europe. Among the most important was the rise of powerful central governments. By the fifteenth century in England, France, and Spain, the authority of the feudal lord was yielding to that of the crown, and this political development created, among other things, new commercial opportunities. Feudalism rested in part on the power of local lords, but with the advent of stronger, larger political units and eventually modern nations came more opportunities for engaging in regional, national, and even international commerce. Stronger central governments, for instance, brought a greater measure of security and uniformity (as in such important items as weights, measures, and currencies). Rulers emerged who were interested in furthering business activity and the spread of trade as a way of obtaining funds to support the central governments and their armies and navies.

As capitalism slowly replaced feudalism, mercantilism became the doctrine of political economy that blended old feudal customs with new business attitudes and provided a transition into the modern age of business. Mercantilism was not a set philosophy but rather an approach that dominated European economic thought between about 1500 and 1800. The purpose of having a business system, according to mercantilist theory, was to enhance the power of the state, not the individual. This emphasis on the community reveals mercantilism's feudal origins. When the British established businesses in North America and settled in the New World, they did not necessarily come as individuals seeking personal gain, but instead were either trying to establish a new commonwealth in the New World or to work on behalf of the interests of the British crown. Only toward the end of the eighteenth century did the idea spread that the goal of a business system was to enlarge the wealth of individuals and the general population.

Mercantilists sought to have the government intervene vigorously in business affairs in order to increase the power of central rulers over traditional feudal allegiances and to improve the government's ability to wage war and make alliances. Mercantilists espoused several main ideas, all of which involved close government regulation of business opportunities to ensure that the state benefited from commerce. They emphasized that a nation should have a favorable balance of trade, that is, it should export more than it imports. To help bring about this situation, they argued that the government should pass laws to encourage exports and should maintain a strong navy to protect traders. The government should also sponsor agricultural and industrial advances, mercantilists believed, through subsidies called bounties, and should enforce laws to keep skilled artisans and industrial processes at home, out of the hands of rival countries. Finally, mercantilists favored the establishment of colonies, for they viewed them as sources of raw materials not found in the mother country and as markets for their products. A vibrant and growing trade, not simply the possession of treasures of gold and silver, lay at the heart of mercantilists' formulas for national success.

British Mercantilism, British Business, and British Colonies

Because mercantilist philosophy encouraged the establishment of colonies, it was one of the factors behind the great exploratory voyages of the fifteenth and sixteenth centuries that led Europeans to the shores of southern Africa, the Americas, and parts of Asia. Another factor was the growth of Turkish power on the Mediterranean Sea, which reduced commercial opportunities for Europeans along traditional trade routes. Thus the Italian Christopher Columbus, funded by the Spanish crown, began the exploration of the Americas in 1492, searching for an alternative route that traders could follow to Asia. Similarly, Vasco da Gama of Portugal sailed around Africa to India in 1498, and Ferdinand Magellan's expedition returned home to Seville, Spain, in 1522, completing the first trip around the world.

The British crown also encouraged overseas expeditions, and British mercantilism, which eventually led to the settlement of Jamestown, Virginia, in 1607, took a special institutional and business form. By the middle of the sixteenth century, the London government was chartering joint-stock companies to entice private individuals to invest capital in overseas business ventures and thereby help augment British power. Those joint-stock companies were businesses in which, by sharing ownership, individual investors

The first English colonists were closely tied to the sea, for ships brought supplies and manufactured goods to them from Europe and carried back their profitable crops and raw materials. This scene depicts the early stages of settlement at Jamestown, the first permanent British settlement. (Virginia State Archives and Library)

spread their risk; they were legal devices whereby individual investors could readily enter, or leave, a business venture. To encourage trade expansion, the government charter typically granted the joint-stock companies exclusive trading rights in a particular area of the world. The Muscovy Company (1555), the Eastland Company (1579), the Africa Company (1588), the Levant Company (1592), and the East India Company (1600) were all ventures in which British merchants, with the support of their government, sought new trading opportunities by looking for alternatives to traditional medieval trade routes. In the case of the most famous of those firms, the East India Company, the crown granted the firm the right to colonize and govern South Asia in the name of the English king or queen. Meanwhile, the growth of the company's commerce and profits effectively added to the power of the central government.

Chartered in 1606, the Virginia Company was a joint-stock company that, along with several others, the London government expected would further British interests in North America. In a sense, the Virginia Company was part capitalist, part mercantilist, and part feudal. It was a capitalist venture in that the London merchants and landed gentry (wealthy landowners) who invested in the firm's stock anticipated making quick profits. The investors hoped that the firm would discover the fabled Northwest Passage, a water route thought to cross North America, and use it to open a lucrative trade with the Orient. The investors expected the firm to exploit North America's natural resources, especially its gold and furs. Finally, the investors, observing that the land called Virginia was at the same latitude as the Mediterranean, hoped to grow citrus crops to supply the British market. The English government, in turn, chartered the Virginia Company with mercantilist ambitions. The political leaders favored the "planting" of settlements as a way of blocking French and Spanish ambitions in North America. The crown expected the colony to strengthen England by supplying products that the nation otherwise had to import from the merchants of rival nations.

The Virginia Company was also, however, partly feudal. The people that the company sent to Jamestown were not expected to reap individual rewards but to work on behalf of the common good—for the company, and especially for the British crown. The instructions issued to the first colonizers concluded, in addition to an admonition to serve and fear God, with the following words: "Lastly and chiefly, the way to prosper and achieve good success is to make yourselves all of one mind for the good of your country and your own. . . ."

The Failure of the Virginia Company and the Success of the Virginia Colony

The initial expectations of the investors in Virginia proved unfounded. The climate of Virginia was unreceptive to the cultivation of citrus fruits. Nor did the adventurers find a Northwest Passage, for no such route exists. Ore sent from Jamestown to England proved to be worthless iron pyrites, not gold and silver. As if the failure of the initial business expectations was not enough of a blow, social problems arose. Disputes over leadership and land rights divided the settlers. Physical and mental disorders, caused by a poor diet and isolation from home, racked them. Conflict with native Americans gravely injured them, culminating in 1662 in attacks in which the Indians killed nearly one-half of the English residents.

As a result of those problems, the Virginia colony very nearly failed at the start. It experienced a "starving time" that almost wiped it out. In 1607–1608, some 70 of the 108 colonists died. The firm recruited replacements, but in the winter of 1609–1610, about 440 of the 500 settlers perished. In all, only 1,200 of the 6,000 people who migrated to Virginia in the years 1607 through 1624 remained alive in 1625.

These difficulties led to reorganization of the Virginia Company, for the original company proved unable to attract new capital investments. At a time when London merchants put almost £2 million into the East India Company, the Virginia Company could secure only £40,000. In 1609, the Virginia Company began offering its stock free to anyone who would move to Jamestown. Each such stockholder was to receive a hundred acres of land as a dividend after working for the company for seven years. Nine years later, the Virginia Company moved still further in the direction of private rather than corporate landownership by introducing the headright system, giving fifty acres to people paying their own passage to America. At the same time that the company instituted new systems of land ownership, it delegated more and more responsibility for running the colony to those in Virginia.

Yet the basic problem of developing a profitable enterprise remained unsolved, as various experiments in growing different crops failed. Tobacco ultimately provided Virginia with a profitable export, despite admonitions from King James I to avoid a custom "so vile and stinking" as smoking. The development of the tobacco trade required time, however, with most of the growth taking place after 1620. London's annual imports of tobacco rose from £61,000 in 1620 to £2 million just eighteen years later.

In the meantime, the Virginia Company was earning no profits, and in 1624 it was disbanded. From that time on, the Virginia Colony existed as a royal colony with its governor appointed by the English crown (a colonial legislature known as the House of Burgesses, set up in 1619, advised the governor on how best to rule the colony). As the investors in the Virginia Company painfully discovered, developing a plantation economy was a much more costly and difficult process than simply opening trade with a distant land.

Thus the founding of Jamestown as a business enterprise was only symbolic of the importance that business was to have in the history of American civilization. The experience of the Virginia Company revealed moreover that the New World was inhospitable to old feudal customs. Ancient European traditions of allegiance did not fit the wilderness condition, especially when the leaders resided far away. The colonists' aim was to gain title to the land that they worked as individuals. It was the promise of individual reward that eventually ensured the success of the Virginia Colony.

The Massachusetts Bay Company

If the failure of the Virginia Company and the eventual success of the Virginia Colony were symbolic of the importance of business in the founding of American civilization, the story of British settlement in New England began another theme of American business history—the struggle within the colonies, and eventually throughout American society, to reconcile the sometimes competing interests of individual entrepreneurs and the larger community of which they were a part.

The Massachusetts Bay Company was a joint-stock venture chartered in 1629 to allow a group of English Puritans to establish a new community based on religious values. The Puritans were religious dissenters who sought to purify the Church of England by simplifying its rituals, among other matters. Unlike the Virginia Company the investors themselves traveled to America in 1630 to establish Boston and other towns. The Puritan settlers, led by John Winthrop, envisioned building a new society free from external pressures in which every man respected the worth of every other man—what Winthrop termed "a city upon a hill" that would demonstrate Christian precepts to all people. Winthrop advised his followers to meet one another's needs "in the bond of brotherly affection." In the new land Winthrop believed that "the care of the public must oversway all private respects."

Although Massachusetts Bay was established as a joint-stock company, the first leaders of the colony disdained the commercial practices of merchants who sought profits, if these profits came at the expense of other citizens. So the Puritan's Christian ideals of brotherhood and community soon came into conflict with the ambitions of merchants. The clergymen in control of the colony sought to establish just prices through regulation, for example. They believed, moreover, that men of means should give their wealth to their brothers according to need and regardless of ability to repay.

These Puritan ideals, however, soon encountered practical difficulties. The Massachusetts settlers needed to import numerous commodities from Britain and so had to pursue local business opportunities to raise the necessary cash. At first they obtained furs for sale abroad but soon had to find other means of harvesting the region's resources in order to earn a livelihood. The Puritans, in short, required the services of merchants. Moreover, other settlers not imbued with Puritan doctrines came to Massachusetts who were eager to earn profits from those services. Disagreements between merchants and the Puritan clergy led eventually to changes in the government of the colony, whose charter was finally revoked in 1684; Massachusetts was thereafter under royal authority.

The Puritan ideal of "a city upon a hill," however, had lasting repercussions. Throughout the subsequent history of business in America, events would occur and issues arise that revealed how business entrepreneurs themselves had mixed motives, commercial and communal. Nor were business owners alone in that respect. Throughout American business history there have been and still are occasions when business interests conflict with what Americans define as the public or general interest. Conflicts between ideas of the public interest and the commercial interests of entrepreneurs, firms, and entire industries have become a significant part of the fabric of government-business relations.

Other Colonies

The Massachusetts Bay Company and the Virginia Company were unique in American colonial history. The British government did not establish most of its North American colonies by chartering joint-stock ventures. Most British settlement in the seventeenth century occurred in *proprietary colonies*, in which the crown granted a large tract of land to a proprietor in exchange for favors. The proprietors, of course, encouraged settlement on their lands, hoping to gain tax revenues—the "quitrent"—for their troubles. Lord Baltimore of Maryland saw that colony as a haven for Catholics from the religious disputes sweeping Britain. William Penn sought not only British settlers but Germans and other continental Europeans to emigrate to Pennsylvania.

Although most of the colonies were proprietary, feudalism never took root in North America. The British government encouraged colonization under the doctrines of mercantilism, and spurred by the necessity of trade with the mother country, capitalism flourished. As the settlers overcame the initial trials of their new environment, the colonial American economy began to prosper, and with that prosperity, business opportunities expanded.

134685

BUSINESS IN COLONIAL AMERICA

Once successfully founded, the colonies experienced an uneven growth in population and commercial opportunity. Initially the colonies grew as new settlers migrated to them, but after 1740, more significant growth occurred as opportunities to trade with Great Britain and southern Europe expanded. By the eve of the American Revolution, the colonists had achieved one of the highest standards of living of any people in the world: a population only one-third of England's could boast of an economic output equal to nearly 40 per cent of the mother country's. The colonists had advantages over their compatriots overseas. In America, land was more abundant, water purer, diseases rarer, and energy sources more available than they were in the mother country. The quality of life became higher in the colonies than in the mother country. By 1776, the thirteen colonies had a population of about 2 million whites, 500,000 blacks, and 100,000 native Americans.

Colonial Trade and Business Opportunities

Most colonial Americans lived near the seacoast, and the importance of ocean commerce between the colonies and Europe reverberated throughout the colonial economy. Overseas trade stimulated chances for farmers to prosper from their labor and investments, and opportunities for other colonists to enter overseas trade, which led to the creation of many business firms. As farming developed, artisans appeared; these skilled workers made goods and also, as small business owners, sold those goods. American-owned ships sailing the Atlantic linked the Old and New Worlds; in colonial ports, American-owned merchant firms organized cargoes and arranged banking, shipping, and insurance services. By the 1760s and 1770s, some 20 per cent of the colonists' income originated directly from their overseas exports, and colonists spent about 25 per cent of their income on imports. Table 1.1 lists the exports crucial to the economic advance of the colonies. Foodstuffs and other agricultural goods lead the list.

This substantial overseas trade stimulated regional specialization in colonial agriculture. The colonists learned which crops their areas grew best and produced them for sale in the markets of the British Empire and Europe. The Virginia settlers turned to tobacco as their staple export crop, and a tobacco culture spread throughout Virginia and Maryland in the Chesapeake region. The Carolinas and Georgia grew rice and indigo, a plant used by British textile manufacturers in making blue dye. Farmers in the middle colonies like Pennsylvania produced more diversified crops, with wheat emerging as an important export. After 1750, the population of Europe increased, without a corresponding rise in farm production. Colonial American farmers grasped the opportunities to enlarge the production of grain, flax, salted meat, and even beeswax. In the Chesapeake region, its soils exhausted by tobacco, planters shifted to newly profitable wheat. The relatively rocky soil of New England precluded intensive commercial agriculture, but New Englanders exported codfish, whale oil, furs, naval stores, and lumber.

Table 1.1
The Value of Major Colonial American Commodity Exports, 1768–1772
(yearly average, in thousands of pounds)

Food grains		
Bread and flour	£410	
Wheat	115	
Indian corn	83	
Rice	312	
Total		£920
Tobacco		766
Fish		154
Wood products		135
Indigo		113
Meat		72
Horses		60
Iron		58
Naval stores		48
Whale oil		46
Flaxseed		42
Potash		35
Rum		22

SOURCE: Gary Walton and James F. Shepherd, *The Economic Rise of Early America* (Cambridge: Cambridge University Press, 1979), pp. 194–195.

Shipbuilding, shipping, and shipping services like insurance also bolstered the economy of New England.

Although overseas trade was the most powerful engine of colonial business, domestic developments were becoming significant by the eve of the American Revolution in 1775. Marketing networks were reaching out from Philadelphia, Boston, New York, and Charleston to nearby towns and farms; farmers sent their produce via middlemen to towns and cities for sale in both domestic and overseas markets. In business terms, those networks consisted of hundreds of small specialized firms providing services. For many colonists—a growing proportion as time progressed—"getting and spending" within a commercial economy was the way of life.

The commercial spirit extended to the interior and to the family farm, especially after 1750 with the expansion of foodstuff sales to the growing European population. Before the second half of the eighteenth century, commercial opportunities were limited for many; farmers and artisans (skilled workers) in remote regions, isolated from easy access to the Atlantic, were obliged to engage in a simple barter economy to satisfy their needs. In the area around Kent, Connecticut, for instance, before 1750 only one-third of the farms produced any surplus for sale; farmers and artisans bartered, using no middlemen. The value of maintaining the close-knit family farm and links to the local community was important and persisted even as commercial opportunities expanded. The growth of commercial opportunities, especially in providing farm products for European markets, did not substantially change the way of life on the family farm. Instead, farmers successfully expanded the production of surplus foodstuffs, which they then exported through networks of middlemen.

Colonial Businesses as Family Enterprises

Except in isolated areas where subsistence farming was the way of life, business enterprises flourished in colonial America. Like most European businesses, colonial American businesses were family businesses. American merchants relied heavily upon family members, who served as clerks in their offices, as captains of their ships, and as their representatives in distant cities. At a time when communications were slow and unreliable, merchants had to trust those with whom they worked, and one way to ensure that trust was to conduct business through family networks. Often, artisan businesses and plantations also operated as family ventures. Ties of blood and marriage bound the colonial business world.

In all of these businesses, wives played roles shaped by colonial ideas of the family. In the colonial period, European and American ideas about the family were patriarchal, and when women engaged in commercial activities, they did so within that framework. Husbands were in charge, wives in a subordinate position. Within the patriarchal family, however, as long as women's actions aimed at strengthening their families and did not conflict with the wishes of their husbands, wives could and did enter the business world.

In particular, a wife was expected to serve as a business deputy for her husband should circumstances prevent him from filling his position. The wives of fishermen and small merchants, who traveled with their goods, often managed their husbands' businesses in their absence. In 1710, Elizabeth Holmes of Boston met Patience Marston of Salem to settle accounts resulting from a voyage to Newfoundland, though neither woman had been on the ship. They were acting as proxies for their husbands—Captain Robert Holmes, who had commanded the ship, and Benjamin Marston, the shipowner. In a few localities women as deputy husbands became the norm, as in Nantucket, where men were often away for lengthy periods on whaling or trading voyages, leaving their stores and shops in the hands of their wives. Elsewhere, widows continued family businesses in coachmaking, shipbuilding, rigging, horseshoeing, painting, engraving, and the making of fish pots and fishnets.

There were four main types of businesses in colonial America in addition to the family farm. In the seaboard towns of the North, entrepreneurs engaged in general mercantile activity. In the Chesapeake region and the southern colonies, there were prominent planters who organized businesses. In the towns, there were skilled artisans who made and sold items, and throughout the colonies, there were itinerant peddlers who bought and sold goods on a small scale.

The Merchant

Colonial Americans usually reserved the word "merchant" for a person conducting an overseas wholesale trade, and in the northern and middle colonies, the largest businesses were those of such merchants. These merchants resembled the Italian merchants of medieval times. The most important colonial merchants were sedentary.

They had an office in one city and did not travel from place to place with their goods. The merchant called his office a "counting house," and colonial Americans used the term "house" to describe the merchant's business. Boston, New York, Philadelphia, and lesser cities were the homes of the leading merchants: the Cabots, Lowells, Browns, Jacksons, Hancocks, Beekmans, Willings, Binghams, and Whartons, among others. Colonial merchants operated as single-owner proprietors or as members of partnerships. The partnerships might be short-lived, limited to the single voyage of a ship, or long-lasting, continuing for a generation or more. Unlike the British, colonial American merchants did not organize joint-stock companies.

The nerve center of the merchant was the counting house, but it was not an elaborate office, even though many different types of entrepreneurial activities originated there. Colonial businesses functioned without a complex hierarchy of managers and officers. Only the largest merchants employed even a bookkeeper and a few clerks. In the counting house the merchant recorded his transactions, the largest firms using the Italian double-entry method. There he arranged the collection and shipment of various cargoes to different overseas markets. For example, merchants sent salted fish to the West Indies, imported molasses, distilled rum, and sold or exported the spirits. Large merchants supervised the wholesale of goods to smaller merchants, and they operated retail stores. Some merchants participated in the slave trade, supplying the colonial economy with involuntary labor.

Some merchants of colonial times were involved, however, in much more than trading commodities. They provided a wide variety of services essential to the colonial business system. Many owned or shared ownership in ships. They entered the field of shipbuilding, a lively industry in New England by the eighteenth century. They had interests in wharves and supplied naval stores (lumber, ships' masts, turpentine, and so forth). They engaged in insurance services: the first insurance enterprise in America, Thomas Willing and Company of Philadelphia, was formed in 1757. No commercial banks existed in colonial America, but leading merchants performed banking functions by lending money at interest to each other and to smaller business enterprises. Finally, many colonial merchants were deeply involved in real estate projects, both in their cities and on the frontier. Quick profits might come through speculation or steadier incomes from rents.

The counting house was the nerve center for the business activities of the colonial merchant. Even the most important merchants, however, employed only a handful of clerks in their counting houses. (The Library Company of Philadelphia)

The House of Hancock: A Colonial Merchant

The House of Hancock, the largest colonial business, illustrates the ties between family and business so important in the colonial period. The very use of the word "house" to describe the firm suggests the close connection between family and business life. An eighteenth-century Boston merchant, Thomas Hancock relied heavily upon family and friends in carrying out his far-flung business ventures.

Born in 1703, Hancock was the son of a Puritan minister. Trained as a bookseller and binder, Hancock entered these trades as a small businessman at the age of twenty-one, probably using funds from his father as his initial capital. From the start, Hancock moved in the polite society of Boston and was soon making the personal contacts necessary for business success. In 1730, he married the daughter of Daniel Henchman, a prominent bookseller and merchant, thus solidifying his social and economic position in the city.

Competition in Boston's book trade greatly increased in the 1730s, and Hancock was soon diversifying his business. Over the next few decades, he became one of the leading general merchants in the colonies. He added a growing line of products to the imported books sold in his retail store, and eventually got out of the book business altogether. By 1755, clothing made up two-thirds of his sales, but he also sold such items as brass compasses, fire-making steels, hourglasses, swords, and tea. Still more important was Hancock's wholesale trade, the backbone of his business. From his Boston office he resold the goods that he imported from England to country merchants throughout New England. To do so, Hancock had to offer liberal credit terms, up to a full year, to these smaller merchants. He had to accept the products of the countryside acquired by the country merchants—wheat, corn, whale oil, and less likely items such as harnesses—in payment for their debts to him. In return, Hancock exported these products to England and the rest of the world.

To assist him in making foreign sales, Hancock maintained foreign agents, often friends or family members, in London, Amsterdam, Lisbon, and other cities. Personal ties linked Hancock to his agents; for instance, one agent sent his son to live with the Hancocks for four years. Hancock taught him accounts, and Mrs. Hancock grew so attached to him as a family member that she did not want to part with him when his apprenticeship ended. On another occasion, Hancock's Jamaica agent asked Hancock to take on his son as a boarder: "Let me know what you would Ask with him & I'll remit you sugar or Molasses for that purpose."

Hancock took part in other business activities as well. He dabbled in real estate, for example. In addition to owning one of the major wharves in Boston, he purchased an island off the coast of Nova Scotia with the idea of establishing a fishery there. Hancock was also interested in mining and manufacturing opportunities. He invested in copper and iron mines, only to find operational difficulties frustrating his search for profits in these ventures. For a twenty-year period Hancock, joined by several partners, tried intermittently to set up and run a paper-making factory, until he was finally defeated by a lack of good raw materials. Hancock's various activities, especially his trading activities, made him one of New England's leading merchants, and on his retirement, his work was carried on by other family members, most notably John Hancock, the signer of the Declaration of Independence.

The Philadelphia Merchants of Late Colonial Times

Thomas Hancock was a general merchant, a jack-of-all-trades who engaged in a wide range of business activities. Like him, many of the most important merchants of colonial America were general merchants, particularly in the early colonial period. In most of the colonies, markets were too small and too greatly separated by poor transportation to allow merchants to earn large profits from specialized businesses. Moreover, financial institutions were not well enough developed to allow widespread specialization. However, by the close of the colonial period, mercantile specialization was becoming increasingly common in some of the larger colonial cities. An increase in the size of markets and an improvement in financial facilities made specialization possible, and merchants with relatively little capital found in specialization a way to enter and advance in business; to enter a multitude of lines of work simultaneously required too much capital for most. Nowhere in the colonies did mercantile specialization proceed further than in Philadelphia in the years after 1750.

As a rapidly growing city with a prosperous hinterland and expanding overseas trade, Philadelphia had a large number of merchants: 230 in 1756, 320 by 1774, and 514 in 1785. These were not grocers selling food or shopkeepers running small stores but wholesalers active in overseas trade. About 52 traders, organized into thirty-seven firms, dominated the wholesale trade on the eve of the Revolution. They were the "great oaks" of the Philadelphia merchant community. The hundreds of smaller merchants, "lesser trees," who labored in their shadows were much smaller wholesalers. While the large merchants clearly stood out from most Philadelphians by their ownership of luxurious townhouses, country estates, and carriages, the smaller merchants enjoyed lifestyles that were not much different from the better-off artisans, grocers, and shopkeepers.

By the time of the American Revolution, Philadelphia's overseas trading area embraced New England, England, southern Europe, and the Caribbean. Whether importing or exporting, few individual merchants or partnerships enjoyed sufficient capital to trade with all of this vast region, so specialized trading relationships with one or two areas were the norm. Specialization by type of trade also occurred; different groups of merchants came to handle the exportation of foodstuffs (mainly wheat and flour) from Philadelphia and the importation of dry goods (cloth and buttons), hardware, and other manufactured items into Philadelphia. By the 1770s and 1780s, this differentiation by function was pronounced, only the very largest merchants dealing with more than one type of commodity.

Specialization divided the Philadelphia merchants into two distinct groups. About 250 merchants acted as importers of dry goods from five to ten suppliers in England. They sold the goods, in turn, through extensive networks of retailers in small towns around Philadelphia. Some 90 per cent of the sales to retailers were made on credit extended for as long as twelve months, and bad debts of retailers often threatened the livelihood of the wholesalers. Most of the other Philadelphia merchants took part in the export trade, conducted mainly on a cash basis. Exporters sent out one or two ships (only the larger firms owned more than two ships) on regular shuttle runs between Philadelphia and one or two overseas destinations year after year, hoping in this way to establish a secure source of stable profits. In addition to shipping and selling on his own account, a merchant might act as a commission agent for other merchants. To fill the holds of their ships, some merchants even promised to leave port on a stipulated day, whether or not their ships were full, and they advertised the regularity of their sailings. Thus, the idea of scheduled voyages, fully established by New York packet lines in the early 1800s, was present in embryo in late-colonial Philadelphia.

The Colonial Plantation

The counterpart to the merchant of the middle and northern colonies was the wealthy planter of the Chesapeake and southern colonies who dominated the business systems of the South. Except for Charleston, South Carolina, cities whose businesses served the hinterland never developed in the colonial South. Instead, the population dispersed along navigable waterways, and most business activity centered upon the plantation, often located at a desirable spot near the headwaters of a river. In the Chesapeake region, specialized merchants supplementing the plantation business appeared after 1740 and helped organize both the domestic coastal trade of the region and overseas export trade. By the eve of the American Revolu-

This painting by an unknown artist shows a typical southern plantation. In the southern colonies, planters operating from their plantations often assumed the role of merchant, buying and selling goods for their smaller neighbors. (The Metropolitan Museum of Art. Gift of Edgar Williams and Bernice Chrysler Garbisch, 1963, 63.201.3)

tion, some American entrepreneurs even challenged the British merchants who controlled the tobacco trade.

The southern planter produced staple crops for sale within the British Empire. The planter, like other colonials, held no political authority over that economic and political system, which was governed from London. The planter could not control the prices or the markets of staple crops and depended on British supplies of desired manufactured goods and credit. As a result, the largest, wealthiest planters, always dependent on the importation of luxury goods, followed a strategy of self-sufficiency in everyday items and pursued profits through a variety of entrepreneurial activities.

The heart of the southern plantation was agriculture. Tobacco became the most profitable crop in the tidewater region of the Chesapeake during this period. The cultivation of tobacco, however, was labor-intensive; that is, it required much more in the way of labor than capital to clear the land and grow the tobacco. So in the seventeenth century, planters began importing large numbers of black African slaves to work their fields. In addition, tobacco cultivation rapidly exhausted the soil, so the planters constantly sought to open new lands in the interior. They sent overseers with slaves to live on and work inland fields. Their base, however, remained the plantation and its wharves reached by ocean-going ships.

The wharf at the tidewater plantation was a center of business activity. From the wharf went the area's exportable produce, and to it arrived manufactured goods from England. There the planter conducted sales from slave ships that called. There too he often maintained a warehouse and a store to service his less-well-off neighbors. The major plantations were impressive indeed: in Virginia, Robert Carter's Nomini Hall had thirty-three outbuildings and looked like a village.

Although the planters grew tobacco, rice, and indigo to earn income from the export trade, they sought self-sufficiency in many other respects. The wealthier planters sometimes owned iron foundries, breweries and distilleries, and flour mills. They housed artisans who spun thread from wool, wove textiles, sewed clothing, and tanned leather to make shoes and harnesses. Plantation blacksmiths fashioned and repaired tools. Cabinetmakers produced furniture; coopers made barrels. (By the eighteenth century, the planters had trained slaves to perform these tasks.) The planters sold manufactured goods to neighbors, sometimes bartering for tobacco, which they in turn exported. Nevertheless, planters suffered from a chronic imbalance of trade because of the luxury goods and manufactured items they had to import from Europe.

As time progressed, planters came to depend increasingly upon others for their needs. Southern farming, like colonial trade, became more and more specialized from the mid-1700s on. By the 1760s, for example, tobacco-growing plantations in the upper Chesapeake were surrounded by smaller farms that sold them foodstuffs and were themselves exporting foodstuffs, hemp, flax, and forest products to Great Britain.

George Washington: Planter-Businessman

George Washington's Mount Vernon plantation on the banks of the Potomac River in Virginia in many ways typified the plantation enterprise of the eighteenth century. At the age of twenty-five, Washington owned 3,000 acres of land, which he supervised from his home. The land of Mount Vernon, however, was of poor quality, eroded and exhausted from earlier tobacco cultivation. In his search for income, therefore, Washington sold goods and services to his neighbors and produced profitable export commodities. He was also heavily involved in land speculation in the West, and he sent slaves to till farms near Mount Vernon.

A pioneer in experimenting with agricultural techniques, Washington cultivated a variety of crops under different conditions and raised animals not common to Virginia, especially sheep and mules. He learned how to grow a high grade of wheat on his tidewater lands and, since wheat was too bulky to ship long distances profitably, entered the flour-milling business. One of his main sources of income came from exporting flour to customers in the West Indies.

From this agricultural base, Washington diversified into a range of business activities. He operated a fishery on the Potomac, supplying the West Indies with dried and salted fish. In 1774, Washington paid taxes on 135 slaves over the age of sixteen, among whom were coopers, smiths, carpenters, spinners, and knitters. His coopers made barrels in which other slaves packed fish, flour, and whiskey. Still other slaves made bricks from local clays and constructed buildings for the plantation. Washington provided services to his neighbors, shipping their produce from his wharf, where he maintained a small store for the retail sale of items he imported. His neighbors paid Washington in kind, usually one-eighth of their wheat for milling or tobacco for shipping. Washington also operated a distillery and, for a time, a ferry service to Maryland.

Like the general merchants operating farther north, Washington diversified his entrepreneurial activities. Both the southern planters and the northern general merchants invested their capital in varied activities, because the opportunities for profit in any one specialized activity were limited. Unlike the northern merchants, Washington used his slave-run plantation as his base. But, like Hancock, he was successful not only through hard work and entrepreneurial acumen but also because of family connections and inherited wealth.

Artisans and Manufacturers

Although most of the goods manufactured in the Chesapeake region, and farther south, came from the hands of slaves, there were opportunities elsewhere for small-scale craftsmen to satisfy local markets. Small towns from Pennsylvania to the northernmost fringe of settlement had their gristmills, sawmills, tanneries, and smithies. As a growing population broadened markets in the late-colonial period, some of these ventures became of more than local importance. By 1770, some 140 distilleries clustered in the northern ports, using molasses imported from the Caribbean as their raw material, produced nearly 5 million gallons of rum, about 60 per cent of the total consumed in the colonies. In the same year, 26 refineries produced sugar. In the Brandywine valley near Wilmington, Delaware, a complex of water-driven mills took form in late-colonial times: 60 gristmills, 6 sawmills, 4 paper mills, 2 snuff mills, a barley mill, a cotton mill, an iron-slitting mill, and several fulling mills (cloth-making establishments).

In the larger towns and cities, skilled artisans, investing small sums in simple tools, worked as silversmiths and coppersmiths. Printers like Benjamin Franklin published newspapers, pamphlets, and books. Near Franklin, a William Will operated his pewterer's shop, where he sold, at wholesale and retail, mugs, plates, washbasins, and the like that he imported from London or made himself. Such opportunities multiplied many times over in eighteenth-century Philadelphia and other towns as the colonial business system prospered.

Large-scale manufacturing to supply more than local markets was rare because of the high cost of transportation, but there were initial efforts in a few fields. Between 1763 and 1775, colonial ship-builders launched 40,000 tons of ships, of which 18,600 tons were sold abroad. Most iron made in the colonies was destined for local use, but some entered intercolonial and international trade. Smelted with charcoal made from America's plentiful hardwood forests, the pig iron was produced at iron "plantations" located in the country-side. (Americans called them "plantations" because of their rural nature; they even grew food crops to feed the ironworkers.) By 1775, the American colonies possessed at least 80 furnaces and 175 forges making iron, numbers that exceeded those of the corresponding facilities in England. With an annual output of 30,000 tons, these installations in the colonies produced one-seventh of the world's iron—an amount that placed colonial America behind only Russia and Sweden as a manufacturer of iron.

Peddlers

Roaming through the colonies were small-scale merchants known as peddlers. Carrying their trade goods on their backs, on packhorses, or in small wagons, they joined the seaport cities with the inland areas. Bartering their goods for local produce and craft items wherever they went, the peddlers provided entrepreneurial links, however primitive, between city and countryside that would not otherwise have existed. Every medium-sized town supported one or two young men who made their living as peddlers, but the number of peddlers more than doubled as economic opportunities broadened at the close of the colonial period. Peddlers sometimes became resident merchants in the interior when they observed trading opportunities at strategic points along rivers.

The Conduct of Business in Colonial America

Several general features characterized the colonial American business system as a whole, whether the entrepreneur was a merchant or planter. As we have seen, commercial people looked outward to the ocean and the British Empire rather than inland to the North American continent. For colonial Americans, most of whom lived along the coast, the larger markets lay overseas because their homeland was still underpopulated. Internal transportation and communication facilities were slow and poorly developed. In 1723, for example, Benjamin Franklin required four days to travel the one hundred miles from New York to Philadelphia. Thus, it was an overseas economy rather than internal commerce that provided merchants and planters more significant opportunities for profit. The southern crops went to market in Europe, and George Washington and his fellow planters did business with English merchants, called "factors," who sold their goods, lent them money, and filled orders for finer-quality manufactured goods. Without staple crops to export profitably, New England merchants harvested the ocean, built and operated ships, and provided naval stores for the British fleet. Like their southern counterparts, they imported expensive items from Britain and often had to deal with associates abroad.

The overseas nature of many of the business opportunities available to colonial Americans brought considerable risks. Ocean travel was slow; sailing ships took from four to six weeks to cross the Atlantic Ocean (more if the weather was bad). Piracy, shipwreck, and weather-ruined cargoes were risks that all overseas traders had to face, and planters like Washington faced additional hazards of crop failures. Nor was success guaranteed, even to a ship that survived the perilous ocean crossing. When a ship arrived at a port laden with goods, an oversupply might have depressed prices.

Furthermore, the American business system was a colonial system, which meant it was supposed to operate mainly for the benefit

As the British colonies grew, their prosperity remained dependent on overseas commerce. This scene shows the town of Boston with its busy harbor in 1723. (The American Antiquarian Society)

of the mother country. The British government sought supplies of raw materials and markets for finished products in order to enrich itself, not its colonies. The net cash flow went from the colonies to England and, as a result, American entrepreneurs were frequently short of money. William Byrd II, a well-known Virginia planter, boasted in 1726 that "half-a-crown [an English coin] will rest undisturbed in my Pocket for many Moons together," in part because his plantation was nearly self-sufficient and in part because the colonial business system operated, of necessity, with little cash. Entrepreneurs, like Washington's neighbors, paid for services in kind (a barter arrangement). Merchants endorsed bills of exchange, just as their Italian counterparts had centuries earlier, which circulated as a kind of currency.

Largely because of the overseas nature of American business in the colonial period and the shortage of cash, business relationships were personal and informal, and the pace of business was necessarily slow. A simple exchange of correspondence could take up to half a year. In towns and cities, merchants transacted business informally among friends in taverns and coffee houses.

As the colonial economy grew after 1740, however, business practices began to change somewhat. More of the merchants felt the need to use double-entry bookkeeping. Bookkeeping manuals came into widespread use, and by the mid-1750s, one such guide, *Bookkeeping Methodiz'd* by John Mair, had a section devoted to colonial needs. Merchants' handbooks—guides to standard business practices around the world, arranged alphabetically by city name—helped regularize business methods. Colonial newspapers came to carry more specialized shipping information, local trade statistics, and local commodity prices. In imitation of their European counterparts, late-colonial merchants supported the publication of two types of specialized business newspapers—marine lists and lists of current commodity prices. As specialization took hold in the business system, brokers of various sorts—real estate, insurance, commodity, shipping, and exchange—brought together buyers and sellers. By the close of the colonial period, in some cities brokers met in set places, taverns or "exchange alleys," to make it easier for customers to find them.

Merchant Leadership and the American Work Ethic

The merchants were profit-oriented men who believed in the accumulation of wealth. They took risks and ventured into new fields because they were imbued with the commercial spirit so vital to a capitalist society. As the colonial society matured in the eighteenth century, moreover, the merchants became the highest social class, usually closely tied with British colonial officials. Merchants sometimes were elected to colonial legislatures and town councils, and they also advised the royal governors. The merchants and southern planters set themselves apart by living in grand houses, dressing in the latest London finery, and enjoying luxury goods imported from abroad. Not everyone admired their success, or the means by which they achieved it, but their very ability to succeed showed that American society tended to encourage and reward hard work and entrepreneurship.

Ironically enough, the encouragement of hard work and the reaping of its benefits were a Puritan legacy—although perhaps not the one most hoped for by the idealistic settlers whose main goal was to build "a city upon a hill" to serve as a model of Christian precepts. The Puritans followed the theology of John Calvin, a sixteenth-century Swiss cleric who argued that God was so powerful, His wisdom so infinite, that He knew who among humankind had achieved salvation. God, in this view, was omnipotent, and the individual human powerless to determine his or her ultimate fate. Calvinists reasoned that individuals should accomplish good works while on earth as an indication that they were among those whom God had elected to salvation. Hard work, in the eyes of Calvinists, was an important sign of salvation. This view, known as the Protestant ethic, instructed individuals to lead their lives according to the Lord's teachings and to bring forth the fruits of the earth and create wealth.

The Puritans were relatively few in number, but their ideas influenced both colonial society and the course of American history, for they meshed nicely with the needs of a vital, growing country and thus became part of the American culture and the system we know as capitalism. Their ideas were popularized in the writings of Benjamin Franklin, a successful Philadelphia printer who belonged to no church and became both a respected pillar of Philadelphia society and an important political leader. Franklin expressed Puritan values in pithy aphorisms, such as "a penny saved is a penny earned," which became permanent fixtures of the American language. In his *Autobiography,* Franklin admonished American to practice "INDUSTRY. Lose no time; be always employ'd in something useful; cut off all unnecessary actions." Such prescriptions promoted the creation of wealth and the growth of the American business system.

THE NAVIGATION ACTS

Despite the vitality of the colonial economy, neither the merchants, the manufacturers, nor the farmers of colonial America were free to pursue business opportunities wherever they found them. Beginning in 1650, the British government, through a series of laws called the Navigation Acts, attempted to regulate business for its own benefit, in accordance with the prevailing mercantilist philosophy. Colonial American entrepreneurs were expected to help make Britain strong while weakening her rivals. (Other European nations had similar regulations, by which they hoped to weaken Britain.) Although the Navigation Acts did little to affect actual business opportunities overall, by the end of the colonial period some colonists saw them as important symbols of British arrogance and power that could be used as instruments to repress them.

The Navigation Acts regulated commerce in four major ways.

Map 1.1 Atlantic Trade Routes

Major points of trade
Major trade route
Intercoastal trade route

EUROPE

Glasgow
ENGLAND
Bristol London
SPAIN
Cadiz
Lisbon
PORTUGAL
MADEIRA IS.

AFRICA

IVORY, GOLD, SLAVE COASTS

NORTH AMERICA
Boston
New York
Philadelphia
ENGLISH
COLONIES
Charleston

CUBA
HISPANIOLA
JAMAICA
WEST INDIES
GUADELOUPE
MARTINIQUE
BARBADOS

SOUTH AMERICA

Linens, horses
Fruit, wine
Wine, fruit
Wine
European products
Molasses, fruit
Slaves
Rum
Slaves
Slaves

Fish, furs, naval stores
Manufactured products
Manufactured products
Tobacco
Rice, indigo, skins
Manufactured products
Meat, fish, rum, lumber, grain
Manufactured products

Fish, livestock, flour, lumber
Slaves, molasses
Slaves, molasses
Slaves

First, most trade between the colonies and the rest of the world had to be carried out in English or colonial ships manned primarily by English or colonial crews. Second, most goods destined for the colonies had to pass through England, even if they had originated in other countries. Third, many items exported from the colonies had to go first to England, even if their final destinations lay elsewhere. These products, "enumerated articles," included molasses, indigo, and tobacco. Finally, bounties or subsidies were paid for the production of certain goods, like indigo and naval stores, and restrictions were placed on some forms of manufacturing in the colonies, such as finished iron products. (See Map 1.1.)

The Navigation Acts helped shape business opportunities for colonial Americans. Clearly, the bounties increased opportunities for producing the selected goods. The requirement that merchants conduct trade in English ships probably stimulated New England's shipbuilding industry, one of the largest in the world by the mid-1700s. The regulations reduced opportunities in other areas, however. Tobacco exporters in Virginia might have preferred selling tobacco directly to the continental European market, rather than going through British merchants, who charged high commissions for their services.

On the whole, however, the British mercantile regulations affected economic growth very little. At most, the Navigation Acts retarded economic growth in the colonies by 1 or 2 per cent of the total income in any given year. For the most part, business opportunities would have occurred as they did without the regulations because the economy of the British Empire was the strongest in the world by the eighteenth century, and colonial American entrepreneurs, as part of that system, enjoyed many advantages. The colonial American entrepreneurs were mostly Englishmen with strong ties of culture and language to the homeland. Southern planters shipped their tobacco to England because of the regulations, but also because they had ties to British merchants who provided credit and desired English books, clothing, furniture, and many other fine manufactured products in return.

The Navigation Acts were intended to benefit British entrepreneurs, not to harm them. Therefore, the rules contained important exemptions that allowed considerable business opportunities for the Americans. Northern merchants sent fish, flour, and rum directly to West Indies markets within the empire and to southern Europe outside of the empire. Trade to these two areas was exempt from the regulation that colonial exports and imports pass through England. Furthermore, in one important measure, the Molasses Act of 1733, British officials allowed violations. In order to help molasses production in the British West Indies, the law placed a prohibitive tariff on the importation of foreign molasses, primarily that made in the French West Indies. This regulation posed a problem to American entrepreneurs, for the supply of British molasses was insufficient to satisfy the American market, and the tariff made French molasses prohibitively expensive. So Yankee traders bribed customs officials in the New England port to allow them to smuggle in French molasses.

Also in accordance with mercantilist philosophy, the thirteen colonies suffered from an imbalance of trade with England: they imported more than they exported. (See Figure 1.1.) But the colonials made up nearly all of the trade deficit through "invisible earnings." The colonies came to supply many of the ships and shipping services for the British Empire, and the earnings from those sources (called "invisible" because they were less apparent than direct returns on trade) helped reduce the annual negative balance of payments with Britain to only a small sum by the close of the colonial period.

Throughout American history, business and politics have been intertwined, as the Navigation Acts demonstrate. The Navigation Acts provided the political framework within which the colonial American economy developed, along with the economy of the rest of the British Empire. The acts were designed to strengthen England, but this consideration did not mean that they hurt the colonies. In reality, the Navigation Acts had relatively little impact on the colonial economies. The economies of the various colonies probably would have developed as they did with or without the Navigation Acts.

Notions of mercantilism went far beyond the Navigation Acts. The British imperial government created a postal service in 1751, with Benjamin Franklin as postmaster, to operate mail routes from Boston to Charleston. The British colonial governments aided the fledgling business system, building wharves and harbors in port towns and constructing roads to facilitate commerce. Governments organized the rapid exploration, surveying, and sale of land, encouraging the transfer of land into private hands. Public loan offices, often called land banks, provided credit to businesses in a credit-hungry economy. Colonial governments minted and printed money, increasing the stock of the circulating exchange medium.

Figure 1.1
Colonial American Commodity Exports to and Imports from England, 1721–1770

SOURCE: Based on data from James F. Shepherd and Gary M. Walton, *Shipping, Maritime Trade and the Economic Development of Colonial North America* (Cambridge: Cambridge University Press, 1972), p. 42.

THE CLOSE OF THE COLONIAL PERIOD

If the Jamestown settlers had by some miracle lived to see the American colonies at the close of the colonial period in the 1770s, they would have found them unrecognizable. Prosperous farms and bustling towns and cities stood along the seacoast. What wrought these changes? The clearing of land for farms and the building of businesses by thousands of individuals were responsible. The settlers of 1607 might have recognized the entrepreneurial motives and capitalist mentality of later generations of Americans, but they could not have foreseen how much their business activities would enrich the material well-being of the resulting society.

North America proved to be a hospitable environment for the conduct of business. Geography and abundant natural resources played important roles in the colonial period, as they would after the founding of the new nation. Colonial Americans were the beneficiaries of seas teeming with fish and whales, virgin forests supplying timber for ships and lumber for buildings, land capable of sustaining diversified agriculture, and rivers capable of transporting the resulting crops and goods. Colonial Americans were also helped by being part of the largest, most powerful European empire, and of a world economy that was in fact growing and thereby adding to entrepreneurial opportunities. By the eighteenth century, the British political system, on the whole, was conducive to business growth and the further development of capitalism.

By the 1770s, the business system of the American colonies was emerging from its infancy, its core in prosperous farms and plantations, with merchant houses serving as conduits for the sale of their products. Trade mechanisms connecting the colonies to the rest of the world were well developed. America's economic dependence upon Britain was rapidly lessening. Yet the business system of the colonies was far from fully developed, even in the late-colonial period. Although considerably improved over earlier years, internal transportation systems remained primitive, hindering the growth of domestic trade and business specialization. A business infrastructure of insurance companies, banks, and shipping services was just beginning to develop in the years after 1750. Artisans and manufacturers, while significant, would become a more important part of the economy in later years.

As their economy developed, some Americans living in the 1770s came to see the desirability, even the imperative, of breaking with the homeland and establishing a new nation. This break, of course, was primarily a political, not a business, event. During the Revolution and in the founding of an American government, however, would be born new institutions and ideas about political economy that would unleash business activity capable of transforming the North American continent and the world economy.

Selected Readings

For an overview of the economic development of Europe, see Carlo Cipolla, *Before the Industrial Revolution: European Society and Economy,*

1000–1700 (New York: W. W. Norton, 1976). Edwin Perkins presents a broad-ranging overview of the colonial economy in *The Economy of Colonial America* (New York: Columbia University Press, 1980), as do Gary Walton and James Shepherd in *The Economic Rise of Early America* (Cambridge: Cambridge University Press, 1972) and John J. McCusker and Russel R. Menard, *The Economy of British America, 1607–1789* (Chapel Hill, N.C.: University of North Carolina Press, 1985). A second edition of Perkins's book will soon be published. On the origins of industry during the colonial period see James Mulholland, *A History of Metals in Colonial America* (University, Ala.: University of Alabama Press, 1981). Stuart Bruchey, ed., *The Colonial Merchant: Sources and Readings* (New York: Harcourt, Brace & World, 1966), offers an introduction to that topic. Bernard Bailyn, *The New England Merchants in the Seventeenth Century* (New York: Harper & Row, 1964), and Frederick B. Tolles, *Meeting House and Counting House* (New York: W. W. Norton, 1963), deal with the social and political as well as the business activities of the merchants. Thomas M. Doerflinger, *A Vigorous Spirit of Enterprise: Merchants and Economic Development in Revolutionary Philadelphia* (Chapel Hill, N.C.: University of North Carolina Press, 1986), examines the Philadelphia merchant community.

Standard studies of colonial American businessmen include William T. Baxter, *The House of Hancock* (Cambridge, Mass.: Harvard University Press, 1945); Stanley Chyet, *Lopez of Newport* (Detroit: Wayne State University Press, 1970); and J.R. Dolan, *The Yankee Peddlers of Early America* (New York: Bramhall House, 1964). A standard biography is Douglas Southall Freeman, Mary Wells Ashworth, and John Alexander Carroll, *George Washington* (New York: Charles Scribner's Sons, 1948–1957), 7 vols. Caroline Bird, *Enterprising Women* (New York: W. W. Norton, 1976), and Laurel Thatcher Ulrich, *Good Wives: Images and Reality in the Lives of Women in Northern New England, 1650–1750* (New York: Alfred A. Knopf, 1980), examine colonial businesswomen.

IMPORTANT EVENTS, 1763–1791

1763   The French and Indian War ends with Britain victorious.
        The Proclamation of 1763 declares the temporary
        western boundary for colonial resettlement.

1764   The Sugar Act imposes new duties on some imports into
        the colonies.

1765   The Stamp Act requires tax stamps on most
        printed materials.

1767   The Townshend Acts impose taxes on British trade goods
        imported to the colonies.

1773   The Tea Act aims at changing how British tea is sold in
        the colonies; colonists react against the Act with the
        Boston Tea Party.

1776   The Declaration of Independence is adopted by the Con-
        tinental Congress on July 4.
        Adam Smith publishes *The Wealth of Nations*.

1781   The Articles of Confederation are ratified by the states.
        Robert Morris founds the Bank of North America.

1783   The Treaty of Paris ends the American Revolution.

1784   Direct trade between the United States and China begins.

1788   The Constitution is ratified.

1789   The federal government begins operations.

1791   The First Bank of the United States is chartered.
        Alexander Hamilton presents his report "On Manufac-
        tures" to Congress.

2

Business
in the
Revolutionary
Era

The formation of the United States of America as a result of the Revolution had significant repercussions in the business, as well as the political, sphere. Not only did businessmen participate in the Revolution as political leaders, they also helped fashion a federal political structure capable of enlarging and shaping business opportunities. The American leaders were members of a generation that had begun to reject mercantilism, and they established in its place a new political economy that promoted capitalism. The founding fathers of the United States believed that government should rest on popular consent and that the purpose of the business system was to enlarge material well-being, not enrich the state or its hereditary rulers. In their view, freedom and the success of the new nation depended on a virtuous and independent citizenry who owned property and enjoyed business opportunities. In the 1780s and 1790s, there was dispute about the best methods of fostering opportunity and about what kinds of business to encourage, but there was also much consensus that entrepreneurial opportunity was desirable, even necessary, for the survival of the Republic and the general welfare of its citizens.

The very formation of the United States as one political entity was as significant for the development of entrepreneurial opportunity as the new political economy that leaders eventually instituted. The thirteen colonies, as we have seen, were already among the wealthiest areas of the world by the 1770s. Entrepreneurs successfully exploited both North America's natural resources and the benefits of being part of the British Empire to achieve that wealth. The Revolution, of course, ended benefits of the British imperial system, but in doing so established other, ultimately more significant, benefits. The United States became the largest free-trade area in the world. Entrepreneurs could operate over a vast territory whose peoples, for the most part, spoke a common language and held a common legal tradition. Political freedom, at least for white males, also meant unprecedented occupational freedom. Common political institutions, abundant natural resources, and occupational freedom resulted in a society with expanding entrepreneurial opportunities.

Planters and merchants, angered by new British economic policies, were among the most important leaders of the Revolution. However, they could not fully foresee the changes that independence would bring to their businesses. Cut off from the British Empire, they had to develop new trade routes and business institutions. They also had to establish government policies for business development, a task that sorely tried the new American government and led to conflict between its two great leaders, Alexander Hamilton and Thomas Jefferson.

BUSINESS AND THE AMERICAN REVOLUTION

Business and the Coming Revolution

Economic complaints helped cause the American Revolution, and business leaders—colonial merchants like John Hancock, a nephew of Thomas Hancock, and planters like Washington and Jefferson—played major roles in the movement for independence. Objectively viewed, British actions were not oppressive, but many business operators saw them as such. Moreover, the colonists came to look upon English economic regulations as part of a general plot against their liberties.

Changes in British mercantile policy prompted the first large-scale complaints. Before 1763, few colonists had complained of the Navigation Acts, but this situation soon changed dramatically. In 1763, England emerged as the winner in a world war fought in

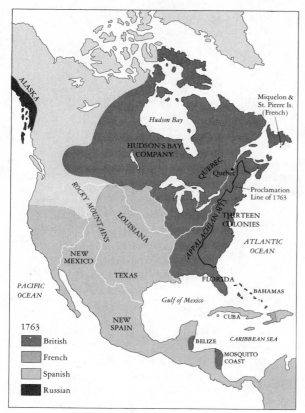

Map 2.1   *European Claims in North America*
After the French and Indian War
SOURCE: From John P. McKay et al., *A History of*
Western Society, 3rd ed. Copyright © 1987 by
Houghton Mifflin Company.

Europe, Asia, and the Americas against France. Called the Seven
Years' War in Europe and the French and Indian War in the colonies, the conflict was costly. The British found the price of victory
great, and England's public debt soared.

The British government responded to those new political and
economic conditions by trying to control the costs of defending its
larger empire while raising additional revenue to pay for that defense. In order to establish peaceful relations with the Indians, the
Proclamation of 1763 forbade settlement west of the Appalachian
Mountains. This decree outraged colonial Americans, especially
southern planters speculating in western lands, who saw it as un-

duly limiting their opportunities. Even worse in the eyes of colonial American merchants was the shift in the goals of the Navigation Acts that occurred after the victory over the French. Parliament passed new postwar measures designed to raise revenue from the colonies, not just to regulate their trade as before. The first of the new laws was the Sugar Act of 1764. This measure actually reduced the duty on molasses imported from the French islands in the Caribbean. For the first time, however, the government strictly enforced the tariff and prosecuted smugglers, whose actions had earlier been tolerated. The Sugar Act hurt New England merchants who dealt in molasses and distilled rum. Another tax, the Stamp Act of 1765, required the colonists to affix stamps of various prices to legal documents, newspapers, pamphlets, playing cards, and dice. Two years later, the Townshend Acts placed import duties on tea, glass, paper, and several other items. Finally, the Tea Act of 1773 allowed the British East India Company to establish a monopoly on the importation of tea into the colonies. This measure lowered the cost of tea to consumers by eliminating middlemen, but it outraged the colonial merchants who had earlier handled this trade.

Although the colonists' complaints were business-related, they were essentially political in nature. Many Americans complained about these new British policies because they disliked Parliament passing laws limiting their freedom without being able to influence those measures. Americans elected no representatives to Parliament, and so could try to influence British policy only indirectly, through friends, political agents, and business associates in England. The colonial grievances involved more, thus, than purely business concerns; "no taxation without representation" was a familiar cry from Americans.

Economic grievances combined with political considerations to convince some leading planters and merchants that they needed a new American government to insure the representation of their interests, a system they could influence directly. By the 1770s, rebellious Americans perceived Parliament's measures as a plot to destroy freedom and profit in the colonies. By then, the colonists also had a growing confidence in the development of their land. Those who would declare independence and found the new nation were coming to envision an American empire, in which a new republican government would protect American commerce, encourage American agriculture, help develop American industry, and promote the settlement of lands in the West—all separate from the British Empire.

The language and images that Americans used to protest the British policies that precipitated the Revolution were often vicious. Here Bostonians gleefully pay the British tax collector with unwanted tea, accompanied by tar and feathers. (Library of Congress)

Colonial merchants and planters led the resistance to English actions. After the passage of both the Stamp Act and the Townshend Acts, they called upon colonists to boycott English goods. They drew up and enforced agreements that proved remarkably effective in causing substantial declines in the importation of British goods into the colonies. Parliament repealed both the Stamp Act and most of the Townshend duties because of this pressure. The colonial merchants and planters also led the way in petitioning the British government for a redress of colonial grievances. For example, John Hancock participated actively in politics throughout the late-colonial period. The merchants and planters proved adept at securing a fair degree of public support. They succeeded, for instance, in organizing mobs who tarred and feathered officials trying to enforce the unpopular Stamp Act of 1765.

The road to revolution and independence was nonetheless tortuous, and not all merchants trod it easily. The merchants in Philadelphia, for example, were reluctant revolutionaries. Philadelphia merchants feared British infringements upon American rights and were prepared to make financial sacrifices to oppose them. However, their opposition was qualified and inconsistent, and the merchants never offered united, sustained resistance to the British. The British measures after 1763, while disliked, did not lead to any unusual economic hardships. Philadelphia's merchants remained apolitical, accustomed to attending to their commercial affairs. In Pennsylvania other groups—wealthy lawyers, clerics, landed gentlemen, and artisans—were most important in leading the opposition to Great Britain.

Business During the American Revolution

The clash of economic and ideological interests led to the outbreak of war in 1775 and an assertion of American independence a year later. The war disrupted American business, as the British army and navy at various times occupied all of the important towns. Most established merchants, especially the larger ones, suffered from the war. For example, Philadelphia merchants experienced the war's decimation of their opportunities in both coastal and transatlantic trades, as shown in Table 2.1. The Philadelphia merchant community declined from 320 active members in 1774 to only 200 by the

Table 2.1
Ships Entering Philadelphia

Origin	1773	1781
Coastwise	293	13
West Indies	286	106
Europe	172	21

SOURCE: From *A Vigorous Spirit of Enterprise: Merchants and Economic Development in Revolutionary Philadelphia*, by Thomas M. Doerflinger. © 1986 The University of North Carolina Press and published for the Institute of Early American History and Culture. Reprinted by permission.

close of the war. Only a few merchants were able to take advantage of new opportunities during the war years, supplying American troops with food and war materiel.

Robert Morris was an exception who combined patriotism with private gain. The junior partner of a leading Philadelphia merchant house, Morris was elected to the Continental Congress in 1775 and became a member of committees dealing with trade. At the low point of American military fortunes in 1776 and 1777, Morris was instrumental in maintaining essential American trade in the Atlantic basin but also used his inside knowledge to build up a personal fortune through trade. Always ambitious, Morris resigned from Congress in 1778, left the merchant house with which he had been associated, and participated in nine new business ventures over the next three years. Morris invested in tobacco shipments, military contracting, importation of dry goods, and land speculation, and by the early 1780s, he was the commercial king of Philadelphia.

With the American government in dire financial straits, Morris reentered governmental service. Taking charge of finances for the government, in 1781 Morris formed the Bank of North America in Philadelphia. Morris used deposits of government funds to start the bank, which then provided credit services to the government and merchants. The bank proved to be profitable, paying a 14½ per cent return on its capital stock in 1783. Soon other Americans established banks, making American merchants less dependent than before upon British creditors.

Business After the Revolution

The Revolution greatly affected the business opportunities for Americans, and with the advent of peace in 1783, a new business system emerged. American independence meant that American merchants were excluded by the Navigation Acts from trading with much of the British Empire. The British severely restricted trade with the West Indies colonies, for instance, forcing a substantial decline of American exports to that region. During the early 1790s, the British West Indies absorbed only 10 per cent of American exports, whereas in late colonial times American traders had sent 27 per cent of their exports there. This exclusion hurt many merchants in the short run. However, in the long run it forced traders to develop new business activities, many of which proved to be very profitable. For instance, southern planters and Philadelphia merchants began shipping American tobacco directly to European mar-

Yankee Pedlar, *by an unknown artist, shows an itinerant peddler displaying his wares in a home. The business enterprise that this peddler represents extended into the countryside as the young nation developed. As settlers moved inland, peddlers followed. (Collection of the IBM Corporation)*

kets, by-passing the British and Scottish merchants through whom they had earlier been forced to work. By the early 1790s, direct trade with northern Europe took 16 per cent of American exports. Trade with Britain declined from 55 to 31 per cent of America's exports in the same period.

A dramatic new opportunity was the China trade. In 1784, after the war was over, New York merchants dispatched the *Empress of China* to Canton with a cargo of ginseng root, which the Chinese believed to be an aphrodisiac and general cure-all, and the merchant adventurers earned a 25 per cent return on their investment. (More typically, voyages elsewhere earned a 6 to 10 per cent return.) News of this success soon spread, and the scramble to enter the China trade was on. American merchant ships sailed around South America, traded with the native Americans of the Pacific

Northwest for furs, especially sea-otter pelts, and then exchanged them in Canton for tea, silk, porcelain, and other fine products. During colonial times the Navigation Acts had prevented direct American trade with China, but soon wealthy Americans decorated their homes with directly imported Chinese rugs, wore fine silks, and sipped Chinese tea. In the early nineteenth century, American and British merchants exported opium from Turkey and India to China in exchange for desirable Chinese goods.

The opening of the China trade and the direct export of tobacco were the most spectacular examples of new opportunities, but there were others as well, particularly within the United States. The war cut off access to British manufactured goods, which encouraged some entrepreneurs to develop domestic manufactures. During the war, American artisans supplied the army with clothing, gunpowder, and guns. Nor did manufacturing opportunities collapse with peace and the return of trade with Britain. By 1790, American mills were supplying paper for an expanding production of newspapers and magazines, and a domestic glass industry had become firmly established. American entrepreneurs felt optimistic that freedom from British mercantilism would mean ample opportunities for the development of internal manufacturing. Tench Coxe, their leading spokesman, told a Philadelphia audience in 1787 that the "useful arts" and manufactures "must afford the most comfortable reflection to every patriotic mind, to observe their progress in the United States, and particularly in Pennsylvania. . . . The list of articles we now make ourselves, if particularly enumerated, would fatigue the ear, and waste your valuable time." Coxe then named a long list of products anyway. (See Figure 2.1.)

ADAM SMITH AND THE ECONOMICS OF FREEDOM

Adam Smith's Ideas

America's Declaration of Independence, so eloquently worded by Thomas Jefferson in 1776, was not the only major document produced that year. The Scottish philosopher Adam Smith published a book entitled *The Wealth of Nations* that over a generation's time revolutionized the way educated persons thought about economic affairs and the relationships between government and business. Smith summarized what some scholars and men of affairs—the two were

Figure 2.1
Destinations of Exports to Overseas Areas from the
Thirteen Colonies (1768–1772) and the United
States (1790–1792)

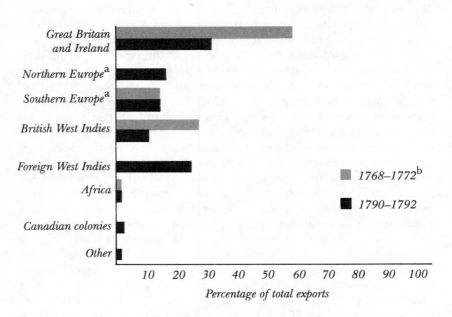

Percentage of total exports

[a]Northern Europe includes Continental European countries north of Cape Finisterre. Southern Europe includes Spain, the Canary Islands, Portugal, Madeira, the Azores, the Cape Verde Islands.
[b]In 1768–1772, there were no exports to Northern Europe, the Foreign West Indies, or the Canadian colonies.
SOURCE: Based on data from Gary M. Walton and James F. Shepherd, *The Economic Rise of Early America* (Cambridge: Cambridge University Press, 1979), p. 190.

often the same in the eighteenth century—were thinking about mercantilism and its faults, and his ideas influenced Thomas Jefferson, Alexander Hamilton, and other American revolutionary leaders, as well as subsequent generations of American business owners and politicians. The new American government never followed Smith's prescriptions exactly, but his ideas were so powerful that for more than two centuries they influenced how Americans thought about government policy toward business.

The lugger—here flying the American flag—was a vessel of French design. Americans bought several of these from the French during the American Revolution and deployed them against British merchant ships. Their design influenced later ship construction in the United States. (Courtesy of Peabody Museum of Salem. Photo by Mark Sexton.)

Adam Smith rejected mercantilist thought and practice at a time when other philosophers were also beginning to question it. In France "physiocrats" developed the notion of laissez faire—a belief that governments should keep their hands off the economy because government regulations inhibit the growth of wealth, which always comes from the soil. Smith adopted their idea of discouraging government regulations, added his own keen insights, and argued that the proper goal of economic policy was the material well-being of citizens, not an increase in state power.

Smith viewed the economy as dynamic. Individuals who tilled the soil, manufactured useful articles, or engaged in trade created wealth. The "invisible hand" of the market—the unstructured system through which individuals bargained for the production and exchange of goods and services—would regulate relationships among persons, not governmental edicts. Smith envisioned only a minimal role for government: the provision of police forces to keep the peace, military forces for national defense, and educational institutions. Smith reasoned that the laws of supply and demand best governed business relations—by determining the prices and production of goods through the demands of purchasers and the supplies of goods and services. Smith thought that allowing the interaction of supply and demand would result in a self-regulating economic system capable of producing larger and larger amounts of wealth. The free interplay of the "invisible hand" of the market, moreover, should occur among nations as well as within a nation if economic well-being were to advance. Under international free trade, Smith reasoned, each nation would specialize in what it could do best (today the concept of "comparative advantage"), and the efficiency and productivity of the economies of nations throughout the world would rise. Free trade, Smith asserted, would benefit everyone.

The Significance of Smith's Ideas

Smith's ideas confirmed the notions of individualism and democracy that the American political revolution expressed, and they were very attractive to Americans. If the individual was entitled to certain political freedoms and a certain form of government, so too should he be free from government or other institutional restrictions on his business life, and this freedom would provide the greatest wealth for human society. Thus, laissez faire in economics and democracy in politics came to be coupled in a framework of thought that the Americans and British in the nineteenth century called "liberalism."

Much of the amplification, explication, and adoption of Smith's ideas, however, remained for the future. In America, few members of the revolutionary generation, whether they were farmers, planters, merchants, or politicians, quickly cast off the old mercantilist habits of thought. Some leaders, including Thomas Jefferson and Alexander Hamilton, read *The Wealth of Nations* and found that it helped them comprehend the workings of the economic system. Most Americans agreed with Smith's proposition that the purpose of the business system should be to enlarge the wealth of the people, not the power of government, which in the American view, came from the people in any case. Nevertheless, they continued to think that government policies directing the economy were desirable in order to augment the numbers of propertied, independent citizens. In fact, Americans never consistently and systematically applied the core ideas of laissez faire to government-business relations.

ESTABLISHING THE TRADITION OF GOVERNMENT-BUSINESS RELATIONS

The Creation of the New Government

The revolutionary decision to break with England and its empire was emotionally difficult for Americans, most of whom thought of themselves as British subjects. The Declaration of Independence was one matter; ahead lay great problems of statecraft. The American revolutionaries still had to decide on the appropriate form the republic should take, the proper roles of the state and federal government, and the kind of political economy best suited for a nation with diverse interests.

The men who gathered at the Continental Congress in Philadelphia to announce their independence from Great Britain and form a new government demonstrated their hostility to the policies of British rule by creating a weak central government for the United States. The first American constitution, called the Articles of Confederation (finally ratified by all thirteen states in 1781), left most authority in the hands of separate states. The Articles of Confederation permitted the federal government to provide for the armed forces and international relations. The federal government also established a postal system, issued a currency (which quickly became worthless), and began a program for the sale and settlement of western lands.

However, the federal government lacked many important powers, and this situation soon distressed many businessmen. It had no power to levy taxes and depended largely on assessments voluntarily contributed by state governments, assessments not often paid in full. Lack of funds made it difficult for the federal government to support a navy, something merchants wanted to protect their ships from piracy. Nor did the federal government have the power to regulate commerce between the different states and, to the dismay of business entrepreneurs operating beyond the boundaries of their own states, some states enacted tariff laws to protect and promote local manufacturing. Individual state governments also passed their own navigation acts in attempts to direct overseas shipping to their ports and issued their own paper currencies, again distressing entrepreneurs seeking to operate in more than one state.

A number of important American leaders came increasingly to see this first federal system as unsatisfactory. These men, who by the end of the 1780s called themselves Federalists, had during the Revolutionary War developed a vision of a strong central government capable of asserting American interests against the self-serving practices of European mercantilism. The Federalists envisioned their new nation as a great free-trade area, an arena in which all Americans would be free to engage in commercial activities with one another under common sets of rules and a common currency. The Federalists were especially concerned with financial matters: the establishment of a stable and uniform currency for the conduct of business, government assistance in the creation of capital needed for funding new ventures or expanding old ones, and the financing of naval protection of merchant ships. By 1784, the debt of the federal government stood at $40 million, and there was little revenue coming in to retire it, much less to conduct current governmental activities. By then, merchants had established banks, one each in Philadelphia, New York, and Boston, to provide short-term credits for overseas trade. But those three banks had neither the will nor the resources to support capital expenditures within the nation or to fund the national debt. Congress, in the meantime, had to borrow additional funds just to pay interest charges on the outstanding notes.

The dissatisfaction with the Articles of Confederation thus revolved to a considerable extent around questions of political economy. The Federalists were, for the most part, wealthy men of affairs—merchants from the seaboard cities, ambitious entrepreneurs, and planters from Virginia—who sought a new federal system able to meet the needs of business and commercial agriculture. A nationalist vision bred during the war tied this elite group together. Eventually, they met in Philadelphia, ostensibly to discuss revisions in the Articles of Confederation. Instead, they drafted an entirely new Constitution, which specially elected conventions in each of the states debated and finally ratified in 1788. The new federal government, divided into executive, judicial, and legislative branches, began to oversee the country from New York City, the provisional capital, in 1789.

The new Constitution included a number of provisions important to the development of American business. One provision granted Congress the power to impose import duties and raise revenues. Funds thus were potentially available for naval protection on the seas and military security for westward expansion. Congress assumed the sole authority to impose tariffs and conduct foreign relations, and its ability to adjust tariff rates could be a powerful weapon for encouraging foreign powers to allow American businesses to penetrate their markets. The Constitution also granted the federal government the exclusive right to coin money and issue currency, which meant that a national medium of exchange was possible. (However, states could still charter banks that issued notes that circulated as money.)

In addition to its fiscal and foreign relations measures, the Constitution provided the political framework for the creation of a national market. States were prohibited from restricting the flow of commerce or from passing laws that impaired contracts between businesses. Bankruptcy laws had to be uniform, assuring creditors that state bankruptcy laws would not be used against them. A postal system, guaranteed by the Constitution, provided all citizens (and business firms) with a reliable means of communication. Patent and copyright laws were authorized that eventually would serve to protect the rights of the pioneers of new technologies. Under the new Constitution, both investment capital and labor (except for the slaves in the South) were free to move within the United States according to the needs of the market. Nowhere in the world in 1789 was there a basic legal framework more conducive to the free flow of goods and people over such a large area—a framework, in other words, favorable to entrepreneurial activity.

The decision for a new governmental structure still left many questions unanswered. Differences of judgment regarding federal economic policy, differences rooted in conflicting political theories as well as varying business interests, soon appeared. By the 1790s, those differences centered on the personalities of Thomas Jefferson and Alexander Hamilton. In part, they involved disputes over how the new, more powerful federal government should best use its resources for the expansion of the American economy. Both Hamilton and Jefferson used the insights of Adam Smith to explain how the economic system functioned but, unlike Smith, they were unwilling as practical politicians to follow a consistent program of having invisible market forces alone determine the destiny of American business.

Alexander Hamilton and American Business

The ideas, ambitions, and energetic leadership of Alexander Hamilton led to the first major conflict over government-business relations in the new national government. Born in the West Indies in 1755, Hamilton grew up in an impoverished family, but his aunts arranged for him to go to New York in 1772. In 1773, he entered King's College (now Columbia University), and in 1774, at the age of nineteen, he wrote widely read pamphlets attacking the British Parliament. Hamilton received an artillery commission in the Continental Army in 1776, and the next year George Washington appointed him his personal secretary. In this post, which he held until the battle of Yorktown in 1781, Hamilton served as an important manager for the American army. After the war, he became a lawyer and settled in New York City, where he established a successful practice. Hamilton was one of a group of war leaders dismayed by the weakness of the federal government, and in 1787 he arranged for the state of New York to approve the calling of a constitutional convention, to which he won appointment as a delegate. He played a small role in the convention, but afterward was instrumental in persuading the state to ratify the new Constitution.

Hamilton earned recognition as one of the ablest men in the young nation, and George Washington appointed him the first secretary of the treasury in 1789. In this position, which he held until 1795, Hamilton provided bold initiatives for the federal political economy, initiatives that sparked much of the political controversy of the 1790s. Disputes over his policies helped divide Americans into their first political parties.

Hamilton was primarily interested in strengthening the nation through the promotion and preservation of both private property and the means of accruing wealth. The main purpose of government, he thought, was not just to protect property but to provide a legal structure for its expansion. Hamilton had little trust in democracy. He believed the success, even the very survival, of the new government and the American nation depended on its wealthiest citizens identifying their economic interests with preservation of the government.

The linchpin of political economy, Hamilton believed, the key to ensuring that the rich and well-born tied their fortunes to the survival of the government, was government credit. The failure of the government under the Articles of Confederation to pay even the interest on the national debt was a complaint that attracted men to

The First Bank of the United States issued this ten-dollar bank note in 1796. The crosses probably mean that the note was redeemed or turned in for gold or silver. The holder's name and the date were written on the note. (John Carter Brown Library)

the idea of writing a new Constitution in the first place. So Hamilton worked quickly and ably to develop a proposal for the funding of the national debt and for assumption by the federal government of the state revolutionary war debts. If government credit was good, he believed, wealthy men would support the government. If merchants, manufacturers, and bankers believed that the government really would make good on its notes, then they would trade in government securities. Such confidence would provide a medium of exchange and, most importantly, substantially enlarge the supply of capital for the financing of new business ventures.

Hamilton also proposed the creation of a Bank of the United States. Under his plan, which Congress adopted, the bank combined public and private ownership, with the federal government holding one-fifth of its stock. By selling the remainder of the stock to wealthy men, the personal economic interests of these men were linked to the stability of the new government and to its promotion of economic growth. The bank provided a place for the government to deposit its funds, and through the establishment of branches (eventually there were offices in eight important commercial cities), it created a mechanism for transferring money from one place to another. The bank's notes circulated as part of the nation's money supply, easing commercial transactions. The Bank of the

United States also acted as a general commercial bank, accepting deposits from and making loans to businesses.

Hamilton's economic policies proved highly controversial. They were intentionally designed to attract the wealthy merchants in the eastern seaports to the support of the government and did not reach out directly to the small property holders, who were in the majority, or the southern planters, who used the services of the merchants to export staple crops. Many Americans thus viewed Hamilton as a politician advancing the interests of one privileged class.

Moreover, Hamilton favored a pro-British foreign policy. He worked and developed close personal ties with merchants who had made their fortunes exporting American materials to England in exchange for manufactured goods. Hamilton wanted to preserve and promote that trade. This commerce was essential to his economic program, for the British trade provided the largest source, some 80 per cent, of the tariff revenues needed to service the national debt and operate the government.

Hamilton's desire to promote the export trade, as well as his personal and political ties to the wealthy merchants of the eastern seaports, became clear in the last of his great proposals for the American political economy, his famous report "On Manufactures." This report, which had a long and tortuous history, was first drafted by Tench Coxe, a wealthy Philadelphian who served as assistant secretary of the treasury. Coxe called for a vigorous government program to foster a new surge of internal manufacturing to enable Americans to compete successfully with British manufacturers. Hamilton, however, reformulated the report to recommend governmental provision of funds to his merchant friends to produce items for the export trade.

Although Hamilton discussed manufacturing enthusiastically in his report, he offered no program to help manufacturers obtain the needed capital to expand or start industries. He offered little to help develop the domestic market for home manufacturers. He opposed tariff barriers lest they reduce the income of the government so essential to retiring its debt. The report "On Manufactures," unlike Hamilton's other recommendations, was never adopted by Congress, and the men, including Coxe, who were most interested in establishing a political economy favorable to manufacturing and internal business development eventually opposed Hamilton politically. They turned to Hamilton's opponent, Thomas Jefferson, to provide the leadership for using government to enlarge business opportunities for the development of domestic commerce.

Thomas Jefferson and Agrarian Democracy

Thomas Jefferson's background contrasted sharply with Hamilton's. Jefferson was born in 1743 in Virginia, where his father was a large landholder on the western fringe of settlement. In 1757, Jefferson inherited 2,750 acres of land and an established position in his community. As a young man, he developed wide literary, scientific, and architectural interests, but emotionally he always remained rooted in the agrarian community from which he came. He was a slave owner, and his plantation, Monticello, produced, among other goods, tobacco for the export trade.

Deeply involved in the independence movement and the Revolution, he served as Governor of Virginia from 1779 to 1781. After the war, Jefferson also served as an American minister to France from 1784 to 1789, where one of his main goals was negotiating a free-trade treaty between America and France. He had read *The Wealth of Nations* and agreed with Adam Smith's ideas about free trade. The theory of free trade fit in with Jefferson's democratic beliefs because it was, in effect, evenhanded. Free trade, after all, meant the absence of policies benefiting particular nations or special interest groups within a nation. The American Revolution gave France access to markets previously closed by the British Navigation Acts, so Jefferson saw France as a logical trading partner of the United States. After the French Revolution of 1789 created a republic similar in some ways to America's, Jefferson saw France as a potential partner in establishing free world trade.

In his hope of achieving a commercial treaty with France, however, Jefferson was frustrated. The United States eventually negotiated a commercial treaty with Prussia, but that small German state was of little consequence to American merchants. The weakness of the American government under the Articles of Confederation made it impossible to bring any significant pressure to bear on the European powers during negotiations, and Jefferson's awareness of the situation led him to support the writing of a new Constitution that established a stronger federal government.

In 1789, Jefferson returned to America to accept the post of secretary of state under President Washington. As secretary of state, Jefferson almost immediately clashed with Hamilton. The two men held fundamentally different views on important questions of political theory, federal economic policy, and foreign policy. Jefferson's ideas about economic policy were less clear-cut than Hamilton's, and over his long political career, they changed as circumstances changed. Although poorly focused at times and inconsistent on occasion, Jefferson's ideas in general embodied democratic values that contrasted sharply with Hamilton's aristocratic tendencies. The clash between the two men eventually led to the formation of the nation's first political parties and, after Jefferson became president in 1801, to a reversal of some of Hamilton's most cherished accomplishments.

Jefferson served as Washington's secretary of state from 1789 to 1793. His main responsibility was foreign policy, but because the United States was a trading nation whose well-being depended on overseas commerce, Jefferson inevitably confronted questions of political economy. He was deeply disturbed by Hamilton's desire to link the wealthiest class of merchants to the fortunes of the federal government and by Hamilton's insistence that the new nation maintain friendly relations with its most important trading partner, England.

Jefferson had a preference for an agrarian society. This preference did not mean that he believed agriculture to be the source of all wealth but rather that the bulwark of a republic consisted of independent farmers. Jefferson's observations of the factory system in Europe led him to fear that it encouraged rulers to engage in tyranny in order to control the underpaid workers. He was convinced that manufacturing centers were a source of corruption in Europe, and he was afraid that industrial workers, unlike independent farmers capable of self-sufficiency, would become dependent on the caprices of the marketplace.

Jefferson was also appalled by what he saw as Hamilton's favoring of Britain. Hamilton's close ties with the mercantile establishment seemed to result in a pro-British foreign policy and a fiscal policy favoring the wealthy. The two prongs of Hamilton's bias were, of course, interrelated, and they rankled the Virginian, who strongly believed that America should retain her hard-won independence from the British.

The Conflict Between Jefferson and Hamilton

Jefferson's dispute with Hamilton grew more bitter in the first years of the Washington administration, especially their disagreement over tariff policy. To Hamilton the tariff was an essential element in raising the revenue without which his entire fiscal program would collapse. Hamilton therefore wanted to encourage trade with England through the commercial ties that were already established. Jefferson, on the other hand, wanted to use the tariff as a political weapon in diplomatic negotiations. His objective was free trade; his means toward that objective were negotiations of reciprocal trade agreements that would break down old mercantilist barriers. Jefferson was thus willing to have the United States impose tariff barriers, even mercantilist-style restrictions, on foreign trade as weapons to persuade European nations to negotiate reciprocal trade agreements.

The Bank of the United States, so important to Hamilton's program, was another point of bitter dispute. Jefferson was dismayed by its creation, his complaints kindled by his suspicions about the handling of higher finance and his dislike of public debt. He disapproved of the speculation and fraud he observed and thought it was only the speculators, the creditors, and the wealthy bank stockholders who benefited from a public debt that, in the final analysis, wrung its repayment from the sweat-stained shirts of honest taxpayers. The bankers, claimed Jefferson, had no stake in general prosperity or public well-being except insofar as they generated tax revenues to pay the interest charges that enriched them. The bank and Hamilton's entire fiscal program seemed to Jefferson to have been created to serve merchants and speculators, not those Americans who invested capital and toil in the improvement of land and buildings.

Constitutional as well as economic issues separated Jefferson from Hamilton. The Tenth Amendment to the Constitution stated that any power not specifically granted to the federal government was reserved to the states or the people. Jefferson interpreted the measure as restricting the power of the federal government. He said, for instance, that the federal government had no power to charter the Bank of the United States. Hamilton, on the other hand, interpreted the amendment more broadly, believing it gave more power to the federal government. Jefferson's views on these matters eventually proved more popular than Hamilton's program. The rivalry between the two men resulted in Jefferson's resignation as secretary of state in 1793. (Hamilton left his treasury post in 1795.) In the late 1790s, Jefferson and his supporters formed a Democratic-Republican party (not to be confused with later parties), and in 1800 Jefferson was elected the nation's third president.

As president, Jefferson showed his practical side. With the Louisiana Purchase, which added vast tracts of land to the United States, and the dispatch of the Lewis and Clark Expedition to the Pacific Northwest, he helped open the North American interior to development. Those actions were consistent with his background as a nationalist and with his advocacy of an agrarian society. His policy of free trade, however, changed according to the practical realities of world politics. In 1805, with Europe in the turmoil of the Napoleonic Wars and American commerce threatened, Jefferson advocated tariff protection. In 1807, in response to British attacks on American ships and to restrictions imposed on neutral American ships by both England and France, Jefferson and Congress ordered an embargo on the export of American foodstuffs and the import of British manufactured goods. By this time, Jefferson was seeking a domestic equilibrium of agriculture, commerce, and manufacturing so that America could be more self-sufficient in a world fraught with dangerous warfare.

As a politician, Jefferson attracted the support of those Americans who wanted to develop the interior of the country and local manufacturing. The nation's leading advocate of a political economy favorable to manufacturing, Tench Coxe, who once served under Hamilton as assistant secretary of the treasury, eventually became a Jeffersonian. Coxe realized that Hamilton would retard the development of American industry, because Hamilton feared domestic manufacturing might reduce imports to the United States and therefore lessen the federal government's tariff revenues. In 1811, the Jeffersonians, under the leadership of President James Madison, allowed the charter of the Bank of the United States—one of Hamilton's most prized creations—to expire.

THE LEGACY OF THE
REVOLUTIONARY GENERATION

Enduring Ideas and Principles

The death of Hamilton's Bank of the United States and the pragmatic response of the Jeffersonians to the issues of tariff protection and domestic manufacturing may appear to have closed a chapter in the history of the American political economy with one side victorious over another. In one sense, this was the case, but in another, more important historical sense, it was not. The dispute between Hamilton and Jefferson was superficially a debate between conflicting personalities, but more fundamentally it involved recurring questions of federal policy.

The principles underlying Hamilton's program appeared in later debates concerning the political economy. Although Hamilton left public service in 1795 and died in 1804, his ideas of using the federal government to expand the capital resources of the nation and of creating a Bank of the United States to stabilize and direct the allocation of capital resources continued in succeeding generations. So too did the notion of benefiting the nation through policies that directly helped its leading businesses. "Hamiltonianism," as this philosophy has been termed by historians, lived on a general body of ideas supportive of strong federal intervention in the economic system to assist the expansion of business.

If Hamilton's vision eventually became a shorthand description of a particular political economy, so too did Jefferson's reaction. While Hamilton seemed to advocate policies enhancing the wealth and power of a merchant aristocracy, a myth arose of Jefferson as a great democrat (even though he was a wealthy slaveholder). Jefferson sought policies to promote free trade and a fiscal system that was evenhanded. Those were democratic ideals. So too, in a sense, was his later support of protection for American manufacturing, for in the nineteenth century a persuasive ideology emerged in support of federal economic policies designed to grant Americans the ability to develop their own industries and business firms, free from ruinous foreign competition.

Institutions

If the revolutionary generation left a legacy of dispute in the American political economy, it also left institutional factors basic to the future development of the American business system. The most important result for American business of the formation of the United States, especially after the adoption of the Constitution in 1789, was the gradual creation of the world's largest internal market. At the end of the eighteenth century, the United States was already a wealthy nation by world standards, but unlike the nations of Europe, it embraced a huge geographical area—an area, of course, later to become even larger. In the 1790s, the internal market, still largely unreachable and underpopulated, existed only as an exciting possibility whose time had not yet come.

A second legacy of the revolutionary generation was the creation of a political system that sanctioned private investments. Under the Constitution, individuals were free to invest in business enterprise, although some ill-formed ideas were expressed about the need for occasional regulation. The freedom to lend money at interest went unchallenged. Under their new government, Americans could hold land or other property for appreciation. The basic features of capitalism were protected by the same political system that provided what became the world's largest market.

A third legacy was occupational freedom. The wealthy merchants and planters occupied the top niche of society, but social classes were less sharply defined in the United States than in Europe, where they were made more rigid by ancient, inherited feudal customs and prejudices. In America, people could rise (or fall) in their social standing according to their acquisition of wealth. White males were free to move from one occupation to another. There was a desire for a classless society to differentiate the new nation from the old world of Europe. Talented Europeans could bring their skills to mills, shops, offices, and farms in the United States and thereby enrich the nation. This freedom, this geographical and occupational mobility, was a basic policy upon which all political factions agreed, and it provided a fluidity of human resources in the conduct of business. The absence of occupational and political freedom for black Americans, however, would increasingly rack the nation's conscience and divide its politics. Moreover, the decisions of entrepreneurs to invest in new ways of manufacturing goods in the nineteenth century would eventually destroy the artisan class.

INTO THE NINETEENTH CENTURY

Later generations of Americans took for granted the gifts bestowed by their revolutionary forebears. The freedom from distant mercantilist restrictions, the ability to influence governmental policy through institutions of representative democracy, the high esteem for the rights of property, and a geographically large and wealthy internal market provided a framework within which American business institutions changed, entrepreneurs adapted to new opportunities, business prospered, and wealth increased over the course of the next two centuries.

While Jefferson, Hamilton, and the others were debating fundamental features of the new political economy, furthermore, important, as yet unappreciated, changes were beginning to occur that would prompt unprecedented entrepreneurial opportunities and vitally affect the American business system. Those features included technological innovations, the birth of the Industrial Revolution in the United States, and a large expansion of agricultural enterprise. They also included a westward expansion of the American nation, so that within half a century, America was geographically and physically a very different place than it had been during colonial and revolutionary times.

Selected Readings

The importance of economic grievances as a cause of the American Revolution is discussed in Marc Egnal and Joseph Ernst, "An Economic Interpretation of the American Revolution," *William and Mary Quarterly,* 29 (January 1972): 3–32; Allison Olson, "The London Mercantile Lobby and the Coming of the American Revolution," *Journal of American History* 69 (June 1982): 21–41; and Joseph Reid, Jr., "Economic Burden: Spark to the American Revolution?" *Journal of Economic History* 38 (March 1978): 81–100. Curtis P. Nettels, *The Emergence of a National Economy, 1775–1815* (New York: Holt, Rinehart & Winston, 1962), provides a useful overview of economic developments. Drew R. McCoy, *The Elusive Republic: Political Economy in Jeffersonian America* (Chapel Hill: University of North Carolina Press, 1980), is a sophisticated treatment that explains how important the political economy was to American revolutionary thinkers and politicians. Broadus Mitchell, *Alexander Hamilton* (New York: Macmillan, 1957 and 1962), 2 vols., is a thoroughly researched biography; and Merrill D. Peterson, *Thomas Jefferson and the New Nation: A Biography* (New York: Oxford University Press, 1970), is a balanced, sympathetic account. The standard account of the Bank of the United States is in Bray Hammond, *Banks and Politics in America from the Revolution to the Civil War* (Princeton: Princeton University Press, 1957). For a fresh view of Hamilton and manufacturing, see: John R. Nelson, Jr., "Alexander Hamilton and American Manufacturing: A Reexamination," *Journal of American History* 65 (March 1979): 971–995. See also: Jacob E. Cooke, "Tench Coxe, Alexander Hamilton, and the Encouragement of American Manufacturers," *William and Mary Quarterly* 32 (July 1975): 369–392.

PART 2

Business
Development
in the
New Nation

1790–1850

IMPORTANT EVENTS, 1789–1853

1789   Samuel Slater brings plans for cotton textile machinery to America.

1793   Eli Whitney invents the cotton gin.

1807   Robert Fulton operates a steamboat on the Hudson River.

1813   Boston Associates found the Boston Manufacturing Company to produce cotton textiles.

1828   The Baltimore & Ohio Railroad is chartered.

1831   Cyrus McCormick demonstrates the first workable reaper.

1834   The Harpers Ferry armory produces rifles with interchangeable parts.

1837   Samuel Morse invents the telegraph.

1853   The British study the American system of manufacturing.

3

The
Expansion
of
American
Business:
Agriculture,
Commerce,
and
Industry

In the autumn of 1784, George Washington departed on a seven-hundred-mile horseback journey through the wilderness into the interior of the United States. Like many other leaders of the revolutionary generation, Washington foresaw the internal development of North America, and he had bought some land near the head-waters of the Ohio River. The fifty-two-year-old planter, now a national hero because of his military leadership during the Revolution, left on the arduous journey to inspect his investments and in-sure that trespassers were not falsely claiming his fertile forests and fields. He also hoped to discover and explore navigable waterways between the Potomac and Ohio river basins.

For more than twenty years, Washington had advocated the westward extension of navigation, believing that internal shipping routes were crucial to the development of the country. Washington was convinced that someday a great waterway would connect New York State's Hudson River and the Great Lakes. Such a canal would enormously expand business opportunity in the American North, and Washington believed that a similar canal to the South would have a like effect. He hoped for a commercial route from Mount Vernon across the Appalachian Mountains that would branch south to New Orleans and north to the Great Lakes and Detroit. Now, with the American nation and the peace secured, Washington sought not just to enrich himself but to provide commercial opportunities for other investors.

When Washington returned from his travels, he reported his findings and recommendations to the Virginia government. He suggested the chartering of a Potomac Company to construct canals around the falls of the Potomac River, clearing the stream of obstacles to make it navigable, with a road from the headwaters across the mountain barriers that divided East from West. With the cooperation of friends from Virginia and Maryland (the Potomac River runs through both states), Washington secured the necessary charter, invested $10,000 of his personal funds, and embarked on the great project.

Washington lived to serve as the new nation's first president, but he did not live to see the completion of his hoped-for water route. At his death in 1799, entrepreneurs still found most of their business opportunities in overseas commerce. However, Washington's vision, his dream of the westward expansion of settlement and commerce, was realized within three generations.

Between 1800 and 1860, the American economy developed explosively, and with that development came several crucial changes. The general merchant of colonial times disappeared, replaced by many specialized firms serving the needs of an internal market. In 1860, some Americans still looked outward, toward the seas, for commercial opportunities, as entrepreneurs always have; but many more looked inward at the great prospect of developing business within the continental expanse of the United States. New inventions powered transportation, communication, agrarian, and industrial revolutions of lasting significance. American capitalism bloomed in the early nineteenth century, and Americans worked and prospered as never before. Entrepreneurs increasingly invested in specialized opportunities, and thereby helped create a new American business system, one regulated by the laws of supply and demand (Adam Smith's "invisible hand of the market"). The market governed both the allocation of capital to private firms and the flow of goods and services through the system. The government got involved in business activity by developing commercial opportunities, convinced that developmental opportunities helped the entire community.

ECONOMIC GROWTH

Economic growth accounted for the emergence of the specialized business firm in the first part of the nineteenth century. The general merchants and planters of colonial times had invested their capital in a variety of enterprises because they could not expect a good return on their investment if they sank all their money in one business venture. As the country grew, however, the situation changed, and more opportunities for profitable specialization emerged. The growth of the United States was remarkable. When Congress declared independence in 1776, the new nation had about 2.5 million inhabitants. In 1815, it had 8.5 million people, and in 1860 the population had reached 31 million. This dramatic expansion of population caused an equally dramatic enlargement of the domestic market, which in turn created more and more business opportunities.

What caused such dramatic changes in the new country in such a relatively short period of time? Forged in the crucible of an eighteenth-century political revolution, America was further molded by three nineteenth-century revolutions of another type: in transportation and communications, in agriculture, and in industry. Each of these revolutions resulted in important changes in entrepreneurial opportunities, and each spurred growth in the nation's wealth. The growth in material wealth was not always steady: there were significant downturns in the business cycle (Americans called them "panics") in 1819, 1837, and 1857. And, as we shall see, sometimes the changes associated with the Industrial Revolution initially hurt the well-being of the men and women and their families who toiled in the new factories. Overall, however, business publicists and political leaders characterized the period as one of optimism and energy. Between 1839 and 1859, for instance, America's per capita real gross national product (the measured amount of all goods and services produced in a nation, adjusted for inflation and deflation, divided by the number of people in the nation) rose by 37 per cent. American business success earned the country one of the highest standards of living in the world.

THE TRANSPORTATION REVOLUTION

At the start of the nineteenth century, overland transportation was so difficult that businessmen looked toward the oceans for trading opportunities. As late as 1816, shippers could bring a ton of goods three thousand miles from Europe by sea for about $9, but the same sum would move a ton of goods inland by wagon only thirty miles. George Washington was among the American leaders who recognized that overcoming the barriers to inland transportation was a necessity for the commercial growth of the domestic American market. Therefore, Washington and other entrepreneurs, often in alliance with government officials, set out to lower transportation costs through what they called internal improvements.

Roads

The construction of improved roads was one of the first internal improvements Americans made in the early nineteenth century. Most of the nation's original roads were nearly impassable: severely rutted, axle-deep in mud during rainy weather, and usually single-lane. Americans made a start in overcoming such obstacles to travel with several major improvements, called turnpikes, constructed in the early 1800s. The most famous road was the National Road, which reached from Baltimore across the mountains to Wheeling on the Ohio River by 1818. However, these roads were still primitive; contractors building the National Road, for instance, were permitted to leave any tree stump less than eighteen inches tall in the roadway. And the roads charged tolls to defray their costs. The roads speeded travel somewhat, but the cost of moving goods over them was still high.

Steamboats

The primitive highway technology meant that most people regarded waterways as the best hope for internal improvement. The interior of the United States contained a vast river system that, once

The stagecoach in this early engraving proceeds along a road in western Pennsylvania, with a newly cleared field to the right. Travel by stagecoach was slow, uncomfortable, expensive, and unreliable in bad weather. (Old Sturbridge Village. Photo by Henry E. Peach)

made navigable, could allow plentiful commercial opportunities. But making that river system navigable was not easy. When Americans first settled the transappalachian West, they built rafts and floated cargoes downstream to the port of New Orleans. Traveling upstream, however, was another matter. One technique of ascending the rivers was for twenty to thirty men to pull keelboats—squat, cargo-carrying vessels—against the current by harnessing themselves to long lines and trudging upstream on the riverbank. Under those conditions, the round trip from Pittsburgh at the headwaters of the Ohio River to New Orleans near the mouth of the Mississippi River took 130 days. During 1807, more than 1,800 boats or rafts arrived downstream in New Orleans, but only 11 departed upstream.

The solution, clearly, was to develop some way of moving boats against the river currents mechanically. Robert Fulton successfully demonstrated a steam-driven boat on the Hudson River in 1807, and the steamboat era began. Steamboats were first introduced on the Mississippi River in 1811; by 1860, there were 800 on western waters. During the high water of springtime, enterprising captains even drove their steamboats up small tributaries to earn extra profits.

The successful development of the steamboat provided important new business opportunities in the American interior. Owning and operating the boats was one such opportunity. Entrepreneurs, usually operating singly or in partnerships, could purchase a medium-sized riverboat for about $20,000, the grander versions for $40,000 to $60,000. Some steamboats ran as tramp steamers, stopping for cargo and passengers wherever they were available. Other owners joined together in packet lines to provide scheduled service. As the number of operators increased, competition among them drove down the cost of service, allowing farmers and manufacturers along the nation's rivers, lakes, and bays more opportunities to reach customers profitably.

The river system and the mountain barriers to overland transportation from the eastern seaboard prompted the early development of manufacturing in the interior. In Pittsburgh, for instance, favorably situated at the confluence of two major rivers, merchants began investing in manufacturing, so that by 1810 the city produced goods worth over $1 million. Iron was the main industry. Local entrepreneurs established smelters, where the area's plentiful iron ore was melted down using coal mined from the local hills. In 1811, the city's first rolling mill was built. It produced iron bars for sale to local artisans and blacksmiths, who fashioned iron goods and tools that were then shipped to customers downstream. There were many other examples of productive opportunities along the navigable waterways. Along the Ohio River at Cincinnati, for instance, a few businesses specialized in brewing, purchasing 40,000 to 50,000 bushels of barley from the countryside annually. As a center of the meat-packing industry in the Ohio Valley, Cincinnati also became known as "Porkopolis."

Canals

As important as steamboats were, the realization of Washington's dream of canals linking the Midwest with the Atlantic seaboard was a more dramatic development. Washington correctly surmised that a logical route existed across New York from Albany to Buffalo.

The Erie Canal inaugurated east-west commerce when the *Seneca*

These pictures of Cincinnati graphically illustrate how transportation improvements helped spur economic growth and business development in the United States during the nineteenth century. Steamboats plying the Ohio and Mississippi rivers connected the city to other regions in the United States. (Top: The Cincinnati Historical Society. Bottom: From the Collection of the Public Library of Cincinnati and Hamilton County.)

Chief, carrying Governor De Witt Clinton, entered it from Lake Erie on October 26, 1825. A steamer took the boat in tow at Albany, and when the *Seneca Chief* arrived in the port of New York on November 4, the governor poured a keg of lake water into the sea. He and the crowds of well-wishers who greeted him at every stage of the trip well knew that significant new commercial opportunities had appeared.

The Erie Canal was an instant success. Even before it was finished, hundreds of thousands of barrels of flour, bushels of grain, gallons of whiskey, and millions of board feet of lumber began arriving in New York's port annually. Entrepreneurs built flour mills, sawmills, distilleries, and other enterprises in towns along the canal route, and farmers opened new fields to commercial cultivation. Other persons entered the shipping business. In 1831, for example, one small entrepreneur built a forty-nine-ton canal boat for less than $1,500, operating it with two horses along the towpath. Boat operators paid tolls for their passage, and the revenues soon covered the construction and maintenance costs of the Erie Canal.

The success of the Erie Canal in opening commercial opportunities sparked a flurry of canal building elsewhere. In the 1820s, for instance, Ohio launched two projects to connect the Ohio River and Lake Erie. By 1840, the United States had over 3,000 miles of canals. In 1833, a firm in Nashville, Tennessee, reported that it received New York goods most *cheaply* via sailing ship to New Orleans and steamboats chugging upriver on the Mississippi, Ohio, and Cumberland rivers. However, the same goods arrived most *quickly* when sent across the Erie Canal and Lake Erie, down the Ohio Canal to Portsmouth, and then by steamboat on the rivers. After 1833, canal rates fell, and more and more trade followed the interior route. By 1852, it was cheaper for Cincinnati entrepreneurs to ship tobacco through the Erie Canal to New York than by the longer route on the river and seas, and the goods arrived in better condition.

Railroads

Speed of passage was the major advantage of the east-west route that the Erie and other canals provided. Still, overland travel was slow. When Abraham Lincoln retired from Congress in 1849 and returned home to Springfield, Illinois, he left Washington, D.C., on a new device, the railroad. He traveled 178 miles to Cumberland, Maryland, where he caught a stagecoach on the National Road,

Map 3.1 Major Canals in 1860
SOURCE: From *The Transportation Revolution, 1815–1860*, by George Rogers Taylor. Copyright 1951 by George Rogers Taylor. Reprinted by permission of Mrs. Mary L. H. Taylor.

which he rode about twenty-four hours to Wheeling on the Ohio River. Then he went by steamboat, first down the Ohio River and then up the Mississippi River, finally reaching home on another stagecoach. The entire trip took eleven or twelve days. Twelve years later, in 1861, Lincoln left Springfield for his March inauguration as president and made the entire trip by rail. He stopped en route to greet well-wishers, but if he had gone directly, he could have reached the capital in a little more than two days. The trip by river was impossible, in any case, because in March the nation's northern waterways were icebound.

Lincoln's two trips illustrate why American entrepreneurs favored the railroad for overland transportation. Railroads came into use in England in the early 1800s, first to carry coal and somewhat later for general transportation. In fact, the first locomotives used on American railroads were constructed in England. As early as 1828, Baltimore merchants, lacking a good water route to the West, chartered the Baltimore & Ohio Railroad, the nation's first major line. They saw that the railroad offered potential advantages of speed, reliability, and flexibility over water transportation. By 1840, American business firms had laid 3,000 miles of track. The first routes fed passengers and freight to and from navigable waterways, but by the 1850s, railroads were linking one region to another with trunk lines, which were the major railroads connecting East Coast cities to Chicago. By 1860, the country had over 30,000 miles of track.

The advantages of railroads lay not only in their speed and all-season reliability but also in the fact that builders could locate tracks in many places where streams were not navigable or canals were impractical. Unlike waterways, railroad technology did not allow small-scale ventures into the transportation business, but the railroads did create an expanding horizon of commercial opportunities for nineteenth-century Americans. For instance, as we shall see later in this chapter, it was the transportation improvements resulting from a great railroad network that enabled Cyrus McCormick to sell reapers (mechanical devices used to harvest wheat) produced in his Chicago factory to farmers throughout the Midwest. By 1860, Americans had invested about $188 million in canals and $1.1 billion in railroads. The next five decades would see additional investment in the construction of an eventual total of 254,000 miles of track. The development of the railroad network in the 1850s and thereafter, as we shall see in Chapter 5, ushered in a new era for American business.

Map 3.2 Major Railroads in 1860

ATLANTIC OCEAN

GULF OF MEXICO

CANADA

L. Superior

L. Huron

L. Michigan

L. Ontario

L. Erie

Mississippi R.

Portland
Boston
Providence
New York
Philadelphia
Baltimore
Washington
Norfolk
Wilmington
Charleston
Savannah
Jacksonville
Buffalo
Pittsburgh
Cleveland
Toledo
Detroit
Milwaukee
Chicago
La Crosse
St. Joseph
St. Louis
Cairo
Memphis
Louisville
Cincinnati
Richmond
Chattanooga
Atlanta
Mobile
New Orleans
Galveston

0   100   200   300 miles
0   200   400 kilometers

89

Even before the Civil War, Chicago had become an important hub in the nation's burgeoning railroad system. This scene from a lithograph made in the 1860s shows the railroad operating along the shore, between Lake Michigan and Michigan Boulevard. (Library of Congress)

Communications

Improvements in the transportation network allowed corresponding improvements in the communications system of the country. In 1790, there were only 75 post offices serving about 2,000 miles of routes. Although most mail was still carried by stagecoach or on horseback, steamboats began to carry some as early as 1813, and the first railroad mail car was introduced in 1837. By 1840, there were 13,468 post offices serving 155,739 miles of routes. However, mail service was still slow and expensive. It took seven days to complete an express delivery between New Orleans and New York in 1825, and until 1845 it cost at least fifty cents to send two sheets of paper over 400 miles. By 1851, however, rates were reduced to three cents for letters going under 300 miles, and in 1863 free city delivery began.

A second major development in communications was the telegraph. Invented by Samuel F. B. Morse in 1837, the telegraph provided rapid communication between most of the eastern states by 1846, and its wires reached all the way to California in 1861. Although significant for all Americans, the telegraph was especially important for business. By the 1840s and 1850s, railroad executives were using the telegraph to schedule the movement of trains. Within one or two more additional generations, many other types of business people came to see the telegraph as essential in coordinating the operations of their companies. The speed of the telegraph in transmitting messages helped bring predictability to America's business world.

THE AGRARIAN REVOLUTION

The transportation revolution opened up the American interior and made possible the development of its vast agricultural potential. From the early days of colonial settlement, as we have seen, entrepreneurs invested in opportunities to harvest the agricultural resources of the continent. The opportunities to sell grain and other produce profitably in European markets that had arisen in the colonial period continued to seem attractive to American farmers. George Washington wanted to open a water route to the Ohio River valley, not just, as he reported to the Virginia governor, "for the fur and pelting trade" but also "for the produce of the country." The first cargo carried on the Erie Canal to New York was agricultural produce and liquor manufactured from grain. Clearly, the midsection of the country was a resource just waiting to be tapped.

It was not long before commercially minded American farmers tapped the rich resources of the transappalachian frontier. To expand their wealth, farmers made tremendous efforts to clear the forests that dominated the landscape of the region. The dominant belief was that the acquisition of wealth, especially as expressed in the ownership of land, was desirable. At first, farmers tried to be as self-sufficient as possible, to save cash for further land purchases. In the northern states (outside the thin and rocky soils of New England) market opportunities for farmers steadily expanded, so that by the 1850s a market-oriented agriculture, in which farmers thought of themselves as small businesses selling commodities for manufactured goods, was clearly the dominant type of farming.

In the first half of the nineteenth century, the commercial crop that had the largest impact on the American business system was cotton. Cotton cultivation expanded westward from the sea islands off the Carolina and Georgia shores in the 1790s, through the belt of rich black soil in Alabama and Mississippi, and on into Louisiana and Texas by the time of the Civil War. In this period, cotton was the largest American export item in both volume and value, and the organization of the cotton trade, made possible in part through the transportation revolution, changed the way many Americans conducted business.

Eli Whitney and the Cotton Gin

The agrarian revolution in the South owed much to an inventor-entrepreneur from New England named Eli Whitney, born in 1765. During the American Revolution, Whitney manufactured nails and knife blades at his family's Massachusetts farm workshop, only to have cheaper British imports challenge his thriving business with the return of peace. A versatile person, Whitney shifted to the production of hatpins and walking sticks. However, bored by the drudgery and isolation of farm life, he left the farm for an education at Yale. There, Whitney moved in polite society, met socially prominent people, and made personal connections that would help him later in life. In 1792, he graduated from Yale and now twenty-seven, used his connections to win appointment as a tutor to the children of a planter in South Carolina.

Whitney invented the cotton gin in 1793 while at this post. There was a large and growing market for cotton at the time in Britain, but American farmers could not profitably supply it. The problem was the type of cotton that could be grown in the American interior: it had short fibers that were expensive to remove from the seed when done by hand. Whitney's invention changed that situation. The cotton gin removed the seeds from the cotton fibers mechanically. In doing so, the gin greatly reduced the cost of processing the raw cotton, making possible the profitable cultivation of cotton, which soon became the major crop of the South.

To satisfy the ever-growing market for cotton, plantations and the slave system they depended on spread westward across the South into Alabama and Mississippi to exploit virgin soils. The emphasis on cotton production caused the plantations to become much more specialized than those of colonial days. Planters continued to grow food or to purchase foodstuffs from neighboring farmers, and some slaves continued to work as artisans, fabricating goods for use on the plantation or for sale elsewhere, but concentration on cotton production tended to occur, and most manufactured items were purchased from entrepreneurs located elsewhere, in Europe or the North. Southern spokesmen referred to King Cotton because the crop was the basis of the region's business system.

Northern Merchants and the Organization of the Cotton Trade

The emergence of cotton as the nation's largest export provided new opportunities to organize and profit from its trade. At the time Whitney invented the cotton gin, the South produced about 3,000 bales of cotton a year; on the eve of the Civil War, production had risen to almost 4 million bales a year (a bale weighed about 400 pounds). The organizing, supplying, warehousing, insuring, and financing of this tremendous output provided new and specialized business opportunities that did much to reshape the nature of the American firm. Northern merchants, especially those from New York, led the way.

Northern merchants were able to organize the cotton trade of the South because they supplied essential shipping and credit services. New York merchants pioneered so-called packet lines of ships that sailed on appointed, scheduled days. By the 1820s there were regularly scheduled shipping services in the coastal trade between New York, Charleston, Savannah, Mobile, and New Orleans. The availability of packet services meant that shippers did not have to hold valuable cargoes in warehouses while waiting for ships to appear, an important consideration when a single bale of cotton might be worth $50.

Cyrus McCormick and the Reaper

Although cotton was the biggest export from the United States in this period, the agrarian revolution also occurred elsewhere. Commercial farming greatly expanded as a business enterprise, thanks to the lowering of transportation costs brought about by the steamboats and canals and because of the development of a mechanical reaper by another inventor-entrepreneur, Cyrus McCormick. In a sense, McCormick did for the North what Whitney did for the South.

From time immemorial, harvesting grain had been a backbreaking, time-consuming task. When a field of grain ripened, farmers had to walk through it, cutting the stalks with hand tools before the kernels spoiled or were ravaged by weather. By 1830, harvest technology had improved only slightly from ancient times; a man could reap only two acres of wheat a day, limiting the acreage planted. Even with those primitive techniques, grain production was important to the American business system. After McCormick's contribution, however, opportunities for expanding the production and processing of grain grew dramatically.

Born in 1809, Cyrus McCormick grew up on a farm in Virginia's Shenandoah Valley, a wheat-growing region. He observed both the laborious tasks of harvesting wheat and his father's frustrating efforts to develop a mechanical reaper. The younger McCormick took up the task and in 1831 demonstrated a workable mechanical reaper that he had assembled in the farm workshop. Drawn by a team of horses, the reaper derived its power from a wheel that was turned by coming into contact with the ground. The wheat was then cut by blades arranged on a circular wooden frame that turned constantly as the horses pulled the reaper along. For a time, McCormick diverted his attention to an iron-mining venture, but in the 1840s he began manufacturing and marketing his reaper, guaranteeing that the machine would cut two acres an hour. He moved to Chicago in 1848 and in 1849 made 1,500 reapers; production soared to 4,500 machines just nine years later. Over time, McCormick set up a network of franchised dealers who sold, financed, and repaired his machines. His successful device and his system of producing and marketing machines allowed farmers in the Midwest and later on the Great Plains to enlarge greatly the acreage under wheat cultivation. McCormick's skill as both inventor and businessman earned him a fortune; he was a millionaire by 1858.

The expansion of the grain trade, already under way even before the mechanical reaper was developed, created business opportunities in the North and West just as the cotton culture had in the South a generation earlier. Millers located themselves at strategic intersections of navigable waterways to grind the grain into flour. Servicing the farm economy with credit, transportation, and merchandise became significant areas of enterprise for many business people. For instance, lumbering grew to be the second largest industry in the United States. Ships laden with lumber sailing the Great Lakes were second in number only to those hauling grain, as the farmers and townspeople of the Midwest bought lumber to build farms, houses, stores, and workshops. Farming brought people to the interior of the continent; by 1840, 40 per cent of the population lived west of the Appalachian Mountains. More people with more money meant a growing domestic market for goods, and entrepreneurs seeking to satisfy that market sparked the third of the three great nineteenth-century revolutions that so transformed the ways Americans worked and lived.

THE INDUSTRIAL REVOLUTION

In 1789, an English mechanic named Samuel Slater arrived in New York, eager to enter textile manufacturing. Slater was a harbinger of the coming of the Industrial Revolution to the United States, a revolution that transformed manufacturing. New technologies for fabricating goods provided significant new business opportunities during the first decades of the nineteenth century. Opportunities to organize industrial production attracted merchants to invest capital in new kinds of factories and encouraged the general trend of specialization in the American business system. By 1850, American entrepreneurs had built one of the leading systems of industrial enterprise in the world. (See Figure 3.1.) While the majority of Americans continued to earn their livelihood on the farm, entrepreneurial decisions were dramatically changing how goods were made and how the men and women who fashioned manufactured commodities lived.

Textiles and the Industrial Revolution

Samuel Slater's arrival in New York was a significant event in American business history because he was knowledgeable in the new techniques of textile manufacture that British entrepreneurs had developed in the second half of the eighteenth century. These entrepreneurs had observed that there was a large market for comfortable cotton clothing to replace scratchy, uncomfortable woolen and linen garments. The problem, however, was that the spinning of cotton thread and the weaving of cotton textiles, when done by hand, was too slow and costly for the products to garner a wide market.

The development of two ingenious machines overcame this problem. The spinning jenny quickly spun thread from cotton fibers, and the power loom wove the thread into cloth. British entrepreneurs placed those machines, which were driven by giant water wheels, in factories and trained workers to operate them in return for wages. These techniques were successful, and British businesses soon dominated the world textile market with their cheap cotton goods. Their success in organizing industrial textile mills created the great demand for cotton that sparked the agrarian revolution in the American South.

The British sought unsuccessfully to protect their industrial leadership. The London government's mercantilist regulations included

Figure 3.1
U.S. Labor Force Shares by Industry, 1810–1980

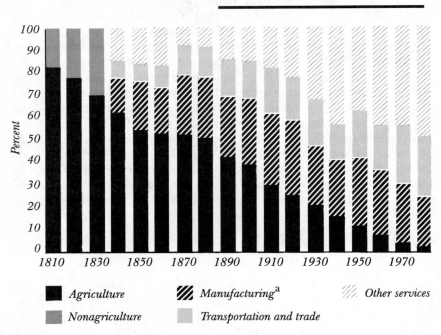

Agriculture   Manufacturing[a]   Other services

Nonagriculture   Transportation and trade

[a] Also includes fisheries, mining, and construction.
SOURCE: *Economic Report of the President, 1988* (Washington, D.C.: U.S. Government Printing Office, 1988), p. 190, based on data from Department of Commerce and Department of Labor.

bans on the export of advanced machinery and the emigration of skilled mechanics. When Samuel Slater left for America, he violated those rules. After arriving in New York in 1789, Slater contacted Moses Brown, a Rhode Island merchant who had failed to establish a successful textile mill. Brown agreed to provide Slater with the capital to build a spinning jenny to make cotton yarn. Slater completed the machine in 1791, and, tended by nine children, it began to make yarn. The firm put out the yarn to workers who wove cloth in their homes. By 1801, the mill was a success, employing more than a hundred children and adults. The Industrial Revolution was under way in America.

This scene of a weaving room in a water-powered cotton textile factory reveals that capital investment in industry was already substantial by the 1830s. This engraving, from A Memoir of Samuel Slater, *also shows that both men and women worked in the mill. (Old Sturbridge Village. Photo by Henry E. Peach)*

From these early beginnings in Rhode Island, Slater and other New England merchants, such as Francis Cabot Lowell, developed the textile industry further. Lowell came from a trading family, and when Harvard University suspended him for making a bonfire in the university's Yard, he went into business, specializing in trade with Europe. Lowell enjoyed success as a merchant, soon forming partnerships with other Bostonians to trade with China and ·India. Political events, however, brought their business to an abrupt halt. In 1807, President Jefferson ordered an embargo on imported British goods in an effort to make the London government respect American trading rights. Disputes between America and Britain eventually led to the War of 1812. By cutting off trade with England, the source of most cotton goods that Americans imported, the embargo and war also created a demand for domestically manufactured cotton textiles.

Pushed and pulled by international events, Lowell, like many other merchants, used the capital he had made in trade to enter manufacturing. In doing so, he was joined by Boston merchants whom he knew personally: Patrick Jackson, Israel Thorndike, John and James Lloyd, Nathan Appleton, and others. Calling themselves the Boston Associates, this group set up the Boston Manufacturing Company in early 1813. The company was capitalized (had financing of) at $400,000, a very large sum in those days. Lowell had visited British textile mills in 1810, and he used the information he picked up then, together with his own ideas, to establish the Boston Manufacturing Company's factory at Waltham, Massachusetts. By 1815, the Waltham mill was using waterpower to turn out cotton cloth. From the outset, the company was a success, making money on the sale of both the cloth (which was marketed through another firm controlled by Appleton) and the textile machinery made in its machine shop. By 1817, the Boston Manufacturing Company had sales of $34,000 and paid its investors a dividend of 17 per cent.

The Boston Associates reinvested their profits and founded America's first new factory town, Lowell, Massachusetts. Completed in 1823, the manufacturing center consisted of six factory buildings grouped together to integrate, or link, the different steps in making textiles. In this one center, machines spun yarn, wove the yarn into cloth, and finished the cloth through bleaching and printing. The firm made and maintained its own machinery as well, and wherever possible, the owners substituted machines for hand labor. The firm provided boarding houses, attracting women from the surrounding countryside to work in the mills with wages higher than those in any other occupation open to them.

So well put together was the Lowell enterprise that it prospered, even under competition from British mills. In fact, cotton textiles proved to be the largest manufacturing opportunity in the United States prior to the Civil War. Entrepreneurs like the Boston Associates made fortunes from the business, and reinvested their profits not only to advance textile manufacture but also to further the emerging railroad, insurance, and banking industries.

The Nature of the Industrial Revolution

The textile industry illustrates some of the changes in the organization and technology of manufacturing that characterize the Industrial Revolution. Before the Industrial Revolution, men and women made yarn and cloth at home, with simple, hand-powered machinery; the industrial production of textiles used complex machinery tended by men, women, or children working in factories. Water wheels drove the first textile machines; by the 1840s, American entrepreneurs were using water turbines to provide power.

The social system that accompanied the industrial production of textiles also changed. The businessmen who formed the textile industry reorganized the ways in which humans worked. In the preindustrial manufacture of textiles, a worker at home might card wool, spin it into yarn, and weave the cloth from which he or she made clothing. The worker would then use the clothing or would market it through the local area's system of merchants. In the industrial processes at Lowell and elsewhere, work was organized much differently. Individual workers earned wages, paid to them by the owners, in exchange for accomplishing specialized, and usually routine, tasks of tending machines. The firm organized the individual workers into groups and employed foremen to supervise those groups, which accomplished just one part of a much larger task. The Industrial Revolution tended to separate the individual worker from the finished product and to reduce his or her ability to control the pace, technology, and quality of production.

Other industries took similar advantage of other technological advances. The steam engine, invented by James Watt in Scotland in 1769, was first used to pump water from mines, using coal for fuel instead of horses for power. As steam-engine technology improved, entrepreneurs used steam engines to drive machines in factories. Other technological innovations included the widespread use of the mineral resources of the earth. Men began to substitute iron for wood in machinery, and later, they began using iron and steel instead of timber to support buildings. Iron became a symbol of the new industrial age.

Thus industrialization changed the way goods were produced in three fundamental ways. First, machines—tireless, precise, and rapid—replaced handicraft labor in making things. Second, new raw materials and new sources of power gained importance in the production process. Finally, workers became concentrated in factories away from their homes. The new industrial organization of manufacturing eventually eliminated independent artisans as persons who played an important role in the economy.

One dominant characteristic connected the industrial, transportation, and agrarian revolutions: the availability of customers, the market. Americans desired cotton textiles. The American population was large enough by the 1820s, and linked well enough together by a transportation system, to justify the expansion of industry that Lowell represented. Industrial manufacturing drove down the cost of textiles and thereby enlarged the number of customers who could afford them. Moreover, the mills created a demand for raw cotton that merchants and planters could supply. The development of the domestic market created the opportunities for Americans to organize the industrial revolution in textiles, and that same market would do so for other industrialists.

Merchants and Manufacturers

The success of the Boston Associates illustrates a common trend in the development of manufacturing: merchants were central figures in organizing industrial processes. The pattern usually followed one of two routes. One was the direction that Lowell and the Boston Associates took as wealthy merchants—risking their personal funds in a new textile venture because they saw an opportunity to seize a market. New York City's merchant elite followed this pattern, supplying craft entrepreneurs with the credit necessary for organizing industrial factories. One result was that New York became the most productive manufacturing city in the United States by 1850. The other direction was for an individual versed in mechanical innovations to observe the opportunity for lower production costs through the use of machines and to turn to merchants for assistance in financing factories and distributing their products. In either route, bankers were seldom involved at the early stages of industrialization, for their resources went into funding the nation's trading system.

The industrial transformation of shoemaking in Lynn, Massachusetts, was an important example of the changes of the first half of the nineteenth century as merchants invested capital to reorganize the fabrication of goods. The merchants' investment decisions changed the lives of individuals and families, and even the dynamics of an entire community. Shoemaking was originally a handicraft operation conducted in a multitude of household businesses. Working in small shops, master shoemakers owned their tools, organized production from raw materials to finished products, and controlled the pace of their work. Production occurred in family units, with wives and children joined by journeymen and apprentices in small workteams. By 1800, there were two hundred master shoemakers in Lynn turning out 400,000 pairs of shoes annually. The shoemakers sold some of their output to Lynn shopkeepers and distributed shoes to a growing regional market in the Northeast through a network of small consignment merchants and retailers.

The industrialization of shoemaking that changed this production system occurred in three stages, in each of which merchants were the principal innovators. First, after 1814 the master shoemakers lost their autonomy to the shopkeepers. Opportunities to market shoes were expanding, but the shoemakers lacked the capital needed to purchase the larger volumes of raw materials and to employ more workers to seize those opportunities. The Lynn shopkeepers, however, enjoyed access to capital, credit, and markets, enabling them to begin reorganizing shoe production to take advantage of expanding markets. The shopkeepers used their resources to take control of shoemaking, contracting with skilled artisans for production.

In the second stage, complete by 1830, the merchant organizers sought to standardize production. They moved shoemakers out of their workshops into central shops and broke down shoemaking into separate steps. One worker now performed just one step in producing a shoe, and the capitalist organizer controlled the fabrication of the finished product. As the artisans lost control of the work process to the merchants who ran the central workshops, the family unit lessened in importance in the workplace. By 1830, the central workshops typically employed fifty to one hundred people. With the centralization of production, output soared. Lynn's shoemakers made mostly women's shoes. In 1790, the town's master shoemakers had sold one pair of shoes for every 10 white females in the United States, but in 1837, with the successful reorganization of production by merchants, the shoe workshops sold one pair for every 2.5 white females.

The third stage, which occurred in the 1850s, transformed the central workshops into factories. The introduction of sewing machines powered by steam engines provided a major advance in productivity. The efficiencies thus gained displaced skilled workers almost entirely. The industrialists who organized shoemaking further and further subdivided the production process, so that by the early 1860s, there were forty distinct steps in shoemaking. With introduction of new machinery and the further subdivision of the work process, the shoe factories became larger enterprises; by the 1850s, they typically employed 300 to 500 persons. With the refinement of industrial shoemaking in the second half of the nineteenth century, shoe output per worker tripled over what it had been in the preindustrial system. In fact, between 1855 and 1875, employment in the shoe industry fell by 2,000 workers, but output rose by 7 million pairs.

A second type of relationship between merchants and manufacturers involved a knowledgeable mechanic or artisan striking up an alliance with a merchant, as in the case of Slater and Brown. These alliances were of great mutual benefit, because each member needed something the other had.

Artisan entrepreneurs who wanted to grasp a market opportunity by organizing a new industrial enterprise required long-term and working capital. Long-term capital provided resources to acquire land, construct buildings, and buy machinery. Working capital was necessary to purchase raw materials and pay employees until sales of the factory's products began to earn revenue.

However, it was difficult to secure capital in the early stages of the Industrial Revolution. The United States had an established banking system, and banks provided credit to farmers, to shipowners, to merchants, and the like. But, for some bankers, new factory processes seemed too risky to make the sizable loans required, when trade provided surer profits. So entrepreneurs were forced to turn elsewhere—to the merchants who had accumulated capital from the profits of more traditional trade.

The formation and early growth of the Jones & Laughlin Company proved how workable an alliance between mechanics and merchants could be. Neither Benjamin Jones nor James Laughlin was especially familiar with iron making; yet a successful firm bore their names. The firm began in 1850 when mechanics started a rolling mill on the south bank of the Monongahela River in Pittsburgh (a rolling mill shapes raw iron or steel into products). They had developed an ingenious process that produced a high-quality iron rail, but a shortage of capital soon thwarted their efforts.

The mechanics began to solve their capitalization problem in 1853 when they struck an alliance with two merchants, including Jones, who had bought and sold iron products in Pittsburgh and Philadelphia. Jones was an able financier, and his capital was vital to the firm's success, but more was still needed. Jones arranged a partnership with Laughlin, who had made a fortune as a pork packer and by selling provisions to migrants moving west through Pittsburgh. Laughlin enjoyed considerable personal credit, which he used to supply the steel business with working capital. He became the firm's financial backer, although he played no active part in its management. By 1857, because of reinvested profits and Laughlin's infusions of capital, J & L, as Pittsburghers called the firm, owned blast furnaces making pig iron, other furnaces to refine and prepare the iron, five rolling mills, and twenty-five nail-making machines.

The American System of Manufacturing

Alliances between artisans and merchants did much to advance the Industrial Revolution in the United States. By the 1850s, the nation was second only to Britain in per capita income, due in part to the increasing wealth pouring from American factories. The British were concerned about the successes of their industrial rival across the Atlantic and sent commissions to inspect American factories and observe what they termed the American System. The British approved "the eager resort to machinery wherever it can be applied" and concluded that "the Americans showed an amount of ingenuity, combined with undaunted energy which we would do well to imitate." American industrialists were the world leaders in using both woodworking and metalworking machinery to turn out products with less and less hand labor. Particularly important was the use of machinery in turning (as in shaping gunstocks), sawing, and mortising operations. Behind the growing use of this machinery lay America's machine-tool industry, the use of machines to make the machines that, in turn, produced the industrial goods. America possessed the most advanced machine-tool industry in the world.

The federal government was a major agent in introducing machine production of standardized goods to the United States. Federal armories at Springfield, Massachusetts, and Harpers Ferry, Virginia, needed to make large numbers of standardized small arms (pistols and rifles) for the United States Army. To do so, the managers of the armories arranged special-purpose machinery—lathes, drill presses, turning machines, and the like—in logical sequences. Each machine performed only one task in making an item, such as boring one hole in a rifle barrel. Work progressed in an orderly fashion until all of the parts for an item were made and assembled. By 1834, the Harpers Ferry armory was making rifles whose parts could be interchanged. The parts of the rifles were produced to such close tolerances that any part could be used to make any rifle. Costly and time-consuming hand labor in fitting the parts together to assemble rifles was eliminated.

Many American industries, influenced in part by the federal armories, adopted the use of machinery in their production processes, and it was this widespread use of machinery that caught the attention of British observers. However, in the years before the Civil War, no private company achieved the production of goods with interchangeable or standard parts. Private companies making small arms, clocks, watches, and axes moved in this direction, but all continued to use considerable hand fitting in assembling their final products.

Although manufacturers were not able to achieve full interchangeability of parts, a number of them did design their mills and factories in the interests of maximum efficiency. Oliver Evans introduced a continuous-process, gravity-fed flour mill in Delaware as early as 1795. Grain was poured in the top, and flour packed in barrels came out the ground level, all with little hand labor. The cotton textile mills of the Boston Associates and other investors were laid out in a logical fashion, with nearly all the separate steps in manufacturing performed within each individual mill.

THE INVISIBLE HAND OF THE MARKET

Business Specialization

The expansion of commercial and manufacturing activities made possible by the transportation, agrarian, and industrial revolutions caused significant changes in the American firm, as we have seen. A complex web of business transactions developed, created by the enlarging internal market and transportation system, and presented many opportunities for providing specialized business services. The number of specialized firms grew accordingly. By the 1840s, the general merchant had all but disappeared, replaced by firms that engaged in a much narrower range of tasks than was the case in colonial times.

By the mid-1800s, thousands of specialized mercantile establishments operated in the American business system. Most were relatively small, and thus no single firm controlled its field of business. Despite the progress made in industrialization, the output of industrial products remained low enough in volume for merchants to handle directly. Moreover, most of the early industrial goods were technologically simple enough for the merchants to demonstrate, sell, and service themselves. Market forces—Adam Smith's "invisible hand"—proved to be adequate guides for determining the prices and quantities of goods produced and distributed in the United

Map 3.3 *Cotton Production in the South*

SOURCE: From Mary Beth Norton et al. *A People and a Nation: A History of the United States*, Brief ed., 2nd ed. Copyright © 1988 by Houghton Mifflin Company.

1859

Percentage increase in population, 1821–1859

Under 200%
200% to 499%
500% to 1000%
Over 1000%

• Each dot equals 1000 bales

ATLANTIC OCEAN

GULF OF MEXICO

VA.
N.C.
S.C.
Columbia
Charleston
Savannah
FLA.
GA.
KY.
TENN.
ALA.
MISS.
Mobile
New Orleans
LA.
Memphis
ARK.
MO.
KAN.
INDIAN TERR.
TEXAS

0   100   200   300 miles
0 100 200 300 400 kilometers

States. Only in the 1880s did the business network established before the Civil War break down, changed by the processes set in motion as manufacturing and its products became technologically more complex and industrial output soared.

The complexities of the increasingly large cotton crop initiated the shift toward specialization. Traveling merchants called cotton factors scouting interior plantations marketed the planters' crops and, in turn, provided them with credit and supplies. The factor either arranged sales of cotton to representatives of manufacturers or, more commonly, sent it to merchant firms in large cities such as New York or New Orleans (many of the firms also had branches in Europe) that specialized in marketing cotton. Only rarely did the firms assume ownership of the cotton. Rather, they took the cotton on consignment. They sought to sell the cotton for the highest price possible for the planters. The factors and other middlemen received a commission, usually around 5 per cent, for their services. By 1840, some 381 commission houses were doing business in Louisiana, and 1,044 were open in New York. In the largest port cities, where the amount of trade justified it, yet another specialized institution developed, the brokerage house. For a fee, brokerage houses brought together buyers and sellers of cotton. An elaborate credit system based on advances from one middleman to the next, using the traditional financial instruments of promissory notes and bills of exchange, grew up to service the cotton trade.

Developments in the trade of other agricultural goods, such as wheat, roughly paralleled those in the cotton trade. The trend, again, was toward increased specialization. Farmers sold their grain to local merchants in country stores, who arranged storage and shipment to millers. With the opening of the Erie Canal, these local midwestern merchants shipped the grain and flour to specialized commission houses in Great Lakes cities such as Buffalo for sale and transshipment to points farther east. As in the cotton trade, the commission houses took the produce mostly on a consignment basis and found buyers for it in the eastern United States or abroad. Like the cotton trade also, the grain trade relied on a complex system of financial transactions based on advances in credit carried out through bills of exchange and promissory notes.

The coming of the telegraph and the railroad mandated further changes, as the volume of trade rose exponentially in the 1850s. Commodity dealers, who brought grain directly from farmers, replaced the commission houses. They worked through grain exchanges in major cities like Chicago, buying from and selling to other dealers and brokers. "To-arrive" contracts replaced consignment contracts as the standard way of conducting business in the grain trade. A to-arrive contract, which was paid for in cash, detailed the amount, quality, price, and future delivery date of the grain. This type of contract was a step in the evolution of futures trading. The to-arrive or future-delivery contract required standard grades and language, which helped regularize and stabilize transactions in grain by making them more routine and less subject to negotiations and disputes between different layers of commission merchants. It was made possible by the telegraph and railroad, which insured the prompt, reliable filling of orders.

Specialization also occurred in the selling of manufactured goods, whether imported or made domestically. Leading merchants in large port cities concentrated on importing or exporting. Most merchant houses left retailing to specialize in wholesaling, where greater profits were available, and many came to specialize in handling just one line of goods. The same trends were apparent in the marketing of consumer goods, items bought directly by consumers, and producers' goods, products sold by one manufacturer to another. Both cotton textile manufacturers and pig-iron producers, for instance, relied on wholesale merchants to find markets for their growing outputs.

After short-lived and generally abortive efforts to sell the products of their mills directly to retailers (since mill owners lacked the knowledge of market conditions needed to make their selling successful), cotton textile manufacturers turned to wholesale merchants for help. The New England mills sold their textiles to wholesale commission houses, usually located in New York City. Because these firms specialized in the cotton textile trade, they became known as textile "selling houses." J. W. Paige & Co. was the first modern selling house, established to dispose of the output of four New England mills in 1828. Paige became the sales agent for the entire production of the mills, receiving a 1 per cent commission on most sales. Paige assumed all risks on credit sales, thus relieving manufacturers of a major source of unpredictability in their business. Paige sold the cotton textiles to other merchants and to consumers on credit. If any purchaser defaulted on paying his bill, Paige—not the textile mills—bore the loss. This type of arrangement dominated cotton textile marketing in the years before the Civil War. Manufacturers welcomed it; for, in addition to taking the output of the mills, the selling houses often supplied them with sorely needed capital as advances on goods received for sale.

A new type of merchant—the "jobber"—connected the selling houses with the thousands of country stores and other retail outlets across the nation. Retailers found it time-consuming and tiresome to visit all the cotton textile selling houses looking for bargains. For their part, the selling houses did not like to break up their bales of textiles into the small quantities desired by the retailers and often charged large fees for doing so. Jobbers filled the gap between the selling houses and the retailers, buying in large quantities from selling houses and selling in small amounts to the many retailers. Retailers, whether country stores in villages or small shops in large cities, then sold the textiles to consumers.

Roughly the same situation prevailed in producer-goods industries. Specialized merchants served as crucial links joining separate segments of these industries. They proved essential, for instance, in the expansion of the iron industry. During the colonial period, iron makers either sold their wares directly to consumers or relied on general merchants to handle their goods. These simple marketing arrangements, however, became inadequate for the rapidly increasing output of iron products that poured from American smelters and foundries in the early and mid-1800s, and they gave way to a multi-level marketing system run by specialized iron merchants.

Despite a large increase in output, iron making was largely an unintegrated industry in the pre–Civil War period. Firms like Jones & Laughlin, which combined all or most of the steps of a manufacturing process under one company, were the exception. Usually, different companies were involved in the various stages of the manufacturing process. Furnace companies smelted pig iron; foundry companies cast the pig iron into stoves, hardware, simple machinery, and merchant bars (undifferentiated bars of iron); blacksmiths and toolmakers turned the merchant bars into finished products. Moving the iron from one stage of the manufacturing process to the next was a major problem, for the iron makers lacked the resources and market knowledge needed to produce the iron at the proper times and ship it to the right places. Specialized iron dealers arose to rationalize the flow of iron goods from furnace to foundry. They usually acted as commission merchants, taking the pig iron on a consignment basis and supplying it to finishers. City merchants or iron jobbers, in turn, often disposed of the outputs of the foundries. These merchants, especially the iron dealers, provided the credit and capital, as well as the marketing services, required by the iron makers, particularly the furnace owners, whose business was capital-intensive. (A capital-intensive business is one whose major expense is the cost of capital—money—needed to build expensive plants and to purchase machinery for those plants.) With large blast furnaces and other works, iron making was capital-intensive.

The pattern of manufacturers selling to commission merchants or selling houses that, in turn, sold to jobbers, who then dealt with retailers, was repeated in industry after industry. Most pre–Civil War industrial ventures, like the cotton textile and iron companies, lacked the resources to handle all phases of their operations by themselves. As a result, merchants' knowledge of the country's diffuse markets, combined with their control over scarce capital, gave them dominance over large segments of the American economy during the pre–Civil War years.

Specialization in Service Businesses

Some merchants specialized by leaving the buying and selling of goods altogether and entering new fields of endeavor. During the first half of the nineteenth century, they took the lead in providing banking, insurance, shipping and credit-rating services for America's expanding economy.

Some of the larger sedentary merchants in America's leading seaports dropped most of their earlier mercantile activities and specialized in granting credit to other merchants. John Jacob Astor, Stephen Girard, and Alexander Brown were among those who turned from trade to finance. They were particularly important in financing interregional and international commerce, especially the cotton trade. Brown is an especially vivid illustration of this particular process of specialization. A successful linen merchant in Ireland, he emigrated to Baltimore in the 1790s and there founded a new firm to deal in linen goods. His firm quickly prospered and as it did, the House of Brown (all of Alexander's four sons entered the business) moved into a wide range of commercial activities in Philadelphia, New York, and Liverpool. In the 1820s and 1830s, however, the Browns began to specialize. From general merchandising they restricted their work to buying and selling on commission only. Finally, in the 1840s, the House of Brown developed into the most important international banking house financing the commercial segment of the American economy. As early as 1830, its capital of over $3 million surpassed even that of Baring Brothers & Co., a British firm and the Browns' chief rival in the financing of Anglo-American trade.

In smaller towns and cities, local merchants and other business people entered commercial banking as a moneymaking proposition. Hundreds of small commercial banks operated at the state level during the years preceding the Civil War. Many of these banks were chartered and regulated by state governments, but a large number, called private banks, were regulated by no one. Whether chartered or private, the banks made loans to local businesses and farmers, using real estate, crops, business securities, and personal promissory notes as collateral.

Additional forms of banking began to develop in the early and mid-1800s as well. First started in 1816, savings banks were originally operated by merchants in a few large cities to help the poorer classes, but they were soon taking deposits from people of all incomes. They invested in federal government securities and made personal loans. Savings bank deposits rose from $1 million in 1820 to ten times that amount fifteen years later and continued to increase in later years.

The bare beginnings of investment banking may also be traced to the early and mid-1800s, although the term "investment banker" did not come into common use in the United States until the early 1900s. Investment banking began as part of the efforts of merchants to finance international and interregional trade and took on a new life with the selling of railroad stocks and bonds starting in the 1850s. Investment bankers served the users and suppliers of capital by providing the means by which savings could be moved into long-term investments. They were specialized middlemen linking those with surplus capital with others needing that capital. Merchants in New York organized a "stock exchange office" in 1792, and the New York Stock Exchange opened for business twenty-five years later. It was at these exchanges that the investment bankers met, or worked through brokers, to sell the stocks.

Merchants had engaged in primitive types of shipping and mercantile insurance during the colonial period (sea captains and ship owners bought shares in one another's voyages so as to spread losses in the event a ship sank), but insurance did not develop as an independent enterprise until the early and midnineteenth century. The first company formed specifically to insure ships and their cargoes came into existence in 1792; by 1807, forty such firms were doing business. Fire and life insurance were slower to develop, but by 1860, the United States possessed eighty-one general insurance companies, many of which wrote fire insurance, and forty-three life insurance companies, including the "Big Three" that dominated the industry in the late nineteenth century—New York Life, Mutual of New York, and Equitable Life. By 1860, the life insurance companies had policies worth $205 million in force and possessed assets of $25 million, most of which they conservatively invested in real estate mortgages rather than in the more speculative securities of railroads and industrial enterprises.

The Conduct of Business

In the conduct of business the specialized business people of the nineteenth century showed both important similarities to and striking differences from their colonial counterparts. As in colonial times, most businesses were family enterprises, and a single individual could supervise most firms' operations. The largest American industrial firm in 1860 was the Pepperell textile mill, which employed about 800 people, and even it could be toured and understood by a single manager in a matter of a few hours. Management, therefore, tended to be informal. Partners might divide responsibilities, with one, say, handling sales and the other finances, and with coordination between them occurring in informal conversations. Elaborate managerial hierarchies for the most part did not exist in pre–Civil War commerce and manufacturing.

This informality began, however, to change in some manufacturing concerns before 1860. In the largest industrial firms of the textile industry, the merchants who set up the mills did not always participate in their routine operation. Instead, the owners appointed a company treasurer and factory agents to take charge of daily affairs. Samuel Slater, for instance, found that he and his closest associates could not personally supervise his textile empire, which by the time of his death in 1835 had grown to include ten cotton textile mills, two machine shops, and a wholesale and commission firm, spread across Massachusetts, Rhode Island, and New Hampshire. Instead, Slater hired salaried managers to run his businesses and devoted his attention to coordinating the work of the mills and planning for the future. Thus, as the industrial business advanced, entrepreneurial functions began to separate from daily management.

Another change that the early industrialists had to face involved workers. Industrial work differed from preindustrial work and therefore posed new sorts of problems for the business executives who organized it. Trading firms had few employees, who were easily supervised through personal contact, but industrial firms em-

The factories of Lowell, Massachusetts, were the nation's largest when they were built. As this label shows, the owners of the Merrimack Manufacturing Company were not only proud of their product—printed cotton whose colors would not run when wet—and guaranteed it, but they also displayed their workers and their industrial equipment. (Museum of American Textile History)

ployed many more men and women. Moreover, industrial work depended on the routines of machines, not the rhythms of nature that governed occupations such as farming or fishing. Industrialists had to devise ways of recruiting, training, and disciplining workers for the new industrial mills and workshops; they had to devise a new managerial function.

The organizers of industrial work devised managerial schemes that mixed paternal concern for their workers with harsh discipline. The founders of the Lowell mills tried the paternalistic path first. They sent recruiters into the countryside offering employment to young women, who would live near the factories in carefully supervised dormitories. By the 1840s, however, the owners were experiencing difficulty recruiting workers for their mills, because the women found the industrial life harsh, with long hours and low pay. The women complained of "the yoke which has been prepared for us." A common response of the early industrialists was to demand regimented performance by workers and to dismiss those who refused to accede to the dictates of management. "I regard my work people," one factory agent said, "just as I regard my machinery. So long as they do my work for what I choose to pay them, I keep them, getting out of them all I can."

The new management problems of dealing with workers were not, however, a major source of change in the conduct of business before 1860, simply because industrialism was not yet fully developed. In 1860, America still had more slaves than factory workers. The organization of most firms, therefore, was still informal. And there were other similarities to the ways business had been conducted for centuries. The pace was still slow. Until the advent of the telegraph in the 1840s, communications depended on animal or wind power. It took about eighteen days, for instance, for a large ship to sail the 1,700 miles from New Orleans to New York. Merchants kept their accounts using the Italian double-entry method, and they were only beginning to call counting houses offices.

Although vestiges of the past remained, the future—in the form of a larger, more impersonal business environment—was clearly at hand. The transportation and communication revolutions resulted in farms, villages, plantations, seacoast towns, and interior cities all being interconnected. Personal business networks disappeared. Instead, the world of the specialized businesses of pre–Civil War America was governed by the unseen forces of supply and demand.

The Auction: A Visible Market

Although Adam Smith described the laws of supply and demand as unseen, there was one place where they were clearly visible. New York was the center of auctions, which began when British exporters dumped large volumes of goods on the American market. In the years from 1821 to 1830, auction sales in New York alone accounted for 20 per cent of the nation's imports. The peak year for the New York City auction was 1827, when $24 million of the $79.4 million total of all American imports were sold at the auction. Textiles were the major commodity traded there, but drugs and hardware were auctioned too.

Prices fluctuated rapidly and widely at the New York auction, depending on the available supplies and the desires of jobbers to purchase goods. One observer wrote in 1828 that he had seen textiles that sold in the morning for 65 cents per yard sell for only 43 cents in the afternoon. "I have known," he reported, "an article that was not very plenty [in limited supply] advance in a few days from 35 to 65 cents, by the competition in the auction rooms."

The New York auction began to die in the 1830s as jobbers learned to deal directly with importers, but the same market mechanisms continued to govern business. The prices that entrepreneurs received for their goods depended on the demands of customers and how many rival firms were seeking to supply those demands. One result was that business people cared less about their past experience in their line of trade than about immediate and future prospects. The profits received from moving, say, barrels of whiskey across the Erie Canal depended not so much on the costs of production as they did on the uncertain demand in the city market. Knowledge of the market demand—fresh news—was the key element of entrepreneurial success. Consequently, entrepreneurs paid scant attention, in keeping their accounts, to the costs of production. Advances in accounting techniques much beyond those developed by medieval Italian merchants awaited the rise of modern big-business firms.

A BUSINESS IDEOLOGY

Individualism

Along with the growth in the number of business firms in America, the atomization of the business system, and the vulnerability of businesses to unseen market forces came changes in the ways that Americans thought about themselves, their entrepreneurial activities, their families, and their society. The development of the economy, the growth of specialization, and the increase in wealth that resulted from increased agricultural and industrial production changed the social milieu. Colonial merchants and planters—and their families—had belonged to a relatively well-ordered, cohesive society in which they had accepted roles to play. In fact, Europeans had first settled the colonies as members of group enterprises. After 1790, this well-defined society crumbled and fragmented. Those who seemed to develop the nation, to increase its wealth, were those who risked their fortunes in hopes of gain. The business opportunities the nation now presented seemed to call for strong-willed individualists, and the expansion of opportunities seemed to be producing a nation where commercial values were ascending.

Alexis de Tocqueville, a French political figure and historian who traveled through the United States in the early 1830s, was the most widely read of many European observers who wrote about the young nation. De Tocqueville noted this individualistic enthusiasm for private gain, and he also noticed that an exploitative attitude toward natural resources was widespread among the American people. When he informed pioneers in the Michigan Territory that he wanted to visit the wilderness for pleasure, they thought he was quite mad. Most Americans viewed the wilderness as an obstacle to be overcome in wrenching a living from the earth and as a source of raw materials for humans to put to use. "In Europe people talk a great deal about the wilds of America," de Tocqueville wrote, "but the Americans themselves never think about them; they are insensible to the wonders of inanimate nature and they may be said not to perceive the mighty forests that surround them till they fall beneath the hatchet."

Americans clearly sought to gain individual wealth through this kind of exploitation. George Washington was among those who purchased unsettled western lands, speculating that in time their value would rise as population and commerce advanced. Nor was the optimism that Washington typified confined to real estate. In the winter of 1839–1840, Jay Cooke, who eventually became one of the nation's millionaires, told his family about the bank in which he worked. "My bosses are making money fast," Cooke wrote. "Among our customers are men of every age and every position in society, from the hoary miser to the dashing buck who lives upon his thousands. Through all grades I see the same all-pervading, all-engrossing anxiety to grow rich."

When American speculators and entrepreneurs thought about their pursuit of wealth, they expressed not only a desire for personal gain but a faith in Adam Smith's precepts in the working of market forces as the best route to human progress. Entrepreneurs were confident, when they reflected upon the matter, that they were achieving larger results. Profits, in this view, were not only individual but added to the store of material plenty to which all citizens, if they chose to do so, could contribute, and in which they could share. One of the partners of John Murray Forbes, an early railroad magnate, observed that Forbes "never seemed to me a man of acquisitiveness, but very distinctly one of constructiveness."

Forbes seemed driven by a "dominant passion for building up things."

The faith in "constructiveness" involved more than accumulating personal wealth. It included the notion that business built character and improved the individual. Business success seemed to depend on self-discipline; trade seemed to sharpen a person's faculties. In the atomized business system of the time, successful people needed to develop personal characteristics of honor, trust, and integrity, in this view. Commercial people could not deal with one another and promote the greater good of American society without those attributes. Nor did the belief in building character end at the counting-house door or the steamboat gangplank. Hard work was a virtue that business people encouraged. Discipline extending into the lives of industrial workers was essential for the operations of industrial factories powered by machines.

Exceptions

The victory of individualism and the admiration of commercial activity was far from complete, however. Just as the business system became more complex with the expansion of the American economy in the first half of the nineteenth century, so did the diversity of views and social situations among Americans increase. The individualism that became so large a part of American rhetoric in the first half of the nineteenth century, and that seemed to many observers to define an American character, was often rejected by workers, once in control of their craft but now more subjected to the authority of the business people who organized manufacturing. Individualism seldom extended to women and minorities, who were excluded from full participation in the nation's business opportunities. Social customs and family traditions prevented women from realizing their full potential as participants in the world of business, and the continuation of slavery meant, of course, that black Americans seldom enjoyed any economic opportunity.

The expansion of business opportunities did not benefit all workers. Artisans and those with craft skills who were unable to compete with newer forms of industrial production actually lost a sense of independence. Often they tried to resist changes by clinging to communal values and trying to foster group means of controlling manufacturing. Workers expressed their views by trying to organize unions, even in the early decades of the Industrial Revolution.

The growth of the commercial economy altered economic opportunities for women and American ideologies concerning them. There were two main trends. On the one hand, as work left the home for the factory and artisans became workers whose activities a factory manager controlled, women usually found themselves relegated to lower paying, routinized jobs. The Boston Associates, for instance, were famous for their recruitment of New England farm-girls to leave their homes and work in the mills of Lowell. In that sense, the specialization that swept through economic life lowered the status of women, who seldom found themselves in positions of authority. On the other hand, successful businessmen began to idealize and elevate women as "ladies" who should not soil themselves with business. This concept fully flowered in the middle of the nineteenth century as the "cult of true womanhood." While American rhetoric was promoting individualism for white men, it was idealizing women as the pure, pious, gentle keepers of the home who nurtured children and comforted husbands.

There were exceptions to the general rule, of course. Women continued to work in family businesses. For instance, Rebecca Lukens assumed managerial control of an iron mill on Brandywine Creek in eastern Pennsylvania when her husband died in 1825. During the twenty-two years that she ran the company, it grew from a small craft operation serving a local market to a large industrial firm reaching a substantial regional market. Occasionally women emerged as business entrepreneurs in their own right, not just as family members. And women were vital participants in the family farm's operation as a small business.

If the business achievements of a few women were exceptional, those of black Americans were remarkable, given the fact that in 1860, free blacks comprised only about 10 per cent of America's black population of 4.5 million. Nevertheless, in 1860, there were about 2,300 black-owned businesses in the United States. A few black businesses had existed during colonial times, and in the decades before the Civil War ended slavery, black entrepreneurs entered additional enterprises. Blacks were involved in merchandising, manufacturing, and real-estate speculation, among other fields. Small black family businesses operated as peddlers, blacksmiths, and the like. A few blacks even achieved substantial success. Between 1830 and 1865, twenty-one black businessmen accumulated at least $100,000 in wealth. William Leidesdorff, a San Francisco merchant, became America's first black millionaire, worth $1.5 million at his death in 1848. Like their white counterparts, these entrepreneurs often benefited from inherited wealth, family connections, and apprenticeships in family enterprises.

Social Responsibility

Some of the entrepreneurs who so greatly developed America's opportunities saw themselves as stewards, trustees, or essential leaders in other areas of American society. An elite group of Boston merchants and industrialists went the furthest in this regard. Called Brahmins because of their emphasis on family background and cultural ideals, they sought to improve their city and American civilization in a variety of ways. They hired architects to design attractive offices and homes for themselves. They patronized the arts and funded libraries, scholarships, and scientific projects, making Boston the showplace of American civilization. One of the Brahmins, Nathan Appleton, so important in organizing the industrial revolution in textiles, once wrote, "The truth is that my mind has always been devoted to many other things rather than money-making."

The idea of social responsibility was not confined to the entrepreneurs of Boston, however. For instance, the Tappan brothers, prominent New York merchants, provided sorely needed finances to the antislavery movement. Amos Kendall, who advocated individualism while serving as a close adviser of President Andrew Jackson (1829–1837), later made a fortune in the new telegraph industry and eventually retired from business to found Gallaudet College for the deaf, the first such institution in the world. The list of benefactions in pre–Civil War America was long. Businessmen also served society as political leaders, just as they had in colonial and revolutionary times.

AMERICA'S CHANGING BUSINESS SYSTEM

The business system of the United States underwent vast changes in the seventy years following independence. George Washington would have been astonished by the enormous growth of business activity and the market that supported it, the many specialized firms, and the machine technologies that eased travel, manufacture, and farming. During this period as well arose new ways of conducting business that presaged the methods of the big business firms that were to come. American railroad executives, especially, who were doing so much to overcome the barriers of time and space that had hindered entrepreneurs in Washington's time, were facing and solving unprecedented business problems with new techniques of organization and management.

Washington was prescient in observing the great possibilities for internal improvements. Successive political leaders continued to call for and receive governmental assistance in the financing and construction of roads, waterways, and railroads to open even greater opportunities than Washington had imagined. There remained widespread political consensus on the desirability of having government encourage entrepreneurial opportunities and provide the necessary legal framework for their full fruition.

Selected Readings

Douglas C. North, *The Economic Growth of the United States, 1790–1860* (Englewood Cliffs, N.J.: Prentice-Hall, 1961), and Diane Lindstrom, *Economic Development of the Philadelphia Region, 1810–1850* (New York: Columbia University Press, 1978), examine the expansion of America's business system. George Rogers Taylor, *The Transportation Revolution, 1815–1860* (New York: Holt, Rinehart and Winston, 1951); Albert Fishlow, *Railroads and the Transformation of the Ante-Bellum Economy* (Cambridge: Harvard University Press, 1965); and Cynthia Owen Philip, *Robert Fulton: A Biography* (New York: Franklin Watts, 1985), look at transportation improvements. Paul Gates, *The Farmer's Age: Agriculture, 1815–1860* (New York: Harper & Row, 1960), and Clarence H. Danhof, *Change in Agriculture: The Northern United States, 1820–1870* (Cambridge: Harvard University Press, 1969), are classic studies.

David Hounshell: *From the American System to Mass Production 1800–1932* (Baltimore: The Johns Hopkins University Press, 1984), and Thomas Cochran, *The Frontiers of Change: Early Industrialism in America* (New York: Oxford University Press, 1981), survey the process of industrialization from different points of view. Alan Dawley, *Class and Community: The Industrial Revolution in Lynn* (Cambridge: Harvard University Press, 1976); Robert Dalzell, Jr., *Enterprising Elite: The Boston Associates and the World They Made* (Cambridge: Harvard University Press, 1987); and Gary Kornblith, "The Craftsman as Industrialist: Jonas Chickering and the Transformation of American Piano Making," *Business History Review* 59 (Autumn 1985): 349–68, are useful case studies.

Glenn Porter and Harold Livesay, *Merchants and Manufacturers:*

Studies in the Changing Structure of Nineteenth-Century Marketing (Baltimore: The Johns Hopkins Press, 1971), present a penetrating analysis of business changes in America during the 1800s. The classic account of the cotton trade is in Robert G. Albion, *The Rise of New York Port, 1815–1870* (New York: Charles Scribner's Sons, 1939). For an introduction to the plantation, see Eugene D. Genovese, "The Significance of the Slave Plantation for Southern Economic Development," *Journal of Social History* 28 (November 1962): 422–437. Morton Keller, *The Life Insurance Enterprise, 1885–1910* (Cambridge, Mass.: Harvard University Press, 1963), introduces the early years of the life insurance industry. Claudia Golden, "The Economic Status of Women in the Early Republic: Quantitative Evidence," *Journal of Interdisciplinary History* 16 (Winter 1986): 375–404, examines women in business, focusing on Philadelphia. Juliet E. K. Walker, "Racism, Slavery, and Free Enterprise: Black Entrepreneurship in the United States before the Civil War," *Business History Review* 60 (Autumn, 1986): 343–82, reveals the remarkable story of black business achievement in the age of slavery.

IMPORTANT EVENTS, 1784–1861

1784	George Washington requests Virginia's assistance in connecting the Ohio and Potomac river valleys.
1789	Congress enacts the first tariff law.
1803	Ohio is admitted to the Union. Congress authorizes construction of the National Road. Thomas Jefferson arranges the Louisiana Purchase.
1808	Albert Gallatin calls for a national program of internal improvements.
1811	The Bank of the United States' charter expires. New York passes the first general incorporation law.
1816	Congress charters the Second Bank of the United States.
1824–1838	The General Survey Act provides assistance for planning roads, canals, and railroads.
1825	The Erie Canal is completed by the state of New York.
1832	Andrew Jackson vetoes the rechartering of the Second Bank of the United States.
1844	A telegraph line between Washington, D.C., and Baltimore is completed with federal funds.
1850	Congress authorizes the first federal land grant in support of railroad construction.
1861	Eleven Southern states secede from the Union. California is linked to the East by the telegraph.

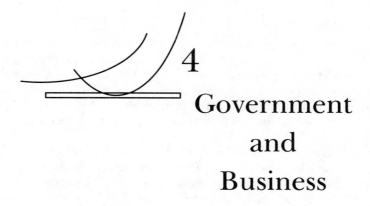

4

Government
and
Business

After George Washington explored possible routes to connect Virginia with the Ohio River valley in 1784, he appeared before the Virginia Assembly to request the state's assistance. The legislators agreed to help. Virginia appointed an official commission to survey routes, chartered the Potomac Company to begin clearing the Potomac River of obstructions, and offered to help finance the venture. The project eventually failed because the available technology and capital were insufficient to maintain navigation on the Potomac River. Thirty-three years later, however, the legislature of New York passed a law to finance, construct, and operate the Erie Canal. On July 4, 1817, De Witt Clinton, then mayor of New York City, ceremoniously lifted the first shovel of earth, and the great project was under way.

The stories of the abortive Potomac Company and the successful Erie Canal illustrate the extent of government involvement in the development of the young nation. In fact, one major aspect of the relationship between government and business after 1789 was developmental. There was considerable agreement among American leaders that the government should assist private entrepreneurial enterprises. This agreement differed from European forms of mercantilism. The mercantilist policies, against which Americans had rebelled, were impositions by a government upon the people it ruled. In the new United States, in contrast, there was no sense that the government was somehow separate from its people. The propertied men who ran the American government were not part of an aristocracy ruling on the basis of ancient feudal privileges. Thus, governmental policies intended to promote business were not policies to benefit some separate ruling class, or some entity called the state, but instead were seen as policies of the people to help the people. The result was initiatives that promoted entrepreneurial opportunity.

If there was general consensus about a developmental political economy, however, there was much disagreement concerning its particulars. We have seen how bitter those disagreements were in the 1790s, and more disputes followed. The growing diversity of specialized business enterprises also meant a growth in competing business interests. The clash of interests meant that local interests tended to prevail over visions of uniform national policy during the nineteenth century. After 1820, the racial and economic institution of slavery began to loom over all other political considerations until by 1861, slavery's Southern defenders, in the most extreme form of localism, felt compelled to secede from the Union. Nor was slavery the only issue in which local and particular interests disjointed the nation. American entrepreneurs and their political representatives disagreed about important internal-improvement, tariff, banking, and land policies as well. These grave conflicts notwithstanding, the overall characteristic of government-business relations during the nineteenth century was developmental, as all levels of government actively promoted business opportunity.

INTERNAL IMPROVEMENTS

The Federal Government

When Thomas Jefferson was inaugurated president for the second time in 1805, he pointed proudly to the success of his fiscal program. "Because of the elimination of internal taxes," Jefferson observed, "it may be the pleasure and pride of an American to ask, what farmer, what mechanic, what laborer, ever sees a tax-gatherer of the United States." A growing revenue surplus from the tariff on imported goods was retiring the debt and freeing the federal government to use its resources for improving "rivers, canals, roads, arts, manufacturing, education, and other great objects." And there was a lot of country to improve now. Concerned about assuring American access to the seaport of New Orleans at the mouth of the

Mississippi, the president had greatly enlarged the size of the United States with the Louisiana Purchase of 1803. Much internal improvement appeared necessary if America were to fulfill Jefferson's promise as a republic resting on a productive, independent citizenry.

In matters of planning for internal improvements, Jefferson's most brilliant adviser was Secretary of the Treasury Albert Gallatin. Born in Switzerland in 1761, Gallatin emigrated to America in 1780. In 1786, he moved to southwestern Pennsylvania, where he attended the convention of 1788 that discussed the ratification of the new Constitution, and he became a member of the state legislature in 1790. As a member of Congress from 1795 to 1801, Gallatin was part of the faction opposing the military and fiscal policies of President John Adams. Gallatin's proposals for financial reform, to have Congress more cautiously appropriate money, made him Jefferson's logical choice for the important cabinet post of treasury secretary.

As secretary of the treasury, Gallatin became the nation's first economic planner in matters of internal improvement. Whereas Hamilton had looked outward toward overseas commerce as the key to the nation's economic health, Gallatin the Jeffersonian looked inward. With the movement of population westward across the Appalachian Mountain barrier, the need for overland transportation and communications links was clear. Shortly after 1803, when Ohio was admitted as the first state from the Northwest Territory, as the Great Lakes basin was then called, Congress authorized the building of a road west from Baltimore, Maryland, to provide an overland route to the Ohio River. In 1807, the Senate also instructed Gallatin to draw up a comprehensive report on the need for further public improvements.

Gallatin issued his *Report on Roads, Canals, Harbors, and Rivers* in 1808. In it he described both the needs of the nation and the problems of meeting those needs. According to his national plan for transportation and communications, the country should have "from north to south, in a direction parallel to the seacoast" both "a great turnpike road" and "canals opening an inland navigation for sea vessels from Massachusetts to North Carolina." From east to west, similarly, roads should cross the Appalachian Mountains and extend as far as Detroit, St. Louis, and New Orleans. Waterways, built to improve the navigation of rivers and combine them with canals, should connect the eastern seaboard with the transappalachian interior. At places where there were natural bottlenecks, such as Niagara Falls or the falls on the Ohio River near Louisville, canals should be built to allow boats to pass. Thus, Gallatin planned to open "navigation from Lake Ontario to the upper lakes as far as the extremities of Lake Michigan," with Lake Ontario connected by canal and river to New York City. He estimated this plan would cost $16.6 million. To make it politically palatable to regions that would not directly benefit from improved connections to the interior, he suggested the expenditure of another $3.4 million on "a number of local improvements," which would "do substantial justice and give general satisfaction." The total cost of $20 million, he believed, could be paid in ten years' time from surplus tariff revenues.

When Gallatin presented his sweeping program, he explained why it was necessary for the federal government to embark on internal improvements. He observed that there were two types of projects. *Exploitative* projects went through populated countryside. Private investors saw profitable opportunities for capital improvements in such cases. *Developmental* projects such as those he proposed were different. They were based on the anticipation that, upon completion, settlements and businesses would arise along their paths. Private investors were often reluctant to engage in developmental projects, which promised only remote and uncertain profits. Individuals and private enterprise simply did not have the resources, or the incentive, to embark on such projects, however desirable they were from the viewpoint of the national interest. Gallatin made a key point: "The General Government can alone remove these obstacles."

Gallatin's report came to naught after 1808. The warfare between Britain and France made his scheme for financing improvements impossible. President Jefferson felt compelled to order embargoes on the importation of British goods, and the tariff revenue surpluses upon which Gallatin had based his projections disappeared. The need for internal improvements continued, and the obstacles to private development that Gallatin had noted remained, but the financial and political ability of the federal government to act evaporated in the foreign policy crises that resulted eventually in the War of 1812. The actual construction of internal improvements after the war ended in 1815 fell mostly to state and local governments.

Although the federal government did not build the canals and roads that Gallatin envisioned, it did provide essential help in planning both state and private ventures. In 1802, the army created the Corps of Engineers, located at West Point on the Hudson River up-

Cincinnati, situated on the Ohio River, bustled with commerce along its waterfront even after the railroad came. Merchants and merchandise crowded the levee, and steamboats docked in the shadow of the new railway bridge. (Courtesy of the Ohio Historical Society)

stream from New York City. The establishment of the United States Military Academy, run by the corps as an engineering school until the outbreak of the Civil War in 1861, provided the government with a cadre capable of providing valuable assistance in laying out the routes for roads, canals, and railroads. In 1816, army engineers began to survey western rivers and lakes and to help state and local projects along the Atlantic seaboard.

The federal government enlarged this service under the General Survey Act of 1824. Between 1824 and 1828, a Board of Engineers for Internal Improvements investigated the links essential for the nation's transportation system. President John Quincy Adams thought this work was of "great importance," and the army engineers began to help to build the nation's first railroad lines. When the Baltimore & Ohio Railroad was chartered in 1828, it asked for a government survey, and the army lent three surveying brigades, each told to follow the company's instructions. Army engineers, led by Major William J. McNeill, supervised the construction of the first Baltimore & Ohio line. Eventually, McNeill worked for eight other railroads. After 1828, the government paid only the salaries of the engineers whose services it lent to the railroads, and the companies assumed their other expenses. Under this arrangement, army engineers had made at least ten railroad or canal surveys by 1830, and by 1835 at least twenty railroads were receiving vital federal engineering assistance. This policy lasted until 1838, when Congress repealed the General Survey Act. By that time, army engineers had helped build 1,879 miles of track.

Congress repealed the law because after the general economic depression that began in 1837, there seemed a sufficient supply of civilian engineers to complete the necessary work. But only eleven years later, when Americans began to think about crossing the Great Plains and the formidable Rocky Mountain barrier with iron rails, Congress again began making annual appropriations for military and geographical surveys west of the Mississippi River. In 1853, the government began the Pacific Railroad surveys, which examined four major routes. Actual construction of the first transcontinental railroad was delayed, however, until after the start of the Civil War.

This limited federal assistance for internal improvements was hardly the fulfillment of Gallatin's grand plan. The need for internal improvements remained, and the federal government commanded sufficient fiscal resources to help fund them, but the political will to engage in internal improvements dissipated in the face of the slavery controversy. As the plantation system of the South expanded westward, southern political leaders came to see every national policy issue in the light of its potential impact on the institution of slavery. Much of the South was blessed with rivers that flowed to ports on the Gulf of Mexico. High-value, compact bales of cotton could be sent to market on rafts, barges, or steamboats without resort to expensive improvements. Internal improvements sought by northerners were largely east-west ventures, and the southern planters did not want to pay the higher tariff duties needed to fund them. Southerners saw the tariff as a tax on the South for the benefit of the North and West, and they thought it would serve only to augment the wealth and therefore the power of the sections that were antagonistic to the continuation of slavery. Then, too, debate over a constitutional issue helped limit federal aid to internal improvements. Those opposing federal involvement argued that the Constitution did not give such far-reaching powers to the federal government, that they were reserved, according to that document, to the state governments. In this view, federal funding of internal improvements was simply unconstitutional.

Presidential encouragement of federal support of internal improvements waned in the face of the bitter intersectional rivalry. John Quincy Adams, who served in the White House from 1825 to 1829, was the last of the pre–Civil War presidents to support the idea of federal aid for transportation improvements. His successor, Andrew Jackson, ended sizable federal expenditures for roads and canals, arguing that those projects, under the Constitution, belonged to state and local governments. He turned over the completed sections of the National Road to Maryland, Virginia, Ohio, and Indiana. By the 1830s, Gallatin's integrated plan was no more. In its place stood the more decentralized situation of individual, state, and local government action; localism had triumphed.

There were two significant exceptions to the general pattern of federal retreat from support for internal improvements before the Civil War, however. Both involved the newest technologies of transportation and communication: the telegraph and the railroad. As we saw in Chapter 3, the federal government subsidized the development of communications through the reduction of postal rates and the expansion of postal routes. It went a step further after the invention of the telegraph in 1837. Private investors were unwilling to support the risky venture of building an experimental telegraph line, so Congress appropriated $30,000 to complete a line from Washington to Baltimore in 1844. Some consideration was given to making the telegraph part of the postal system, but instead, once the practicality of the new technology was demonstrated with public funds, it was left to private exploitation. By the end of 1846, most of the eastern states were connected by telegraph line, and California was linked to the rest of the country by telegraph in 1861.

Federal subsidies for railroad construction were even greater than those for the telegraph. Western interests had asked for federal help in expanding railroad mileage in their region, but a combination of southern and northeastern congressmen, who saw no immediate advantage in transferring wealth to the West, had stopped them. That situation changed in 1850 with the proposed construction of the Illinois Central Railroad to link the upper Mississippi River valley and Chicago with the port of Mobile, Alabama. Investors in Boston and New York saw the advantages of such a line connecting to ones they owned running eastward toward Chicago. The result was the first federal railroad land grant, passed by Congress in 1850. This measure granted federal land to Mississippi, Alabama, and Illinois, which they could turn over to the railroad, and which the railroad could then use to back its bonds. The railroad received a two-hundred-foot-wide right of way and a checkerboard of sections of land in a six-mile-wide swath along its path, land which the railroad could either sell or use to secure private loans. In effect, the federal government underwrote the original capital costs of the Illinois Central. In return the railroad was obligated to carry the troops or property of the United States government free from any toll or other charge, and Congress had the authority to set the rates for carrying mail.

This subsidy provided enormous help for the entrepreneurs building the new railroad. The cost of construction and equipment for the Illinois Central was $23 million, only one-sixth of which came from private stockholders. The rest of the funds came mostly from mortgages secured by the lands granted by the federal government. Not only was this policy instrumental in speeding the construction of an important north-south carrier, but it also set a precedent for the future. Once the political power of the South was broken by the Civil War, the way was clear to extend the land-grant system for the support of the construction of transcontinental routes. The first transcontinental railroad, created by linking the track of the Central Pacific building eastward from Sacramento and the Union Pacific building westward from Omaha, was completed under federal incentives and support, including land grants, in 1869.

State and Local Governments

Although the federal government before the Civil War played an important role in planning internal improvements but was thwarted in executing their development by constitutional and political disputes, no such factors retarded state and local government action. In an era when business firms were small and specialized, merchants, manufacturers, commercial farmers, and land speculators tended to influence state and local governments, viewing them as logical entities to meet the needs of economic development. Unlike the situation with the federal government, within each state there were no restrictions imposed by strict constitutional construction on economic activity. Nor were state politicians—often ambitious entrepreneurs themselves—encumbered by laissez-faire theory. Whenever the needs of economic development were critical, state aid was enthusiastically given. Missouri, admitted to the Union in 1820, perhaps best expressed this spirit in its constitution, which stated that "internal improvement shall forever be encouraged by the government of this State." In the absence of legal and theoretical restrictions, it was the state and local governments, responsive to local entrepreneurial ambitions, that gave the most aid to internal improvement projects in the period before the Civil War. This assistance did not follow the national plan laid out by Gallatin, but instead helped projects intended to improve or create local economic advantages.

State and local government aid was instrumental in hurdling the Appalachian Mountain barrier. The aid took several forms, all of which involved available transportation technologies, from roads to steam railroads. Some railroads and canals were built as public works. Others were mixed enterprises that combined public and private funds. The first commercially important east-west transportation link was the Erie Canal. The total original cost of the Erie Canal was $7 million, by far the largest sum ever expended on an internal improvement and one that exceeded the capitalization of the nation's largest manufacturing firm by ten times. The state of New York financed the canal because private entrepreneurs were unwilling to engage in such a difficult and speculative venture. So the state held lotteries and sold bonds to pay for the venture and operated the canal as a public work. The Erie Canal was an immediate commercial success and, as noted in Chapter 3, sparked a veritable craze for canals elsewhere. But most of these other canals failed to generate enough toll revenues to pay for both their capital and maintenance costs.

Since state funds were by far the most important source of capital for canals, the failure of canals to generate revenues sufficient to repay the state caused serious problems. By 1841, for instance, Indiana was carrying over $9 million of debt attributable to internal improvements. These investments were simply not recoverable from canal tolls, and the states that had to pay the bill from tax revenues legislated against any such future investments. After Ohio lost money on its canals, for example, its new 1851 constitution forbade the state or any of its cities, counties, or townships from owning stock, making loans, or raising funds for any internal improvement companies.

This was an extreme reaction to the canal debts, however. There were innumerable instances of states, cities, counties, and towns funding railroad projects in anticipation of diverting or developing trade and thereby enhancing local entrepreneurial opportunities. The best-known example of government support for railroad construction was one of the nation's first lines, the Baltimore & Ohio Railroad, which was a joint public and private venture. The business and political leaders of Baltimore realized that the success of the Erie Canal threatened their long-term prospects, for the canal drew trade to New York City, which rapidly eclipsed its rival ports. Baltimore's leaders wanted to counter this competition by the construction of a railroad west to the Ohio River valley, in effect fulfilling George Washington's earlier vision. The city provided capital for the construction and hoped eventually to reap the rewards of dividends and interest. (Profits were too far in the future to attract the necessary private capital.) The City of Baltimore held a financial interest in the Baltimore & Ohio until 1890, and in another line, the Western Maryland, until 1902.

In the South, as well, much of the investment in railroads came from governments. Southern agricultural production was capital-intensive—that is, it required large monetary investments. Cotton farming exhausted the soil, necessitating investment in new land, and the requirements of the slave system, although generally profitable for its owners, soaked up capital. Private financiers used their resources to fund the short-term needs of agriculture. The result was that southerners often turned to public sources of capital for building railroads. Georgia led the way in 1836 when it launched the Western & Atlantic Railroad as a state enterprise. Between 1841 and 1850, up to one-third of Georgia's budget went to railroad construction. The main line of the Western & Atlantic went to the northwestern region of Georgia, up to then a landlocked and sparsely populated area, and in 1849, it reached Chattanooga, Tennessee. The line carried thousands of cotton bales to market in Savannah during the 1850s, and freight revenues soon began to repay the state's investment. The plan of the Western & Atlantic was not that it would compete with private facilities—they were not being constructed—but that it would provide a focal point for a rail network. Shorter lines constructed by towns and private investors connected to the trunk line, and the Western & Atlantic provided terminals in Savannah and Atlanta for goods originating on them.

Public Investment in Private Enterprise

Georgia and the other states that were building railroads and other improvements did so to expand opportunities for private enterprise. The projects, thus, were not mercantilism in the traditional sense, or some precursor to modern socialism, but developmental

The Erie Canal and other important canal projects were funded by state governments. This is an example of a bond issued in 1839 by the state of New York to provide capital for the Erie Canal. Note that the interest rate was 5 per cent per year. (Smithsonian Institution photo no. 85-0893)

planning ventures intended to foster business and agricultural opportunities for private citizens. Much of the railroad investment came from residents along the lines who hoped not so much for a profitable return as for the benefits of using the facilities.

Public investment in internal improvements was substantial. In the years between 1815 and 1860, about 60 per cent of the total investment in transportation facilities came in the form of government public works. More than half of this investment was concentrated in the seven states that either faced or included parts of the Appalachian Mountain range. In canal construction, about 73 per cent of the funds came from public investment; the federal government granted about 4 million acres of land and $3 million to Ohio, Michigan, Indiana, Illinois, and Wisconsin for canals. For railroads, 25 to 30 per cent of the investment before 1861 was public, not including land grants. All these funds were required, as Gallatin had predicted, either where capital costs exceeded the resources of private entrepreneurs or where profits were too far in the future to entice private developers, given the absence of prior social and economic development.

The results of the public investments were sometimes chaotic. Towns feared, rightly, that if they lacked rail service they might die as viable economic entities, so excessive and wasteful construction occasionally ensued. In retrospect, the shortcomings of relying on state and local government planning for internal improvements, in contrast to Gallatin's national scheme, were clear. In the decentralized system, there were no workable criteria for selecting projects or for assigning particular projects to different levels of governmental responsibility. Nor did governments have effective means of supervising projects. Just as the nation lacked an engineering cadre at the start of the nineteenth century, throughout the period it had no body of public experts and no system of legal agencies capable of overseeing the usage of public funds. Sometimes waste and fraud were the result, although the worst scandals occurred after the Civil War, when the first transcontinental railroad was completed.

BANKING AND THE TARIFF

Although there were areas of strong collaboration between government and business in the pre–Civil War years, as in the funding and building of internal improvements, there were also areas of intense conflict. Controversies over the appropriate use of the federal government's power to levy import duties racked national politics after 1789, as businessmen with competing and changing interests wrangled over the questions of tariff protection for domestic manufacturing from foreign competition. Disputes over banking policies, on the other hand, arose not just from the competing economic interests of businessmen but from the need of officials to provide an adequate currency system for the operation of the government.

Banking Policies

Just as there was a fragmentation of the political economy on policies of federal support for internal improvements, so there was a similar situation in banking policy before the 1860s. As we have seen, the chartering of the Bank of the United States was the most controversial subject in the political economy of the 1790s. That controversy deepened and grew more complex by the 1830s. The charter of the Bank of the United States ran for twenty years, and the Jeffersonians, ever suspicious of the concentration of so much power in the hands of a few private individuals, refused to renew it in 1811. During the War of 1812, the United States had no federally chartered bank, but the ensuing difficulties in maintaining a sound currency led prominent businessmen and financiers, including John Jacob Astor and Stephen Girard, to encourage Congress to charter a Second Bank of the United States in 1816.

Businessmen like Astor and Girard wanted a Second Bank of the United States, and Congress agreed, because the absence of such an institution had led to chaos. State governments chartered banks—so-called state banks—in which the federal government deposited its funds after 1811. Both businesses and the government borrowed from the state banks, which issued notes redeemable in specie (gold or silver) that circulated as currency. When borrowing increased, as it did during the War of 1812, the amount of currency flowing into the economy rose. When the economy boomed, optimistic bankers freely loaned money, liberally printing more notes, sometimes without regard to their ability to redeem them in specie. Bank notes—the nation's currency, in other words—became suspect, adding to the risks of conducting business.

Congress tried to correct this situation when it created the Second Bank of the United States. The Second Bank was like its predecessor, except that the government appointed five of its twenty-five directors, and the directors enjoyed considerable power to control the nation's currency. When the federal government collected revenue, mostly from tariff duties, in bank notes, it deposited them in the Bank of the United States. The bank, in turn, could require their redemption in specie, and thus provide a powerful brake on state banks that might otherwise overexpand their credit. In other words, the Bank of the United States indirectly regulated the supply of credit and the volume of currency available. The new scheme worked well for a time, but by the 1830s, the Bank of the United States encountered vociferous complaints from agrarians, who suspected all banks and all paper money, and from optimistic financiers, who wanted to promote rapid economic expansion.

The Bank of the United States, especially after Nicholas Biddle became its president in 1823, was very helpful to established businesses. Business people could count on the value of the currency they received because Biddle, from his office on Philadelphia's Chestnut Street, tried to insure that the state banks did not extend their credit beyond their assets. Moreover, the Bank of the United

States supplied about one-fourth of the nation's currency, and its branch offices—there were twenty-nine by 1830, all in commercial centers—facilitated interregional monetary exchange. The Bank of the United States also operated as a commercial bank, accepting deposits and making loans.

If Biddle's policies were helpful to the conduct of business, however, agrarians, especially in the West and the South, and many state bankers questioned them. Agrarians, eventually championed by Andrew Jackson, who was elected president in 1828 and reelected in 1832, were suspicious of all paper currency and the power of so few men to manipulate its value. Jackson denounced the bank for its failure to establish "a uniform and sound currency," by which he meant an entirely metallic currency whose volume of circulation and value would not fluctuate. Some bankers, on the other hand denounced Biddle's policies as "coercion" and "oppression." Calling themselves "Democrats by trade," they promoted the virtues of free enterprise and laissez faire and exalted the rugged individualism of the entrepreneur and the pioneer. Alexander Hamilton's son, ironically, was a leading Democrat who sought the destruction of Biddle's power in order to gain more freedom for a large bank on New York's Wall Street, controlled by him and his friends.

The controversy, sometimes summarized as one between Wall Street and Chestnut Street, concluded in the 1830s with the New Yorkers and the other Democrats victorious. President Jackson vetoed the rechartering of the bank in 1832, complaining that it made "the rich richer and the potent more powerful." Then the federal government withdrew its deposits from the Bank of the United States. The result was a bonanza for state banks, which increased in number. The Wall Street bankers seized this opportunity to increase their power, expecting that the assets of the American business system would begin to concentrate in the nation's leading port and largest city. Lending policies were liberal in the absence of any central control and, true to the expectations of the New Yorkers, assets began to concentrate in their banks. Efforts on the part of some western states to allow only a metallic currency proved futile. It was not until the 1860s that the federal government devised a new banking policy. Until then, Americans often had to question the worth of the notes they received in payment of goods and services.

These developments in banking were an important part of the larger American business scene of the pre–Civil War decades. They

GENERAL JACKSON SLAYING THE MANY HEADED MONSTER.

"General Jackson Slaying the Many-Headed Monster." The cartoonist here depicts the Bank of the United States as evil by portraying it as a snake. Clearly the evil bank had already appeared in many places and thus was difficult to exterminate. (Library of Congress)

were evidence of sentiments that reflected the growing diversity of the American business system. The nation's political leadership was unable, in banking as in transportation, to develop uniform, consistent, long-range policies that brought together the divergent economic interests of western farmers, southern planters, cotton factors, nascent northern manufacturers, and Wall Street bankers. The net effect, however, of the transportation and banking policies was the promotion of speculative, optimistic business enterprise.

Tariff Controversies

The longest-running controversy in the political economy of the nineteenth century concerned the tariff. This controversy resulted in a further retreat by the federal government from intervention in the free flow of goods among markets. The retreat was the product of a concern with holding the Union together; it was a political compromise, not the result of any growing consensus regarding free-market economic theory. Federal tariff policy came to reflect not so much the needs of domestic industries as the potent political power of commercial agriculture, especially of the southern planters. As in the other areas of political economy before the Civil War, the growing size and diversity of the American business system prevented agreement in favor of planned federal intervention.

At its simplest level, the debate about the tariff raged between those Americans, led before the Civil War by the planters in the South, who were consumers of manufactured products and exporters of raw materials and foodstuffs, and those who saw the tariff as essential for the encouragement of manufacturing within the United States. The debate involved Adam Smith's idea of comparative advantage and was complicated by the fact that the tariff was the principal source of revenue for the federal government at that time. The issue of the tariff affected the outcomes of elections and helped separate Americans permanently into two political parties. By the end of the 1850s, the Democratic party, with deep southern roots, generally stood for a tariff "for revenue only," while the new Republican party argued for a protective tariff to promote industrialization.

The first piece of legislation enacted by the new Congress that met after ratification of the Constitution was the Tariff Act of July 4, 1789. It established precedents for both future legislation and heated debates on the subject. One purpose of the law was to raise revenue for the new government. The tariff generally placed a tax of 5 per cent on the value of items imported to the United States (so-called *ad valorem* duty) and, for special items listed, specific duties regardless of their value. Boots, for instance, were taxed at 50 cents a pair. But this first legislation expressed more than the desire to raise revenue for the government. Among its declared purposes was "the encouragement and protection of manufactures." The specific rates selected for items like boots were intended to protect American producers from foreign competition. The protective features of this first tariff act were ineffective, but they marked the beginning of heated dispute that saw political leaders try to shape American development and individual business people or their organizations seek special favors through legislation.

Disputes over the tariff grew more vociferous and more complex as American merchants invested their capital in manufacturing.

Manufacturers, when having to compete with more advanced firms abroad, especially in Great Britain, claimed the high patriotic ground of protecting the internal American market for American producers. Their opponents, usually agrarian or other business interests who bought manufactured goods, promoted Adam Smith's arguments that it was best to allow self-interest to operate through the invisible hand of the free market. Advocates of protection dismissed those arguments as "abstract and theoretical" ideas spoken by "foreign speculative writers."

The shifting needs of producers and consumers complicated tariff politics and divided business leaders. For example, the burgeoning railroad network used large quantities of iron rails. Before 1860, the British exported rails to the United States at prices American manufacturers could not match. Thus, one of the battles over tariffs involved conflict between the railroads, as consumers of rails, and the American iron makers who wanted to produce them. The iron makers, led by Abram S. Hewitt, began petitioning Congress in 1849 for protection; although they could raise money for publicity and lobbying, they could not translate those funds into the necessary popular voting strength to change legislators' behavior. The railroads struck an alliance with western and agrarian interests that sought the expansion of their regional railroad facilities and kept the duties on British rails low. As manufacturing businesses appeared west of the Appalachian mountains, however, politicians from states like Ohio sometimes took up the protectionist cause.

The result was a welter of confusion in national politics, exceeded in emotion prior to the Civil War only by the slavery controversy. Congress passed deliberately protectionist measures in 1824, 1828, and 1832, but in 1833, after Vice President John C. Calhoun dramatically resigned and returned to his native South Carolina to lead resistance to the protectionist tariff, a compromise was reached to achieve a tariff for revenue only. When the new Republican party took power in 1861, it launched the nation on a determined course of using the tariff to help American industrialists.

LAW AND BUSINESS DEVELOPMENT

The Nature of American Law

These conflicts over banking and tariff policies were due in part to the country's federal system of government, in which power is separated into different branches and levels. Groups gaining access to political power in these different areas might have very different business interests, depending on their region or local forms of business development. Within the welter of conflict, confusion, and diversity, however, two factors stand out as important for the development of American business institutions. First, there was a tendency in the federal law, especially as it was clarified by court decisions, to give individuals wide latitude in using their entrepreneurial talents. Second, there was support for the rights of individuals to gain, hold, and use property in order to earn profits. The chief exception to the second factor was the antislavery movement. The abolitionists, however, did not propose to destroy capitalism as the basis of the American economic system but to place the ownership of humans outside the boundaries of what was acceptable.

The Supreme Court and Business Development

In the first half of the nineteenth century, two great chief justices of the Supreme Court of the United States left an indelible stamp on American constitutional law and vitally affected the framework in which American business institutions developed. John Marshall, the first of these justices, served on the court from 1801 to 1836, when he was succeeded by Roger Taney, the other greatly influential justice. Marshall matured during the American Revolution and expressed the federalist viewpoint of the men who wrote the Constitution. His decisions protected federal supremacy over the states. Taney, in contrast, was embroiled in the Jacksonian politics of a later era. His decisions tended to reduce the power of government to restrict business enterprise, and thereby to enlarge business opportunities.

Marshall's main contribution to American constitutional law was the care he took to assert the Supreme Court's right of judicial review—the Court as the final authority on the Constitution—and its independence from the legislative and executive branches of government. With respect to the development of the American political economy, three of his decisions stand out. In the case of *McCulloch* v. *Maryland* (1819) the court ruled against the effort of the state of Maryland to impose a tax on the Second Bank of the United States, and Marshall asserted his famous dictum that the power to tax was the power to destroy. Not only did this decision protect the bank from an important source of opposition but it also provided a doctrine that allowed the federal government, if it so chose, to create instruments such as the bank to govern or promote business enterprise. The second case, *Dartmouth College* v. *Woodward* (1819), involved the question of the states' power to change corporate charters. Dartmouth College was a corporation chartered by the British crown in 1769. When New Hampshire sought to change the charter to make it a public institution, Marshall ruled that corporate charters were contracts that the states could not "impair." Rather than preventing state regulation of corporations through charter changes, however, the effect of the decision was to encourage the states routinely to place clauses in corporate charters stating that they could be changed. Such action in effect, made the possibility of change part of the contract. *Gibbons* v. *Ogden* (1824), a case involving the commerce clause of the Constitution, which grants the federal government exclusive authority to govern business among the states, was even more significant. Aaron Ogden was a steamboat operator who enjoyed a monopoly, granted by the state of New York, to operate a ferry service across the Hudson River between New Jersey and New York City. Thomas Gibbons set up a competing line, and Ogden sued. Marshall decided the case in favor of Gibbons. A state, the chief justice said, may regulate commerce within its boundaries but not transactions that cross state lines. In such matters, national authority prevailed. This decision affirmed the commerce clause and asserted the importance of the national market over the states' more parochial desire to promote their self-interests. Marshall's ruling would have far-reaching consequences in the future, both for the development of a national market, which businesses could tap without state government restrictions and, eventually, for allowing federal regulation of business. Neither result occurred immediately, however, as legal disputes and political wrangling lasted over a century.

Marshall's successor on the bench, Roger Taney, brought conservative convictions of hard money and respect for private property to the Court. His most significant decision for the expansion of the American business system conformed to a growing spirit supportive of free enterprise. In *Charles River Bridge Company* v. *Warren Bridge Company* (1837), the Court attacked monopolistic privilege. It was common in the earliest days of internal improvements for states to grant monopoly privileges to corporations in order to encourage private investment. The Charles River Bridge Company, which operated a toll bridge across the Charles River at Boston, had an implied monopoly privilege. When a free bridge threatened its investment, the toll-bridge company sued. Taney ruled against it. The charter for the toll bridge was, he said, no insurance against competition. Taney's opponents worried that he was in effect ruling against private property rights, but such was not the case. Taney was concerned with promoting entrepreneurial opportunity. For instance, in 1848 Taney upheld the right of the states to use their power of eminent domain to take property for public use, which meant, in practice, enlarging public facilities, such as railroad rights-of-way, so as to create greater entrepreneurial opportunity. Taney's most controversial and famous decision came in 1857 when he protected the slave investments of the planter class.

One further development important for business growth occurred while Taney was chief justice. After the new government was first formed in 1776, English common law became American common law in the states, but it was left for the federal courts to formulate a national common law. In one decision, *Swift* v. *Tyson*, written by Associate Justice Joseph Story in 1842, the Court enunciated a doctrine important for the conduct of business on a national scale. The justices ruled unanimously that in civil suits the federal courts could ignore state precedents in favor of developing their own rules. This doctrine stopped state courts, which reflected local prejudices and interests, from preventing out-of-state creditors from recovering their debts. Businesses, in other words, could now enjoy a reasonable assurance of their rights when they made contracts and loans across state lines. Eventually, as we shall see, the court's decision allowed corporations to escape state governmental restrictions by settling disputes in the federal courts.

Corporation Law

Other laws passed by other levels of government also aided business. The use of the corporate form of business organization, for example, quickly became much more widespread in the United States than it was abroad, as the state governments chartered corporations to achieve public goals. Corporations were legal entities created to bring individuals together for a specified purpose. Between 1776 and 1800, some three hundred companies were incorporated by state governments. About 60 per cent of these corporations were located in New England, with an additional 15 per cent in New York and Pennsylvania.

Businesses organized as corporations possessed advantages not held by single-owner proprietorships or partnerships. Most importantly, the corporation had a life of its own under law, separate from that of its owners who held shares of stock in it. When a shareholder died, his stock could be sold to someone else without affecting the affairs of the corporation. A partnership, in contrast, had to be dissolved and reorganized whenever a partner died or withdrew from the business, a costly and time-consuming process. Moreover, incorporation sometimes granted limited liability to investors in a business, though this situation became more common in the mid and late 1800s. That is, shareholders were not held personally responsible for the debts of a corporation and could lose only the amount of their investment in a company that failed. Partners, however, were personally responsible for any debts incurred by their partnerships and might lose their homes and personal possessions, should their businesses fail. Indeed, they might end up in debtors' prison! The promise of limited liability served as a strong inducement for investment in corporations. This situation made it easier for corporate businesses to raise the capital needed for their expansion, just at the time that larger markets were inducing such growth. Finally, the state charters possessed by corporations gave the business some promise of immunity from governmental interference in their affairs, and this circumstance also appealed to potential investors.

In return for these advantages and privileges, the American public initially expected corporations to serve the public interest as well as the interests of their private stockholders. The concept that the corporation would serve the public interest originated in the Middle Ages, when towns granted the privilege to incorporate had some degree of political and economic freedom from feudal lords. In England many of the chartered joint-stock companies of the 1500s and 1600s took the corporate form and were set up with the mercantilistic goal of increasing that nation's strength. In colonial America, some towns, church groups, and educational organizations such as colleges and universities incorporated, gaining thereby rights of self-governance. Of the business corporations organized in the early United States, two-thirds consisted of transportation firms, toll-road companies, bridge companies, and canal businesses (banks and insurance companies composed most of the remainder), all of which had a clear public purpose of enlarging commercial opportunities for citizens.

However, as the nineteenth century progressed, the public-service aspect of the corporation gradually dissipated in favor of policies that enhanced individual business opportunities. The corporation became simply a legal device, available to more and more Americans, to mobilize capital for business enterprise. Instead of implying public restraint, incorporation became a way to free the company from public or governmental control. The gradual adoption of general incorporation laws by the states opened these paths. Originally, an individual act of each state legislature chartered each corporation. Not only was the process cumbersome, but fears grew that the process enhanced the privileges of the well-to-do. New York legislators, who desired to foster economic growth, responded in 1811 to these concerns by passing the nation's first general incorporation law for manufacturing firms. Under this law, no special legislative act was needed; certain types of companies could incorporate whenever they met a few simple requirements. Between 1811 and 1848, 228 textile manufacturers, 63 metal products firms, and 15 glassware companies incorporated under the law's administrative procedures. Other states emulated New York with general incorporation statutes. Connecticut passed a general incorporation law for all types of businesses in 1837. By 1870, nearly every state had some type of general incorporation law.

The willingness of the states to sanction the corporate form of business was evidence of the widespread desire for governmental support of business development. The passage of general incorporation laws especially demonstrated the eagerness of Americans to use legislation to encourage business growth. The state legislature intended the laws, at least indirectly, to augment the general prosperity.

Contract Law

The states also gradually changed contract law in the early nineteenth century in a way that fostered business development. In the more traditional society, the community had maintained its right to judge the fairness of contracts. Thus, if a jury felt that a price charged for something was higher than its objective value, the jury had the power to redress the grievance of the buyer. But by the 1840s the courts began moving to a new doctrine—*caveat emptor:* let the buyer beware. Under this new doctrine, the community could no longer intervene in the determination of prices. Business entrepreneurs now had the advantage in selling scarce goods, because the new court doctrine disallowed suits from purchasers claiming that prices were too high. The effect was thus to allow entrepreneurs opportunities to reap large rewards in developing the country's economy.

Property Law and Eminent Domain

American law also helped entrepreneurs to establish new ventures for the creation of wealth by removing some traditional property rights that stood in the way of growth. This form of assistance became even stronger after the 1820s as the states developed the legal doctrine, called the right of eminent domain, that they could take a person's land for some public purpose.

The use of the right of eminent domain varied from state to state, but the general pattern promoted industrial development and new technologies at the expense of vested farming interests. By the 1820s, the states generally held that sovereignty included the right to eminent domain but that this right could not be exercised without some clear public purpose and without "just" or "fair" compensation. Eminent-domain powers were important both for state-promoted internal improvements, such as canals, and for private projects. States often granted private corporations, in their charters, eminent-domain powers for the construction of roads, bridges, and railroads. The use of the power of eminent domain to help manufacturers spread in the 1830s.

THE POLITICS OF GROWTH

The use of eminent domain was but one indication that public policies deliberately fostering the growth of private business opportunities were widespread in the United States in the first half of the nineteenth century. All three branches of the federal government promoted business, but governmental aid was especially pronounced at the state and local level. Government supported private entrepreneurial action to produce burgeoning agricultural growth, an internal system of transportation and communications, the beginnings of an industrial system of production, and the spread of an urban network.

Although government at all levels tended to support business enterprise in general, particular policies were often controversial. As the United States experienced economic growth, it also witnessed the appearance of diverse economic interests, each of which made different demands on the government. Any particular government economic policy inevitably involved taxing some citizens for the benefit of others. Gallatin's hope that the "General Government" would be able to make internal improvements in the national interest proved futile in the face of the growing number of special and local interests.

As a result, the growth of American agricultural, industrial, and commercial enterprise in the pre–Civil War period took place without any overall direction or planning from the national government. Through the middle decades of the nineteenth century, Americans struggled to define more precisely the nature of their federal system and the appropriate powers of the national government versus the state governments. By midcentury this constitutional question crystallized around the slavery issue, and that issue was settled only by a civil war. The relationship between the national government and the nation's economic development was part of the constitutional contest, and misgivings that powerful federal intervention with the intent of fostering economic growth might lead to tyranny at worst or, at best, was inappropriate for a nation with striking regional differences restrained the national government. Unlike the federal government, states and municipalities were not restrained from economic intervention by constitutional questions of federalism, and their political economies were often frankly interventionist and developmental.

The American political economy changed after the Civil War. Government policies fostering business opportunities continued, but as new business institutions emerged to mobilize capital and organize the flows of production and distribution, new tensions appeared in American society that were reflected in the political economy. The development of a managerial revolution fundamentally changed the American business system.

Selected Readings

Stuart Bruchey, *Roots of American Economic Growth, 1607–1861* (New York: Harper & Row, 1968), is a good description of America's political economy. Carter Goodrich, *Government Promotion of American Canals and Railroads, 1800–1890* (New York: Columbia University Press, 1960), remains a standard reference on the role government played in the development of internal improvements. E. A. J. Johnson, "Federalism, Pluralism, and Public Policy," *Journal of Economic History* 22 (December 1962): 427–44, examines the importance of federalism in the fragmentation of government economic policy. John Lauritz Larson, "'Bind the Republic Together': The National Union and the Struggle for a System of Internal Improvements," *Journal of American History* 74 (September 1987): 363–

87, illuminates the political considerations behind the failure to adopt a national plan for internal improvements. Robert A. Lively, "The American System: A Review Article," *Business History Review* 29 (March 1955): 81–96, reviews the studies that demonstrate the great extent of government support for business development. Carter Goodrich, "Internal Improvements Reconsidered," *Journal of Economic History* 30 (June 1970): 289–311, evaluates the scholarship that appeared after the publication of Lively's essay.

Bray Hammond, *Banks and Politics in America from the Revolution to the Civil War* (Princeton: Princeton University Press, 1957), provides a solid overview of the politics of finance and banking. John Dobson, *Two Centuries of Tariffs* (Washington, D.C.: United States International Trade Commission, 1977), is a brief, readable account of the tariff controversy and legislation. James Willard Hurst, *Law and the Conditions of Freedom in the Nineteenth-Century United States* (Madison: University of Wisconsin Press, 1967), argues that legal decisions created opportunities for business in the nineteenth century. On the changing nature of the corporation and corporate law, see James Willard Hurst, *The Legitimacy of the Business Corporation* (Charlottesville: The University Press of Virginia, 1970). Donald J. Pisani, "Promotion and Regulation: Constitutionalism and the American Economy," *Journal of American History* 74 (December 1987): 740–68, includes a treasury of citations to scholarship regarding the relationships between law and economic development and regulation.

PART 3

The
Rise
of
Big
Business

1850–1920

IMPORTANT EVENTS, 1855–1901

1855   Daniel McCallum of the New York & Erie Railroad issues a statement on the "general principles" of management, one of the first efforts to standardize management practices in a big business.

1869   The Union Pacific–Central Pacific, America's first transcontinental railroad, is completed.

1872   Montgomery Ward is founded.

1876   The telephone is first demonstrated publicly.

1880   More workers are employed in nonfarm jobs than in farm jobs.

1882   The Standard Oil Trust begins.

1895–1904 The first major merger movement in the United States occurs.

1898   Blacks form the North Carolina Life Insurance Company.

1900   General Electric establishes the first industrial research laboratory in the United States.

1901   United States Steel, the first billion-dollar U.S. corporation, is founded.

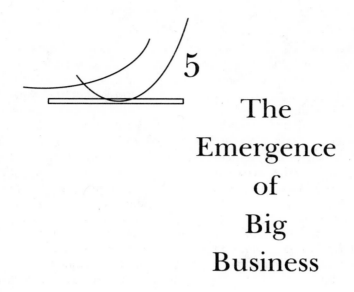

5

The
Emergence
of
Big
Business

On October 5, 1841, as a result of a scheduling error, two trains collided in western Massachusetts. One conductor and one passenger were killed; seventeen other passengers were injured. This accident horrified the public and provoked an investigation by the Massachusetts legislature. Clearly the great promises of overland travel by steam power also held the potential for human tragedy. In response to the accident, officials of the Western Railroad, responsible for operating trains along a hundred-and-fifty-mile line between Massachusetts and New York State, began to define a new approach to business—what scholars would later call the managerial revolution. It was apparent that the old informal business practices had become unsuitable. Business executives now realized the necessity of having firm, exact, human control over the new railroad technology, and this realization led to a gradual unfolding of new methods of doing business. The managerial revolution that began in the railroad industry after 1841 changed forever the way business was conducted in America and began the process known as the rise of big business.

An event that occurred six decades later in New York City symbolized the second grand theme in the rise of big business in America. In 1901, J. P. Morgan, America's best-known and most powerful investment banker, purchased Carnegie Steel and combined it with other firms in the steel industry to form United States Steel, capitalized at over $1.4 billion. The formation of the world's first billion-dollar corporation was a signal that big business had achieved a permanent institutional status on the American scene. Morgan organized United States Steel from firms that had earlier competed in the marketplace. Now those firms could cooperate, and through their combined size, control of iron ore, and efficiencies of production, Morgan expected they would dominate the nation's steel industry, reducing if not ending price competition. With the rise of giant companies such as United States Steel in the post–Civil War years, the personal management of earlier years gave way to bureaucratic management (management through organizations such as committees), as big-business executives designed new corporate structures capable of controlling the vastly enlarged outputs of their companies' plants and factories.

The nature of economic decision making in the United States also experienced major changes with the rise of big business. Decisions previously made through the free play of market forces came to be internalized within the new, gigantic business firms. The invisible hand of the market gave way to the visible hand of business management in ordering and coordinating the American economy. In some key industries, oligopoly developed and competition lessened, as big businesses grew in importance. (In an industry characterized by oligopoly, a few companies are so large and powerful that they can influence the market, especially the prices, for their products.) In fact, the United States began developing a dual economy in which big businesses dominated the center of the economy, with smaller firms at the periphery, a trend that continued well into the twentieth century.

RAILROADS: PIONEERS IN BIG BUSINESS

Railroads and the Problems of Growth

By the 1850s, individual railroads had become the biggest businesses of their day. Even before the Civil War, the trunk-line railroads controlled about 500 miles of track each and employed hundreds, indeed sometimes thousands, of workers. During the late

1860s and early 1870s, trunk-line railroads such as the New York Central and the Pennsylvania established control over through routes to the West, and entrepreneurs completed America's first transcontinental lines. Building these lines was an expensive task; the trunk-line railroads connecting the East with the Midwest were capitalized at from $17 million to $35 million each. Other pre–Civil War businesses paled by comparison. Even the largest textile mills employed fewer than a thousand people, and only a handful were capitalized at more than $1 million.

Railroads continued to grow in size and complexity after the Civil War. Hungry for capital before the war, the railroads became voracious after it; for example, the Pennsylvania Railroad issued $78 million worth of securities to help finance its expansion in the 1870s. In the 1880s, Americans built an annual average of 8,000 miles of track, so that by 1890, the nation had 166,000 miles of track, and a growing number of large cities were linked by a national transportation network. The construction of over 254,000 miles of track finished the system by 1916, but even by the end of the 1880s, an integrated, nationwide railroad network was available to farmers, manufacturers, merchants, and passengers. In 1883, railroads (not the government) established the four time zones in the United States as a way of standardizing their schedules, and three years later, railroads in the Southeast joined those in other regions in adopting a standard-gauge (uniform width) track, thus allowing car interchanges and through freight traffic between different sections of the nation.

New or improved forms of communications accompanied the development of the railroad network. The relationship between the railroad and the telegraph evolved symbiotically in the 1840s and 1850s, with the telegraph serving to help managers schedule trains and the railroads allowing the telegraph to use their rights-of-way for its poles and wires. In 1866, the nation's three leading telegraph companies merged to form Western Union, and by 1915, this company had 1.6 million miles of wire in operation. The use of the telegraph quickly spread beyond railroad executives, as business executives across the United States used it to control their own far-flung business empires and to communicate with managers in other firms. Similarly, the telephone, first publicly demonstrated in 1876, came into use as an instrument of business in the late nineteenth and early twentieth centuries. The Bell Company which grew to dominate the industry, had 8.3 million telephones in use by 1920, and independent companies operated an additional 5 million.

As this 1917 photograph shows, women almost exclusively operated the switchboards of the nation's telephone system. The women standing behind the operators are their supervisors. (Courtesy of AT&T Archives)

Because of their rapid expansion, railroads faced unprecedented managerial problems. They were much larger—in terms of people employed, regions served, and capital invested—than any other companies of the period, even the biggest textile mills. Moreover, their operations were more complex and much faster than those of other businesses. Canal traffic, for example, was much slower. And each canal boat was individually owned. Unlike railroads, canals did not need to be run as unified, coordinated systems. Decisions that affected the lives of people over ever-larger regions needed to be made quickly and accurately in the railroad business, and suitable ways of making such decisions had to be developed, as the 1841 disaster on the Western Railroad all too clearly demonstrated. Even more complex were strategic problems. The unparalleled demands for capital by their lines meant that top railroad executives found themselves spending much of their time in arranging for financing. Moreover, as America's railroad network expanded, railroad officers had to deal more and more with the question of how to anticipate and respond to the moves of their competitors.

Map 5.1   Major Railroads in 1910

Railroads and the Beginning of Modern Management

Clearly, business executives could not run railroads in haphazard ways and hope to survive very long. The complexities of both the operating and the strategic problems—especially those faced by the trunk-line railroads like the Baltimore & Ohio, the Pennsylvania, and the New York & Erie—called for the installation of systematic management methods. Railroad executives solved their problems through the establishment of business bureaucracies, the first in American history. For the most part, railroad officers acted as innovators in setting up new management systems in response to specific business problems. To a degree, however, some railroad executives were influenced by the example of another bureaucracy, the United States Army. By the 1820s and 1830s, the army had a fairly sophisticated structure in which there was a separation between staff officers, who made strategic decisions at headquarters, and the widely scattered line officers, who carried out the decisions in the field. Precise recordkeeping allowed headquarters to stay abreast of events in the field. Whether working on their own or influenced by the army, railroad executives changed the nature of business management in America.

The Western Railroad was one of the first to institute bureaucratic management practices. Both military officers and civilians had surveyed and built the Western Railroad in the 1830s, with the military engineers in the technical positions and the civilians in charge of business matters, and the system of reporting and accounting later adopted by the railroad closely resembled that used by the army. A bureaucratic structure developed, in a process hastened by the accident of 1841, that comprised three geographical divisions whose operations were coordinated by a headquarters in Springfield, Massachusetts. Each division had an assistant master of transportation, a roadmaster, and a senior mechanic, all reporting to headquarters. New regulations tried to eliminate ambiguities in daily operations by laying out definite lines of authority and responsibility. Employees were required to file frequent, detailed reports about their work for the central office.

Like the Western Railroad, the Baltimore & Ohio Railroad was aided in its development by the military. The army engineers who surveyed the route for the Baltimore & Ohio introduced army accounting and reporting techniques during the 1830s, and their military experience enabled them to advise the railroad's management on how best to define the specific duties and responsibilities of the firm's officers. Although it was important in the Baltimore & Ohio's early years, army influence became less significant in the late 1840s when Benjamin Latrobe, the line's chief engineer and a man without military experience, organized his own bureaucratic structure to run the railroad. Latrobe set up an administrative structure that separated the responsibility for the activities of the Baltimore & Ohio into two parts: a finance department to handle the internal and external financing of the line and to take care of other matters of grand strategy, and an operations department to run the trains. The operations department was divided into geographic divisions. Each geographic division, in turn, possessed three managers—one in charge of transportation (scheduling and running the trains), a second in charge of constructing and repairing the roadbed, and a third in charge of repairing machinery. All three functional managers reported to their respective functional superiors in the central office where the railroad's general superintendent coordinated the work of the different managers.

Daniel McCallum of the New York & Erie added still further refinements to railroad management. Taking over as the Erie's general superintendent in the 1850s, he sought to cut the railroad's soaring operating expenses. In doing so, he issued "general principles" of management, which stressed the clear definition of responsibilities for each railroad officer, and drew up one of the first organization charts in the history of American business. McCallum emphasized that lines of authority should also be lines of communication within his company and required daily reports from his conductors, agents, and engineers. Monthly statements prepared from these reports allowed McCallum to assess accurately how his railroad was doing financially and proved very useful in setting its rates.

The Pennsylvania Railroad became known as the "standard railroad of the world" because of its good management. Herman Haupt, a West Point graduate, helped develop its bureaucratic organization during the 1840s and 1850s in his position as the railroad's superintendent of transportation and as its general superintendent. This structure was then more fully developed by J. Edgar Thomson, the railroad's president. In 1857, Thomson enlarged the central office of the line by separating the accounting from the treasury department and by creating a secretary's office and a legal department. Thomson also clarified relations between the head office and the railroad's operating divisions and began moving in the direction of fully demarcating the duties of its officers. In the 1860s and 1870s, he completed the task of separating the responsibilities of the executives in the central office from those of the managers in the railroad's three regional divisional offices, and he installed financial controls by which the executives in the central office could monitor and coordinate work throughout all of the divisions.

Three hallmarks of modern business management stand out in the steps taken by these railroad executives. First, they began to separate policy making from operations—they began to divide strategy and tactics. Different groups of executives were in charge of overall planning and of operational details. It came to be the job of top management to plan for the future of the lines and to coordinate the functions of different parts of the lines. Second, and directly related to the first point, the railroads began to build bureaucratic organizations staffed by middle managers. These middle managers were essential to the development of the railroads as big businesses. While the top management in the central office concentrated on grand strategy, the middle management in the divisional offices attended to the operational details. These middle managers received reports from conductors, station managers, and the like, digested them, and then made their own reports to the top management, forming a chain that connected the various levels of the railroad bureaucracy. And if they were the chain, better financial reporting—the third hallmark of modern business management—was one of the major links. Railroad executives developed new types of accounting methods to hold together and analyze the work of their ever more complex business empires. These new accounting techniques were of three types.

In financial accounting, railroad officers moved beyond the relatively simple profit-and-loss statements of double-entry bookkeeping to the use of operating ratios to analyze their companies' profitability—the first American business managers to do so. Operating ratios relate companies' earnings to their volume of business, and even today are the basic standard by which profitability is assessed.

Before the advent of the railroad, America possessed few capital-intensive businesses. That is, for the vast majority of businesses the cost of labor, not the cost of capital, was the major expense. Railroads, with their enormous demand for funds, reversed this situation. Not surprisingly, then, railroads were the first companies to develop systematic capital accounting. By the 1870s, railroad executives were charging the repair and replacement of equipment against their operating revenues, an early form of depreciation.

Finally, railroad executives developed cost accounting. They divided their companies' costs into various categories of fixed costs (such as those of roadbeds and tracks) and variable costs (such as that of labor). Because their fixed costs were much higher than their variable costs, railroad managers sought to run as many fully laden cars as possible. And they used cost accounting to pinpoint problems in their companies' operations and to aid in setting profitable railroad rates. The men responsible for railroad accounting thus pioneered in administering prices, as opposed to allowing invisible market forces to determine them.

The adoption of bureaucratic methods by railroads marked a fundamental shift in how American business people conducted their affairs. The personal business world of the merchant gave way to the more highly organized and impersonal world of modern big business, a trend that continued in the late nineteenth and twentieth centuries, and came to characterize many firms beyond the railroad industry.

Railroads and the Rise of Big Business

The changes occurring in railroad management were important not only for the railroad industry but also for a vast array of other businesses and industries in the United States. As their companies grew in size and complexity during the 1870s and 1880s, America's industrialists sought new management methods and structures by which they might control them. They found them, in part, in their nation's railroads. The general idea of bureaucratic rather than personal management and specific methods of accounting and statistical controls spread from the railroads to other industrial ventures.

As railroads increased in size and their executives perfected new techniques of business management, the railroads became the first businesses in the United States in which the visible hand of management replaced the invisible hand of the market. What the managers of railroads decided to do became more important than market forces in determining what happened on the railroads. Here, too, the railroads provided a model for other businesses.

Railroads were important in the rise of big business in the United States in yet another way. Economic growth created new opportunities for businesses to expand the scope of their operations, and the building of America's railroad network lay at the heart of this busi-

The nation depended on "the iron horse" for economical and efficient inland transportation. Railroad operations light up the night at this busy switching yard scene published in 1885 by the popular engravers Currier and Ives. (Library of Congress)

ness expansion. As we saw in Chapter 3, the transportation revolution spurred business development in the pre–Civil War years, and the completion of the national railroad system continued to power business expansion after the Civil War. The internal development of a vast land rich in natural resources was far more important than foreign trade in America's economic growth in the late nineteenth and early twentieth centuries. Central to the exploitation of these resources was the railroad, for it created a large domestic market for industrial goods. By 1890, railroads carried twice as much freight as all other forms of transportation in the United States, and railroad freight traffic more than tripled over the following twenty years.

THE SPREAD OF BIG BUSINESS

The growth of the U.S. population and its concentration into cities linked by the railroads was an important change that allowed entrepreneurs to construct big businesses. The population of the United

States rose from 31 million people in 1860, to 63 million in 1890, to 106 million in 1920, and most of that growth occurred in the cities. In 1860, 16 per cent of Americans lived in towns or cities greater than 8,000 in population; in 1900, the proportion had risen to 33 per cent. The growth in population combined with the railroad system to create unprecedented business opportunities.

Andrew Carnegie and Carnegie Steel

The story of Andrew Carnegie and the steel industry illustrates the importance of railroads and expanding cities to the rise of big business. Carnegie benefited directly from the example of the railroads in organizing his steel business; the railroads and urban construction projects provided significant markets for his steel mills. A Scottish émigré who moved with his family to Pittsburgh in 1848, Carnegie owed much of his success to what he learned in the railroad business. In Pittsburgh, Carnegie held several low-paying menial jobs, including that of bobbin boy in a textile mill, before becoming one of the city's leading telegraph operators. It was while he was working as a telegrapher that Carnegie was hired in 1852 by Thomas Scott, the superintendent of the western division of the Pennsylvania Railroad, as his personal telegrapher and secretary. When Scott became a vice president of the line seven years later, Carnegie succeeded him as superintendent of the railroad's western division, a position he held until he resigned in 1865 to pursue other business interests.

Introduced to the world of high finance by Scott, Carnegie became an investor in numerous enterprises—a railroad sleeping-car company, an oil company, and a bridge company, among others. Benefiting from inside information about many of these enterprises from his railroad contacts, Carnegie became a very rich man. As early as 1863, Carnegie's investments were bringing him $45,000 annually, and Carnegie could tell a friend triumphantly, "I'm rich, I'm rich." Over the next decade, however, Carnegie's outlook changed. He still wanted to make money, but wealth alone could not satisfy him. "The amassing of wealth is one of the worst species of idolatry," he wrote in 1868. He wanted to create something of lasting importance, and it was this desire that led him to forsake his career in finance and enter the steel industry.

When Carnegie entered the steel business in 1872, he brought with him several important lessons from his railroad experience. He was aware of the large and expanding market for steel that rail-

First used by Carnegie Steel, Bessemer converters greatly lowered the cost of making steel. Andrew Carnegie was always quick to invest in new technologies, reasoning that in the long run the profits resulting from technological innovations would more than offset the costs of installing them in his plants. (Library of Congress)

roads were creating with their requirements for track, bridges, and locomotives. In fact, one of his first major sales was steel track to the Pennsylvania Railroad. Moreover, in managing his steel company Carnegie took to heart the obsession of railroad executives with low-cost, high-volume operations. Like the railroads, steel was a capital-intensive business, and Carnegie sought always to lower the costs and increase the volume of production of his steel mills.

Like the executives of the Pennsylvania Railroad, he installed sophisticated cost-accounting and recordkeeping systems in his company, systems he used both to locate production inefficiencies and to reward (or penalize) his plant managers. Take care of the costs, Carnegie believed, and the profits would take care of themselves.

Carnegie's policies proved successful. He created the largest steel company in the world and, with other American steelmakers, established the United States as the leading steel-producing nation. By 1900, America's output of pig iron had risen to 15 million tons, surpassing Great Britain's. The output of steel in the United States soared from 70,000 tons in 1870 to over 4 million tons just twenty years later, as steel went into America's expanding railroad network and into skeletons for the buildings of the nation's growing cities. By 1900, American steel production had leaped to nearly 12 million tons, and in 1920 it reached 47 million tons. By the latter date, the United States was producing about 60 per cent of the world's steel.

Big Business in Industry

Big business developed in American industry when some entrepreneurs took advantage of the new national market and improvements in technology to combine mass production with mass distribution. A few entrepreneurs did so even before the Civil War. Cyrus McCormick set up a large factory to mass-produce reapers in Chicago in 1848, and he established a nationwide network of franchised dealers to demonstrate, sell, and service them in the 1850s and 1860s. Most big businesses, however, had to await the integration of the national market by the railroad and the development of new technological processes in production. When they did develop, big businesses grew up quickly, in just one or two generations. In 1860, no single American company was valued at $10 million; by 1904, some three hundred were.

Mass Distribution

The creation of a national market through improvements in transportation and communications revolutionized the marketing and distribution of goods in the United States. Major changes occurred in wholesaling and retailing, and these alterations affected the handling of both agricultural and industrial products.

As we saw in Chapter 3, the use of the telegraph and the railroad led to significant alterations in the organization of the wheat and cotton trades during the 1850s and 1860s. Commodity dealers using to-arrive contracts and working through established exchanges came to dominate both businesses. These institutions were further developed in the late nineteenth and early twentieth centuries. Futures trading grew out of the to-arrive contract, and large commodity firms and dealers supplanted the traditional merchant in the trade in agricultural goods. By 1921, some 60 per cent of the cotton crop of the United States was handled by only twenty-four firms. The establishment of the New York Cotton Exchange by New York cotton merchants in 1871 regularized trading in cotton by setting up formalized channels for the necessary transactions.

Still more dramatic changes occurred in the marketing of manufactured products. Jobbers increased in importance as a link between manufacturers and retailers. Instead of working on a consignment basis as they had before the Civil War, jobbers bought the goods they handled. More than in earlier times, they also set up extensive purchasing networks throughout the nation and established close relations with retailers, such as country stores in farming areas and specialized retail outlets in big cities.

The jobbers soon found their control over marketing in America challenged by mass retailers, firms that saved money by purchasing directly from manufacturers and by emphasizing speed and volume, rather than high profit margins, in making their sales. Mass retailing developed first in the large cities, the biggest markets. Department stores came into existence in cities across the nation during the 1860s, 1870s, and 1880s: Macy's, Bloomingdale's, Marshall Field, Abraham & Strauss, Wanamaker's, Lazarus, and I. Magnin. Big-city department stores pioneered a new way of selling. Traditional retail establishments were often dingy and crowded, and carried only a limited line of goods; haggling over prices was common, and clerks harassed customers to make purchases. In contrast, the new department stores created inviting public places filled with attractive displays of tempting merchandise. One-price shopping replaced haggling and harassment. Customers flocked to the department stores, which became a business institution symbolizing American urban life for the prosperous.

Meanwhile, for small-town and rural Americans, mail-order companies with national distribution systems appeared, capable of selling goods advertised in attractive catalogues: Montgomery Ward in 1872, and Sears, Roebuck about fifteen years later. Chain stores also began to bring the products of America's industries and farms to customers. In variety goods, beginning in 1879, F. W. Woolworth pioneered the Five-and-Ten-Cent stores that came to both small towns and urban districts. In 1905, Woolworth's sales volume exceeded $15 million, and in 1913, the Woolworth Tower graced New York's skyline as the world's tallest habitable building.

These mass-marketers gradually replaced the older merchants in distributing goods throughout the American economy. They did so by handling high volumes of transactions. By using a set number of workers in certain facilities to distribute a growing quantity of goods, mass-marketers were able to lower their unit costs and widen their markets. Volume and speed of sales came to dominate marketing.

Mass Production

Mass production evolved nearly concurrently with mass distribution, and for much the same reason. The opening of the national market enticed manufacturers into boosting their production, and the development of new technological processes made increased output feasible.

Mass production first appeared in industries processing liquids, where the application of new heat and chemical processes made it possible to produce more product in less time with fewer workers. The use of enlarged stills, superheated steam, and catalytic cracking permitted the development of large-batch or continuous-process production in the oil, sugar, fats, and alcohol industries during the 1870s and 1880s.

Breakthroughs in machinery designs brought mass production to a number of mechanical industries at a slightly later date. The use of a machine to make cigarettes automatically in 1881 transformed that industry. By the mid-1880s, one machine made 120,000 cigarettes per day, many more than the 3,000 that could be made by hand. The adoption of similar continuous-process machinery also remade the match, soap, and grain-milling industries, bringing mass production to them in the 1880s and 1890s.

Finally, the establishment of mass production in the metalmaking and metalworking industries occurred in several steps. First, more complex and expensive machinery was installed to make and work the metal. Using new steel alloys as cutting edges on machine tools greatly sped metalworking processes. Even more importantly, entire plants were designed to ensure as continuous a flow as possible from the suppliers of raw materials through the various production processes to the shipment of goods to market. Inefficiencies and bottlenecks in production were eliminated. As Figure 5.1 on page 167 shows, the rise in U.S. manufacturing production was dramatic.

Mass production owed much to the spread of federal armory

In the late nineteenth century, most U.S. factories were powered by steam. This source of power required elaborate systems of belts to transmit energy to the machines. It was not until the twentieth century that electric power, which was easier to use in many situations, replaced steam power in most factories. (Library of Congress)

practices involving the use of special-purpose machinery discussed in Chapter 3; nonetheless, progress along these lines was uneven. Although some sewing machine companies adopted special-purpose machinery to work metal as early as the 1850s, the industry leader, Singer Sewing Machine, did so only in the 1880s. Similarly, McCormick Reaper turned to armory practices in 1881. For many years, the Singer and McCormick factories were simply oversized workshops in which skilled workers fitted parts together with handheld files. But with the expansion of the American market, made possible by the railroad and the growth of cities, both firms turned to production systems featuring special-purpose machines that made interchangeable parts. When the demand for bicycles grew in the 1880s and 1890s, eastern bicycle-makers (such as the Pope Com-

Figure 5.1
Growth of U.S. Manufacturing Production, 1860–1914
(Indexes based on the year 1899 = 100)

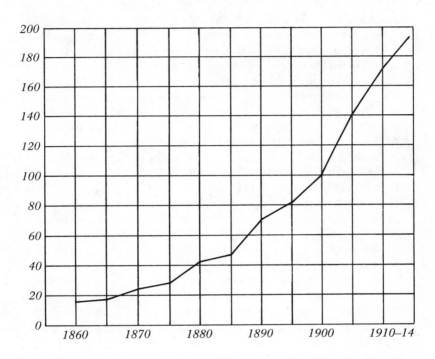

SOURCE: Based on data from U.S. Bureau of the Census, *Historical Statistics of the United States, Colonial Times to 1970,* pt. 2 (Washington, D.C.: U.S. Government Printing Office, 1975), p. 667.

pany) used armory practices from the first, but midwestern companies (such as Western Wheel Works) relied on other methods.

Restructuring the Business Firm

As companies began combining mass distribution with mass production, they became very different from earlier American business firms. As we have seen, the new companies were much larger; they were the nation's first industrial big businesses. In addition to their increase in size, the late-nineteenth-century companies differed from their predecessors in other ways.

More of them were corporations as incorporation became more and more widespread after the Civil War, especially among manufacturing companies. Manufacturing concerns needed to raise vast amounts of capital to build new factories and modernize old ones. The corporate form of organization, with its promise of limited liability for investors, proved particularly attractive to industrialists. As in earlier times, the legal aspects of the incorporation—the fact that, unlike single-owner proprietorships or partnerships, corporations did not have to be dissolved and reorganized if one investor left the business—also appealed to late-nineteenth-century business people. As a result, corporations accounted for three-quarters of all of America's industrial production by 1904.

As they grew larger, the big businesses of the late nineteenth and early twentieth centuries developed internal structures different from those of most earlier enterprises. These structures evolved in response both to the opportunities of the new national market and to the increasing complexity of manufacturing processes and goods. The national market offered glittering possibilities to American business people, but it also presented them with previously unknown perils. The nationwide transportation network broke down local monopolies, intensifying competition across the United States and demanding changes in business methods. At the same time, the tremendous increase in the output of their factories and the growing complexity of goods their factories produced raised additional difficulties for industrialists, giving rise especially to problems in marketing the increasing numbers of technologically sophisticated products.

A dramatic demonstration of the growing significance of the national market came in San Francisco in the early 1870s. During the 1850s and 1860s, San Francisco developed a broad range of industries—ironworks, carriage businesses, and the like—to serve its rising population. Protected from eastern and midwestern business competition by the high cost of overland transportation across the continent, the city's enterprises thrived. But the completion of the transcontinental railroad to San Francisco changed the situation abruptly. In 1868, San Franciscans wondered, along with Henry George (an economist and writer then living in San Francisco), "What is this railroad to do for us, this railroad we have looked for, hoped for, prayed for so long?" A year later the Union Pacific–Central Pacific line connected San Francisco with the Mississippi

River valley and points east, and by the mid-1870s San Franciscans had some answers to George's question. Chicago merchants used the railroad to send manufactured products to San Francisco, undercutting the prices of many locally made goods. Many San Franciscan manufacturers were forced out of business.

Vertical Integration

In an attempt to reestablish control over their destinies—to avoid the fate of the San Francisco merchants—business executives restructured their companies. Vertical integration was one common response to the problems and opportunities of the new national market. In vertical integration a company that initially engages in only one stage of the production and sale of its goods may acquire control of its sources of raw materials and/or the making and sale of its finished products.

Andrew Carnegie's desire to control fully his costs of production while taking advantage of the opportunities offered by the national market for steel led him to construct a self-contained, vertically integrated business empire. Initially, the Carnegie Steel Company depended on other firms for many of its raw materials—iron ore, coking coal, limestone, and the like. This situation displeased Carnegie, because he thought he was being charged too much for the raw materials and, even more importantly, because he could not always secure enough of them during times of peak production. To lower his costs and assure adequate supplies, Carnegie moved to control his sources of raw materials. In the 1880s and 1890s, Carnegie gained control of the Frick Coke Company (a producer of coking coal), the Mesabi iron-ore range, and numerous limestone quarries. Moreover, to carry the raw materials to his smelters near Pittsburgh, Carnegie acquired a fleet of Great Lakes ore ships and put together a railroad system of about a thousand miles of track. He also took steps to control the making and sale of finished steel products. In the 1890s, Carnegie began production of a wider variety of finished goods than in early times, and he set up his own sales offices in major cities in the United States and Canada. Figure 5.2 illustrates vertical integration at Carnegie Steel.

The development of vertical integration at Carnegie Steel and other steel companies marked a fundamental change in the way the iron and steel industry was organized. As we saw in Chapter 3, the pre–Civil War iron industry was mainly unintegrated: different companies controlled different stages of the manufacturing process

Figure 5.2
Vertical Integration at Carnegie Steel

and depended heavily on independent merchants to move their products from stage to stage. As men like Carnegie reorganized the industry, however, the merchants became much less important, and giant companies emerged that coordinated all the steps in making and selling goods. Market forces began giving way to managerial decisions as the controlling factors in the American iron and steel industry. Vertical integration, as at Carnegie Steel, was a major method by which business sought to exploit new marketing opportunities in the late nineteenth century. Business used vertical integration to try to insulate its firms from market forces and to keep all the profits within one company.

Some entrepreneurs also found in vertical integration a solution to problems they encountered in trying to sell their goods through America's network of merchants. Business people who used continuous-process machinery in their factories found that the nation's established network of jobbers and retailers could not adequately market the rapidly growing output of their plants, for they proved incapable of handling the impact of the explosive growth rate of America's post–Civil War factories. As a consequence, manufacturers in some fields—matches, cigarettes, flour, and canned products—moved, almost of necessity, to set up their own nationwide marketing outlets. Producers of perishable goods—beer, meat, and citrus fruits—also set up their own sales systems when the nation's established marketers either refused to handle their goods or proved unable to do so. Finally, the manufacturers of technologically sophisticated products ranging from sewing machines to elevators moved into sales because jobbers could not adequately demonstrate, install, or service the goods. A variety of reasons, then, led industrialists to link manufacturing with sales through vertical integration.

The Swift Company was one of those firms to engage in vertical integration as a way to take advantage of the new national market for perishables created by the railroad and telegraph. When Gustavus Swift, a New England butcher, moved to Chicago in 1875, most western cattle were being shipped east alive in railroad stock cars to be slaughtered near the towns, where the meat was consumed. This process was inherently inefficient, for 60 per cent of the animal was inedible. Swift solved this problem by hiring Andrew Chase to design a refrigerated railcar to carry dressed beef (the 40 per cent of the animal that could be eaten) to market.

Using the speed of the railroad to get his dressed beef to market in good shape and the telegraph to coordinate his business activities, Swift established a large, vertically integrated business empire in the 1880s. He purchased cattle from Great Plains ranches, slaughtered and dressed them in packing plants in six cities on the cattle frontier (the plants possessed large stockyards to hold the cattle), and then shipped the dressed beef in his own refrigerator cars to his branch houses around the United States.

Swift depended on his own branch houses—not on the nation's established wholesalers—to get the beef to consumers. Each branch house had refrigerated storage space, and each was staffed by a sales force whose job it was to persuade local butchers and grocers to sell Swift beef. This was difficult at first. Many railroads, fearful of losing local cattle shipments, refused to ship refrigerated beef. Only the Grand Trunk line would initially handle Swift's refrigerator cars. Local wholesalers, organized as the National Butchers' Protective Association, also fought Swift. Low prices and high quality offered by Swift overcame this opposition, and Swift & Company emerged victorious as the nation's leading meat-packing company in the 1890s. Other meat-packers—Armour, Cudahy, and Morris—soon emulated Swift in setting up their own networks across America. In doing so, the meat-packers followed the nation-wide trend of replacing local with national business enterprise.

The vertically integrated system Swift pioneered had many advantages over the old, decentralized meat business conducted by smaller firms. Swift's firm enjoyed economies of scale in its slaughterhouses; that is, by using large, efficient plants, Swift was able to reduce its unit costs of production. Swift and other integrated packers could use the many animal by-products, and the firms entered fields like soap, fertilizer, glue, and leather. Armour even went into the sandpaper business to find a profitable outlet for the glue it manufactured from animal hoofs.

Horizontal Integration

Horizontal integration provided a second mechanism by which industrialists tried to restructure their companies. In horizontal integration, a number of companies combined forces to control one step in the production or sale or their products. As in vertical integration, the goal of horizontal integration was to bring order to an unstable, highly competitive business situation. Specifically, horizontal integration sought to lessen competition, thus reducing the risks to the capital invested in America's new industrial enterprises. John D. Rockefeller's Standard Oil Company was a classic example of horizontal integration, as Rockefeller and other oil magnates sought to control their rapidly expanding industry.

The growth of the oil industry, like that of the steel industry, was explosive. The first commercial oil well in America was sunk in Pennsylvania in 1859 by E. L. Drake. This strike led to oil booms throughout the East and Midwest during the late nineteenth century, as Americans substituted kerosene for whale oil and candles. Oil discoveries in Oklahoma, Texas, and California in the 1890s and early 1900s further expanded the petroleum industry. In the early twentieth century, oil began gradually supplanting coal as a source of energy for railroad locomotives and some industrial plants. And with the development of the automobile, gasoline emerged as the major oil product in the 1910s and later. Spurred by the growth of new markets, crude-oil production in the United

States rose from 5 million barrels in 1870 to 64 million barrels in 1900, and to 378 million barrels in 1919.

Rockefeller was a pioneer in the oil industry. Born in Richford, New York, in 1839, he had moved to Cleveland, Ohio, by the time he was sixteen years old. There he entered the business world as a bookkeeper in the firm of a commission merchant, earning a salary of fifty cents per day. Using his own savings and a gift from his father, Rockefeller became a jobber of hay, grain, and meat in 1859. Rockefeller took his work very seriously. "Don't be a good fellow," he later warned people. "It is my firm conviction that every downfall is traceable directly or indirectly to the victim's goodfellowship, his good cheer among his friends." Not surprisingly, he was viewed as solemn and humorless. "Oh, young Rockefeller—he's a stick!" noted the son of the Cleveland merchant who first hired Rockefeller. But Rockefeller was successful, and he soon used the earnings made in trade to go into the oil business.

He entered oil refining in 1863, just four years after Drake drilled his well. By 1867, Rockefeller owned a large refinery in the Cleveland area and purchased oil for it from well owners in Pennsylvania and other eastern states. Needing capital for further growth, he incorporated his company in 1870 as the Standard Oil Company. The anticipated expansion occurred. However, oil refining was a very competitive industry, and Rockefeller and his rivals soon found themselves battling fiercely over the national market for kerosene and other oil products. No one really wanted to engage in this competition, which threatened to disrupt operations and lower profits.

To lessen competition, the owners of the Standard Oil Company and forty other oil-refining companies entered into a trust agreement in 1882. They turned over the common stock in their companies to nine trustees. The nine trustees then operated the companies in ways that avoided competition among them. In return for the stock in their original companies, the shareholders received trust certificates, and each year the nine trustees distributed what they thought were equitable shares in the earnings of the refining companies to the shareholders. By the 1890s, Standard Oil controlled over 90 per cent of the petroleum refining capacity of the United States. Figure 5.3 illustrates horizontal integration at Standard Oil.

Additional changes soon took place in Standard's structure. In 1889, New Jersey amended its incorporation law to become the first state allowing one company to own stock in another company—to

Figure 5.3
Horizontal Integration at Standard Oil

become a "holding company." Many large corporations took advantage of this provision to become holding companies by incorporating in New Jersey. Standard Oil was one of these firms. In 1899, Standard incorporated under New Jersey law and purchased the stock of the other members of the trust. In the early 1900s, Standard emerged as a single operating company. Its management sold or closed inefficient plants and rationalized the work of the corporation by uniting offices, such as sales offices, previously operated separately. Once horizontally integrated, Standard turned to vertical integration. In the 1880s, Standard began securing its own supplies of crude at a reasonable cost. Somewhat later, Standard began operating pipelines to transport its oil and sales outlets to market it.

America's First Merger Wave

Business integration—both vertical and horizontal—took place more through mergers of formerly independent companies than through the growth of individual companies. From the 1880s on, mergers became increasingly common, culminating in America's first major merger movement during the years 1895 through 1904. (See Figure 5.4.) Over 2,000 firms disappeared into consolidations in this period. Truly gigantic combinations resulted. When the United States Steel Corporation was formed in 1901 by the purchase of Carnegie Steel and the merger with competing steel firms,

Figure 5.4
Mergers in Manufacturing and Mining in the United
States, 1895–1904

SOURCE: Based on data from U.S. Bureau of the Census, *Historical Statistics of the
United States, Colonial Times to 1970*, pt. 2 (Washington, D.C.: U.S. Government
Printing Office, 1975), p. 914.

United States Steel consisted of 213 different manufacturing establishments, 41 mines, over 1,000 miles of railroad track, and 112 ore
ships. The company controlled 43 per cent of the pig-iron capacity
and 60 per cent of the steelmaking capacity in the United States.

There were many motives for these mergers. A search for
efficiency and predictability in all facets of their businesses led Carnegie and Swift into vertical integration, and the need to demon-

strate and service new, technologically sophisticated products led other manufacturers to integrate vertically, sometimes by merging with established firms. However, a quest for market control lay behind many mergers. In fact, in one-half of the mergers, the consolidations absorbed over 40 per cent of the manufacturing capacity of their industries; in one-third, over 70 per cent of the capacity. Manufacturers in capital-intensive, mass-production fields were especially eager to form consolidations to escape the severe price competition they faced during the depression years of the mid-1890s. Their companies had expanded rapidly in the 1880s and as a result of their extensive capital investments, had high fixed charges. To cover those charges, manufacturers operated their plants at full capacity. However, since their competitors were doing the same and manufacturing companies in any given field were usually evenly matched, the result during the depression years was rampant competition, overproduction, and low prices. It was the desire to dampen this competition and control markets that led to the merger wave.

Events in the telephone industry illustrate the complexity of the motives often involved in mergers and integration. Formed in 1877, American Bell originally relied upon agent licenses and equipment leasing for its revenues, but competition with Western Union quickly led Bell to extend financial support to, and administrative control over, its agents. In 1879, Western Union and Bell agreed not to compete (Western Union abandoned voice communications, and Bell left telegraphy), but despite the lessened competition, integration continued at Bell. The need to centralize switching centers and long-distance services, combined with a key business decision in 1882 favoring consolidation, spurred both vertical and horizontal integration throughout the 1880s. When its patent monopoly expired in 1894, American Bell faced renewed competition and responded with a reinvigorated integration drive. A variety of motives in different time periods thus interacted to speed consolidation and integration at American Bell.

The results of the merger movement soon became apparent to Americans in the form of lessened price competition in many industries. Whereas in the depression years of the mid-1890s there had been violent price competition as production outran demand, the recession year of 1907 brought fewer instances of price cuts, even though production again surpassed demand. In the steel and paper industries, for example, price reductions were few, for these industries had come to be dominated by combinations formed during the merger movement: United States Steel and the International Paper Company. These companies exercised price leadership over their industries, significantly dampening price cuts.

Not all mergers were successful, however. Only about one-half of the mergers lasted for more than a few years. The list of failed mergers was long indeed: American Bicycle, National Starch, U.S. Leather, American Glue, National Salt, National Cordage, United Button, and a host of others. Two elements were often present in those mergers that succeeded. First, the combination achieved production efficiencies as great as or greater than those of the firms remaining outside the merger. Second, the consolidation erected nonprice barriers to entry into its industry. For instance, United States Steel bought up much of the high-grade iron ore in the United States during the opening decade of the twentieth century, making it difficult for any new firm to compete with it on equal terms.

The New Corporate Business System

As their companies grew in size and became fully integrated enterprises, the decisions of business managers played ever-larger roles in determining how the business system of the United States functioned. The visible hand of management replaced the invisible hand of market forces in controlling production and distribution of industrial goods and services. Decisions once made in thousands of independent market transactions became concentrated in the hands of managers of relatively few big businesses. This shift in the locus of control explains the lack of price competition in 1907. Thus, even though supply exceeded demand, little price competition occurred because business managers exercised sufficient control over their markets to prevent it.

By the opening decade of the twentieth century, in fact, key segments of U.S. industry were characterized by oligopoly. That is, in some fields of manufacturing, a handful of companies dominated their markets. Oligopoly was particularly characteristic of the metal, oil, rubber, chemical, tobacco-processing, electrical-machinery, transportation-equipment, and sugar-refining industries. As early as 1904, a few major companies controlled at least half the output of seventy-eight industries in the United States. During the opening decade of the twentieth century, the structure of much of American industry assumed its modern form, oligopolistic and concentrated.

Not all American business became big business, however. Small business continued to be an important aspect of American life. Small businesses remained especially significant in sales, despite the development of mass retailing and wholesaling. In manufacturing, too, small businesses survived and prospered in some fields. In those industries—such as furniture production, the lumber industry, publishing, and the manufacturing of clothing—in which production processes were simple and no special marketing skills were called for, small businesses remained the norm. Market forces still operated to coordinate the production and distribution of goods in these parts of the American economy. Possessing no special advantages in such fields, big business failed to develop in these areas. Also, small businesses often did well by developing proprietary processes (a process owned by the company, usually with patent protection) or by making specialty products. In these ways, small-scale entrepreneurs sometimes protected themselves from the incursions of big businesses into their markets.

The history of Buckeye Steel Castings shows how a small industrial business could successfully carve out a market niche in late-nineteenth-century America. Set up as a partnership in 1881 and reorganized as a corporation five years later, Buckeye manufactured a broad range of cast-iron and steel products for a wide variety of customers in central Ohio. Lacking any specialty item to set it apart from other iron foundries, Buckeye faced fierce competition and nearly failed during the late 1880s. Only with the development of a specialty product, a new type of coupler to join railroad cars, did Buckeye emerge as a success in the 1890s. The development of this specialty item allowed Buckeye to differentiate itself from its competitors and to sell to the large national market for the first time.

The emergence of big businesses in some fields, combined with the persistence of small businesses in other fields, illustrates a key fact about America's business system in this period: it was fast becoming a dual system. The big businesses, "center firms," were at the center of the nation's new business system. Center firms were capital-intensive companies, such as Standard Oil and Carnegie Steel. They often used continuous-processing or large-batch production methods to achieve important economies of scale. Center firms were also usually vertically or horizontally integrated (or both) and frequently exercised some degree of control over their markets. As large ventures in manufacturing, communications, and transportation, the center firms were of tremendous importance to America's emergent industrial economy; the fortunes of a single center firm often had a ripple effect on the nation's economy as a

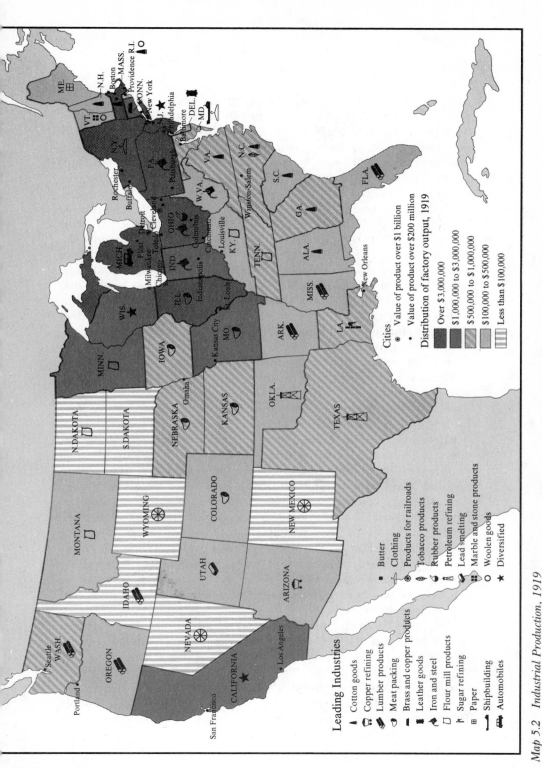

Map 5.2 Industrial Production, 1919

SOURCE: © American Heritage Publishing Co., Inc., *American Heritage Pictorial Atlas of United States History;* data from U.S. Bureau of the Census,

Cities
- ● Value of product over $1 billion
- • Value of product over $200 million

Distribution of factory output, 1919
- Over $3,000,000
- $1,000,000 to $3,000,000
- $500,000 to $1,000,000
- $100,000 to $500,000
- Less than $100,000

Leading Industries

Cotton goods
Copper refining
Lumber products
Meat packing
Brass and copper products
Leather goods
Iron and steel
Flour mill products
Sugar refining
Paper
Shipbuilding
Automobiles

Butter
Clothing
Products for railroads
Tobacco products
Rubber products
Petroleum refining
Lead smelting
Marble and stone products
Woolen goods
Diversified

whole. "Peripheral firms," on the other hand, were smaller, for no production efficiencies resulted from increasing their scale of production. They were likely to be labor-intensive rather than capital-intensive—Buckeye Steel Castings was an exception to this rule—and they usually had no control over their markets. What happened to a single peripheral firm had little impact upon the national economy.

A major distinction between center firms and peripheral firms lay in their degree of commitment to industrial research. Center firms set up the first U.S. industrial research laboratories during the opening two decades of the twentieth century. Company executives tended to engage in research and development, which had high fixed costs and represented large capital investment, to ensure that their factories would have a stream of goods to produce in the future. Only in this way, they reasoned, could high-volume production be maintained and their burdensome fixed charges be paid off. Peripheral firms typically lacked both the incentives and the resources for setting up research laboratories.

There was, however, another important reason for the establishment of research laboratories by the large center firms: center firms used the new products, processes, and patents developed by their laboratories to maintain or increase their market share. Just as many mergers resulted from attempts to control markets, so did the creation of research laboratories. General Electric set up the first such laboratory in 1900 to advance the technology that would maintain the company's domination of the U.S. electric-lighting market. Only after the laboratory successfully fended off threats to the company's markets through the development of the ductile-tungsten light filament in 1911 was it allowed to move on to a broader range of projects. Similarly, American Bell set up its research laboratory in 1911 to further the company's lead in telephone communications through the development of an electronic repeater. The same product, the company's executives hoped, would allow their firm to control radio technology.

Corporate research laboratories took root in the United States between 1900 and 1920. Counting only the eighteen companies employing the greatest numbers of scientists, industrial employment of Ph.D.'s rose from 4 in 1900 to 172 twenty years later. In 1900, only one-tenth of the new physics Ph.D.'s trained in the United States chose industrial employment; twenty years later, one-fifth did. By 1920, some three hundred American companies claimed to have industrial research laboratories. Nearly all of these were large center

Industrial growth and the prosperity of particular manufacturing firms were often dependent on scientific and technological innovations. A. L. Rohrer, pictured here, worked in 1886 at the first West Lynn Works laboratory; this firm eventually became part of General Electric. (The Hall of History Foundation, Schenectady, N.Y.)

firms: Standard Oil of Indiana, DuPont, Kodak, General Motors, and the like. Almost none of the small peripheral firms had them. Nonetheless, smaller enterprises continued to make many product innovations well into the twentieth century.

SERVICE INDUSTRIES

Post–Civil War Expansion

The growth of the national market and the emergence of giant firms that manufactured for and sold to that market provided new entrepreneurial opportunities for service businesses, companies that provided services for other businesses. Large capital-intensive ventures required help in selling their stocks and bonds, insuring their properties, and learning about market conditions. Specialized businesses that could perform these functions—banks, insurance companies, and credit-rating agencies—matured rapidly after the Civil War and continued to develop in importance in the twentieth century.

First started as independent businesses in the late eighteenth and early nineteenth centuries, banks continued to expand in the late nineteenth century. The number of commercial banks (banks lending money to farms and businesses) rose from about 2,000 in 1860 to nearly 25,000 by 1910. Their expansion was paralleled by that of other types of financial institutions. The 149 savings banks in existence in 1860 grew to nearly 2,500 by 1900, a sixteenfold increase. Investment banking, through which businesses sold stocks and bonds, attained maturity in the late nineteenth and early twentieth centuries. Established stock exchanges like the New York Stock Exchange broadened their range of interests as time progressed. First developed to serve the voracious capital needs of railroads in the 1870s, they began to handle industrial securities (stocks and bonds) in the 1890s. Insurance companies also grew in numbers and significance. The United States possessed 81 general insurance companies in 1860 but almost 500 by 1900. The growth in numbers of life insurance companies was even more rapid. Reaching out to new customers by offering new kinds of policies, they increased from 24 in 1860 to over 1,700 by 1900.

As an increasing number of businesses began to operate on a national scale, credit-rating companies increased in importance. In the new national market, business managers were simply unable to gather their own information about companies across the country, and they began to rely on specialized credit-rating agencies for their information. These agencies advised companies about the creditworthiness of other firms, thus allowing the companies to reach rational decisions on whether or not to extend credit or make loans to those firms. Two companies came to dominate this field after the Civil War. By 1880, the credit-rating agency run by R. G. Dun had 69 branch offices in major cities and employed 10,000 credit investigators. The Bradstreet Agency, its main competitor, also operated throughout the nation. These two firms later merged to form Dun and Bradstreet and continued to supply credit information.

All of these institutions—commercial, savings, investment banks, stock exchanges, insurance companies, and credit-rating firms— played important roles in America's expanding business system by helping to channel funds from the general public to the nation's rapidly growing railroads and industrial companies. Nor did the financial intermediaries simply provide capital for new railroad and industrial ventures; they often also played active roles in managing them.

Morton, Bliss & Company

The activities of Morton, Bliss & Company illustrate this kind of involvement. Like many others who formed private investment banking houses in nineteenth-century America, the people who set up Morton, Bliss began their careers as merchants. Levi Parsons Morton, one of the founders, started as a rural retailer in the 1840s, then entered the wholesale import-export trade in the 1850s, and finally turned his attention to transatlantic private banking during the Civil War. As time progressed, Morton's firm, like many other banking-mercantile ventures at that time, became increasingly specialized in its operations. In the late 1860s, it dropped its general banking services to focus all its attention on its growing business in exchange and securities transactions. Morton established two overlapping partnerships in 1869: Morton, Bliss & Company of New York and Morton, Rose & Company of London. George Bliss had been a dry-goods merchant who had moved into international credits and railroads. Rose had earlier served as Canada's minister of finance. With some changes, these partnership arrangements lasted for the next two decades.

Like many private bankers, Morton, Bliss entered the expanding field of railroad financing in the early 1870s. The firm quickly became involved with such lines as the Milwaukee & St. Paul; the New Orleans, Mobile & Texas; and the Illinois Central. Morton, Bliss and other private bankers worked for interregional railroad expansion and integration in the South and West, as well as in the North. These bankers were not simply middlemen arranging financing for the new lines. As directors and as officers in the railroads, they played active roles in setting policies and making decisions for the lines.

A depression in the mid-1870s led bankers still further into railroad operations as they sought to protect their own investments and those of their clients. Morton, Bliss took an active part in the reorganization of the Indianapolis, Cincinnati & Lafayette when that line encountered financial problems: the banking house helped extend the railroad and arrange traffic alliances with other lines. Not all such efforts succeeded. The bankers largely failed in their efforts to establish the New Orleans, Mobile & Texas as the basis of a regional system; in this case, competition generated political maneuvering that defeated them. Despite difficulties, however, bankers remained interested in railroad securities in the late 1870s, and in this period Morton, Bliss and other bankers bid heatedly for the bonds of reputable lines. Securities trading remained at a high level until 1884, when the onset of another recession led to its decline. Then, once again, Morton, Bliss and other bankers entered into numerous railroad reorganization plans tending in the direction of interregional combination.

Investment Bankers and Corporate Management

Morton, Bliss was only one of a number of investment banking houses that grew up to supply the tremendous capital needs of America's rapidly expanding railroads. In the 1890s, the investment banking firm controlled by J. P. Morgan became deeply involved with its railroads to the extent that Morgan's efforts to end competition between the railroads that his company was financing became known as the "Morganization" of the railroad business. A severe depression in the middle of the 1890s left many railroads in bankruptcy and threatened many others with failure. Morgan stepped in to consolidate and reorganize the lines in an attempt to make them profitable again and thus insure his own investments. Moreover, Morgan held a vision of a risk-free, harmoniously operating business system. Chaotic competition, railroad rate cutting, and business failures had no place in Morgan's scheme, and he tried to eliminate them.

The involvement of investment bankers in the affairs of railroads set the stage for their engagement in the activities of industrial companies in the opening decades of the twentieth century. In return for their help in arranging financing for industrial ventures, investment bankers demanded and received seats on boards of directors and could thus oversee and influence the decisions of corporate management. By 1913, just four investment banks—J. P. Morgan & Company, the National City Bank, the First National Bank, and the Bankers' Guaranty Trust Company—held 118 seats on the board of directors of 34 banks and trust companies, 35 seats in 10 insurance companies, and 193 seats in 68 nonfinancial firms. Such concentration of influence probably lessened competition in American industry and may also have dampened innovation. In general, investment bankers were not risk-takers. They wanted steady returns from their investments and so were most interested in order and stability, not new departures.

THE NEW CONDUCT OF BUSINESS

As business firms grew in size and complexity, business executives developed new management methods and structures to control their operations. As we have seen, railroads led the way in substituting bureaucratic for personal management. Other businesses soon followed in the late nineteenth and early twentieth centuries. Companies became too large and complex to be managed as one-man shows. The systematic division of authority became increasingly urgent.

Taylorism: Scientific Management

Management attempts to control industrial firms in new ways were often first apparent at the plant level. A method that came to be known as scientific management or Taylorism, after its creator, offered new methods of organizing work in factories.

Frederick Taylor attended Exeter Academy in New Hampshire as a young man, but soon left to go to work at the Enterprise Hydraulic Company and later at Midvale Steel as a machinist and engineer. Even as boy, Taylor was interested in efficiency, experimenting with the most efficient strides when hiking and the most efficient strokes when playing croquet. Appalled by the chaotic situations he found at his workplaces in the 1870s and 1880s, Taylor set out to make them orderly and efficient. Using a stopwatch, he measured the time it took workers to accomplish tasks on the factory floor. He tried to redesign the jobs so that they might be done more efficiently.

Taylor soon moved beyond examining individual tasks to redesigning the physical layout and the flow of work in entire factories. In doing so, he stressed three factors: the logical positioning of machinery in a plant to move material from point to point in an efficient fashion, accompanied by the minute subdivision of labor; strict recordkeeping to speed the flow of materials through the factory; and detailed internal cost accounting to keep track of exactly what went on in a plant. Taylor spread his ideas through talks and books and by working as a management consultant. His concepts were well known throughout the United States and the world by the early 1900s. Few companies adopted all of Taylor's ideas, but many, especially in the metal-making and metalworking industries, used some of them. Through scientific management, plant managers were at least partly successful in removing bottlenecks standing in the way of mass production.

Company Management

More far-reaching than changes at the level of the individual plant were changes in how entire companies were run. The most widespread managerial change in the late nineteenth century, a change especially common among big manufacturing businesses, was the movement toward the establishment of strong central offices (or corporate offices, as they might be called today) to oversee the operations of the company. These head offices were departmentalized by function. Different people or, more commonly, different committees in the headquarters were in charge of handling different functions for a company. There might typically be separate committees in the head office for production, transportation, and sales. No single person tried to take charge of all of those functions. At Standard Oil Company, for example, which set up a functionally departmentalized central office in 1886, the head office consisted of committees dealing with domestic commerce, foreign trade, containers for oil, manufacturing (refining), and transportation. An executive committee composed of Standard's top officers coordinated the work of these different committees.

This type of management was less personal than that of the past. The large industrial enterprises of the 1880s and 1890s required more administrators to run them than even the largest mercantile concerns of fifty years before. A major consequence of this requirement was the sudden growth in the numbers and importance of middle managers after the Civil War. By the opening years of the twentieth century, Singer Sewing Machine, for example, had 1,700 branch offices across the United States staffed by middle managers. No longer could most business executives personally know their customers, employees, and fellow managers. The personal business world of the merchant had given way to the organized and bureaucratic business world of the railroad magnate and industrialist.

Business Cooperation

Just as business executives sought to rationalize the administration of their individual companies, their desires for profits and stability in a rapidly changing economic environment led them to try to re-structure relations with each other. They sought to replace competition with cooperation as they grappled with the effects of the new national market on their businesses. Pools and trade associations were the major tools by which business executives sought to achieve industrial peace.

As in so many other areas, railroads pointed the way. From the point of view of railroad officials, America's railroad system was overbuilt by the late nineteenth century. There was not enough traffic for all of the lines to remain profitable. To attract more traffic, weak railroads often lowered their rates, setting off rate wars that could injure the profits of all of the lines, even the strong ones. This situation first appeared during depression years in the mid-1870s, and it occurred again as traffic fell off during a recession in the mid-1880s. In 1887, an extreme example took place. Because of a rate war between the Southern Pacific and Santa Fe railroads that year, passengers could travel from Texas to California for only one dollar! To dampen competition, railroad managers resorted to a form of cooperation called pooling.

Albert Fink of the Louisville & Nashville Railroad led the attempts to set up pools. In 1875, Fink established the Southern Railway and Steamship Association to control traffic in the Southeast. Fink later helped set up regional pools in the Northeast and trans-Mississippi West. Each of these pools tried to limit competition by fixing uniform railroad rates, establishing standard freight categories, and setting freight quotas for member lines. None of these pools worked as well as their founders had hoped, for they lacked the force of law. No railroad could be required to join or remain in a pool. Since there was almost always some railroad willing to stay out of or withdraw from a pool and cut its rates to win short-term increases in traffic, the pools did not end the rate wars.

Business executives in a wide variety of fields emulated railroad officers in seeking to limit competition through the formation of pools. As in the case of railroads, however, these pools did not usually achieve their goals. In most instances, someone was willing to break ranks with his fellow industrialists and cut prices. In the steel industry, for example, Carnegie joined pools just long enough to gain information about his competitors. He then left the pools and, using the information obtained from them, engaged in all-out competition with their members.

Failing in their efforts to create workable pools, many business executives turned to the establishment of trade associations as a way of regulating or limiting competition. Trade associations consisted (and still consist) of firms from the same or different industries working together for common purposes. Some early trade associations set prices and production or sales quotas for member companies. More commonly, trade associations tried to limit competition in indirect ways—by spreading market information through newsletters, for instance. Active at both the regional and national levels, trade associations lobbied politicians vigorously for business interests. A few, most notably the National Association of Manufacturers, worked with officials of the federal government to expand markets for U.S. products overseas.

While trade associations were more successful than pools in achieving some goals, trade associations, like pools, could not stop competition between member companies. As we have seen, it was in part the failure of business executives to limit competition through cooperation that led them to try to create fully integrated business firms. Only through the establishment of the integrated business empires, many late-nineteenth-century business executives thought, they could take advantage of the riches offered by the national market while avoiding competition with other companies.

THE CHARACTER OF THE BUSINESS LEADER

Social and Economic Backgrounds

For many late-nineteenth-century Americans, the leaders at the helm of these integrated business empires were heroic figures, industrial leaders to be admired for the fame and power—not simply the wealth—that they had acquired. Popular magazines of the day—*Century, McClures,* and *Cosmopolitan*—and widely read novels depicted business leaders as achieving success by virtue of their strong-willed individualism. The ideology of individualism in business, which had become entrenched in the American mind during the pre–Civil War years, continued to dominate, even as business became more bureaucratic and impersonal.

The 135 pieces of fiction written by Horatio Alger were among the most widely read works of the era. All of these books have the same basic plot. A young man, usually an obscure person of lower-class origins, moves from the farm to the big city to seek his fortune. There he gets ahead through hard work, leading a morally upright life, and luck (such as rescuing the boss's daughter from a fire). In short, through a combination of "pluck and luck," an individual could, according to Alger, rise from "rags to riches." Writers for popular magazines put forward essentially the same ideas; most described business leaders as farmboys from lower- or middle-class backgrounds.

What the writers described and what the American readers wanted to believe was not reality, however. Only a few business leaders rose from rags to riches. Andrew Carnegie, who came to the United States as a penniless immigrant, did. But he was the exception, not the rule. Over two-thirds of America's business leaders of the late nineteenth and early twentieth centuries had fathers who were businessmen or professional men. Most of the men who led the business system came from middle-class or upper-class families and were well educated by the standards of their day. Few were immigrants or the sons of immigrants. Moreover, most spent all of their lives in large cities; few grew up on farms. The heads of the large center firms in America's emerging industrial business system were white and male.

Women found white-collar positions as clerical workers, department-store buyers, and saleswomen, and took blue-collar jobs in such sex-segregated industries as textiles and clothing production, bookbinding, hatmaking, and tobacco and food processing. As in earlier times, most of those few women who made it to the top as managers succeeded in family businesses. Kate Gleason, for instance, began her career in her father's manufacturing firm. Gleason learned the trade of machinist and worked for the company as a saleswoman. After a falling out with her father and brothers in 1913 over business matters, she struck out on her own, first as the president of the First National Bank of East Rochester and later in a variety of businesses, including housing construction. Like many men heading peripheral firms, some women exploited markets ignored by large center companies. Lydia Pinkham succeeded by developing a tonic designed to cure "the ills of women," and marketing it nationally.

The system of racial segregation that characterized American society provided few business opportunities for black Americans. Those few opportunities lay in peripheral businesses. When the white-owned insurance companies turned down black applicants for policies or charged them excessive rates, black entrepreneurs formed their own insurance companies. Commonly, black entrepreneurs used their profits to establish additional businesses of great benefit to black communities. Most influential was the North

Lydia Pinkham's face, which appeared in advertisements and on boxes containing her patent medicine, was one of the most widely distributed images in the United States. Patent medicine companies advertised more heavily than any other type of firm before the Progressive Era. (The Schlesinger Library, Radcliffe College)

Carolina Mutual Life Insurance Company, started by three black entrepreneurs in Durham in 1898. Those forming the company combined a quest for private profits with a desire to use business institutions for the advancement of their race. From their base in insurance they branched out into banking, printing, and cotton milling in the years before World War I. With assets of nearly $120 million in 1970, North Carolina Mutual remained a leading black business in the years following World War II.

There was a wide gap, then, between popular conceptions about the social and economic backgrounds of business leaders and reality. The reason for this difference is that Americans wanted to keep believing that they could achieve success in the business world as individuals at the very time when the spread of business organizations with managerial hierarchies was decreasing their chances of doing so. Believing deeply in individualism, and especially in the ability of the individual to get ahead economically, Americans had (and still have) a difficult time coming to grips with big business and the giant corporation. They found it hard to realize that the personal business world of the merchant was being replaced by the organized world of the industrialist and that there would be less room for individualism in the business bureaucracies of the twentieth century.

The Business Leader and American Society

While most Americans viewed their nation's business leaders as captains of industry who had achieved success through the exercise of their will power, the business owners were less certain of their dominance over the economy of the United States. Many felt insecure in the face of the economic forces that were transforming their country. Far from controlling the course of events, business executives—like other Americans—were often bewildered by them, particularly during times of depression and financial panic. A leading California insurance man expressed sentiments felt throughout the nation when he observed in 1904 that although "business was constantly changing," at the present time "the changes are revolving with such velocity that some of us are made dizzy by the mere contemplation of them."

The same feeling of insecurity that led business executives to restructure their companies and industries also encouraged them to look for stability in society. This quest led them into many avenues, some heavily traveled, some less so. The railroad barons Commodore William Vanderbilt and Leland Stanford turned to mystics and seers as they tried to understand the present and future through spiritualism. (Vanderbilt once even tried to call upon the spirit of Jim Fisk, a notorious stock-market manipulator, for advice on business affairs.) For others the Bible, with its timeless verities, offered solace. For many business people, "natural laws" of economics, whether learned from reading the works of Adam Smith or more commonly from personal observations, provided a rudder in the perilous seas of economic change. Despite the growth of oligopoly in many fields of industry, most business executives continued to believe that the invisible hand of supply and demand could and should determine economic transactions. Even as they formed giant corporations and sought to control competition through pools and trade associations, business executives emphasized the importance of the free play of economic forces in determining how the American economy functioned. For them, no less than for other Americans, the realities of big business were unnerving and difficult to understand.

Perhaps because of their sense of insecurity, some executives resorted to what the American economist Thorstein Veblen labeled "conspicuous consumption" as a way of winning social acceptance for themselves. They spent their money lavishly in attempts to become members of the social elite of America. Those entrepreneurs who made their fortunes in railroads and industry after the Civil War felt this need most acutely, for they faced two interrelated problems. First, they wanted to show people that they were wealthy, no mean feat at a time when large fortunes were becoming more common. (The United States possessed only a handful of millionaires in the 1850s but had 4,074 by 1892.) Second, they yearned for acceptance by America's established social elite—an elite whose inherited wealth was based on trade and commerce and who looked down on new wealth derived from industrial pursuits. Aping the aristocracy of Europe, the newly rich industrialists built houses that were castles and constructed fifty-room "cottages" at oceanside retreats. They used private railroad cars and yachts to travel from place to place. Their parties and dinners, which featured rarities like peacock tongues, were ostentatious. And they wore clothing to these functions that made them stand out in a crowd. A gown worn by Mrs. Jay Gould, the wife of the railroad financier, had $500,000 worth of jewels sewn onto its cloth.

More than just a desire for social recognition motivated these business leaders, however. Nineteenth-century American business leaders believed in the virtues of capitalism and were confident that their efforts added to their nation's plenty and to the well-being of all Americans. "I saw a marvelous future for our country," John D. Rockefeller noted, "and I wanted to participate in the work of making our country great. I had an ambition to build." Or, as the railroad president Charles Perkins asked rhetorically in 1888, "Have not great merchants, great manufacturers, great inventors done more for the world than preachers and philanthropists? Can there be any doubt that cheapening the cost of necessities and conveniences of life is the most powerful agent of civilization and progress?"

Andrew Carnegie best typified this sort of business leader. He took personal pride in the accomplishments of his business and viewed his business as an extension of himself. Carnegie abandoned a very successful career selling stocks and bonds to enter the steel industry because he wanted to build an establishment of permanent value. Once in it, Carnegie identified himself closely with the steel business. When he constructed one of the world's largest blast furnaces in the early 1870s, he named it the Lucy furnace after the wife of his brother. He valued his business for its efficiency and productivity, for its ability to build up America. Carnegie, in effect, equated the development of his steel company with the progress of the United States.

The same desires to improve the United States and to leave monuments of lasting value led business leaders to engage in philanthropy. In a very paternalistic fashion, they believed that they knew what was best for the majority of Americans, and they were determined to use their wealth to change the lives of everyday people. Under the flood of contributions from business leaders, charity was transformed into philanthropy; its aim became less the relief of the immediate ills of the poor than the improvement of the whole quality of life in America. "The best philanthropy," observed Rockefeller, "is constantly in search of finalities—a search for cause, an attempt to cure evils at their source."

Business leaders supported those philanthropies they thought best embodied the values in which they believed. Like other Americans, most business leaders thought that anyone could rise in status through hard work and the acquisition of knowledge. Not surprisingly, they funded educational institutions as a way of making knowledge, especially technical knowledge, available to enterprising young people trying to move ahead. Andrew Carnegie, who had attended night school as a young man, gave millions of dollars to found thousands of libraries across the nation. He believed that libraries would do more to help the poor than direct aid, for they would build character by rewarding those taking the initiative to use them. For much the same reason, other business leaders gave large sums to colleges and universities. Johns Hopkins, a merchant-banker, donated $3.5 million to establish the university bearing his name. Leland Stanford gave $24 million to found Stanford University, named after his son who had died as a young man, and Rockefeller donated $34 million to remake the University of Chicago.

Robber Baron or Industrial Statesman?

While most Americans looked up to business leaders as heroic figures, many disapproved of some of their actions. Big-business

Andrew Carnegie became one of the nation's best-known industrialists in his lifetime. He is shown with two associates near the time of his retirement from steel-making in 1901, after which he devoted his energies to philanthropy. (Library of Congress)

leaders were blamed for financial panics and recessions, for break-ing labor unions and keeping wages lower than they might have been, for engaging in "unfair" forms of competition that destroyed small businesses, for controlling the prices of consumer goods through monopolistic actions, and for many other misdeeds. As early as 1869, the editor of the *Nation* labeled big-business leaders medieval barons. By the 1890s, business leaders were commonly be-ing referred to as robber barons, by which it was meant that they controlled crucial production processes and communications net-works for their own profit rather than for the good of society as a whole.

What of these accusations? Were business leaders robber barons, as their critics charged? Or were they industrial statesmen dedi-cated to building up the economy of the United States, as they and their defenders asserted? Or should they be viewed in yet another manner?

There can be little doubt that late-nineteenth-century business leaders often engaged in what would today be viewed as unethical practices from which they benefited personally. Competition was ruthless and did drive small businesses to extinction. Big businesses were often able to secure secret rates from railroads lower than those given small businesses, and this situation gave the large enterprises a competitive advantage over the smaller concerns. As we have seen, big businesses often sought to control their markets. Big businesses operating on a national scale sometimes engaged in selective regional price cutting designed to drive local rivals out of business. Money lost in lowering prices in one area was made up by raising prices in other regions where less competition existed. The Standard Oil Company was notorious for employing this tactic. George Rice, an independent refiner in Marietta, Ohio, was one of many who complained about Standard's methods. "They could cut only my customers' price, and below cost, leaving the balance of the town, nine-tenths, uncut," Rice observed in 1899. "This they can easily do without any appreciable harm to their general trade, and thus effectually wipe out all competition."

Big-business leaders did corrupt politics. At both the state and national levels they used money to buy favors for their companies and, less frequently, to win election to office for themselves. At one point, Andrew Carnegie tried to bribe the Pennsylvania legislature to get that body to lower railroad rates. But he was outbid! The Pennsylvania Railroad offered larger bribes, and railroad rates stayed high. Business people also used their power, backed up by the courts, to break unions.

As their critics charged, big-business leaders did benefit from these actions. When he died in 1893, the railroad magnate Leland Stanford left an estate valued at $100 million. Carnegie retired from the steel business in 1901 with a fortune of $300 million. When judged by the standards of their day, however, big business executives appear less deserving of blame. Concepts of business ethics and conflicts of interest were not as well developed as they would become later, and business leaders were groping to redefine their relationships to the rest of society in the wake of disruptions caused by the rise of big business.

The emergence of oligopolistic big business had a mixed impact on the general public. Price competition decreased between different businesses in many fields. However, the trend toward oligopoly does not appear to have retarded economic growth in the United States, at least not in the late nineteenth and early twentieth centuries. Between roughly 1870 and 1920, the nation's gross national product increased by a factor of eight, and per capita GNP tripled. (See Table 5.1.) Big businesses contributed to this growth by helping to mobilize capital and by providing organizational leadership for America's expanding industrial enterprises. Moreover, the prices of many industrial products dropped, as the larger, more fully integrated, and more efficient manufacturing concerns passed on some of their gains to consumers. Between 1866 and 1894, for example, the price of one gallon of kerosene fell from 30 cents to 5 cents.

To view America's business leaders of the late nineteenth and early twentieth centuries as either robber barons or industrial statesmen may be misleading. It probably attributes more power to them than they actually possessed. They were not in command of events

Table 5.1
Gross National Product (GNP) in the United States, 1869–1921

	1929 Prices	
	Total (in billions of dollars)	*Per capita (in dollars)*
1869–1873	$ 9	$223
1872–1876	11	254
1877–1881	16	327
1882–1886	21	374
1887–1891	24	388
1889–1893	26	405
1892–1896	30	434
1897–1901	37	496
1902–1906	47	569
1907–1911	55	608
1912–1916	63	632
1917–1921	72	683

SOURCE: U.S. Department of Commerce, *Historical Statistics of the United States* (Washington, D.C.: U.S. Printing Office, 1958), p. 139.

to the extent that most Americans imagined they were. More often, business executives understood only partially and incorrectly the growing complexity of the economic situation in the United States. Rather than mastering circumstances, they were frequently mastered by circumstances. Instead of thinking of Rockefeller, Carnegie, and Stanford as either robber barons or industrial statesmen, it is more accurate to see them simply as business executives searching for opportunities in a difficult and rapidly changing economic situation. Like other Americans, they found it hard to comprehend fully the spread of industry and the rise of big business in their land.

AMERICA'S BUSINESS SYSTEM TRANSFORMED

Although American business executives may have had a difficult time understanding the economic changes occurring in the late nineteenth and early twentieth centuries, the actions they took to deal with those changes permanently altered the nature of business in the United States. Big businesses with managerial bureaucracies replaced many small businesses run directly by their owners. Vertically and horizontally integrated companies supplanted single-unit firms, thus leading to concentration in industry and to the creation of oligopoly in many fields of manufacturing. These developments, in turn, influenced the nature of economic decision making in the United States. With the rise of big business, decisions about the production and distribution of goods that had previously been made by the free interplay of market forces came to be internalized within the business firm. The visible hand of management replaced the invisible hand of the market in determining the functioning of part of the American economy.

The rise of big business also altered the nature of government-business relations in the United States. Federal, state, and local governments continued their developmental policy of aiding businesses as a way to build up their economies—a policy begun in the pre–Civil War years. But after the Civil War, a new element appeared in the realm of government-business relations. Governments, especially the federal government, began regulating business practices. Starting with railroads in 1887, the federal government expanded its regulatory powers to other businesses in the early 1900s.

Selected Readings

Glenn Porter, *The Rise of Big Business, 1860–1910* (Arlington Heights, Illinois: Harlan Davidson, 1973), offers an excellent short analysis of the development of big business in America. Glenn Porter and Harold Livesay, *Merchants and Manufacturers: Studies in the Changing Structure of Nineteenth-Century Marketing* (Baltimore: The Johns Hopkins Press, 1971), examines the same topic in more detail. Naomi Lamoreaux, *The Great Merger Movement in American Business, 1895–1904* (Cambridge: Cambridge University Press, 1985), examines America's first business merger movement. Valuable essays on the evolution of management appear in James P. Baughman, ed., *The History of American Management* (Englewood Cliffs, N.J.: Prentice-Hall, 1969), and Edwin Perkins, *Men and Organizations* (New York: G. P. Putnam's Sons, 1977). On the continued importance of small business, see the essays in Stuart Bruchey, ed., *Small Business in American Life* (New York: Columbia University Press, 1980); James Soltow, "Origins of Small Business: Metal Fabricators and Machinery Makers in New England, 1890–1957," *Transactions of the American Philosophical Society* 55(December 1965): 1–58; and Mansel G. Blackford, *A Portrait Cast in Steel: Buckeye International and Columbus, Ohio, 1881–1980* (Westport, Conn.: Greenwood Press, 1982).

Two good studies of Andrew Carnegie are Harold Livesay, *Andrew Carnegie and the Rise of Big Business* (Boston: Little, Brown and Company, 1975), and Joseph Frazier Wall, *Andrew Carnegie* (New York: Oxford University Press, 1970). Allan Nevins, *John D. Rockefeller* (New York: Charles Scribner's Sons, 1940), 2 vols., and Ralph and Muriel Hidy, *Pioneering in Big Business, 1882–1921* (New York: Harper and Brothers, 1955), look at the history of Standard Oil. Alfred D. Chandler, Jr., ed., *The Railroads: The Nation's First Big Business* (New York: Harcourt, Brace and World, 1965), investigates new managerial practices developed by railroads. Vincent Carosso, *The Morgans: Private International Bankers, 1854–1913* (Cambridge, Mass.: Harvard University Press, 1987), and Dolores Greenberg, *Financiers and Railroads, 1869–1889: A Study of Morton, Bliss & Company* (Newark: University of Delaware Press, 1980), examine links between investment banking and railroads. Robert Garnet, *The Telephone Enterprise: The Evolution of the Bell System's Horizontal Structure, 1876–1929* (Baltimore: Johns Hopkins University Press, 1985); George Smith, *The Anatomy of a Business Strategy: Bell's Western Electric and the Origins of the American Telephone Industry* (Baltimore:

Johns Hopkins University Press, 1985); and Richard Vietor, "Perspectives on the Bell System," *Business History Review* 60 (Winter 1986): 633–40, examine the telephone industry. Leonard Reich, *The Making of American Industrial Research: Science and Business at GE and Bell, 1876–1926* (Cambridge: Cambridge University Press, 1985), is a path-breaking study.

For more detail on the history of banking, see Margaret Myers, *A Financial History of the United States* (New York: Columbia University Press, 1970), and Vincent Carosso, *Investment Banking in America* (Cambridge, Mass.: Harvard University Press, 1970). Morton Keller, *The Life Insurance Enterprise, 1885–1910* (Cambridge, Mass.: Harvard University Press, 1964), examines the history of life insurance.

William Miller, ed., *Men in Business* (Cambridge, Mass.: Harvard University Press, 1952), and Edward Kirkland, *Dream and Thought in the Business Community, 1860–1890* (Ithaca: Cornell University Press, 1956), investigate the relationship between business and society. Walter Weare, *Black Business in the New South: A Social History of the North Carolina Mutual Life Insurance Company* (Urbana: University of Illinois Press, 1973), is an excellent case study of black business development. Margery Davies, *Woman's Place Is at the Typewriter: Office Work and Office Workers, 1890–1930* (Philadelphia: Temple University Press, 1982), examines the entrance of women into business offices. Sarah Stage, *Female Complaints: Lydia Pinkham and the Business of Women's Medicine* (New York: W. W. Norton, 1979), presents a fascinating study of women, patent medicine, doctors, and the history of a company.

IMPORTANT EVENTS, 1864–1897

1864	Congress establishes a system of chartering national banks. Congress uses a land-grant system to help fund the first transcontinental railroad.
1869	Entrepreneurs and workers complete the first transcontinental railroad. State regulation of railroads begins.
1872	Scandal besets the Union Pacific Railroad.
1876	The U.S. Supreme Court begins to ban state restrictions on center firms.
1877	The Supreme Court upholds state regulation of railroads. Railroad strikes disrupt service and alarm the nation.
1886	The Knights of Labor membership peaks at over 700,000. Union Leaders found the American Federation of Labor. The Supreme Court restricts state regulation of railroads.
1887	Congress establishes the Interstate Commerce Commission to regulate the railroads.
1890	Congress passes the Sherman Antitrust Act. The Supreme Court assures center firms of their ability to operate in a national market.
1894	The Pullman strike highlights "the labor problem."
1895	The Supreme Court allows the "Sugar Trust."
1896	Inflationist campaigns culminate with the defeat of Populism.
1897	The Supreme Court forbids railroads to collaborate in fixing rates.

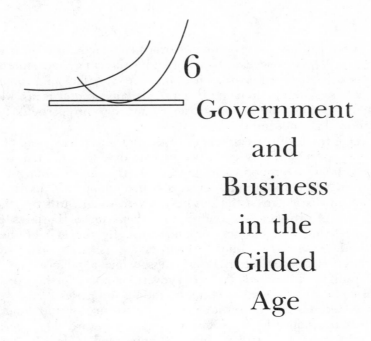

6
Government
and
Business
in the
Gilded
Age

Mark Twain and Charles Dudley Warner, in their 1873 novel *The Gilded Age,* coined a phrase that came to characterize the period from the end of the Civil War in 1865 to the dawn of the next century in 1901. Twain and Warner portrayed not just a national enterprising spirit but what they saw as a veritable rampage to make money that tainted American institutions and democratic customs with materialistic values. Changing business institutions—especially the rise of big business—and the emergence of an urban-industrial society produced new problems in Americans' daily lives and new issues in the nation's political economy. With the emergence of powerful center firms, the localism of the American political economy during the first half of the nineteenth century began to recede after 1850, to be replaced by national policies of the federal government. The federal government remained weak, however, compared to what it would later become. Nevertheless, federal policies regarding tariffs, currency and banking, industrial labor, and especially access to a national market had the overall effect of promoting a business system dominated by large, dynamic center firms, which by 1900 operated on a scale vaster than any entrepreneur had envisioned at midcentury.

One result of the emergence of the new business system of center and peripheral firms was a fiery debate over the very nature of the U.S. political economy. Some Americans began claiming that the growth of corporate power threatened democracy itself. Protest movements aimed at the business system sought to strengthen the power of government to direct the behavior of business people, their firms, and business organizations. By the end of the nineteenth century, the country began taking its first hesitant steps toward federal regulation of business, while a political movement, Populism, advocated outright government ownership of center firms in the railroad and communications industries.

A second result of the increased diversity of the time was a changing stance by some business leaders toward the government. Business groups were traditionally interested in policies that promoted economic growth. Those developmental policies continued in the Gilded Age, but another set of concerns arose: the need for regulation. The burst of economic growth that occurred after the Civil War led Americans with varied outlooks to try to control economic circumstances. They sometimes turned to the government— local, state, and federal—to enact laws; some wanted laws designed to achieve greater stability in an uncertain business environment, and others desired laws to check the power of large corporations.

The Gilded Age was a period of considerable political and social turmoil. The rise of big business and the continuing reorganization of work caused by the spread of industrialization were two critical changes faced by Americans. Other problems seemed to abound. In the nation's cities, mill towns, and mining camps, the social sores of human poverty and degradation contrasted starkly with the opulent lifestyle of the successful. Despite the country's spectacular economic growth, farmers and small business owners sometimes felt that their commercial opportunities were diminishing and that they were losing control of their enterprises to banks and corporations headquartered far from their own communities. The traditional patterns of localism in government remained, even in the face of nationwide innovations introduced by the center firms in railroading, communications, and manufacturing. Governmental institutions did not keep pace with economic changes. In the 1890s, for instance, the Vanderbilt family employed more workers on one estate than the total number of employees in the U.S. Department of Agriculture. Governmental agencies capable of paying expert, continuous attention to business and social problems awaited the twentieth century.

SOCIAL CHANGE AND SOCIAL THOUGHT: THE FLOWERING OF LAISSEZ FAIRE

The rapid technological, social, and economic changes that occurred in the United States in the decades after the Civil War were unprecedented in human experience. The mushrooming of factories, the shifting relationships between human beings and machines that newer technologies required, and the reorganization of daily life that the modern city entailed happened within one or two generations and represented a tremendous uprooting of traditional patterns of human behavior and economic interaction. Americans living during this time turned to laissez-faire economic theory to explain and justify what was happening.

The Gilded Age saw the full flowering of laissez-faire economic thought in America. It permeated judicial decisions (especially in the federal courts), appeared in the writings of social theorists and college professors, and was popularized by thoughtful journalists. In the courts, laissez faire was part of a long heritage of protecting liberty. Judges wanted to prevent those holding governmental power from using it to benefit one group or person at the expense of others. Like Adam Smith a century earlier, these jurists and theorists thought that the best system of political economy allowed for the free interplay of natural economic laws, unimpeded by state interference. Governmental services that benefited everyone—like education or the postal system—met with approval. But on the great questions of the day relating to labor conditions, the tariff, currency, and the "trusts"—the word used then to describe "big business"—the theorists advocated laissez faire.

For business executives, to the extent that they paid attention to economic theory at all, laissez faire provided a theoretical justification for preserving the status quo in social relations, especially in the issues that divided business and labor. Laissez-faire theorists preached that the free market should set wages, hours, and working conditions. If a business manager abused workers, so the theory went, the workers could exercise their freedom and obtain employment elsewhere. Any law protecting the rights of workers or imposing the eight-hour day was seen as an infringement on the individual freedom of the workers to enter into contracts. When industrial workers tried to guard their interests by forming unions, business executives objected on the ground that workers' collective action impeded the operation of market forces. For business owners fighting unionization and seeking lower production costs through new work rules, or trying to survive in a competitive marketplace by lowering wages and providing substandard working conditions, the laissez-faire theory held an obvious appeal. Unencumbered by the necessity of maintaining logical consistency, they might advocate laissez faire with respect to labor laws and at the same time ask for tariff protection from foreign competitors.

Although promoters of business interests and even judges used laissez-faire doctrine inconsistently, it nevertheless remained part of a deeply held faith in the virtues of the republican government established by the American Revolution. During the nineteenth century, judges embedded laissez-faire theory firmly in the law, a development that held particular significance for business interests. In 1842 the U.S. Supreme Court, in *Swift* v. *Tyson,* had asserted the right of federal courts to ignore state precedents in developing federal doctrines. At first, the decision had prevented the states from prohibiting out-of-state creditors' recovering debts, but in the decades that followed, the policy combined with judges' laissez-faire convictions to provide corporations with a federal bastion against unfriendly state laws and regulations.

POLITICS AND PARTISANSHIP

Problems of Politics

A predominant political theme in the nineteenth century was the conflict between localism and the vision of a unified national policy. Within that context, the second half of the century witnessed considerable change in favor of national power, especially as the Civil War ended slavery and established the supremacy of federal authority. Less dramatic, yet critically important for the institutional development of the business system of center and peripheral firms, was the ability of business firms faced with hostile state legislation to obtain redress in the federal courts. The center firms were dramatically changing how the American economy functioned, and they needed the assistance of the federal courts. By 1890, the U.S. Supreme Court had assured center firms the ability to reach a national market, unfettered by local regulation. In short, the localism that had prevailed in the federal system no longer fit the national and international business system that entrepreneurs were establishing.

Although the entrepreneurs organizing the new factories and railroads, and the financiers who assisted them, had a reputation for enormous political influence, they often felt abused by and mistrustful of politicians. Americans whose lives were still rooted in patterns of local economic organization continued to wield enormous influence. Industrialists and financiers faced movements by farmers and local merchants seeking governmental economic policies to protect their interests in the face of more modern and more efficient systems of production, distribution, and transportation. Financiers wanted a currency whose value was stable but other, more numerous Americans, who were debtors seeking rapid growth for their own enterprises, desired inflation. In that setting, business leaders developed techniques of political influence that gained them the unsavory reputation of corrupting traditional American egalitarian institutions.

The uncertainty that business leaders faced from the legislative branch of government and the corruption in which some business leaders were willing to engage became clear in the course of events associated with particular policies. The great issues of the political economy concerned tariffs, money labor, trusts, and internal improvements; as these issues were or were not resolved, the fabric of the political economy was woven.

The Tariff

The tariff once again became a subject of lively controversy in the late nineteenth century. As a major point of contention between the theorists of laissez faire and the practitioners of politics, the issue divided major party platforms and fueled campaign rhetoric. Despite the bitter complaints from some consumers and the attempts, especially of the Democrats led by President Grover Cleveland, to have Congress lower duties, the general trend of American tariff policy remained protectionist. By the end of the 1890s, the Republican party had gained majority standing, in part because it championed the cause of a protective tariff as part of a stronger federal government that fostered economic growth, high wages, and substantial business profits. In the meantime the Democratic party, although it contained important congressional representatives who supported tariff protection, generally asserted the benefits of a tariff for "revenue only."

Underlying the partisan debates over the tariff were conflicting business interests similar to those that had divided American opinion before the Civil War. During the Gilded Age, however, the context of those debates was more complicated. Price deflation was occurring all over the world, partly because the cost of producing many goods was declining with new industrial techniques. In addition, some American manufacturing firms were maturing and seeking export markets for their products; those firms feared that high American tariffs might prompt foreign governments to retaliate. Also, as center firms began to dominate some industries, entrepreneurs in smaller firms complained that the tariff was the "mother of trusts"—the tariff's protective shield allowed big business to avoid competition and grow even more in wealth and power.

There were numerous examples of shifting sentiments concerning the tariff. Railroad magnates had once opposed protective duties on foreign-made rails, but after American producers, led by Carnegie Steel, became low-cost producers they lost interest in avoiding tariff duties on British rails. Similarly, when Carnegie was establishing his steel firm, he favored protecting the American market from foreign competition, but when he became the leading low-cost producer in the world, the lowering of trade barriers was to his advantage. In any case, ironmakers who favored protection always advocated free trade in raw materials.

In the tariff politics of the nineteenth century, thus, there was much intellectual inconsistency. Business people wanted tariffs that were to their advantage, regardless of theoretical principles. As the Democratic senator from Indiana, Daniel W. Voorhees, said in 1883, "I am a protectionist for every interest which I am sent here by my constituents to protect." (Just a year earlier, his party had condemned tariff protection as "unjust.")

The intellectual inconsistency that arose over the tariff was a product, of course, of immediate economic interest. Indeed, there was widespread support for tariff protection. In general, industrial workers believed that the protective tariff allowed employers to pay higher wages—with free trade, the workers feared, low-wage workers in foreign factories would take away American jobs. Moreover, there were American industries—the woolen, hemp, flax, and sugar industries were examples—that depended on tariff protection for their very survival. On the other hand, farmers and other business owners who purchased manufactured commodities believed that free trade was to their advantage, doubly so when they searched for export markets for American goods. The conflicting economic interests involved with the tariff issue meant that politicians were unable to arrange either fully satisfactory compromises in the law or strategies on election day.

The Currency Question

If the recurring battles over the tariff provided more heat than light, issues relating to currency eventually exceeded them in the intensity of political emotions. The currency question arrayed hard money against soft money, a creditor class against a debtor class, and established business people against those interested in new entrepreneurship and speculation. By the 1890s, this issue, along with the rise of center firms and the growing wealth and power of eastern banks and businesses, contributed to a major movement of political protest called Populism, which sought to break up the control of the big corporations to create better opportunities for aspiring entrepreneurs.

The currency controversy arose initially because of the Civil War, when the Union government issued a paper currency called greenbacks to help pay for the war's extraordinary costs. The government required the acceptability of greenbacks; that is, they became legal tender for all debts, public and private, except customs duties and interest payments on the national debt. For those obligations, specie—gold or silver notes—were still required, so that the government could accumulate hard currency. By the end of the war there were $462 million worth of greenbacks outstanding.

After the return to peace in 1865, the continued existence of the greenbacks became controversial. As was the case with the tariff, the debate revolved around the special interests of rival groups of business people. Established manufacturers and merchants tended to favor "hard money"—the abandonment of greenbacks and a return to a currency backed by specie. New England textile producers, for instance, by now established for three generations, wanted both hard money and lower tariff duties, as they operated in an international market. These textile manufacturers imported raw materials, including coal from Nova Scotia and some raw cotton from India, on which they did not want to pay a high tariff. (Their British competitors imported raw materials free of duty.) The New England textile producers, furthermore, disliked the greenbacks, for although they received them as payments, they could not use them to pay customs duties. A lowering of customs duties and a return to hard money, they felt, would help the American textile industry. Other American business executives agreed with this hard-money sentiment—importers, wholesale grocers, commission brokers, and the like. Aspiring entrepreneurs, on the other hand, tended to favor "soft money"—the continuation of the greenbacks—to expand the supply of capital available to boost the opportunity for investment. These entrepreneurs of the late 1860s and 1870s were typified by the Pennsylvania iron men. Their spokesman, Republican Pennsylvania Congressman William D. Kelley, whose nickname was Pig Iron, summarized their view: "The contest is between the creditor and debtor class—the men of industry" and the financiers. Entrepreneurs tended to want soft money, such as greenbacks, which had the effect of enlarging the supply of available capital. They believed that soft money led to a desirable inflation—allowing them as debtors to pay back loans with a currency lower in value.

In the late 1870s, the federal government finally resolved the greenback controversy by limiting their number. Soon a new controversy arose, however, not over printing paper money but over the question of expanding the money supply and reversing the deflationary trend in the economy (prices generally were falling during the Gilded Age), by declaring silver as well as gold an acceptable currency base. The complex question of using silver, which affected American politics until the end of the nineteenth century, arose because American silver production was increasing and silver-mining interests began demanding its use as a currency base along with gold. Wanting a market in the federal treasury, the miners launched a twenty-year campaign to establish a bimetallic coinage, the "free and unlimited coinage of silver" at a ratio of sixteen grains of silver to one of gold.

The campaign of the silver miners, obviously rooted in self-interest, was significant because it was heard sympathetically by discontented farmers and small business operators, mostly in the West and South, who desired an expansion of the money supply and saw bimetallism as the most feasible course. As the discontented westerners and southerners mounted the wide-ranging critique of American business and politics called Populism, they took up the free-silver cry as part of their reform program. The Populists demanded government ownership of the railroads and telegraphs and

William Jennings Bryan (1860–1925) spent much of his life advocating the rights of the ordinary citizen to invest in small business. Bryan traveled widely on the nation's lecture circuit and published popular columns expressing his views against those Americans who, he believed, enjoyed too much wealth and power. Here he is shown delivering his famous "Cross of Gold" speech. (Library of Congress)

inflation through free silver in order to redistribute the wealth and power of eastern bankers and manufacturers to aspiring entrepreneurs. In the eyes of the protesters, deflation operated to the advantage of eastern creditors while it hindered the ability of indebted, independent operators of small businesses and farms to seize opportunities.

The emotions surrounding the silver issue ran high, reaching a climax in the presidential campaign of 1896. The issues resonated most clearly among wheat farmers of the Great Plains and cotton farmers of the South. The farmers who protested in the Populist movement were trying to organize cooperatives that would wrest control of the distribution of farm products from merchants and railroads. The protesting farmers knew that inflating the currency would facilitate the retirement of mortgages and thereby, they believed, ensure the viability of the family farm in the larger economy. The popularity of the Populist rhetoric in the cotton and wheat belts of the South and Great Plains, and the movement's victories at the polls in several states, frightened investors whose fortunes were tied to the railroad industry. Populism's call for government ownership and inflation threatened to destroy the very fabric of the American business system that had evolved after the Civil War. In 1896, silver-inflationist Democrats captured control of their party and nominated William Jennings Bryan of Nebraska for president, as did the Populist party. The Republican platform and its candidate, William McKinley, favored maintaining the gold standard. Inflation, silver versus gold, was a main topic in the campaign that year, and established bankers and corporations rested easy only after Bryan's sound defeat. McKinley's victory, the return to prosperity after 1896, and the opening of new gold mines in Alaska and elsewhere caused the high emotions surrounding the coinage issue to recede more quickly than they had flared.

A National Banking System

During the Civil War, Congress established a new national banking system. The creation of national banks and the subsequent evolution of the financial system were key features of the political economy, although they did not provoke the emotional, long-running disputes of the currency question. Nevertheless, banking and currency policies were obviously related, and the bank laws led to a concentration of financial power in New York City. Thousands of farmers, merchants, manufacturers, and bankers outside of the eastern seaboard centers believed that the banking system operated as a kind of conspiracy of plunder or, more moderately, that it provided unfair advantages to firms and banks that comprised an "eastern establishment."

Salmon P. Chase, secretary of the treasury in the administration of Abraham Lincoln, was the father of the national banking system of the Gilded Age. Responsible for raising the large sums needed by the Union during the war, he considered the system of state-chartered banks and the consequent uneven value of state bank notes to be undesirable. So he set out to devise a system of federally chartered banks (but without a main bank, like the old Bank of the United States, which had proven so controversial in the 1830s). In statutes enacted in 1863 and 1864, Congress provided for the chartering of national banks as a means of financing the war. In this system the government printed national bank notes that a new Treasury Department official, the comptroller of the currency, received in exchange for government bonds. The Treasury Department then used the paper currency to pay the government's bills. The law declared the notes legal tender for all transactions except the payment of custom duties. Meanwhile, an 1865 law taxed state bank notes and drove them out of existence. The result, along with the greenbacks, was the establishment of a new national bank-note currency secured by the debt of the federal government. By 1865, there were nearly 1,300 national banks whose resources included almost $400 million in federal bonds, with a commensurate flow of currency into the economy. Government banking policy thereby encouraged the growth of an important service industry.

The federal government provided little administrative control over the national banks but did place requirements on them intended to insure their soundness. The banks earned profits from lending funds at interest, but bankers could keep only enough cash on reserve to meet withdrawal demands. The law required country banks to maintain a 15 per cent reserve against deposits, three-fifths of which could be kept in either reserve or central-reserve cities. Banks in reserve cities had to keep 25 per cent, half of which they could deposit in a central-reserve city. New York was the only central-reserve city until 1887, when Congress added Chicago and St. Louis. Banks in the central-reserve cities had to maintain 15 per cent of their money on hand to meet depositors' demands.

This system pleased the bankers, but it did not always serve business well. When one bank deposited reserve funds in a reserve bank, it earned interest on the deposits, but the bank that held the money had full use of it. The banks in the central-reserve cities, especially those in New York, thus received enormous deposits that they lent at call. To maintain the ability to repay, those loans were customarily secured by stock securities that could quickly be sold on the Wall Street exchange. This situation operated well during prosperous times, but after the Civil War the economy experienced the ups and downs of business cycles, which the banking system aggravated. At the peaks of the business cycle, with demand for loan funds high, the banks had trouble supplying sufficient credit. When that occurred, depositors, worried about the health of the bank to which funds were entrusted, sometimes made withdrawals. As those withdrawal demands filtered to New York, banks there called in loans based on stock securities, and panics struck the securities exchanges. Wall Street panics in 1873, 1884, 1893, and 1907 helped provoke sharp downturns in the business cycle, as investors in corporate securities encountered a shortage of capital and scaled down their spending on new buildings, plants, and machinery.

This illustration depicting the panic that swept Wall Street in the spring of 1884 indicates just how fragile the banking system was during the Gilded Age. If a rumor or development prompted suspicion of a bank's soundness, then great "runs" would occur, with depositors frantically trying to withdraw their funds before the bank went under. Such panics periodically reverberated through the U.S. economy, triggering depressions, business failures, and unemployment. (Library of Congress)

Not only did the banking system aggravate downturns in the business cycle, but it served the more sparsely settled and agricultural regions poorly during this period. The government had placed a number of restrictions on the banks. For instance, fairly substantial amounts of capital were required for the issuance of corporate banking charters, making it difficult to found banks in small towns and remote regions. Further, the law forbade banks from making loans secured by land, the main asset in agricultural areas. This situation, added to the ambitions of western and southern entrepreneurs and their demands for currency inflation, evoked political complaints about a "money power" entrenched in Wall Street that seemed to manipulate credit and banking to work against the interests and desires of farmers and business firms that were not well established. After the Panic of 1893 fueled the nation's worst-yet economic depression, complete with bankruptcies and widespread unemployment, pressures mounted for reforms in the banking system. None, however, were immediately forthcoming.

Industrial Workers and the Political Economy

In addition to these crucial tariff and banking issues, issues concerning government policy on conditions of work and the relations between employers and employees also arose. In fact, the pain experienced by so many workers and their families in adjusting to the new factory conditions sometimes led to violence and at other times to union agitation and demands for redress from the government. In fact, between 1876 and 1896, there were more strikes and more persons injured or killed in labor protests than in any other nation. The conflicts that occurred between workers and management, "labor" and "capital" in the language of the day, prompted widespread alarm over "the labor question" in the minds of many Americans, including prominent politicians, clergymen, educators, and journalists.

Rapid industrialization left both employers and workers groping for the power to control the conditions of work. Generally in this period, business enjoyed the upper hand in defining the limits of government intervention in controlling hours, wages, safety, and other conditions of work, but that control caused considerable dispute, even violence. The Gilded Age witnessed antagonism between social and economic classes, with industrial workers convinced that employers were intent on exploiting their talents and energies so that investors and managers could live in splendor.

Much of the worker agitation arose from this underlying class antagonism between labor and business. Most hurtful in labor's view was the "wages system" through which the privileged few managed the work of the multitudes. The largest organization giving expression to this complaint was the Knights of Labor, whose leaders

The railroad strike of 1877 was the first nationwide strike in the United States. Striking railroad workers sometimes resorted to violence to prevent strikebreakers from taking their jobs. Although he wished for an amicable settlement of the conflict, President Rutherford B. Hayes ordered troops of the U.S. Army to intervene and preserve order. (Library of Congress)

wanted to alter the way the industrial process was organized. The Knights attracted large numbers of industrial workers and other Americans interested in reforming the industrial system. The Knights envisioned cooperative enterprises in which workers owned and controlled the facilities of production, distribution, and communication. At its peak in the mid-1880s, the Knights of Labor had at least 700,000 members (and many more sympathizers) and owned and operated a coal mine, 62 grocery and retail stores, 11 newspapers, and 55 workshops and factories. The Knights' resources were inadequate for more substantial cooperative enterprises, however, and by the 1890s the Knights of Labor had waned in influence, as other groups were attracting the allegiances of workers and reformers.

In addition to the alternative ways of organizing production the Knights of Labor explored, some workers organized trade unions to protect their interests from the practices of industrial capitalists. These unions, formed mostly by skilled workers, were less concerned with rejecting the wages system than improving the workers' lot within the prevailing industrial order. In 1886, the trade unions organized the American Federation of Labor (AF of L), whose purpose was to support existing unions and help found new ones (it was, and is, a kind of union of unions) so that more and more workers could act collectively in negotiating contracts with employers. This development, and especially the determination of generations of men and women to have unions, provoked ideological and economic conflicts that affected the political economy in both theory and practice for a long time.

The emergence of the trade union movement in the Gilded Age provoked a major confrontation between advocates of the prevailing laissez-faire theory and defenders of business and governmental practices. Laissez-faire theory, which most business people professed to believe in, called for contracts between individual workers and individual employers. If workers did not agree with terms of the contract, including the wages, hours, and working conditions, they were free, employers argued, to seek employment elsewhere. The workers' freedom should serve as a self-correcting mechanism to insure that businesses offered fair terms of employment. Workers, however, realized that in reality they were neither free agents nor on equal terms with employers and that in the impersonal setting of modern industry businesses all too often had incentives to lower labor costs by replacing skilled workers with machines. Workers saw their interests as a class, or as a craft, as distinct and often opposite from the interests of employers, and their trade unions wanted to redress the balance of power in labor contracts by insisting on collective bargaining (workers negotiating as a group with their employer). Unions therefore tried to develop power independent from business, government, or other institutions to allow workers to negotiate agreements for higher wages, shorter hours, and improved working conditions as a group. As Adolph Strasser, president of the Cigar Makers' Union, explained to a Senate committee in 1883, "We are fighting only for immediate objects— objects that can be realized in a few years."

When workers tried to gain those "immediate objects," however, they clashed with business interests and goals. Unions, for instance, sometimes demanded work rules designed to protect traditional crafts, while business executives, wanting to control and improve every aspect of production, insisted on breaking up old craft prerogatives in favor of newer techniques and machines. When managers introduced scientific management principles into their factories in the late nineteenth and early twentieth centuries, as discussed in Chapter 5, they shifted control over work routines from the workers to management, with the workers sometimes becoming mere appendages to their machines. Partly because of management's drive to have tradition yield to efficiency, skilled workers rebelled, a situation that was a major cause of strikes. Moreover, in a deflationary setting, with some industries suffering from overproduction, businesses often lowered labor costs by paying "starvation wages." These were a major bone of contention, but worst of all in the minds of industrial workers were the long, grinding hours of work. Carnegie's steel firm, for instance, demanded that production workers be on the job for twelve-hour shifts seven days a week when the mills were running at full capacity. The cry for the eight-hour day and the forty-eight-hour workweek was the most popular rallying point for the union movement in this period.

The clash between labor and management complicated American politics. Officials in local communities and state capitals often sympathized with the struggles of workers who seemed victimized by powerful capitalists who did not reside in the local mill towns or mining camps. There were thus occasions when unionized workers found that local governments aided their cause. At the very least, union leaders wanted government to remain neutral in disputes. Business managers, on the other hand, frequently complained that work stoppages violated the law, and they demanded forcible government intervention. Powerful corporations succeeded in obtaining help from local and state officials, and they did not hesitate to turn to federal authority when doing so was necessary to suppress a strike. In general, especially as the federal courts assumed more authority to check state and local regulation of economic affairs, the weight of government power in labor-management disputes operated against the interests of trade unions.

The Pullman Strike of 1894:
A Case Study in "The Labor Problem"

There were many strikes during the Gilded Age, and many more would follow in the first four decades of the twentieth century.

Their causes varied from straightforward economic grievances to more subtle conflicts, as managers tried to increase their control over the work process. Usually, the basic issue was the right of workers to have unions and to engage in collective bargaining. Typically, strikes ended when the government applied its power against the unions. One strike in particular, the Pullman strike of 1894, highlighted several of these aspects of "the labor problem," as it was then called.

The Pullman Company, owned by George Pullman, was a major producer of railroad rolling stock, including the sleeping cars that made the name Pullman a household word. The company manufactured the railroad cars in a company-owned town on the outskirts of Chicago and contracted with the major railroads to attach them to passenger trains. Pullman publicized his company town as a model community filled with contented, well-paid workers. But events proved that the Pullman workers disagreed. In response to the depression that began in 1893, the company sought to preserve its profits by lowering labor costs. When the firm slashed its work force from 5,500 to 3,300 and cut wages by an average of 25 per cent, the Pullman workers rebelled. They joined the American Railway Union (ARU) led by Eugene Debs, which was trying to organize rail workers all across the country. The ARU had won concessions from the Great Northern Railway early in 1894, and the Pullman workers looked to it as a chance to weaken Pullman's control over their lives and to restore their wages. To bring pressure on the firm, the ARU asked workers operating trains to which Pullman sleeping cars were attached to stop work and thus halt the trains. The union told the railroads that their trains could operate without the Pullman cars, but the railroads insisted that they had contracts with the Pullman Company requiring them to haul the sleeping cars. The result was an impasse, with railroad workers in and around Chicago refusing to operate passenger trains.

The strike ended with the intervention of the United States Army. The passenger trains also hauled mail cars, and although the workers promised to operate mail trains so long as Pullman cars were not attached, the railroads refused. Pullman and the carriers informed federal officials that violence was occurring and that the mail was not going through. Attorney General Richard Olney, who disliked unions, heard their claims of violence (but not the assurances of local authorities that there was no uncontrolled violence) and arranged to send federal troops to insure the delivery of the mail and to suppress the strike. The union leader, Debs, was jailed for not obeying an injunction that a judge had issued against the strikers.

The Pullman strike was representative of similar, lesser-known events elsewhere during this period when business executives commonly turned to government for assistance in defeating strikes and breaking unions. The use of the federal army was a dramatic exception to the more usual use of local police forces. Most strikes were broken by firms obtaining court injunctions against the unions from friendly local judges. When strike leaders refused to obey the court order, the police and courts intervened, jailing union leaders, destroying union documents, and bleeding union treasuries.

The class conflict and attendant violence that had appeared in American life in the 1890s led to a search by some religious, labor, business, and public leaders for common interests between business and labor. That search would eventually produce reforms and new policies, but those changes had to await the twentieth century, when they would include some of the reforms associated with the Progressive Era.

GOVERNMENT PROMOTION AND REGULATION OF BUSINESS

Tradition and Innovation

The government not only sided with business in breaking labor unions during the Gilded Age but also continued to help in other ways. As we have seen, the government provided significant help for internal improvements before the Civil War. Government aid was especially significant in conquering the Appalachian Mountain barrier during the first half of the nineteenth century. During the second half of the century, government assistance was also important in helping the railroads cross the vast western expanses. Government aid for railroad construction during the Gilded Age was somewhat less important than it had been in the earlier period, when canals and the first railroads were being built, but it nevertheless proved an important factor in linking the Pacific Coast with the rest of the nation.

Even as the government continued to assist the development of business during the Gilded Age, new issues of the control of business began to surface. These new issues related to the use of the railroads, not their construction, and to the emergence of the new

Completion of the transcontinental railroad was cause for celebration; shown here are various dignitaries and workers at Promontory, Utah, where the Central Pacific and Union Pacific lines met in 1869. Moments before, workers had hammered down the golden spike that joined the two railroads. (Union Pacific Corporation)

"big-business" firms. The center firms, which included the railroads, struggled to set prices administratively and to their advantage, while injustices in the eyes of the users of the railroads began to appear. Similarly, the rise of center firms in manufacturing prompted resistance from Americans accustomed to more traditional forms of enterprise. Thus, during the Gilded Age political leaders began to take their first hesitant steps toward a new, regulatory state, eventually refined and expanded in the twentieth century.

The Union Pacific Scandal

Government assistance for internal improvements caused a scandal in the 1860s that revealed the inability of public officials to regulate entrepreneurs, even as they profited at public expense. When the Union Pacific Railroad began to build a line west from Omaha, Nebraska, in 1862, Congress offered the firm land grants of 6,400 acres per mile, and a loan of $16,000 to $48,000 per mile, the amount varying according to the difficulty of the terrain crossed. In 1864, when it appeared that this subsidy would be insufficient to encourage private investment, Congress doubled the size of the land grant and agreed to have its loan become a second mortgage, thus allowing private financiers the first claim on the railroad's assets in case of bankruptcy. The government's loan, as a second mortgage, amounted to little more than a gift.

The promoters of the railroad followed the customary practice of the day and formed a construction company, the Credit Mobilier, not to build the line but to finance it. Credit Mobilier, whose officers were in most cases the same as those of the Union Pacific, proceeded to sell $23 million in stocks and other securities and to raise $150 million in bonds, which came from first-mortgage bonds sold to private investors plus the government's second-mortgage bonds. The $150 million in bonds considerably exceeded the actual construction costs of the railroad, and when Congress, in 1867, threatened to investigate the financing of the road, the officers of the Credit Mobilier sold stock at below market prices to several important politicians, including Vice President Schuyler Colfax. This payoff temporarily averted the investigation, but the scandal broke out anew in 1872. Subsequent revelations ruined the careers of several politicians, including Colfax, and tainted the Grant administration, giving the Gilded Age its aura of speculation, chicanery, and bribery.

The scandal revealed an important weakness: the inability of existing federal institutions to regulate such a crucial business event as the completion of the nation's first transcontinental railroad. In arranging for the railroad's financing, Congress had stipulated construction of a first-class railroad, but instead the promoters built a flimsy skeleton of a track, hardly capable in places of supporting a locomotive. This inadequate work was the result not simply of greed of the line's promoters but also of the inability of Congress to devise an effective system for supervising the affairs of the railroad. Congress had authorized the president to appoint one-fourth of the Union Pacific's board of directors, but they were a minority without special powers to intervene in company affairs. Having rejected an Engineer Office in the Department of the Interior to supervise construction, Congress empowered a governmental board of commissioners to pay the federal subsidy only after it approved each section of road. The commissioners found themselves helpless, in the words of one board member, "to reject an imperfectly built road." They had no authority to "control the materials and workmanship as it progresses" and felt they could not "rely upon a condemnation of the work and a legal controversy after it is finished."

In short, Congress tended to view the building of the heavily subsidized line as another source of patronage. There was simply no tradition of public service, of applying independent public expertise either to the building or the financing of the Union Pacific.

State Railroad Regulation

The practice of applying independent public expertise to the affairs of the nation's railroads began only after they were built. Responding to the materialistic values of the Gilded Age and fearful that they might overwhelm the public good, Massachusetts established in 1869 the first significant commission for the "general supervision of all railroads." A board of three members, led by Charles Francis Adams, grandson of one president and great-grandson of another, exercised an investigatory function for the railroads. The commissioners investigated the affairs of the railroads, including charges for hauling freight and passengers, in the expectation that public exposure would cause the carriers to redress wrongs voluntarily. The idea of using a commission to investigate and publicize the affairs of the railroads spread to other states. In general, their purpose was not to regulate what the carriers actually charged their customers but to focus publicity on the lines.

State railroad commissions with stronger powers, able to instruct the railroads as to the rates they were allowed to charge, came into existence with the so-called Granger laws enacted by the states of Illinois, Iowa, and Wisconsin between 1869 and 1874. Merchants and small business owners in the upper Mississippi River valley, supported politically by farmers in the hinterland who were organized in the Patrons of Husbandry, more commonly called the Grange, pushed for these new regulations, which revealed a change in popular attitudes toward the railroad. When railroads first entered a region, local farmers, merchants, and real estate speculators usually welcomed them as beneficial agents of local prosperity. With the passage of time, however, railroad corporations grew larger, their management more remote from the local scene, and their owners more interested in consolidating rate structures that insured steady usage of their capital plant than in stimulating area prosperity. These occurrences caused local populations to view the carriers as evil dark powers whose tentacles reached out to corrupt the legislative process, endanger the prosperity of the general population through financial manipulations, and damage the well-being of individual farmers, merchants, manufacturers, and towns with discriminatory rates. The response, first expressed in the Granger laws, was to insist that the carriers were a business "clothed with a public interest." According to this view, the railroads served the public, and because that service was vital to the well-being of the community, the public had the right to regulate railroad affairs.

These laws launched a long series of bitter legal disputes, with attorneys for the railroads insisting that they deprived railroads of their private property and therefore violated the fourteenth Amendment to the Constitution, which guaranteed the property rights of all persons, including corporations. The U.S. Supreme Court upheld the constitutionality of the Granger laws in its famous 1877 decision *Munn* v. *Illinois*. But in 1886 the Court reversed itself in *Wabash Railway* v. *Illinois* and forbade the states from regulating traffic that either originated in or went outside the state, so-called interstate traffic. Under this doctrine, only Congress could control the interstate affairs of the railroads.

The Birth of Federal Regulation

Pressures to have the federal government begin regulating the railroads had been mounting well before the *Wabash* decision in 1886. These pressures were a response to the maturation of the American railroad industry in the 1870s and 1880s. When railroads were first built, the lines were, at least by later standards, relatively short ones over which traveled small locomotives and lightweight equipment. Freight rates were accordingly high. After the Civil War, railroad managers interconnected their lines and provided long through routes for hauling freight. At the same time, the introduction of steel rails and, later, air brakes, automatic car couplers, and improved signaling devices allowed longer trains of heavier cars pulled by more powerful, faster locomotives. The costs of operating such trains diminished on a per-mile or unit-of-freight basis, and freight rates for the long haul declined, especially for bulky goods like grain. In contrast, short runs still produced relatively higher charges on a per-mile basis, because the railroads had to recover terminal and switching charges, regardless of the distance the goods were shipped. The result was a chorus of complaints about long- and short-haul rate discrimination from shippers and communities who believed the rate structure placed them at a competitive disadvantage. By the late 1870s, farmers and merchants in upstate New York, for instance, grimly watched trains laden with western grain rumble through their region; the midwestern shippers had to pay

Railroads vied for passenger as well as freight business. The Pullman Palace Car Company supplied the most luxurious passenger equipment. This advertisement demonstrates the comfort provided by an early reclining chair. (Library of Congress)

little more for transportation than their New York competitors. New York City merchants, earlier favored by location, saw their advantage disappear with the growth of cheap, long-haul freight trains and concluded that it was time to initiate federal railroad regulation to prevent the carriers from charging less, per-mile, for a long haul than for a short haul.

The advent of through railroad systems capable of making long hauls introduced another element into the picture: competition. When several railroads were able to provide through connections between distant points, each sought to maintain a steady, high volume of business. The result was a competitive pressure that drove prices downward. By the 1880s, for instance, several systems competed for business between Chicago and the eastern seaboard. One of them, the New York Central, granted to favored shippers 6,000 special rates—prices that were well below its published rates. To prevent price wars from endangering the financial well-being of railroad stock- and bondholders, railroad managers experimented with pooling, a system by which—as we saw in Chapter 5—they could agree among themselves to stabilize rates at profitable levels. When voluntary pooling proved unsuccessful, some railroad executives looked to the federal government for help. Railroad men and many shippers alike pressed for the creation of a governmental body that would stabilize the rate structure and protect their profits.

Neither group received exactly what it desired when Congress enacted the Interstate Commerce Act in 1887 and established the Interstate Commerce Commission (ICC) as the country's first federal independent regulatory commission. (Independent regulatory commissions are agencies separate from the legislative, executive, and judicial branches of government.) The law was the result of a compromise between the competing shipper and carrier interests that left the new commission with little power. Much to the dismay of some railroad executives, it outlawed railroad pools, but its prohibition of long- and short-haul discrimination included an enormous loophole that allowed the practice to continue. The law told the commission to see that freight rates were "reasonable and just" but gave the ICC no enforcement powers. In the 1890s, the U.S. Supreme Court declared that the commission had no authority to set rates and ruled that the railroads could practice long- and short-haul discrimination as a response to competitive conditions. In its early years, the ICC had little impact on the business system; it served mainly as an information-gathering agency. Fulfillment of the vision that somehow it should assert the "public interest" over the behavior of the nation's railroad corporations had to await another generation.

The Antitrust Movement

The concerns that led to railroad regulation in the 1870s and 1880s emerged from the needs and interests of particular business groups. In contrast, the antitrust movement of the Gilded Age and the enactment of the Sherman Antitrust Act of 1890 were deeply rooted in all Americans' conceptions of liberty and political economy. They were the expression of a generalized fear that business developments threatened the very fabric of the country's liberty. Enormous economic growth, the rise of the first giant, vertically integrated firms and the spread of horizontal integration had appeared within the lifetimes of Americans who had matured in a simpler, earlier period when the interactions of thousands of small independent firms governed the marketplace. The emerging business system of center and peripheral firms, in contrast, seemed somehow undesirable, for both the growth of center firms and the alliances among small firms denied traditional opportunities for individual entrepreneurship. In the words of the president of the Grange, spoken at a conference on the trusts in 1899, "the right to acquire, own, control and enjoy the use and income of property, is an inalienable right, that should be enjoyed by each individual." Combinations of firms and vertical integration seemed to threaten that inalienable right.

When Americans voiced complaints during the nineteenth and early twentieth centuries about the "trusts," they used the term in a special way. As we have seen, business owners used a variety of techniques to create greater productivity and security for their firms and investments. Politicians and the general public alike, however, lumped the pools, trusts, and holding companies under the generic term "trusts," which in more modern usage translates roughly as "big business."

The popular dislike of the trusts was clearly rooted in the traditional business system of small independent firms. When center firms appeared in manufacturing, they competed with small enterprises that operated in traditional ways in local markets. The efficiencies of some center firms like the Chicago meat packers drove established local firms like the butchers out of business. Other manufacturers wanted to establish their own company distributors instead of using the services of traditional wholesalers and retailers; I. M. Singer & Company, for instance, employed agents who commanded the technical expertise needed to sell and service complex sewing machines. The response to the intrusion of center firms into local markets typically was not to applaud the competition but to turn to local and state governments for regulations, license fees, and taxes to thwart it.

Enjoying influence with their local and state governments, the merchants being squeezed by center firms experienced considerable if short-lived successes. Missouri used a prohibitive tax to keep Singer's agent out of the state until the U.S. Supreme Court outlawed the practice in 1876. Virginia tried to use license fees in effect to require center firms to distribute goods through independent local wholesalers and jobbers. Again, in 1880 the Court forbade the practice. More dramatic was the formation of the Butchers' Protective Association, comprising firms unable to compete with the Chicago meat packers, which resorted to the tradition of localism in American law. The butchers proposed laws prohibiting the sale of dressed mutton, pork, or beef unless state officials inspected the live animal within a day of slaughter. In 1889, Colorado, Minnesota, and Indiana passed inspection laws to protect local butchers from national competition, and at least a dozen other states considered such proposals. Although the Butchers' Protective Association claimed that such inspection was required to protect the public health, the U.S. Supreme Court saw the measures as a scheme to protect local butchers from competition, and in 1890 ruled the laws unconstitutional. The ruling capped a trend, begun in 1876, of the Court's consciously protecting rights of nationally organized center firms to reach a national market.

While the U.S. Supreme Court was protecting businesses from hostile state regulations and fees and weakening the tradition of localism in American politics, Congress was beginning to assert its authority over big business by passing the Sherman Antitrust Act in 1890. In the debate preceding passage, congressmen expressed concern about the impact of the new business forms on the nation's politics and social character. The trusts, they thought, threatened American traditions of democracy and liberty. Congress should act, according to Senator John Sherman, the law's sponsor, in order to protect "the rights of individuals as against associated and corporate wealth and power." If present business trends continued, he warned, it would not be long before Americans would face "a trust for every production and a master to fix the price of every necessity of life." In Sherman's view, the accumulation of wealth entailed in the formation of trusts produced a concentration of power that threatened the tradition of free, independent, individual action. Such concentrated power affected the social character of Americans in undesirable ways. The beauty of the invisible hand of the market was that it was diffuse, that it could be located in no particular place, and that it operated impartially to grant every American, it was thought, an equal chance of economic success.

Although the Sherman Antitrust Act expressed those general ideological concerns, the statute was inexact. "All that we, as lawmakers, can do," Senator Sherman noted, "is to declare general principles." In general, sweeping language, the law declared "restraints of trade" illegal but gave no precise guidelines for the executive and judicial branches of the government to follow. Congress left it to the president and his Department of Justice to decide whether or not to prosecute a particular business combination for hindering the free exchange of goods.

No great flurry of antitrust prosecutions followed the enactment of the Sherman law. The attorneys general of the 1890s were men generally sympathetic to the needs of business firms to establish control over the market's competitive jungle. They were also hostile to trade unions and, in fact, of the ten cases initiated under the new law between 1892 and 1896, five were against unions, which the administration, and eventually the courts, viewed as restraining trade. For those Americans who wanted a vigorous application of the new law, the first decision of the United States Supreme Court was discouraging. In 1895, in *U.S.* v. *E. C. Knight Co.,* the Court majority ruled in favor of the "Sugar Trust," formally known as the American Sugar Refining Company. This firm dominated its industry and was reaching out to acquire its few remaining competitors. The Court majority saw no violation of the law, which, it observed, applied only to "commerce," not to "manufacture." The Court tried to draw a clear distinction between commerce and manufacturing and ruled that when the Sugar Trust acquired a competing manufacturing plant that did not literally straddle a state boundary, the federal government, authorized only to regulate interstate commerce, had no power to interfere.

Although this doctrine seemed clear in 1895, there remained a large measure of uncertainty. The Court's majority could change, and so it did in 1897 in *U.S.* v. *Trans-Missouri Freight Association.* This case involved railroads, which clearly were engaged in interstate commerce. The decision informed them that they could not collaborate to fix rates. The Sherman law thus remained a potentially powerful weapon against business combinations, and the twentieth century would soon witness highly publicized suits against some of the nation's largest manufacturing firms.

THE DAWN OF A NEW CENTURY

When the twentieth century began in 1901, the American political economy had undergone some significant changes from that of the mid-nineteenth century. Although the federal government was still minuscule and lacking in power as compared to later developments, the federal courts had successfully prevented the nation's traditional localism from preventing operations by center firms on a national scale. Meanwhile, Congress had asserted its authority, albeit with a negligible impact, over those same big business firms. Passage of the Sherman Antitrust Act and the launching of the Interstate Commerce Commission were harbingers of both augmented federal authority and of a desire to promote public expertise to supervise business. As the new century began, the policies of the federal government still tended toward development, as in the case of the protective tariff. Similarly, the debates over the banking and currency systems had given evidence that Americans still wanted federal policies designed to promote and reward entrepreneurship. Nevertheless, significant changes had occurred as the Supreme Court forbade local and state restrictions on the national market and Congress established the first federal regulatory commission and asserted its authority over big business.

Regulation and control of a maturing economy were becoming important matters of concern. Sometimes that concern emanated from small business people and farmers who were aggrieved by the practices of the large corporations, especially the railroads. But America's corporate leaders felt some of the same needs. From a variety of sources, then, modern federal government regulation of business began in the Gilded Age, and the experiences of that time period provided a foundation on which a later generation of Americans, living and working in the twentieth century, constructed a more powerful governmental system to regulate the affairs of business.

Selected Readings

Sidney Fine, *Laissez Faire and the General Welfare State* (Ann Arbor: University of Michigan Press, 1966), is a standard account. Herbert Gutman, ed., *Work, Culture, and Society in Industrializing America* (New York: Alfred Knopf, 1976), analyzes important changes brought by industrialization. Morton Keller, *Affairs of State: Public Life in Nineteenth Century America* (Cambridge: Harvard University Press, 1977), is encyclopedic. Michael Les Benedict, "Laissez-Faire and Liberty: A Re-Evaluation of the Meaning and Origins of Laissez-Faire Constitutionalism," *Law and History Review* 3 (Fall 1985): 293–331, provides a cogent interpretation of the Supreme Court's commitment to laissez faire. Tony Allan Freyer, *Forums of*

Order: The Federal Courts and Business in American History (Greenwich, Conn.: JAI Press, 1979), is a useful study of the relationships between legal history and business history. Two essays by Charles McCurdy stand out in this regard: "American Law and the Marketing Structure of the Large Corporation," *Journal of Economic History* 38 (September 1978): 631–649 and "The *Knight* Sugar Decision of 1895 and the Modernization of American Corporation Law, 1869–1903," in *Managing Big Business: Essays from the Business History Review*, ed. by Richard S. Tedlow and Richard R. John, Jr. (Boston: Harvard Business School Press, 1986), pp. 329–366.

John Lauritz Larson, *Bonds of Enterprise: John Murray Forbes and Western Development in America's Railway Age* (Cambridge: Harvard University Press, 1984), explores the attractions and tensions among a business promoter and local merchants and their communities. George H. Miller, *Railroads and the Granger Laws* (Madison: University of Wisconsin Press, 1971), clarifies a complex subject. The Pullman story is told by Stanley Buder, *Pullman: An Experiment in Industrial Order and Community Planning, 1880–1950* (New York: Oxford University Press, 1967).

Thomas K. McCraw, *Prophets of Regulation* (Cambridge, Mass.: Harvard University Press, 1984), is insightful on government regulation in the Gilded Age and beyond.

IMPORTANT EVENTS, 1900–1917

1900   The National Civic Federation is founded to foster cooperation among business, labor, and the public.

1901   Theodore Roosevelt, an advocate of the supremacy of the
"public interest" over business, assumes the presidency.

1902   The National Association of Manufacturers launches a
campaign against trade unions.

1903   Congress establishes the U.S. Department of Commerce
and Labor.
The Elkins Act outlaws railroad rebates, sanctioning
administrative ratemaking.

1904   The U.S. Supreme Court dissolves the Northern Securities Company.

1906   The Hepburn Act empowers the Interstate Commerce
Commission (ICC) to set the railroads' maximum freight
rates.
The Pure Food and Drug law bans misbranded and adulterated food and drug products.

1907   Immigration to the United States peaks.

1910   The Mann-Elkins Act requires railroads to obtain prior
ICC approval before raising freight and passenger rates.

1911   Ohio pioneers workers' compensation programs.
The Supreme Court breaks up American Tobacco and
Standard Oil under the antitrust law.

1912   Woodrow Wilson is elected president, running on a platform of the "new freedom" from the power of big
business.
The U.S. Chamber of Commerce is founded.

1913   Congress establishes the Federal Reserve system.

1914   The Clayton Act revises the antitrust law.
Congress creates the Federal Trade Commission.

1916   Congress creates the Tariff Commission.

1917   The United States declares war on Germany and Austria-
Hungary, and faces the crises of mobilization.

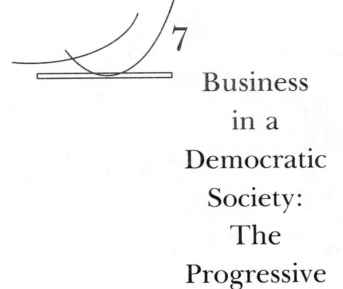

7

Business in a Democratic Society: The Progressive Era

The dawn of the twentieth century saw the advent of new conditions that reshaped the environment in which American business institutions functioned. The return to prosperity after 1897 sparked new waves of immigration, which added not just to the size of the population but to the heterogeneity of the labor force. By the early twentieth century, American employers were recruiting larger numbers of female workers than ever before, blacks from the rural South, white migrants from the rural areas, and newcomers speaking many European tongues. These factors of immigration, urbanization, and the growth in size of some business firms were not new to the twentieth century, but the problems that emerged from the social changes associated with them came to seem particularly acute to both business executives and social reformers after 1900.

American business faced one especially significant development in the early twentieth century: the rise of social reform movements that acted, sometimes through the governmental system and sometimes through private associations, on business institutions and behaviors. The same era saw the inauguration of a new president, Theodore Roosevelt, who, although not antagonistic to the capitalist social and economic system, asserted the primacy of the "public interest" as represented by the government. At about the same time, other leaders from other walks of life, especially from the churches and universities, began seeking new ways to protect the country against what often appeared the corrupt interests of business. The result was the appearance of a frame of mind called progressivism, a set of attitudes and values that optimistically looked toward the erection of new institutions, or the reform of older ones, through which Americans would realize the good society. Among the institutions most affected were business firms and organizations.

Business leaders were important participants in progressivism. Some, in their roles as church and community leaders, joined and supported private associations seeking reform. More directly, the managers in the headquarters of some of the largest firms became inextricably involved in political affairs. The years between the turn of the century and World War I, called the Progressive Era, saw the emergence of "corporatism" (historians sometimes call the phenomenon corporate liberalism), a phenomenon in which leading bankers and industrialists sought to achieve cooperation among business, labor, and government—cooperation that, they were confident, would result in harmonious relations between the social classes and insure prosperity in the general economy. Out of this business involvement with reform came new institutions of government-business relations.

NEW WAYS OF THINKING

The New Political Economy

A new school of political economists emerged in the United States in the 1880s. This new school comprised young men who, in the 1870s, studied German historical and statistical economic thought. Some German scholars had rejected the deductive reasoning of

Adam Smith and his successors in favor of observations of historical and statistical information from which, through inductive reasoning, economists and policy makers believed they could reach conclusions.

The basis of this new school of economic thought lay in the rejection of the assumption of the classical economists that self-interest always governed the actions of humans. Other factors, it was maintained, also affected human behavior: altruism, national honor, and the like. The economists of the new school thus attempted to combine political economy with ethics and, from their pragmatic observations of the realities of economic life, to determine prescriptions regulating business and achieving the public interest.

The leader of the new-school economists in America was Richard T. Ely, who graduated from Columbia College in 1876 and earned his Ph.D. in 1879 at Heidelberg University in Germany. From 1881 to 1892, he taught economics at Johns Hopkins University in Baltimore, after which he spent over thirty years on the faculty of the University of Wisconsin. Not only did Ely write numerous books and essays during his long and distinguished career, but he lectured widely and served on government commissions.

An essential ingredient of Ely's leadership of the new school was his role in founding the American Economic Association in 1885. This association brought together the younger economists influenced by the German theories. Among the charter members were twenty-three clergymen, most notable of whom was Washington Gladden, the father of the Social Gospel movement in America. The Social Gospel was a Protestant church movement formed to help ease the hardships of life faced by the poor and by workers in the factories and cities of the industrial age. When Ely drafted the platform of the American Economic Association, he unequivocally repudiated laissez faire: "We regard the state as an educational and ethical agency whose positive aid is an indispensable condition of human progress. While we recognize the necessity of individual initiative in industrial life, we hold that the doctrine of *laissez-faire* is unsafe in politics and unsound in morals; and that it suggests an inadequate explanation of the relations between the state and the citizens." Those words expressed a sentiment that was to have a profound impact on government-business relations in the Progressive Era.

This rejection of laissez faire doctrine did not mean that Ely or his colleagues believed in state paternalism or socialism. As Ely explained, in a democratic society the government *is* the people, so when the government acts on behalf of the general welfare, it is acting fraternally, not paternally. In this regard, the role of the economist seemed clear. "In a certain sense," Ely noted, "the political economist is to the general public what the attorney is to the private individual." The economist is a guide, helping the people to determine the public interest. In Ely's view, such guidance should direct policy to some middle course between unbridled competition and state socialism. The prevailing business system had produced social evils of poverty and degradation apparent to anyone who cared to observe them, but in Ely's eyes their amelioration had to involve policies that preserved individual freedom.

Theodore Roosevelt and the Ideology of the Public Interest

Important as the new school of economics was to the environment in which American business functioned, the appearance of its doctrines roughly coincided with other, still more important, intellectual and political developments that shaped the Progressive Era. Among those developments was the assertion of an ideology of the public interest, an assertion in which the new-school economists participated but which was by no means confined to their teachings. There was an old tradition in American thought, extending back to the Puritan founders of Massachusetts, that expressed a belief in the desirability of using the government to promote the commonweal, or public good. That tradition lay behind the economic policy of men like Alexander Hamilton and Albert Gallatin in the nation's earlier years. By the middle of the nineteenth century, there were some who claimed that the best government was one that included good men, men whose personal lives and interests transcended the particular needs of the moment and who were capable of acting for the good of all. In the Progressive Era, political philosophers and social theorists like Walter Lippmann and Herbert Croly gave formal expressions to this public-interest doctrine, but no one represented the viewpoint better than a man of affairs, Theodore Roosevelt.

Theodore Roosevelt had achieved public prominence before the beginning of the Progressive Era. The son of a well-to-do family that had amassed its fortune before the Industrial Revolution, Roosevelt decided to devote his life to public service. He entered politics in his native New York State over his family's objection that political office was too corrupt for a gentleman and gained public

President Theodore Roosevelt stirred crowds with his political speeches. He often spoke of the need to accept big business while ensuring that it followed the public interest. (Library of Congress)

attention fighting crime and corruption as New York City's police commissioner. After his well-publicized heroism in the Spanish-American War in 1898, Roosevelt went on to become governor of New York.

Elected vice president in 1900, he assumed the presidency after the assassination of William McKinley in 1901. Roosevelt served as president until 1909, and he unsuccessfully sought a third term in 1912 on a platform he labeled the New Nationalism. Roosevelt was both a thinker in the tradition of defending the public interest and a practical and powerful politician who acted directly to change American business institutions. As president, he tried to enhance the executive power of the government to safeguard the public interest and to create a more moral and orderly society. He was interested in power not for its own sake but for the public good. He tried to establish the supremacy of the government over business and other interest groups and to create a governmental system with orderly procedures of regulating business behavior according to the public interest.

Roosevelt wanted to impose federal power on big business. One practical way he could, as president, regulate business conduct was by enforcing the Sherman Antitrust Act. When warring railroad interests in the Pacific Northwest combined under the leadership of J. P. Morgan and James J. Hill to create a new holding company, the Northern Securities Company, to control the stock of the Great Northern, Northern Pacific, and Chicago, Burlington & Quincy railroads, Roosevelt launched an antitrust suit. The Supreme Court ruled in 1904 that the Northern Securities Company constituted an illegal restraint of competition and ordered it dissolved. Roosevelt encouraged a fanfare of publicity about the prosecution and hailed the outcome as a great victory. The significance of the case, for him, was not the practical result—Morgan and Hill found other unchallenged ways to control the Burlington railroad—but its symbolic nature. The ruling was a successful assertion of the supremacy of government over business. When Roosevelt announced the suit, Morgan left New York for Washington to ask if the president had intentions to attack his other interests. Roosevelt assured the financier that he did not, so long as the firms were not guilty of misconduct.

Meanwhile, in 1903, Roosevelt maneuvered a bill through Congress that created a new cabinet-level Department of Commerce and Labor, which contained a Bureau of Corporations whose function was to investigate corporate practices. Soon a series of "gentlemen's agreements" evolved, in which representatives of big business, especially partners in the House of Morgan, collaborated with the Bureau of Corporations. Under these informal gentlemen's agreements, firms granted the government access to information; the government, in return, approved mergers when it found them to be in the public interest. For Roosevelt the importance of these arrangements was the implicit recognition of the supremacy of public power over private interests.

At their core the actions of the Roosevelt administration were not new to the political scene; governments had always stated their watchfulness over the general welfare. What was new with Roosevelt was the vigor and publicity with which the executive branch took action. The vigorous expression of a clear sense of the rights and wrongs of business behavior endowed the Progressive Era with a character far different from that which prevailed during the Gilded Age.

Efficiency and Corporatism

The notion of the government acting energetically to safeguard the public interest plus the new economic theories that credited human beings with more altruistic motives than that of profit alone gave the Progressive Era its unique quality. That was not the end of the story, however. The early twentieth century also witnessed ideological and institutional developments that produced a modern system of government-business relations.

The Progressive Era saw the growth and widespread acceptance of the idea that science and engineering principles held the key to discovering the public interest. The new-school economists thought of themselves as scientists, dispassionately uncovering data about socioeconomic conditions from which the wise, applying Christian ethics, could learn the public interest. Engineers also participated in this trend. Scientific management, first proposed by Frederick Taylor and other mechanical engineers, put forth, as we have seen, principles for changing working conditions inside the factory. Taylor and his disciples believed that scientific management provided efficient coordination among all of the components of a factory, both men and machinery. Through the principles of engineering science the factory could become a harmonious whole, it seemed. The theory of scientific management extended beyond the factory gates to encompass a social philosophy in which all the components of society could be made to mesh smoothly with one another. According to this ideology, engineering principles, when applied to society, could end conflicts among the social classes and between business firms and industries.

The theory of scientific management, and its concomitant goal of applying engineering principles to all of society, received widespread publicity, especially after 1910. There was general acceptance of the ideology of efficiency, because it conformed to the perceived needs of business people who were attempting to devise new mechanisms of control over their affairs. Financiers, typified by J. P. Morgan, tried to arrange "communities of interest" among firms within industries to restrain unbridled competition in favor of protecting the large sums of capital invested, ensuring the best service for customers, and promoting higher levels of prosperity, including higher wage levels. Within firms, executives developed new systems of accounting and management controls. Small-business owners, working in industries that were not susceptible to the merger movement or to vertical integration, organized private trade associations to arrange new systems of interfirm cooperation. By the Progressive Era, the institutional thrust of American business was clear: it was toward control of the uncertainties and instabilities of unbridled price competition by the use of systematic, rational management systems.

The ideology of efficiency and the impulses toward managerial control within industries combined in the Progressive Era to form corporatism, a frame of mind or point of view expressed by some business people, government officials, scholars, scientists, and reformers. The advocates of corporatism looked for a new kind of partnership between government and business and, in some cases, between business and labor, one that emphasized reason and cooperation, not confrontation, to solve practical problems of business strategy. Some spokesmen thought that prices were best determined through management science, not the uncontrollable workings of the market. Similarly, disputes between business firms over such matters as the allocation of available markets or transportation costs were thought to be best resolved through dispassionate, scientific investigation. The result should be not only higher levels of general prosperity but a society of harmony. America, in this vision, could become a nation whose component parts fit together smoothly and efficiently.

Woodrow Wilson and the Ideology of the New Freedom

Vigorous promotion of the public interest and widespread faith in efficiency became significant themes of government-business relations in the Progressive Era. There was, however, another somewhat contradictory theme as well: the desire to strengthen the government so that it could strictly limit the size of business firms and ensure that price competition governed business behavior. Woodrow Wilson, who served as president from 1913 to 1921, most eloquently expressed this view in the presidential campaign of 1912. Sharply differentiating his ideas from the "new nationalism" expressed by Theodore Roosevelt in the same campaign, Wilson ran on a program of "new freedom."

Wilson was hostile both to the concentration of assets in fewer and fewer institutions—the "trusts"—and to Roosevelt's policies of allowing that concentration so long as public officials determined that the behavior of giant corporations conformed to the public interest. Wilson feared that the growth of big business tended to undermine traditional American freedoms. The concentration of wealth in a few firms meant that individual entrepreneurs might be squeezed out of business or that they would simply not enjoy the opportunities traditionally accorded to Americans. "I don't care how benevolent the master is going to be," Wilson declared. "I will not live under a master. That is not what America was created for. America was created in order that every man should have the same chance as every other man to exercise mastery over his own fortune." The new freedom, Wilson believed, would result when the government used its antitrust powers to break up big businesses into smaller firms.

Although Wilson expressed a desire to break the trusts and scorned Roosevelt's program of accepting big business upon its good behavior, as president he engaged in little "trustbusting." Center firms, as we have seen, arose from innovative business practices, and it was difficult to prove that their growth resulted from illegal actions. In fact, between 1890 and 1915, antitrust law was actually used less against the new center firms than against combinations of peripheral firms. Although there were well-publicized actions against prominent center firms, most notably court orders breaking up Standard Oil and American Tobacco in 1911, these actions were far overshadowed in number by cases in which the federal government prosecuted small firms for agreeing to fix prices and allocate markets. That pattern began before Wilson became president, and it continued through his two terms.

NEW INSTITUTIONS

Associationalism

Important institutional developments accompanied the growth of new ways of thinking associated with the Progressive Era. For example, the number, size, and variety of private associations of all kinds, but especially of business associations, proliferated after the turn of the century. Government officials often saw business associations as desirable devices for disseminating information, while business people saw them as agencies through which they could influence government policy.

Business associations, groups of executives, and firms that typically watched over some particular interest, were not new in the twentieth century. Business associations of various sorts had promoted their own specific interests on the questions of railroad regulation during the 1870s and 1880s, and individual industries had formed organizations to lobby in Washington for favorable tariff legislation. The national and state bodies of the nineteenth century, however, had usually comprised smaller firms seeking protection from the integrated firms that competed so successfully in the market. Local business associations continued to be important in the twentieth century, but it was then that national associations started to grow significance. By 1900, there were 3,000 commercial organizations in the United States, at least a hundred of which were national bodies. In 1912, the federal government reported the existence of 3,356 local, 183 state or territorial, and 243 interstate business associations. Not only did the number of associations grow, but new types of business societies emerged to bring together business people at the local, state, and national levels to promote their larger interests, as opposed to the narrow interests of particular trade association.

The National Civic Federation

By the turn of the century, the idea that business leaders should recognize their responsibility toward society was beginning to appear among the ranks of some of the nation's wealthiest, most powerful corporate leaders. This attitude encompassed traditional forms of philanthropy, which expanded in the twentieth century as industrial fortunes enlarged, and also involved the idea that corporate leaders had responsibilities for the commonweal. "The larger the corporation becomes, the greater become its responsibilities to the community," observed George W. Perkins, a representative of the Morgan banking interests and a director of both United States Steel and International Harvester.

The National Civic Federation (NCF) was the first important institution that arose to give expression to these desires. After the Pullman strike of 1894, a group of Chicago business and civic leaders began the Civic Federation to bring together corporate officers, union leaders, and public representatives to discuss ways to solve the "labor problem." From its meetings emerged the idea of a National Civic Federation, which was organized in 1900. Marcus A. Hanna, a prominent coal operator who served as a Republican party leader and a United States senator from Ohio, became its first president. The NCF followed a tripartite program of bringing together representatives of capital, labor, and the public. In 1903, about one-third of the nation's largest corporations were members, as were union leaders, most prominently Samuel Gompers, president of the American Federation of Labor, and John Mitchell, president of the United Mine Workers. At one time or another, the NCF executive committee included Grover Cleveland, William Howard Taft, and some of the nation's leading names in education and the professions.

During the Progressive Era, the NCF went through three periods in which it developed different programmatic emphases. Until 1905, the NCF was most concerned with mediating labor disputes, trying to find ways for unions and corporations to cooperate democratically. It helped negotiate some contracts between industries and unions but was more successful in promoting an ideology of labor-management cooperation than it was in obtaining the acceptance of collective bargaining by the nation's large manufacturing firms. Between 1905 and 1908, the NCF emphasized "welfare work," a form of paternalism in which firms consciously sought a sense of identification between employer and employee by trying to integrate the daily life and leisure activities of workers with the operation of the corporation. NCF leaders saw welfare work as a substitute for the recognition of unions and collective bargaining contracts; if only workers could voice their grievances and air their views, they believed, they would have little desire to join an independent union. Finally, after 1908, the NCF became more involved in legislative activities. It commissioned studies that helped shape revisions in antitrust law and the creation of the Federal Trade Commission in 1914. It developed model workers' compensation laws and sought to have them enacted by state legislatures.

The most important accomplishment of the NCF, however, was not the achievement of any specific measure. The organization transcended individual firms and industries and brought together some of the nation's most important financiers and industrialists to consider the broader needs of the business system and solutions to some of the social problems that had erupted with the impact of the Industrial Revolution and the growth of cities. The NCF served, thus, as a key instigator of corporatism. In the meetings of its commissions and committees some of the nation's most influential business and professional leaders, politicians, and educators learned from one another and came to realize that the United States needed new agencies and systems of cooperation through which experts could apply their knowledge to the workings of the capitalist order.

The National Association of Manufacturers

In sharp contrast to the activities of the NCF and the ideological expressions of its leaders about corporate social responsibility stood the National Association of Manufacturers (NAM). The NAM was an older organization, founded in 1895 by small, mostly midwestern manufacturers who lobbied for federal policies that would encourage the expansion of foreign trade. However, the NAM remained a small organization until 1902, when David M. Parry, a militant antiunionist, took over its presidency. The NAM had about 1,000 member firms in 1900, but by 1914, due largely to the popularity of its new antiunion activities, 3,500 firms belonged.

Under Parry's leadership, the NAM began coordinating the antiunion activities of American business. To reduce the power of unions (the membership of the unions affiliating with the American Federation of Labor had risen from 278,000 in 1898 to 1,700,000 in 1904), if not to eliminate their influence altogether, Parry and the NAM embarked on a determined campaign to enforce the open shop, or what the business leaders called the American Plan. The employers in an industry or in a community allied, with the help of locally based Citizen's Industrial Alliances, which were NAM offspring, and agreed to hire only workers who would sign a pledge to refrain from either joining a union or trying to organize one. The firms hired private detectives to spy on workers and developed elaborate systems of keeping track of known agitators. With the help of friendly local politicians, the employers tried to break up unions where they existed. A common technique was to provoke a strike, obtain an injunction from a sympathetic judge against union activities in support of the strike, and upon the union leaders' refusal to obey the injunction, call in the police, who would arrest the offenders and pillage union headquarters. By such means businesses could drain union treasuries in legal disputes and sap their strength.

So in the first years of the twentieth century, two significant national business organizations developed. Both the NAM and the NCF, in very different ways, expressed significant business responses to the conditions of a maturing industrial economy. The importance of the NCF as an organization waned after World War I as more specialized organizations took over its work. The NAM, although it later moderated its record of antilabor excesses, continued to express the interests of a significant portion of American manufacturers.

The United States Chamber of Commerce

The federal government was directly involved in sponsoring the formation of a third association in the Progressive Era, the United States Chamber of Commerce, whose goal was to represent the interests of American business in general. On the local scene, businesses had associated in "commercial clubs," "boards of trade," "chambers of commerce," or similarly named groups, for years. But there was no national organization that seemed to voice the views of American business as a whole.

The absence of such an association concerned officials in the new Department of Commerce and Labor, created in 1903, one of whose missions was to "foster, promote, and develop the foreign and domestic commerce." Government officials enjoyed easy access through personal contacts to the nation's large, integrated big-business firms. However, there was no simple way for those officials to reach small- and medium-sized firms, and it seemed especially important to establish lines of communication with them in regard to foreign trade. American leaders were concerned over the ability of the nation to remain economically competitive abroad, especially in the face of growing German business prowess. Both business leaders and government officials thus saw the desirability of having organized mechanisms through which the Commerce Department and the State Department could transmit information about foreign markets to American business firms. Large firms had their own representatives abroad, but smaller firms depended on the government.

The key figure in solving this problem was Charles Nagel, a St. Louis lawyer and businessman who served as secretary of commerce and labor in the presidential administration of William Howard Taft (1909–1913). Nagel sought to enlarge the role of his department and to provide better service to American business so that it could improve its competitive position in world markets. He especially wanted business support for federal policies that would subsidize the merchant marine and protect firms that were trying to expand overseas operations from antitrust suits at home. He was particularly interested in a national chamber of commerce.

The United States Chamber of Commerce was officially born in 1912 at a national commercial conference called by President Taft. Seven hundred delegates from 392 commercial associations in nearly every state came to the meeting in Washington, D.C. Taft told the delegates that the federal government needed "constant and intelligent cooperation" with "the great industrial forces of our country." Nagel spoke of the need to have sound advice from business leaders if the government was to regulate their affairs intelligently. Regulation, in his view, should involve intelligent cooperation, not adversarial conflict. The delegates responded by writing a plan for organizing the United States Chamber of Commerce and circulating it to 1,250 associations and individuals around the country, who approved it. The national chamber held conferences and issued publications to spread information and ideas among business leaders and between them and government officials in the Department of Commerce. One important function of the organization was to present issues of federal economic policy to its members and to hold referendums on those issues to clarify general business views for both legislative and executive officials.

The National Civic Federation, the National Association of Manufacturers, and the United States Chamber of Commerce gave evidence of a renewed desire on the part of both business leaders and politicians in the Progressive Era to enlarge and institutionalize the ability of business people to help shape desirable public policies. Other national associations played important roles in government-business relations during this period, but these three organizations were particularly noteworthy because they represented attempts to deal with important general concerns about the larger economic system. Associations also formed around more specific needs and interests regarding federal policy that played an important part in devising new systems of federal regulation of business in the Progressive Era.

GOVERNMENT REGULATION OF BUSINESS

New Forms of Regulation

In addition to the government-business cooperation symbolized by the associations, new forms of federal regulation of business also characterized the Progressive Era. Sometimes this regulation came from administrative agencies in the executive branch, like the Bureau of Corporations, but more typically it involved some form of independent commission that combined the functions of policy-making, administration, and adjudication. The first commission, as we have seen, was the Interstate Commerce Commission. In the years between the turn of the century and World War I, Congress expanded the powers of the ICC and created two important new agencies, the Federal Reserve Board and the Federal Trade Commission. Each was created to deal with specific industries or specific problems, and thus, although their impact was sometimes widespread, none was responsible for the overall regulation of America's business system.

Each specific area of government regulation that emerged in the Progressive Era had complex sources within American society, but in general they were a response to three trends we have already noted as characteristic of the period: the idea of carefully observing economic activity and thereby deriving policies in the public interest, the reassertion of the power of the government to watch over the commonweal, and the growing conviction of the desirability of developing new avenues of government-business cooperation so that America would become more efficient and harmonious. Each area of government regulation was also a product of associational activity—of business people, farmers, and workers expressing their needs and interests and pressuring government officials through associations of various kinds. Finally, the growing role of the federal government in supervising business affairs meant that the tradition of localism, so powerful during the nineteenth century, was beginning to diminish.

Railroad Regulation

The railroad industry was the first recipient of this new form of government regulation in the 1880s, and in the Progressive Era the revival and redefinition of railroad regulation led the way toward establishing what became the fourth branch of government, the independent commission. Legislation in the Progressive Era enlarged the Interstate Commerce Commission and made it powerful enough to enforce railroad rates and to adjust them after careful investigation.

The growth of the American economy in the Progressive Era complicated railroad politics. Prosperity meant that the carriers faced heavier demands for service, demands that required them to modernize their track and equipment. At the same time that the carriers faced a larger volume of business, price inflation made it more difficult to raise the necessary capital for improvements. While the carriers' costs were rising, the opposition they faced from the powerful shippers' associations made it difficult to raise freight rates and thereby either to generate capital from internal savings or to borrow it in financial markets. The result was a kind of impasse, with the railroads, especially after 1908, seeking higher freight rates, and with the farmers and business people, themselves facing higher costs, trying to hold down the carriers' charges.

The Progressive Era legislation regarding railroads initially helped the carriers but then was revised to grant considerable power to the business owners and farmers who depended on railroad service. In 1903, the Elkins Act, written by Senator Stanley B. Elkins, in effect legalized pooling. The law required the railroad companies to adhere to their published rates and punished railroads and shippers who gave or received rebates. The creation of a rational, administrative—as opposed to market—price structure pleased the railroad corporations but was not satisfactory to shippers, who could exercise little control over the charges. The complaints of business owners and farmers, especially in the South and West, led Congress in the Hepburn Act of 1906 to enlarge the Interstate Commerce Commission to seven members, empower it to control the carriers' bookkeeping, and permit it to set maximum freight rates. This situation still pleased many railroad executives, however, because the law allowed them to set rates administratively ("pooling," in the language of the day). Moreover, the railroad officers could raise charges and collect higher revenues until the ICC rescinded their rates.

Congress completed the Progressive Era system of railroad regulation in 1910. That year saw two important events in railroad politics: the passage of the Mann-Elkins Act and the insistence by the ICC on scientific management before the railroad firms could raise their freight rates. The Mann-Elkins Act made a basic change in the regulatory system by requiring the railroads to demonstrate the necessity of higher freight rates prior to their imposition. This provision pleased shippers, for the burden of proof was now placed on the railroads, and the shippers were convinced they could persuade the Interstate Commerce Commission to act reasonably and take local and regional interests into account in its decisions.

The result of this legislation was that rates were still set administratively, but the carriers' actions were now supervised by the federal commission. Railroad executives expressed pleasure over the construction of a rational system of ratemaking, but they were displeased by some of the Interstate Commerce Commission's most publicized decisions. When the Panic of 1907 threatened railroad revenues, George W. Perkins, representing the Morgan bank and investor interests, negotiated an agreement among eastern railroads for a general freight rate increase of 10 per cent. Shippers were alarmed, both at the prospect of having to pay higher charges and at the inequities in competitive relationships among industries, regions, and communities that such a general increase threatened.

The two sides were granted a hearing before the ICC, which became known as the Eastern Rate Case of 1910. Midwestern shippers organized a new association, the National Industrial Traffic League, to represent them. New England shippers sent Louis D. Brandeis, a prominent attorney who had a reputation as a "people's lawyer," to represent their interests. Brandeis called Harrington Emerson, an efficiency engineer, as a witness, and Emerson testified that with the proper application of scientific management principles, the railroads could save $1 million a day. This argument persuaded the ICC that no general rate increase was necessary pending a more thoroughgoing attempt to achieve cost savings. The decision, in effect, said that with the application of scientific and engineering principles to business, the public interest could be served and conflict between business firms, as here between railroads and shippers, could be resolved harmoniously.

This hope proved ephemeral. By 1913, it was apparent to the ICC that the carriers, which faced large traffic volumes and burdensome capital expenditures as well as higher operating costs, required additional revenue. Shippers began having to pay higher rates, but always as a result of a decision-making system wherein they had an important voice. By 1917, the railroad unions (called brotherhoods) were sending attorneys to commission hearings, allying with the railroads in the belief that higher rates would mean higher wages. Railroad executives voiced displeasure, of course, when they lost rate cases before the commission. But the railroads, on the whole, did not oppose this Progressive Era system of rate-making, for it provided protection from the fierce competition that had damaged the industry in the late nineteenth century. The railroad industry set about the tasks of influencing the ICC and, by establishing a new science of public relations, of reaching the general public, the business community, and the politicians with their message of need.

Food and Drug Regulation

Railroad regulation concerned a broad spectrum of Americans, simply because anyone who wanted to travel or ship goods long distances was dependent on railroad service. Food and drug regulation also affected nearly every citizen, although its origins were less obviously rooted in business and farmer associations. Local regulation of foodstuffs extended back into the colonial period, but the modern movement for legislation requiring pure food and drugs stemmed from an increasing dependence on packaged goods sold through impersonal distribution systems.

The problems of adulteration and mislabeling were manifold. Traditional American medicine had not rid itself of quackery; the snake oil salesman with his traveling medicine show was a national institution. Entrepreneurs supplied the market with a large variety of nostrums, usually containing substantial proportions of alcohol, which were supposed to cure all ills. These "patent medicines" may have promised much, but they delivered nothing (except for hangovers and other alcohol-related diseases) and were an affront to the modern sciences of medicine and pharmacy that had emerged in the late nineteenth century. Similarly, food adulteration was a major problem. Some disreputable processors and packagers sought to deceive customers in the interests of quick profits; others lacked technical expertise and thereby used harmful chemicals to preserve meats, fruits, and vegetables.

Harvey W. Wiley, who served as chief chemist in the U.S. Department of Agriculture after 1883, led the campaign for passage of a federal regulatory bill. Wiley conducted experiments that demonstrated the existence of undesirable impurities in foodstuffs and exposed the fraudulent nature of many packaged medicines. He also worked with manufacturers who wanted their disreputable competitors run out of business. By the early twentieth century, Wiley had gained the help of several popular writers, the best known of whom was Upton Sinclair. The 1906 publication of Sinclair's *The Jungle,* which contained graphic stories of noxious practices in the meat-processing industry, produced a public outcry strong enough to allow Wiley to push a compromise measure through Congress.

The 1906 Pure Food and Drug and Meat Inspection laws, which forbade interstate and foreign trade in adulterated and misbranded foods and drugs, were important regulatory achievements in the Progressive Era. The laws relied largely on the power of disclosure for their effectiveness; underlying the laws was the belief that once consumers knew the contents of a product, the good would drive the bad from the marketplace, but they also contained some stringent measures. Federal inspectors employed by the Department of Agriculture henceforth would grade meat before it went on the

Before passage of the Pure Food and Drug laws of the Progressive Era, patent medicines sometimes posed serious threats to consumers. If Hamlin's Wizard Oil really did cure "all pain in man or beast," its powers probably could be attributed to a large dose of opium or alcohol. (Library of Congress)

market. The large meat packers saw such activity as desirable, because it lent an assurance of quality that was especially important in export trade. Similar measures helped protect food canners with substantial investments in factories and brand names from fly-by-night operators. Although the system was far from perfect, its achievements were substantial. These laws seemed to prove that the application of scientific knowledge through government agencies could both protect the public interest and help responsible business firms.

Banking and the Federal Reserve Board

Other businesses also came under increased regulation during this period. Banking and currency policy disputes, as we have seen, had plagued the American political system since the earliest days of independence. The Progressive Era witnessed the major resolution of those disputes with the creation of the Federal Reserve System in 1913. Bankers, other executives, and politicians reached agreement on the proper relationship between the government and banking and on a system for providing both a flexible currency and policies grounded in expert knowledge.

The legislation of 1913 came only after years of disagreement between bankers and other business leaders and among the bankers themselves over the types of assets acceptable as a currency base and the control of the banking system. The controversy over assets arose because the debt of the federal government was shrinking, while the volume of transactions in the economy was growing enormously. The system established during the Civil War had provided for banks to issue currency secured by federal bonds. Now that the number of bonds was shrinking, the bankers were pressing for a so-called assets currency, one in which high-grade corporate bonds— the numbers of which enlarged with the economy's expansion— would serve as securities. Country bankers, from those thousands of institutions that had emerged to service the needs of the agrarian economy, insisted that the assets currency should include real-estate securities, which were in plentiful supply in rural areas.

Complicating the matter still further was the issue of control. The banking system that evolved in the Gilded Age concentrated deposits in the huge banks located on New York's Wall Street. In fact, the concentration of wealth on Wall Street was so great as to prompt widespread complaints about a "money trust"—the idea that a small, privileged, private group of men with offices in New York and an informal national and international network of communications controlled most of the nation's wealth. Such a concentration was disliked by many bankers and business people outside of New York, who believed that it should be federal policy to disperse control and allow greater influence to bankers in cities like Chicago, Detroit, and Cleveland.

These issues fermented as a result of the Panic of 1907. The banking system created in the Gilded Age turned out to be susceptible to occasions when depositors withdrew their assets quickly, forcing banks to sell securities suddenly and threatening the entire financial system with collapse. In 1907, when withdrawal demand threatened to wreak havoc on banks and corporations, J. P. Morgan organized resources to shore up institutions faced with bankruptcy. Morgan saved the system but also confirmed the suspicions of the inordinate power enjoyed by a few financiers. The panic led to demands for change: first for an emergency measure to allow banks to issue currency secured by high-grade corporate bonds, and second for the establishment of a National Monetary Commission to study reform proposals and recommend a revamping of federal banking policy.

The studies of the National Monetary Commission, headed by Senator Nelson W. Aldrich of Rhode Island, eventually led to the creation of the Federal Reserve System, but only after a long, tangled political controversy. The commission consulted closely with Wall Street bankers and in 1911 recommended the creation of a central bank in New York City with fifteen regional branches. The private banks would control the central bank, which would be authorized, among other matters, to issue a currency based on high-grade corporate securities. These recommendations were unacceptable to many bankers and business leaders, for they failed to address the issue of the "money trust." They did not create a decentralized system that granted power to bankers outside of New York or to the business people who depended on banking services. Country bankers disliked the failure to recommend the use of real estate as a currency base.

Finally, Representative Carter Glass of Virginia arranged a compromise that pleased most bankers. The Federal Reserve Act of 1913 created a Federal Reserve Board with five members, each from a different district, appointed by the president. Instead of creating a single central bank, the law established twelve district Federal Reserve banks, each owned by the banks of its region. National banks were required to join the system; state banks might do so. Each district bank had a nine-member board: three members were appointed by the national Federal Reserve Board, three were bankers from the district, and three were nonbankers. The board in Washington directed overall policies. The law met the needs of the banking industry by allowing decentralization and an assets currency. The Wall Street bankers were the most influential men in the new system; President Wilson made certain that they were represented on the Federal Reserve Board, and all foreign transactions were to go through New York's district Federal Reserve bank. The demand of country bankers for authorization to issue currency based on real-estate assets was not met until 1917. Still, the system was so popular that almost all banks rushed to join it.

The Federal Trade Commission and the Antitrust Movement

In 1914, Congress created a new regulatory agency, the Federal Trade Commission (FTC), and passed a new antitrust law, the Clayton Act. Like other forms of regulation, both events involved compromises, and both were a product of agitation and associationalism among different sectors of the business community.

By 1914, the business community had reached a general consensus on the desirability of having a Federal Trade Commission. Small business people—retailers, grain dealers, and the like—desired an agency with broad investigatory powers that could order a halt to the monopolistic practices by big companies threatening to bankrupt their small firms. Big business sought a depoliticization of the trust issue and a structure that would lend continuity to federal trust policy. Partners in the House of Morgan were particularly upset by the breakdown of the gentlemen's agreements they had arranged with the Roosevelt administration. In looking for new federal regulation, they were reacting against the policy of President William Howard Taft.

Unlike Roosevelt and Wilson, Taft was in fact a trustbuster. Under his administration (1909–1913) the Department of Justice launched many new prosecutions and brought others begun under Roosevelt to successful conclusions. In 1911, for example, the Supreme Court ordered the Standard Oil trust and the American Tobacco trust dissolved. Taft also launched a prosecution of United States Steel that especially enraged the Morgan interests. The House of Morgan had secured the approval of Roosevelt's Bureau of Corporations for the acquisition of the Tennessee Coal and Iron Company by United States Steel, an acquisition that gave the Pittsburgh-based firm a dominant interest in the southern steel industry. Taft dissolved the agreement and began an antitrust suit that accused United States Steel of unfairly monopolizing the industry because of this acquisition.

Executives of center firms and large banks wanted to remove such matters from the arena of informal private meetings with administration officials, who might change with the next election and who were always susceptible to the whims of public sentiment. Regulation of business, in their view, was best left to a nonpartisan body removed from day-to-day political considerations. Congress attempted to meet these wishes by creating the FTC in 1914. Each of the commission's five members was appointed for a seven-year term, and these staggered terms ensured long-running policies independent of shifting election results. Congress also granted the commission broad investigatory powers. When the FTC found violations of the antitrust law, it could order them stopped, subject to court appeals.

The Federal Trade Commission Act had a companion, the Clayton Act of 1914, which revised the antitrust laws. The Sherman Act of 1890 had proved to be too vague to satisfy either business or its opponents, so Congress tried to clarify matters in the new bill. The Clayton Act outlawed interlocking directorates in financial firms capitalized at over $1 million; such firms were not allowed to own stock in other companies if the effect was to reduce competition. The law also forbade "tying contracts" in which large firms prevented their suppliers from doing business with their competitors. And it condemned price discrimination that tended to limit competition. Further, it declared that trade union activities and farm cooperatives did not constitute "combinations in restraint of trade."

Although the Clayton Act gave more clarity and structure to antitrust law, Congress, because of the great diversity of the business interests concerned, was unable to make the law as precise as some wished. The law was neither an affirmation of Wilson's earlier call for a "new freedom" for the individual from the center firms, nor did it forbid, as some reformers wished, any firm from capturing more than a specified share of an industry's market. Instead, Congress empowered the FTC to conduct the day-to-day work of trust regulation and the attorney general to seek court rulings to clarify policy.

Tariff Politics and Federal Regulation

The tariff issue continued to plague national politics in the early twentieth century, but in the Progressive Era tariff politics became intertwined with the trust issue. Business associations and reformers began to call for a system of determining tariff rates "scientifically," apart from the pressures of special interests. At the same time, advocates of tariff reform interacted with those who were calling for vigorous antitrust prosecutions.

Some reformers insisted that the tariff was the "mother of trusts" and that adjustments in tariff rates could restore competition to the American business system. The tariff, in their view, contributed to inequities in the distribution of wealth in American society. Some industries that enjoyed protection from foreign competition seemed to enjoy high profits. In the meantime, American consumers paid high hidden taxes when they bought needed imported items. In the eyes of the reformers, a "scientifically" derived tariff schedule designed with the public interest in mind would lower if not eliminate these "regressive taxes" on American consumers. At the same time, the reformers argued that the federal government should impose income taxes on wealthy Americans, a "progressive" tax levied according to the ability to pay.

The ideas of the reformers were not new to the Progressive Era, but received more publicity and serious attention from politicians than before. The National Association of Manufacturers began pressuring for a system of having a business-dominated commission determine tariff rates flexibly, with promises to lower American duties when other nations allowed American goods to enter their markets freely. After it was organized, the United States Chamber of Commerce also took up the call for a flexible system of tariffs designed to ensure greater free trade for American exporters. Even the American Federation of Labor, no longer convinced that high American duties protected high American wages, supported tariff reform.

Tariff reformers enjoyed some successes in the Progressive Era, although the tariff issue was, as always, embroiled in partisan politics. The Payne-Aldrich Act of 1909 provided little relief from existing protective measures, but it did contain some innovations, such as allowing the president to raise American duties by 25 per cent when he determined that another nation was restricting American exports. The measure also called for a constitutional amendment to allow Congress to impose an income tax. The law failed to establish a tariff commission to advise the president, however, so President Taft appointed his own Tariff Board to give him expert advice. Congress was reluctant to cede authority over the tariff—and the potential favors to constituents—to a commission, however much the NAM and other business groups advocated the idea.

Tariff reform came only after Woodrow Wilson and the Democratic party assumed control of the government in 1913. Then Congress enacted the Underwood Tariff, which substantially lowered duties. Although it was not a free-trade measure, the Underwood Tariff did reduce rates to the lowest level since the Civil War. With the passage of the income tax amendment in 1913, Congress was able to make up for lost revenue by imposing taxes on the wealthy (the highest tax rate was 7 per cent, and there was no withholding tax). But the law also took away the flexibility of the Payne-Aldrich Act, and Congress still declined to establish a tariff commission.

The final Progressive Era contribution to tariff politics came on the eve of the nation's entry into World War I. With the European war disrupting international trade and President Wilson pushing the measure, Congress finally created the United States Tariff Commission in 1916. Like the FTC, the terms of office of the bipartisan commission were staggered to ensure continuity of policy. Under the leadership of its first chairman, economics professor Frank W. Taussig, the commission pursued an advisory role. Taussig believed that elected officials should establish the direction of tariff policy and that the commission should ensure that the policy was put into practice fairly and dispassionately. Congress allowed the commission to work on lowering or raising duties, but elected officials always retained final authority over the tariff.

State Regulation of Business

The creation of the Tariff Commission at the end of the Progressive Era was the last instance of reformers turning to the federally organized commission format for the regulation of business before World War I. The use of commissions as responses to the wishes of business associations, the findings of economists, and the complaints of reformers during the Progressive Era also occurred at the state level, however, where many political leaders looked for fresh ways to shape local business environments.

In the period before World War I, almost all state governments used the commission as a device for regulating business, especially railroad freight and passenger rates and utility rates. By the second decade of the twentieth century, in fact, railroad managers were complaining about their "forty-eight masters." Prior to 1914, state commissions sometimes set rates to benefit local shippers at the expense of distant competitors, but in that year the U.S. Supreme Court clearly forbade states from controlling freight rates so as to have any impact on interstate commerce. After this ruling, the states limited themselves to local rates—some also served as advocates of local shippers before the ICC.

Many national corporate leaders disliked state regulation, not because it was directly hostile to business interests, but, first, because it was difficult for a firm doing business in several or even all states to conform to regulations emanating from many different state capitals at once. This was the source of the railroad managers' complaints of "forty-eight masters." And second, state regulation was usually designed to foster the interests of local, and usually smaller, firms and to protect them from competitive pressures from large, vertically integrated, efficient manufacturers and distributors. This situation was particularly acute in the South and the trans-Mississippi West. Up to the middle of twentieth century, those regions suffered from a kind of colonial dependency, sending agricultural goods and raw materials to the cities and factories of the North and East in exchange for finished products. Southern and western entrepreneurs interested in boosting local manufacturing allied with local politicians in attempts to use state regulation to redress the balance.

The use of state antitrust statutes demonstrated this approach clearly. Texas was active in the antitrust field because many of its business and political leaders were convinced that eastern interests thwarted local development. In the nineteenth century, Standard Oil enjoyed a near monopoly in the oil industry. But after the opening of vast new oil fields in Texas after 1901, Texas law restrained Standard's activities in the state and promoted the development of two new major oil companies, Gulf Oil and The Texas Company.

State Regulation of Working Conditions

State governments also regulated working conditions during the Progressive Era. The Supreme Court maintained that conditions inside a factory were a local concern, outside of Congress's power to regulate interstate commerce. When Congress outlawed the employment of children, for example, the Court ruled the measure unconstitutional. Nevertheless, many Americans considered unregulated factories undesirable places for the employment of both children and women. Northern states passed laws, for instance, restricting the hours and regulating the working conditions of female employees. They also forbade the hiring of children under the age of fourteen and under the age of sixteen for night work.

Reformers enjoyed notable successes in furthering the cause of industrial safety by the end of the Progressive Era. Economists and other observers wrote about the rates of injury, which were high in this period, and the harmful effects of injuries not only on individual workers but on their families and communities as well. They also worked for systems of state regulation that would effectively force employers to improve safety conditions in plants. The result was the creation of state systems of workers' compensation, either through private insurers, or as pioneered by Ohio in 1911.

The workers' compensation reform tied the economic interests of business firms to programs to improve industrial safety. Before the reform, when a worker was injured on the job, he or she could sue for damages in the courts. Businesses were usually able to rebuff

Lewis Hine, a progressive reformer, skillfully documented in his photographs the hardships associated with the Industrial Revolution. His pictures, including this example of boys laboring in coal mines, helped persuade Americans to pass laws forbidding the employment of children. (Library of Congress, photograph by Lewis Hine)

their complaints by citing the common law argument that the injured worker had accepted the possibility of injury as part of the job and was therefore responsible for his or her injury. Nevertheless, juries sometimes granted large awards to injured workers. Led by the new-school economist John R. Commons, the reformers created a program designed to give workers a safer environment. Under workers' compensation, the state government insured workers against injury and adjudicated damage claims through an administrative agency (not the courts) according to a schedule of payments rated by types of injuries. Workers' compensation required employers to purchase state insurance, but their premium costs went down when they cooperated with government experts to devise safer working conditions. This program appealed to business as a practical solution to a real labor problem, and associations like the NAM promoted the idea in many state capitals.

State regulation thus became an important factor in the day-to-day lives of many employers and their workers. The problem, from the point of view of business, was that passage of a law in one state could work to the competitive disadvantage of local firms in another state. Federal measures were unlikely to survive a Supreme Court test, given the judicial climate of the day, so the only alternative seemed to be uniform state legislation. One important activity of business associations, thus, was to attempt to have states enact "model" regulatory laws. The idea behind the movement for uniform state legislation was simple: if each state passed the same law and imposed the same regulatory costs, no firm would have a competitive advantage stemming from the fragmented nature of the American governmental system. Business associations spent much time and energy on this matter, but uniform legislation was difficult to achieve in the face of the multitude of special and local business interests characteristic of American society.

The Supreme Court and Reform

The business firms and associations that wanted to resist the efforts of reformers and regulatory agencies often found an ally in the federal courts. Court actions, in fact, had profound impact on the regulation of business. In the early twentieth century, the Supreme Court often ruled against regulatory measures, especially, as we have seen, those concerning labor. Between 1899 and 1937, the Court used the doctrine of "substantive" due process to strike down state regulatory measures in 184 cases. When the Court found that the "substance" of a law was to deny a corporation its right to life, liberty, or property, it declared the law invalid. This doctrine discouraged both federal and state attempts at regulation.

The Court had an especially profound impact on the antitrust movement. As we saw in the case involving the American Sugar Refining Company in 1895, the Court ruled that a monopoly in manufacturing was not a restraint of trade under the Sherman Act. The Court asserted that a manufacturing monopoly enacted in one state did not "directly" affect interstate commerce even though the factory's products were sold across state borders. This decision caused a furor, and Theodore Roosevelt warned that it would effectively nullify the antitrust law. Not long thereafter, in 1899, the Court ruled that small firms in the same industry could not arrange contracts to control interstate sales. The net effect of these two decisions was to encourage the late-nineteenth-century merger movement, for though it seemed legal for one firm to dominate an industry, it was clearly illegal for smaller firms to control an industry through some arrangement of private associations.

In the Progressive Era, the Supreme Court still retained its prerogative of deciding what "trusts" were legal. In the Northern Securities case of 1904, the Court dissolved the combination of three railroad systems in the Pacific Northwest and thereby asserted the supremacy of federal power. In 1905, the Court ruled against practices of integrated meat-packing firms that amounted to collusion and price fixing. Most dramatically, the Court ordered the Standard Oil and the American Tobacco trusts dissolved into smaller units in 1911. Rockefeller's firm was required to split into seven smaller oil companies. In these cases, the Court enunciated a "rule of reason" doctrine under which it declared that large firms that did not have an undue impact on competition were allowable. When it applied its "rule of reason" to Standard Oil and American Tobacco, the Court found that those combinations were illegal, because they were so large as to prevent competition. This doctrine allowed the Court flexibility in future cases, and in the 1920s it refused to dissolve other large integrated firms when they operated without monopoly control over pricing in their industries.

BUSINESS, REFORM, AND THE IMMIGRANT LABOR FORCE

The New Immigration

American business and its reformers became intimately involved in another important movement during the Progressive Era: Americanization. The involvement came about as a result of the confluence of two major historical trends. With the return to prosperity after 1897, the United States witnessed a flood of new immigrants. During the Progressive Era, the prevailing flow of migration was from southern and eastern Europe, as Italians, Slavs, Greeks, and Jews sought economic opportunity in America's bustling industrial centers. The immigration reached flood tide in 1907, when 1 million newcomers arrived in the country. Immigration was as old as American history, but these "new" immigrants added to the mixture of cultures in America as never before. The immigrants arrived, moreover, while a second trend was under way: the increasing

The success of the Industrial Revolution in the United States created wealth and jobs, attracting millions of immigrants—including these East Europeans debarking in New York City in 1905. The flood tide of immigration peaked in 1907; in 1924, Congress passed strict limits on the number of immigrants. (International Museum of Photography at the George Eastman House)

mechanization and routinization of American factory production. The mines, mills, and factories of the industrial workplace offered numerous opportunities for semiskilled and unskilled workers, occupations for which businesses often recruited the newcomers from Europe.

The arrival of the "new" immigrants seemed to pose special problems. To social reformers—educators, nurses, church leaders, social workers, and the like—the problems involved adjustment to American conditions. The immigrants too often arrived in poverty, without the resources and skills necessary to obtain adequate housing, food, and care for themselves. To many other Americans the strangeness of immigrant ways was perceived as a threat to a culture rooted in British traditions. Out of these various concerns arose widespread worries about how American institutions would cope with and care for the flood of newcomers. The immigrants had to be taught the English language, learn American customs and laws, and adapt their traditional lifestyles, which were usually rooted in peasant ways, to the routine and rigor required for survival and advancement in a complex urban-industrial society. Employers had a special interest in this educational process. Factory work was very different from the agricultural work the newcomers were accustomed to, and they had to be taught its requirements. The immigrants needed instruction in simple matters, such as how to take the correct streetcar at the right time to check into the factory at the appointed hour, and they had to learn the importance of punctuality, sobriety, and regular work attendance, no matter what the season or what traditional folk festival might be occurring.

Americanization

The result of these educational needs was the Americanization movement, led by Frances Kellor, a well-educated woman who committed her life to social reform. Kellor edited a magazine devoted to Americanization and enlisted the support of intellectuals and other reformers for her programs. She also worked with the federal government to establish a bureau to promote the education of immigrants and to aid local communities in their own efforts.

Kellor was especially interested in working closely with business firms, both to meet their needs for training and controlling the work force and to satisfy her wish to deal directly with the newcomers. She and other reformers helped the Chamber of Commerce establish its Immigration Committee, which worked to have businesses establish classes inside factories in which immigrant workers were taught English and the necessity of punctuality, regular work routines, and humility toward overseers. The Chamber of Commerce and Kellor recruited volunteer teachers from the YMCA and YWCA to concentrate their Americanization efforts in a so-called industrial zone—the area bounded by the Potomac, Ohio and Mississippi rivers. In response to this campaign, individual firms provided space for Americanization classes and required immigrant workers to attend.

The paternal spirit that underlay the Americanization movement also led business people to contribute funds and serve on the boards of social-service institutions, to play an active role in reforming public school systems, and to engage in various philanthropic activities. Just as there was an emerging system of government-business cooperation regarding the "trust" question and the control of price competition during the Progressive Era, so was there a growing involvement of business in broader social affairs.

MOBILIZATION FOR WAR

The Economic Problems of War

This cooperation reached its zenith when the United States declared war on Germany and Austria-Hungary in April 1917. Suddenly, the nation was confronted with an unprecedented situation: the necessity of rapidly and efficiently mobilizing its industrial resources for a major European war, for America's British and French allies urgently needed its munitions, weapons, and foodstuffs. Peacetime market forces could no longer be permitted to govern the flow of goods and services and the allocation of capital in the American economy. New administrative means had to be found quickly to replace many customary business practices.

The problem with turning from an economy still governed partly by market forces to one operated by administrative agencies was that those agencies did not exist, at least in government. Although government bureaucracies had grown with the reforms of the Progressive Era, they hardly had the resources to administer full-scale economic mobilization. To raise and equip its own armed forces and supply its allies, the federal government had to construct a host of new agencies and had to turn to business volunteers to staff them. America's large vertically integrated firms, and to a lesser extent the trade associations, were populated by experienced cadres of administrators. They volunteered for public service, often as "dollar-a-year men" (so called because the government paid them a token salary while they remained on private payrolls).

Wartime Agencies

The new wartime mobilization agencies evolved slowly as business and government leaders struggled to avoid too much government direction while achieving the needed results. Eventually, the intervention of government in business life was enormous. In October 1916, before the American declaration of war, President Wilson formed a cabinet-level Council of National Defense with a seven-member advisory commission. Four of the Commission members were prominent businessmen, two were well known in the engineering and medical professions, and the seventh, Samuel Gompers, headed the AF of L. The task of the commission and the council was to recommend policies for improving the nation's preparedness in event of war. Following the advice of Bernard Baruch, a Wall Street speculator who sat on the commission, the council called on private industry to form cooperative committees for every line of trade, committees with which the government could work in coordinating military procurement. Soon a multitude of committees and subcommittees emerged, each composed of leaders from private industry and coordinated by a designated member of the advisory commission. The committees' original purpose was to make detailed studies of their industries, but when the United States entered the war, they became responsible for coordinating production and sales to the military.

The fairly informal system did not work very well. Soon after the declaration of war, the economy was in chaos, with the armed services competing with one another desperately for supplies and business people trying to position themselves favorably in the new market. Firms tried to arrange rules to their advantage. As the problems mounted, however, the solutions started to come. In the summer of 1917, Wilson appointed a successful mining engineer, Herbert Hoover, who had gained popularity for his work in organizing European food relief, to head a new Food Administration. Hoover's task was to implore Americans to produce and conserve foodstuffs and especially to coordinate the flow of agricultural products to places in desperate need. Then, at the end of 1917, Wilson asked Congress to federalize the railroads and place them under the control of a U.S. Railroad Administration. The nation's transportation system was breaking down, with railroads burdened with large flows of traffic toward seaports. The task of the new Railroad Administration was to sort out the mess, impose efficiencies on an industry whose firms were accustomed to competing for traffic, and coordinate the arrival of freight trains and ships. For this task the government used experienced railroad managers who divided the nation into districts and made certain that equipment and traffic were shared. To coordinate and boost the production of energy, the government also created the U.S. Fuel Administration.

The new mobilization agencies took their final shape in March of 1918 with the appointment of Bernard Baruch as head of the War Industries Board. Under Baruch's leadership, the board avoided issuing commands and encouraged voluntary cooperation. The government worked closely with private associations in allocating contracts and setting production priorities. No believer in an economy operated through free-market forces, Baruch ensured that a close partnership between government and business emerged in which government assisted business people in the private associational activities of administering the economy.

The Wartime Legacy

After the war ended in 1918, most of the special business agencies of coordination and administration began to disband. The values and ideas they represented, however, remained. The American economy had been successfully mobilized in a short period of time to support a large U.S. armed force abroad and to bring critically needed supplies to the nation's allies. This mobilization was impressive, as it was accomplished by cooperation, planning, and administrative coordination. Mobilization had required abandoning the "invisible hand" of market coordination in sectors of the economy still characterized by peripheral firms. The owners of most of these firms believed they had benefited from the wartime partnership with the government as it had involved cooperative planning in allocating and pricing goods and services. As we shall see in Chapter 9, business executives and government leaders thus sought to continue these benefits in peacetime.

TOWARD A MODERN BUSINESS SYSTEM

The American business system changed fundamentally in the years of the Progressive Era and World War I. Those changes did not involve so much the pattern of business organization, which had emerged with the rise of integrated big-business firms of the 1880s and the merger wave of the 1890s, but instead occurred in the relationships among businesses and between business, government, and society. Associationalism grew rapidly, peaking during the war. So too did the values of cooperation, not competition. Government regulation of business increased.

In many lines of manufacturing and transportation, the benefits of replacing the invisible hand of the market with the visible hand of management seemed clear, and business managers and prominent politicians sought ways of bringing those benefits to sectors in which economic and technological circumstances had not led to the rise of giant firms. By the start of World War I, they seemed to be reaching their goal. The Supreme Court had announced its "rule of reason," which seemed to grant legal sanction to many big firms. The decades-long controversy over the "trusts" seemed to be ebbing. Even the tariff issue that had so long plagued American politics might, it seemed, be susceptible to "scientific" solutions by an expert commission.

It was during this period too that business began involving itself with local communities and social problems in new ways. The idea of using the administrative bureaucracy of the business world to deal with social and political problems was deeply implanted by 1917. Business leaders encouraged "efficiency" and the bureaucratic application of expert knowledge to schools, local governments, churches, and other social institutions. Business firms and associations were also instrumental in helping the nation cope with the Americanization of its new arrivals.

The experience of business executives during World War I had a profound effect on the conduct of business in the United States, especially in the center firms. The war disrupted business and the American economy, but it also created new opportunities. After the war, firms supplying consumer durable goods, especially automobiles, came to the forefront of the business system. American executives pioneered in arranging decentralized, diversified big businesses suitable for the new conditions of a more affluent nation.

Selected Readings

Robert H. Wiebe, *The Search for Order, 1877–1920* (New York: Hill and Wang, 1967), is a good introduction to the Progressive Era. More directly concerned with the themes of government-business relations are Samuel Haber, *Efficiency and Uplift: Scientific Management in the Progressive Era, 1890–1920* (Chicago: University of Chicago Press, 1964); Edward Berkowitz and Kim McQuaid, *Creating the Welfare State: The Political Economy of Twentieth-Century Reform* (New York: Praeger Publishers, 1980); Martin J. Sklar, *The Corporate Reconstruction of American Capitalism, 1890–1916* (New York: Cambridge University Press, 1988).

Other studies that provide insights into this period include Wiebe, "The House of Morgan and the Executive, 1905–1913," *American Historical Review* 65 (October 1959), 49–60; Mansel G. Blackford, *The Politics of Business in California, 1890–1920* (Columbus: The Ohio State University Press, 1977); K. Austin Kerr, *American Railroad Politics, 1914–1920* (Pittsburgh: University of Pittsburgh Press, 1968); Robert Cuff, *The War Industries Board: Business-Government Relations During World War I* (Baltimore: The Johns Hopkins University Press, 1973); and Thomas McCraw, *Prophets of Regulation* (Cambridge, Mass.: Harvard University Press, 1984).

PART 4

The
Development
of
Modern
Business

1920–1945

IMPORTANT EVENTS, 1913–1945

1913–1915 Ford Motors introduces the moving assembly line, used in the construction of the Model T.

1920 More Americans live in cities and towns than on farms and in small villages.

1920–1922 A recession exposes managerial weaknesses in large businesses.

1920–1924 General Motors and Du Pont adopt decentralized management.

1925 Sears, Roebuck opens urban retail outlets.
Black entrepreneurs found the Chicago Metropolitan Assurance Company.

1925–1931 The United States experiences its second merger movement.

1929 The Stock Market Crash signals the beginning of the Great Depression.

1940 Some 110 universities enroll 100,000 students in business courses.

1942 U.S. production of industrial war goods surpasses that of Germany, Japan, and Italy combined.

1945 Henry Ford II becomes president of Ford Motors.

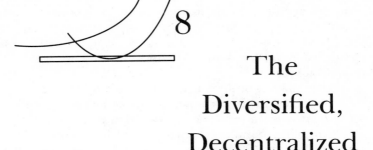

8

The
Diversified,
Decentralized
Company

Looking back over his long career at General Motors, Alfred P. Sloan, Jr.—who as president reshaped the company's management structure in the 1920s—commented on what he considered his major contribution to the firm and to American business as a whole: "My thoughts . . . have always revolved around one concept which contains considerable complexity in theory and reality—the concept that goes by the oversimplified name of decentralization." Led by General Motors and other firms during the 1920s, 1930s, and 1940s, some businesses moved from centralized to decentralized management systems as they became increasingly larger and more complex. In setting up decentralized management structures, business executives like Sloan also unknowingly established models for additional reorganizations of big businesses after World War II.

The development of new management structures by individual firms was symptomatic of the changing nature of the nation's business system. Two trends stood out. First, managers interested in rationalizing their diverse businesses replaced the entrepreneurial empire builders, the robber barons or industrial statesmen of the nineteenth century. As the first generation of big-business leaders stepped down, a new generation with less of a personal stake in the companies they ran took their place. The separation of ownership from management, which had started in the nineteenth century, accelerated in the twentieth. As the separation of ownership from management proceeded, business executives began claiming the mantle of professionalism. Asserting that they were similar to lawyers, doctors, and clergy, they maintained that their mission was not simply to make a profit but to serve society. They issued codes of business ethics, made corporate contributions to philanthropy, and became involved in professional education for business.

Second, the country experienced another major merger movement during the 1920s, and oligopoly came to characterize a growing number of American industries. America's system of capitalism, as a result, contained fewer elements of competition than before. In 1909, oligopolistic industries produced 16 per cent of America's industrial goods. By 1929, they made 21 per cent.

CHANGES IN THE AMERICAN BUSINESS SYSTEM

General Trends in the Economy

Business opportunities changed dramatically following World War I, as America evolved from a producer-dominated to a consumer-oriented society. Opportunities also varied with the ups and downs in the general economic climate of the United States. The onset of the Great Depression in 1929 in particular affected every American institution in the decade following. The economic growth rate during this period was much lower than it had been during the previous fifty years. Between 1921 and 1946, America's real GNP doubled, but GNP per capita rose only 79 per cent. (See Figure 8.1.) As in the past, economic growth was affected by both domestic and foreign developments.

In foreign trade, the United States became a strong creditor nation during World War I and maintained that position throughout the following three decades. During this period, America's exports exceeded her imports except during the depression years of 1934 through 1940. Reflecting America's emergence as the leading industrial power of the world, the nation's exports came increasingly to be composed of industrial items, while its imports consisted more and more of raw materials.

These changes in foreign trade notwithstanding, the internal do-

Figure 8.1

U.S. Gross National Product, 1921–1946 (in billions of dollars, 1929 prices)

SOURCE: Based on data from U.S. Bureau of the Census, *Historical Statistics of the United States, Colonial Times to 1957* (Washington, D.C.: U.S. Government Printing Office, 1960), p. 139.

mestic market remained, as it had been in the nineteenth century, the most important factor in the economic prosperity of the United States. In the mid-twentieth century, the national market became even more lucrative as it was further unified by new forms of transportation and communications—automobiles, trucks, airplanes, telephones, and the radio—and as the population rose from 106 million in 1920 to 141 million in 1946. Business institutions continued to develop in order to tap this ever-growing market. Chain stores, for example, greatly expanded. By 1929, A & P had 15,418 stores in America, Woolworth 1,825, J. C. Penney 1,395, and Safeway 2,660.

Structural shifts in the American business system begun in earlier years also continued in the second quarter of the twentieth century.

In 1920, for the first time in the country's history, more people lived in towns and cities than on farms or in small villages, and the contribution of farming to the economy declined in relative terms as the United States completed its transformation from a rural agricultural society to an urban industrial one. Manufacturing, which suffered during the depression years of the 1930s, picked up as factories shifted to the production of war goods in the early and mid-1940s. Service industries continued to grow in significance, a trend that would become even more pronounced after World War II.

Sears, Roebuck

The continuing growth of the internal market provided new business opportunities, as the history of the nation's leading retailer reveals. Mail-order houses like Montgomery Ward and Sears, Roebuck, which had grown up in the late nineteenth century to serve the farm market, found it necessary to modify their business strategies as cities became more important. Both companies moved into the rapidly growing urban market by opening retail outlets across the United States, but the experiences of Sears illustrate particularly well this shift in marketing approach.

Richard Sears founded the company that would become Sears, Roebuck to sell watches through the mail in 1886. Alvah Roebuck, who originally joined him in this venture as a watch repairman, worked to broaden the firm's offerings. In 1893, Sears, Roebuck was incorporated, and throughout the 1890s the company increased its sales, mainly to farmers who could not easily reach urban stores. Farmers selected merchandise from the company's catalogues, placed their orders through the mail (Sears maintained a central warehouse in Chicago from which the orders were filled), and received their goods by railroad.

Sears continued to grow in the early twentieth century, but problems surfaced. Richard Sears was a promotional genius, but he failed to establish the organization needed to run the expanding business. Because of disagreements over how to manage the company, Roebuck left the firm in 1895. Sears then brought Julius Rosenwald, a Chicago clothing merchant, into the business as a source of new capital. Together, Sears and Rosenwald built up Sears, Roebuck into a large national company, with Sears focusing on marketing and Rosenwald on administration. With sales of $10 million, Sears, Roebuck outstripped its rivals to become America's leading mail-order house by 1900. Twenty years later, the sales of

Mail-order firms were an important innovation in the nation's retail distribution system. The 1927 cover of the Sears, Roebuck catalog featured a painting by Norman Rockwell, who depicted a couple studying a catalog of the industry's most successful firm. (Sears Archive)

Sears topped $200 million. By this time, Richard Sears had left the company, and it became a publicly held corporation.

The growing importance of the urban market in the 1920s and 1930s led the managers at Sears to reassess their company's operations. Robert Wood, who joined Sears in 1925 and became president three years later, took the company into the city. Although it continued to serve farmers through its mail-order business, Sears began opening retail outlets in 1925, and over the next three decades the company built its stores at the intersections of busy traffic arteries, where they could be easily reached by automobile, in medium-sized and large cities all over the nation. Montgomery

Ward, which continued to emphasize the farm and small-town market, fell steadily behind Sears. Wood complemented his new selling strategy with a new buying strategy: by working closely with its suppliers, Sears was able to provide its stores with a steady stream of high-quality goods designed to the company's own specifications.

The results of Wood's actions were dramatic. By 1929, retail sales accounted for 40 per cent of Sears's total sales, and a decade later they composed two-thirds of them. When Wood retired in 1954, Sears had become the world's largest merchandising operation. The company operated 694 retail stores and 570 catalogue sales offices. These outlets employed 200,000 people and generated sales of $3 billion.

General Trends in Manufacturing

In manufacturing, new consumer goods industries developed, and older ones became more oriented to the production of consumer durables (items purchased by consumers for use for more than a year or two). General Electric and Westinghouse, for example, began producing electric stoves, refrigerators, washing machines, and other appliances in addition to their original electricity-generating equipment. From its pre–World War I base in black powder and chemicals, Du Pont branched out into the making of synthetic fibers like rayon and nylon in the 1920s and 1930s. The radio industry was born and reached a robust adolescence in the single decade of the 1920s.

Most remarkable, however, was the tremendous expansion of the automobile industry. Henry Ford's success in using the assembly line to produce the Model T greatly lowered the price of automobiles, making them affordable to many farmers and most middle-class Americans and thus bringing "mass automobility" to the country. In 1915, there were 2.3 million automobiles registered in the United States; by 1929, the number had risen to over 23 million. The development of the automobile industry spurred the growth of a host of related industries—steel, oil, glass, and rubber. In the rubber industry, for example, Goodrich, Goodyear, Seiberling, and United States Rubber (later Uniroyal) came of age as big businesses to supply the automobile industry.

As a generalization, it can be said that in the nineteenth century Americans built their factories and that in the twentieth century those factories began turning out an increasing number of products for use by consumers. Behind this shift lay important technological and scientific breakthroughs in chemicals, metallurgy, and other fields. Perhaps most important for the continued industrialization of the United States was the adoption of electricity—a more flexible and efficient power source than steam in many situations—in factory work. By 1939, electric motors accounted for 90 per cent of the power used in manufacturing.

In short, America began changing from a producer-dominated to a consumer-oriented society, a shift that continued after World War II. Nowhere was this new orientation clearer than in the development of a car culture. Like radios and electric appliances, cars became more than luxuries for many Americans. They were increasingly viewed as necessities, and the use of automobiles came to affect nearly all aspects of life. By bringing a new mobility to Americans, cars linked the farm with the city. Urban and rural differences lessened, and life became standardized throughout the United States. Widespread jokes, especially about the Model T, indicated just how central the automobile had become to American culture. A man about to die, it was said, asked to be buried in his Model T—because he had never yet been in a hole that his car could not get him out of. Not all folklore was so favorable. One ditty declared, "Of all the noises there is none worse than a Model T going in reverse"—a reference to the Ford's transmission.

Oligopoly, Administered Pricing, and a Dual Economy

The trend toward concentration and the growth of oligopoly, which had begun in the late nineteenth century, continued in the twentieth. The United States experienced its second major merger movement in the 1920s (as discussed in Chapter 5, the first merger movement took place between 1894 and 1905). More than in the past, the mergers of the 1920s occurred among large and medium-sized, rather than truly giant, companies. Altogether, 5,846 mergers took place in the years 1925 through 1931. (See Figure 8.2.) As a result, industrial production in America became increasingly concentrated in the factories of big businesses. The 100 largest manufacturing concerns in the United States increased their share of the nation's manufacturing assets from 36 per cent in 1925 to 44 per cent six years later. These big businesses continued to develop most of America's private industrial research laboratories. In 1933, some 113 of the nation's largest 200 industrial companies operated research laboratories; by 1948, some 164 did.

Figure 8.2
Mergers in Manufacturing and Mining in the United States, 1920–1933

SOURCE: Based on data from U.S. Bureau of the Census, *Historical Statistics of the United States, Colonial Times to 1970*, pt. 2 (Washington, D.C.: U.S. Government Printing Office, 1975), p. 914.

With this growth in the concentration of American industry, price competition between manufacturing firms decreased (competition based on advertising, service, and quality continued). Prices in oligopolistic industries made up of center firms became less flexible, less responsive to market forces. A drop in demand no longer automatically led to a fall in prices. Administered pricing—the setting of prices by managers of center firms—replaced price setting by market forces in many fields of manufacturing. The visible hand of management, already significant in the 1880s and 1890s, grew in importance during the 1920s. This practice of administered prices allowed some companies to survive the Great Depression, for prices generally fell less in oligopolistic industries than in industries characterized by competition. For instance, General Motors, America's largest automobile company in the 1930s, responded quickly to the depression by slashing salaries and wages, laying off workers, and cutting back its production of cars by almost three-quarters. The company was slower in lowering the prices of its cars, and even in the depths of the Great Depression continued to earn a profit.

Although they declined in significance in many fields of manufacturing with the merger movement of the 1920s, small businesses remained an important part of the American business system. They continued to be particularly significant in industrial areas in which they could carve out market niches for specialty products—in some fields of metalworking, for instance. Small businesses also dominated industries in which there were no inherent economies of scale—furniture making, leatherworking, garment making, and the like. And as in the past, small businesses continued to be important in sales, both wholesaling and retailing. As in earlier times, small businesses tended to be labor-intensive rather than capital-intensive. In the peripheral industries composed of small businesses there were no advantages in large firm size.

The growth of oligopolistic big business combined with the continued persistence of small business made the distinction between center and peripheral firms even more pronounced. The differences between large and small enterprises became more noticeable, and America's business system increasingly became divided into separate spheres along those lines.

Alterations in farming mirrored the changes taking place in the U.S. economy as a whole. During the first five decades of the twentieth century, two types of farming developed side-by-side; small family farms found it increasingly difficult to compete with a growing number of large, highly capitalized farms using the most advanced scientific methods and machinery. Between 1920 and 1945, about 3 million more Americans left farming than entered it. Fewer farmers produced more food for U.S. consumption and for export. Moreover, larger farms produced a greater and greater share of the total farm output. By 1948, the largest 10 per cent of America's farms accounted for 24 per cent of the nation's farm output; the smallest 20 per cent of the farms raised less than 3 per cent of the total output.

The Rise of Advertising and Marketing

During the 1920s, advertising matured as an important industry, and marketing emerged as a conscious business strategy. The maturation of advertising in the 1920s and the creation of marketing departments and marketing strategies by major firms both promoted consumer values in American society and reflected the rise of the consumer society. In 1919, advertising costs were 8 per cent of total distribution costs in industry; by 1929, the share was 14 per cent. In 1929, advertising costs reached nearly $3 billion.

The content of advertising messages shifted in the early twentieth century. Before 1910, advertisers mostly sought to inform customers about products; after 1910, the main goal was to create a desire to purchase products. By the 1920s, advertising executives recognized that theirs was a business to make consumers want products, and they deliberately sought to break down popular attitudes of self-denial and to foster the idea of instant gratification through consumption. Moreover, the introduction of new techniques for printing advertisements in color opened new possibilities of suggestion and persuasion. As a result of the growth of advertising expenditures in the 1920s, not only did the magazine business prosper but business executives were able to inject attitudes favorable toward consumption more than ever before, even for products for which there was no need. The makers of Fleischmann's yeast, for instance, claimed that the product, in addition to leavening bread, cured "intestinal fatigue" when eaten directly. One advertisement for Listerine, which promoted fears about a disease newly discovered by copywriters, "halitosis," suggested that "unpleasant breath" was the main "obstacle to pleasant business, professional, and social relations" and urged Americans to use the mouthwash as a way of climbing the social and economic ladder.

At the same time that the advertising industry was flourishing, a few business firms launched innovative programs in "commercial research," or what later generations called marketing. A representative of the *Saturday Evening Post,* then a widely circulated weekly magazine, was unhappy with the way advertising space was being sold, because the magazine's space salesmen had no knowledge about their customers' needs or the effectiveness of advertisements. The publisher hired Charles Coolidge Parlin to use social-science techniques to study those questions—the first market research. In 1916 the nation's largest rubber firm, U.S. Rubber, had established a market research department, and the Swift meat-packing concern followed suit in 1917. These efforts pioneered attempts by American manufacturers to integrate systematic knowledge of markets with advertising and the design and production of goods.

In oligopolistic industries, as price competition lessened, marketing techniques and advertising messages became increasingly important ways for companies to differentiate their products and to promote sales. General Motors, for instance, led the automobile companies in instituting annual model changes that were primarily cosmetic in nature. Style became increasingly important in selling goods. The development of consumer credit accompanied the evolution of marketing and advertising. Paying for goods in monthly installments rather than with a lump sum became more and more common as America's consumer-oriented society expanded. General Motors set up the General Motors Acceptance Corporation in 1919 to help people finance car purchases, and Ford Motors established a similar agency about ten years later. By 1929, installment buying accounted for 90 per cent of sewing machine and washing machine purchases, about 80 per cent of all sales of radios, refrigerators, and vacuum cleaners, and 60 per cent of car sales in the United States.

BUSINESS DIVERSIFICATION AND THE SPREAD OF DECENTRALIZED MANAGEMENT

Conditions Leading to Decentralization

The changing economic conditions of the United States had a major impact on the nature of the management of the nation's business firms. The broadened range of consumer goods produced by many companies, which resulted from sustained efforts at diversification, required the institution of new management methods. As late as 1910, even the largest manufacturing companies still produced only one or two major items for a few primary markets. Functionally departmentalized central management systems were adequate for those companies, for officers in the head office could handle the relatively uncomplicated operations of their firms. However, as companies grew in size and especially as they increased the number of goods they produced and the markets they served, centralized management no longer sufficed. A few officers, or even a few committees, in a head office could no longer manage well the growing complexity of their company's work. They could not oversee the daily operations of their firm and simultaneously plan for its future.

A sharp postwar recession that began in the summer of 1920 and lasted into early 1922 revealed the inability of centralized management systems to handle complexity and spurred business leaders to revamp their management structures to take advantage of the new consumer markets. This recession showed, above all, that corporate officers were still so caught up in the daily affairs of their companies that they were not preparing for the future. None had any plans for dealing with the drop in demand that their products faced during the recession. Because of this lack of planning, few businesses could adjust to new conditions quickly enough. The consequences were traumatic. Julius Rosenwald was forced to use his personal funds to save Sears, Roebuck from bankruptcy. J. Ogden Armour had to yield control of the meat-packing company founded by his father. Ford Motors, General Motors, Goodyear, Du Pont, and many other concerns faced severe financial difficulties.

In coping with their problems, some of these companies adopted decentralized systems of management: the head office concentrated on planning for the entire company and delegated authority over most daily operations to semiautonomous divisions organized around product lines. (Decentralized management is sometimes referred to as federalized decentralization. It is also called the M-form of management, with M standing for multidivisional. Centralized management is sometimes called the U-form of management, with U standing for Unitary.) As part of their reorganizations, these firms also greatly improved their market forecasting and financial controls by obtaining more accurate sales information. No longer did a handful of people in the head office attempt to run all aspects of their company's operations.

As we saw in Chapter 5, many railroads divided managerial responsibility with policy decisions handled by executives in the central office and operational decisions made by executives in the divisional offices. One railroad, the Pennsylvania, developed a fairly elaborate system of decentralized management under the leadership of its president, J. Edgar Thomson. To solve managerial problems caused by a rapid increase in the size and complexity of his company, Thomson divided the Pennsylvania into three regional systems and placed a general manager in charge of each of the regions or divisions. These general managers had direct responsibility for all the operations within their areas: scheduling trains, maintaining the roadbed, purchasing equipment, and hiring personnel. Each of the three major regional systems was further divided into subsystems of trackage. Each subsystem had a manager of operations, who reported to the general manager of his major regional system. The managers of these divisions and subdivisions—known as line officers—handled the routine work of running the trains, and they were given considerable autonomy in accomplishing this task as long as they followed the general guidelines, policies, and procedures of their company. Freed now from the need to make routine operating decisions, the managers in the head office (known as the corporate officers) of the Pennsylvania—the president and three vice presidents—were able to turn their full attention to strategic decision making. They oversaw the work of the regional managers and made plans for their railroad as a whole. They decided where to expand or contract operations, how to deal with competing railroads, and how to arrange financing for their line.

Although the railroads pioneered decentralized management, the executives of industrial companies, led by Du Pont and General Motors, brought it to maturity in the 1920s, 1930s, and 1940s with little reference to those earlier efforts. Instead, each company arrived at a similar solution for a similar problem: how to control complex business operations. The experiences of Du Pont and General Motors illustrate a cardinal point about the history of business in the United States: corporate structure follows business strategy. Those companies that chose to grow through diversification found themselves almost forced to adopt the new structure of decentralized management. Those that expanded without increasing the number or complexity of their products or markets found that centralized management systems could handle their needs and therefore made few changes in their management methods.

The Du Pont Company

The Du Pont Company, one of the country's oldest firms, was the first industrial concern to create a plan to decentralize its management, although not the first to implement one. Founded in 1802 on the banks of Brandywine Creek in Delaware as a small gunpowder company, Du Pont remained a producer of gunpowder and other explosives throughout the nineteenth century. Family members ran the company in an informal manner. In 1902, the company's senior partner, Eugene Du Pont, died, and the five remaining family partners, all older Du Ponts, uncertain about what to do, considered selling their firm to a rival company. Alfred Du Pont objected, and with the aid of his cousins Pierre S. and Coleman Du Pont, he persuaded the five elder Du Pont partners to sell out to the three younger Du Ponts.

Pierre quickly emerged as the leader of this trio and soon took the company into a dynamic period of growth and diversification.

Du Pont expanded steadily as a producer of munitions and explosives until the outbreak of World War I, when growth soared. Between 1914 and 1918, the number of workers at Du Pont rose from 5,300 to over 85,000, the gross capital employed by the company climbed from $86 million to $310 million, and net profits totaled $238 million. At the same time, Du Pont started diversifying its production as its officers sought investment outlets for the wartime profits and worried about a slump in demand for munitions once the war ended. As late as 1913, all but 3 per cent of the company's sales were in explosives, but over the next six years Du Pont entered new fields. By 1919, Du Pont had moved beyond explosives into chemicals, dyes, paint, and artificial fibers such as rayon.

The management structure of the Du Pont Company lagged behind these changes in business strategy; in 1919, it was still centralized. The company consisted of four major functional departments (production, sales, development, and treasury) and several minor ones whose work was, in theory at least, overseen and coordinated by an executive committee in the head office, which was guided in making its decisions by a flow of financial data from the departments and by advice from personnel, legal, and real estate officers. In the realm of finance, major improvements had been made in cost accounting, and under Pierre the Du Pont Company pioneered in employing the principle of rate of return on investment in deciding which operations to expand or contract (those that yielded the greatest profits per unit of capital invested were most likely to be expanded). Figure 8.3 illustrates Du Pont's administrative structure in 1919.

Advanced though it was in its day, this management structure broke down, overwhelmed by the combination of rapid growth and diversification. The executive committee in the central office found it difficult to establish broad policies for the diverse company and also failed to provide the needed coordination between key departments. Moreover, problems soon developed within the departments. People in sales, for instance, found it hard to handle a multitude of products designed for different markets. Selling smokeless powder was not like selling paint.

Du Pont's problems deepened with the coming of the postwar recession. In the second half of 1921, the company lost $2.5 million. Of its many products, explosives alone continued to show a profit. It was at this point—in September 1921—that the Du Pont Company adopted a decentralized, multidivisional management system. In the new management structure, the central office was composed

Figure 8.3
Du Pont's Management System in 1919

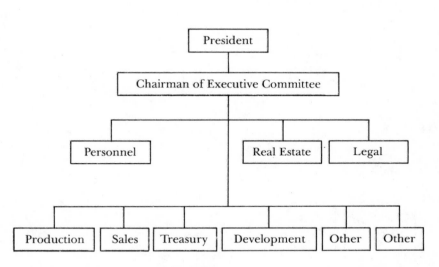

SOURCE: From Alfred D. Chandler, Jr., *Strategy and Structure* (Cambridge, Mass.: MIT Press, 1962). Copyright © 1962 by Massachusetts Institute of Technology.

of general corporate officers advised by staff officers who were experts in such fields as law and finance. The central office planned for the future of the entire corporation and coordinated the work of its different parts but did not supervise the details of the daily operations of the firm. Those became the province of the company's various divisions. Each division was based on a product line and contained within itself departments responsible for making and selling its own goods. As at the Pennsylvania Railroad in the 1870s, a separation occurred between the duties of the central office and those of the divisions. The head office, now freed from involvement in daily operations, could concentrate on the overall policies, the strategy, of the company. The general managers of each division, who were known as line officers, took care of the daily work, the tactics, of producing and selling goods. Figure 8.4 outlines Du Pont's decentralized management system.

The decentralized structure, with divisions based on product lines, served Du Pont well into the 1970s. It made it possible for the

Figure 8.4
Du Pont's Decentralized Management System in 1921

SOURCE: Adapted in simplified form from Alfred D. Chandler, Jr., *Strategy and Structure* (Cambridge, Mass.: MIT Press, 1962).

company's managers to handle the growing size and complexity of Du Pont's operations, something the older centralized management structure had failed to do.

General Motors

Although it was the first industrial company seriously to consider the adoption of a decentralized management system, Du Pont was not the first to implement it. Instead, the General Motors Company, influenced by events at Du Pont, established a decentralized management system eight months before Du Pont, and the General Motors management structure, studied and publicized by business writers, became an important model for other big businesses.

William Durant was the father of General Motors. A carriage maker in Flint, Michigan, Durant first became interested in automobiles in 1904, when he took over the faltering Buick Company in his hometown. Durant redesigned the car made by Buick and built new factories to produce it. By 1908, Buick was the largest automobile manufacturer in the United States, with an annual output of 8,487 vehicles. Excited by the prospects of growth, Durant used Buick as his base to found General Motors. Between 1908 and 1910, he brought together over twenty-five previously independent companies—including Olds, Oakland, and Cadillac—as the General Motors Corporation. Always more interested in expansion than profits, Durant failed to provide rational management for his growing agglomeration. When General Motors experienced financial difficulties in 1910, he lost control of the company to a group of Boston and New York bankers, who provided the firm with sorely needed infusions of new capital.

The bankers ran General Motors conservatively over the next five years, liquidating $12.5 million of unprofitable parts of the firm. Although they expanded production to 100,000 cars annually by 1915, they failed to keep pace with the still more rapid growth occurring at Ford Motors. Under their regime, the company's share of the American automobile market fell from 20 per cent to only 10 per cent.

A resilient businessman, Durant resumed control of General Motors in 1916. He did so by first working with Louis Chevrolet to build and market a light car to compete with Ford's Model T. Durant then used the Chevrolet Company to win back control of General Motors by acquiring a controlling share of General Motors stock. Durant dismissed the bankers and again took over as president of the company. This time, he shared his responsibilities with Pierre S. Du Pont, who acted as the chairman of the board of directors at General Motors. (Looking for investment opportunities for its wartime profits, the Du Pont Company had started purchasing General Motors stock. By early 1918, the Du Pont Company owned 24 per cent of the common stock of General Motors, and by the end of 1919 its share amounted to 29 per cent.) Caught up in the problems of diversification and reorganization at the Du Pont Company, however, Pierre paid scant attention to the activities at General Motors, despite his firm's growing investment in that company.

Once again, Durant pushed the company into another period of expansion. Between 1918 and 1920, he added Chevrolet, Fisher Body, a tractor company, an electric refrigerator company, and a number of smaller concerns to General Motors. And once again, Durant failed to establish a workable management system for the business. He tried to run the company as a one-man show, making both grand policy and daily operating decisions by himself (as late as 1918 the central office at General Motors consisted of only Durant and several personal assistants). Not even someone as energetic as Durant could adequately oversee such a large company's varied operations. As a result, major decisions on investment, expansion, marketing, and the like often simply were not made. As Alfred Sloan later wrote, "Mr. Durant was a great man with a great weakness—he could create but not administer."

As happened with Du Pont, the postwar recession revealed the managerial weakness at General Motors. Cars continued to sell well during the opening months of 1920, but in September the automobile market collapsed. New-car sales were 21 per cent lower in 1921 than in the previous year. General Motors was not prepared for this precipitous decline.

Three related managerial problems surfaced. First, lacking any form of market forecasting, each division continued to invest in new plants to build more cars. The central office, which still consisted mainly of Durant and his assistants, had no criteria by which to evaluate divisional requests for capital improvements, and most were approved with little analysis. In late 1919 and early 1920, the central office approved over $10 million more in capital improvements for Buick, Chevrolet, and Samson Tractor than had originally been scheduled, without any attempt to assess the effect of these extra expenditures on the company as a whole. Second, each division, again without meaningful control from the head office, continued well into 1920 to buy large inventories of raw materials with which to produce cars. By October of that year, the divisions had on hand $209 million worth of inventory, $59 million more than had been approved by the head office. Finally, cash-flow difficulties made these two problems even worse. Each division maintained its own bank accounts, making it very hard for the head office to move funds internally within the company. Buick, in particular, was reluctant to give up its cash to the head office, even when that cash was desperately needed to keep the company afloat.

Underlying these various problems was the basic problem of control. The head office was unable either to plan for the future of the company or coordinate and supervise the work of its different parts. The divisions were out of control. By October 1920, many General Motors managers were having trouble raising cash to pay invoices and payrolls, and in that month the company had to borrow $83 million from banks in short-term notes. Durant's personal financial difficulties compounded the seriousness of this perilous situation. Trying to support the market price of General Motors stock, Durant had by this time borrowed $30 million from bankers to buy the company's stock. (Durant used General Motors stock as the collateral for his borrowing.) Despite his efforts, the price of the stock continued to drop, and Durant could not repay his debts.

In late November 1920, Durant resigned as president of General Motors, never to return to the company. The Du Pont Company and the J. P. Morgan Company stepped in to assume Durant's debts and to take over most of his General Motors stock. Pierre S. Du Pont, recently retired from the Du Pont Company, became the new president of General Motors.

In saving and then rebuilding General Motors, Du Pont was greatly assisted by Alfred P. Sloan, Jr. A graduate of the Massachusetts Institute of Technology, Sloan went to work in 1895 for Hyatt Roller Bearing, a company making metal antifriction bearings for a wide variety of manufacturers. Something of an engineering and managerial genius, Sloan rescued Hyatt from imminent bankruptcy (aided by an infusion of cash from his father) and became the company's president. As Hyatt began to produce a growing proportion of its bearings for the automotive market, Sloan became concerned about its future independence. Realizing that Hyatt's prosperity depended on the whims of just a few major customers, Sloan arranged to sell Hyatt to General Motors. When this agreement was completed, Sloan became a vice president and major stockholder in General Motors.

Frustrated by Durant's chaotic way of doing business, Sloan prepared an "organization study" that contained a plan to revamp the management of General Motors even before the crisis of 1920. Durant ignored the plan, but Pierre Du Pont and others in top management adopted it at an executive committee meeting on December 30, 1920. This plan introduced a rational system of decentralized management to General Motors by clearly delineating the duties and responsibilities of the head office and the divisions and by providing for effective communications among the different parts of the company. Sloan's goal was to combine divisional autonomy with supervision by a strong central office. Over the next four years, Du Pont and Sloan labored to put this organizational plan into practice, modifying parts of it as they proceeded. By 1924, it was fully implemented.

They began with significant changes in their company's management at the operational level. For the first time each division—

Buick, Cadillac, Chevrolet, and the many others—became clearly defined by a distinct product line. Market segmentation in modern industrial firms, in fact, began at General Motors. As the automobile market matured, Sloan and Du Pont recognized the need to differentiate their cars from each other and from those of their competitors. So they eliminated overlap in the prices, products, and markets of the divisions. No longer did they compete with one another in selling their cars and other goods to the American public; each aimed at a precise market segment defined by price. Advertising and annual model changes identified each make of car. Run by a general manager, each division possessed its own engineering, production, and sales organizations, and each enjoyed a considerable degree of freedom in its daily operations, though not as much as had been the case under Durant. To ensure cooperation and coordination in the work of the divisions, Du Pont and Sloan created the office of group vice president. Freed from specific daily operating responsibilities, the group vice presidents supervised the work of related groups of divisions and helped set policies for the entire company. Four groups were established: accessories, affiliated companies, export, and car and truck. The officers in these divisions and groups were line officers.

Sloan and Du Pont also created a strong central or head office (today called the corporate office) for General Motors. General officers, working through executive and finance committees, coordinated the work of the four groups, made policy decisions for the company, and planned for its future. In doing so, they were assisted by a vastly enlarged staff made up of financial and legal experts. Neither the general nor the staff officers concerned themselves with daily operating matters.

To try to arrive at cooperation and understanding between management in the divisional and the central offices, a number of interdivisional relations committees were established. Officers from all levels belonged to these and met at regular intervals to discuss common problems. Both staff and divisional engineers, for instance, composed the general technical committee that sought solutions for common engineering problems the different divisions encountered in designing and producing cars.

Finally, Sloan and Du Pont, borrowing from earlier advances made at the Du Pont Company, established solid financial reporting and statistical controls at General Motors. In doing so, they created a model still followed by modern corporations. Like the officers of the Pennsylvania Railroad fifty years before, those in the head office of General Motors found the possession of statistical information to be absolutely essential for rational decision making. Three innovations made the collection and analysis of this information feasible. First, the central office received weekly and monthly production reports from each group and division. Under Durant, no such data had been available. Second, the central office received reports every ten days from dealers on how many cars were actually being sold, and this information made market forecasting possible (the ten-day period of reporting sales is still the standard period in the automobile industry). Finally, the work of each division was assessed by the central office, using new accounting techniques that measured its rate of return on investment, making it easier for those on top to decide where to expand or contract the company's operations. Figure 8.5 outlines how this sophisticated system of decentralized management worked.

The decentralized management system instituted at General Motors by Du Pont and Sloan generally worked well. The company's share of the American automobile market rose from 19 per cent in 1924 to 43 per cent three years later, by which time its annual net profit amounted to an impressive $276 million. The Great Depression provided the acid test for the new organization. Although sales fell by two-thirds between 1929 and 1932, the corporation reacted quickly to the situation and continued to show a profit and to pay dividends every year throughout the 1930s. With only minor changes, the decentralized management structure pioneered in the early 1920s remained the basic administrative framework of General Motors through the 1970s. Sloan continued as the firm's president until 1937 and as its chairman of the board for an additional nineteen years, after which he stepped down to devote the rest of his life to philanthropy. He died in 1966 at the age of ninety.

The Spread of Decentralized Management

Both the Du Pont Company and General Motors switched to decentralized systems of management when their operations became diverse and complex, but they were hardly the only ones. The more complex and diversified their products and markets became, the more likely companies were to employ decentralized management systems modeled on those of Du Pont or General Motors. Diversity of operations, not sheer size, was the factor most likely to cause the adoption of decentralized management. As noted at the beginning

Figure 8.5
General Motors' Decentralized Management Structure in 1924

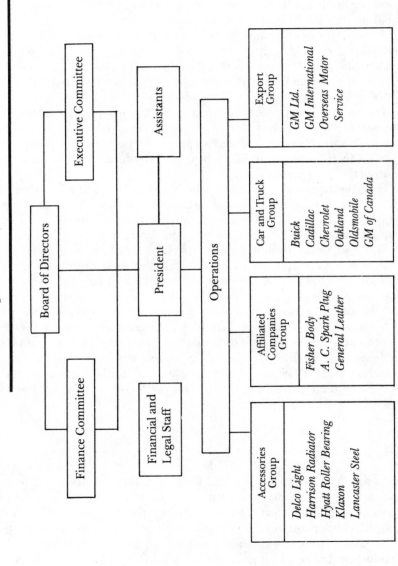

SOURCE: Adapted from *Management and Administration* 7 (May 1924): 525.

of this chapter, structure followed strategy; that is, a company's growth strategy was very likely to influence its management structure.

Companies in three fields most readily established decentralized management systems. In the electrical industry both General Electric and Westinghouse moved beyond making equipment to generate electric power and light by diversifying into the production of a broad range of appliances for consumers. As they entered new consumer markets, they set up decentralized management systems whose divisions were based on product lines—Westinghouse did so in 1934, General Electric in 1950. Growth and diversification in the chemical industry led Hercules and Monsanto to follow Du Pont's lead in adopting decentralized management before World War II; other chemical companies did so after the conflict. The power machinery and automobile industries also witnessed some spread of decentralized management. After investigating the General Motors experience, International Harvester followed suit in 1943. However, only after World War II did other major companies, Chrysler and Ford among them, turn to decentralized management.

Not all big businesses adopted decentralized management systems. Those whose product lines and markets remained relatively simple and few in number usually did not. For them the functionally departmentalized system of centralized management developed by Standard Oil and other companies in the late nineteenth century remained sufficient. Companies in the metals industries, for example, retained centralized management structures. Copper companies—American Smelting & Refining, Anaconda, Kennecott, and Phelps Dodge—and nickel companies such as International Nickel turned out just a few types of products for well-defined markets. With no need to alter their management methods, they kept centralized management systems in place. Steel companies, most notably United States Steel, and aluminum companies, such as Alcoa, did partially adopt decentralized management as they diversified their products, but none went as far as Du Pont or General Motors.

Henry Ford and Ford Motors

More was involved in decentralization than the logic of products and markets. Personalities played an important role too in determining the speed with which businesses set up decentralized management systems. Entrepreneurs who had built up their companies from scratch—people like Durant at General Motors—were often

This 1914 photograph, taken outside the Ford Highland Park factory, shows the final assembly stage as workers attach a car body, which has just slidden down a ramp, onto the Model T chassis. Henry Ford developed the assembly line that lowered the price of his Model T dramatically over the years. (Henry Ford Museum)

reluctant to share responsibility and authority with others. They continued to try to run their companies as one-man shows long after the complexity of their operations suggested that decentralized management might be more appropriate. Henry Ford was such a business leader.

In technology, Ford was very innovative. Building on the earlier efforts of many industrialists to speed the flow of work through their factories, he brought the concept of assembly-line production to maturity, first applying it to the production of his Model N in 1908. The parts needed to assemble the car were laid out in sequence on the factory floor, the car frame was put on skids and pulled along by a tow rope until the axles and wheels were attached, and the car was then rolled from work station to work station until fully assembled. With the Model N, Ford established the cardinal principle of assembly-line production: the work goes to the worker; the worker does not waste time and energy moving to different places. Ford developed this system fully with the building of the Model T, his most famous car. At his new Highland Park plant in Detroit, he installed continuous conveyor belts in 1913–1915 to carry materials to the assembly lines, and added still further refinements with the construction of his gigantic River Rouge complex just southeast of Detroit in the early 1920s. Along the assembly lines, single-purpose machines, similar in concept to those developed in the federal armories ninety years earlier, worked the metal in making the parts for the cars. By 1927, when production of the Model T finally ended, 15 million of them had rolled off the assembly line.

His technical accomplishments won Ford renown at home and abroad, and he became a popular folk hero. In 1916, even though he refused to campaign, Ford won the presidential preference primary of the Republican party in Michigan. A few years later, Ford-for-President clubs sprang up spontaneously across the United States; they collapsed only when Ford announced his support of Warren Harding. Ford was equally well known outside of America. Germans referred to mass production as "Fordismus," and Adolf Hitler once remarked, "I am a great admirer of Ford. I shall do my best to put his theories into practice." In the Soviet Union, which purchased 25,000 Fordson tractors between 1920 and 1927, Russians named agricultural communes and even babies after him.

Yet, Ford was a complex man. He could be obtuse and irrational. He was a virulent anti-Semite. He associated Jews with bankers, whom he hated, and denounced them in a newspaper he owned. He suspected academics and considered "book-learning" impractical; for years no one with a college degree could get a job at Ford Motors. The person most responsible for bringing modern mass production to the world, Ford yearned for what he imagined were simpler times in the past. He built Greenfield Village, a collection of historic shops and homes, near Detroit to bring his version of the past alive. He even tried to revive square-dancing, which he viewed as more civilized and wholesome than the bunny hug, Charleston, and fox trots of the 1920s. (At one point Ford hired a dance instructor for his executives, constructed a ballroom in the engineering laboratory, and kept an orchestra in permanent attendance to play for company officials on his demand.)

Above all, Ford was stubborn. He was determined to run Ford Motors by himself with no outside interference. He bought out minority stockholders, refused to participate in federal plans for industrial recovery during the Great Depression, and violently opposed attempts by the United Auto Workers to unionize his company. (Ford Motors was not unionized until 1941, several years after the other automobile companies.) Ford's stubbornness and his unwillingness to share managerial authority with others nearly destroyed Ford Motors.

The post–World War I recession found Ford Motors, like General Motors under Durant, overextended. Henry Ford was in the process of both building his River Rouge production complex and purchasing stock the Dodge brothers held in his company. By April 1921, Ford needed $58 million, but he had only $20 million available. To raise cash quickly, he took several steps. He forced his dealers to buy Model Ts for cash, even though they could not sell them, or risk losing their Ford dealerships. He sold every nonessential tool and fixture in the company, including 600 telephones. Finally, he fired half of his middle managers, office force, and engineers. Ford saved his business in the short run, but the steps he took to do so nearly ruined the company in the long run.

By the late 1920s, Ford Motors was a company in decline. The Model T had become outdated and, lacking enough good engineers, Ford was slower than its competitors to introduce new cars. In addition, the company had marketing problems. Henry Ford envisioned the Model T as a "universal car," good for all people for all times. He did not understand that as the automobile market matured, people would want a broader range of cars to choose from, and so he lagged far behind General Motors in introducing a full line of cars. Moreover, Ford's dependence on single-purpose machines made it difficult for the company to retool for new car lines. When Ford finally ceased production of the Model T in 1927, it had to scrap or change one-half of its 32,000 machine tools—a situation that helped delay the introduction of the Model A for nearly two years. By way of contrast, General Motors, which relied more on general-purpose machinery, made model changes much more easily.

Even more basic were managerial difficulties. Ford Motors had grown too large and complex for Henry Ford to run by himself, but he was unwilling to share responsibility with others. The result, as at General Motors under Durant, was chaos. There was little coordination among the purchasing, productions, and marketing departments. Market forecasting was almost nonexistent, being based on the informal comments of dealers. Asked about the gains Chevrolet was making at one point in the 1920s, Ford characteristically replied, "I don't know how many cars Chevrolet sold last year. I don't know how many they may sell next year. And—I don't care."

These weaknesses deeply wounded the company. Once the industry leader, Ford Motors trailed other companies in new-car sales by

1936. In that year, General Motors had 43 per cent of the American market, Chrysler had 25 per cent, and Ford had only 22 per cent. And, unlike General Motors, Ford Motors incurred losses throughout the 1930s. Difficulties continued into the 1940s. Because of its paucity of engineers and middle managers, Ford Motors experienced more trouble than other automobile companies in converting to wartime production. By 1945, when Henry Ford stepped down as president of Ford Motors in favor of his grandson, Henry Ford II, the company was losing millions of dollars each month.

Henry Ford II reversed the company's decline in the postwar years. He brought in new managers, many of them from General Motors, to rebuild the firm's organizational structure. One of his most effective moves was the hiring of the "Whiz Kids," a group of ten former air force statistical analysts. This group included Robert McNamara, who became president of Ford Motors and, later, secretary of defense under President John Kennedy. These men brought modern management methods to Ford Motors for the first time. Henry Ford II also presided over the introduction of new car lines that caught the imagination of the American public and sold well: Mustang, Maverick, Pinto, and others. Finally, he increased his company's involvement in the world marketplace. Under his leadership, Ford Motors regained second place among America's automobile companies and, at times, challenged General Motors, the industry leader.

Multinationals

Yet another form of diversification undertaken by U.S. corporations was represented by the spread of multinational operations. A multinational corporation is a company that does business in more than one country. It is usually defined as a firm having direct investments in the form of productive installations, such as plants and factories rather than just sales outlets, abroad. Although U.S. multinationals experienced rapid expansion after World War II, their growth began much earlier.

Even before World War I, the United States possessed some fairly well-developed multinational enterprises. U.S. multinationals had considerable foreign investments in mining, manufacturing, agriculture, and oil by 1914. In fact, the total direct foreign investment of U.S. companies comprised a sum equal to 7 per cent of the GNP of the United States, about the same proportion as in the mid-1960s, although U.S. multinational enterprise had not yet assumed its modern shape. Because of their later start, U.S. multinationals still trailed those of Great Britain, France, and Germany in terms of total overseas investments. Moreover, most American investments were in areas close to the United States—in Canada, Mexico, the Caribbean Islands, and Central and South America. As yet, United States companies had relatively few direct investments in Europe, Asia, or Africa.

Between 1914 and 1930, U.S. multinationals continued to expand their operations. As we have seen, the United States emerged as the chief creditor nation of the world during and immediately after World War I. It was during this time that U.S. multinationals began successfully challenging European, and especially British, businesses over growing areas of the globe. United States investments in Canada exceeded those of Great Britain for the first time in 1922, and by 1929 the investments of United States companies in Latin America had also surpassed those of Great Britain. American investments expanded in Asia and Africa, as well, but the most noticeable change occurred in Europe. The direct investments of American businesses in Europe nearly doubled during the 1920s, until by the close of the decade they were nearly as great as those of U.S. companies in Canada or South America and were larger than the sums invested by U.S. firms in the Caribbean. In short, as the economy of the United States prospered, American companies continued to push overseas.

The years of the Great Depression and World War II, however, witnessed a slowdown in the activities of U.S. multinationals. The decline of the world's economy combined with the destruction of American property overseas during the war restricted multinational expansion. By 1946, the direct foreign investment of U.S. multinationals had fallen to an amount equal to only 3.4 per cent of the United States GNP, a proportion considerably lower than that of thirty years earlier. Further expansion of multinationals had to wait until the postwar years.

THE PROFESSIONALIZATION OF BUSINESS

The Divorce of Ownership from Management

Alterations in the character of business leaders paralleled the changes in their companies. As big business began maturing, a separation between management and ownership took place, as many of the original founders—people like Durant, Carnegie, Rockefeller, and Armour—retired from the active control of their businesses. In most cases, managers who owned little stock in their companies replaced the owner-managers. This divorce between ownership and management became noticeable in the railroads by the 1870s and 1880s and in many large industrial ventures by the 1920s and 1930s. As early as 1914, Walter Lippmann, a leading American journalist, observed, "The real news about business is that it is being administered by men who are not profiteers. The managers are on salary, divorced from ownership and from bargaining."

As the growth strategies of America's leading companies altered, the backgrounds of their executives also changed. Before 1920, executives who had backgrounds in manufacturing ran a majority of the nation's hundred largest companies. By 1949 the situation had been dramatically altered. Personnel with backgrounds in sales, finance, and general management had largely replaced those in manufacturing as the presidents of the firms—reflecting the increasing importance of the domestic consumer market for the companies. Not everything changed, however. The leaders of big businesses continued to be white males. Opportunities for women and minorities to become executives remained limited to small peripheral firms, many of which continued to be family operations.

The garment industry was a case in point. Entry into the manufacture of clothing required relatively small amounts of capital. As part of the peripheral economy, the garment industry offered opportunities for advancement to women. Ida Rosenthal and her husband started Maidenform as a family business in the 1920s to manufacture a new product, brassieres. By the same token, Nell Quinlan, with her husband's support, formed a company to make stylish but inexpensive clothing for women to wear at home under the label of Nelly Don. By the 1920s, the company was grossing as much as $3.5 million annually.

Blacks also sometimes found opportunities in markets overlooked or spurned by large center firms. As in the years before World War I, black businesses often had more than profits as their goal. They also sought to build up the black communities within which they operated. In 1913, Herman Perry of Atlanta founded the Standard Life Insurance Company, developing it as one of the nation's largest black insurance companies in just a few years. From his base in insurance, Perry branched out into real estate, publishing, banking, construction, and many other fields in the early 1920s. Poor management led to the collapse of many of these enterprises in the mid-1920s (Standard Life passed into white hands), but some survived this crisis to form the basis for black business advances in Atlanta in later years. Black entrepreneurs formed the Chicago Metropolitan Assurance Company in 1925. In addition to employing blacks as clerks and agents, this insurance company benefited Chicago's black community through its involvement in the operation of a black radio station, magazine, professional baseball team, and ballroom.

The shifts in the management of companies, especially the divorce of ownership from management, raised questions about corporate goals. Corporations had traditionally been seen as devices to earn profits for their owners, who also ran them. The divorce of ownership from management introduced uncertainties into this way of thinking, especially for the new corporate managers. Since they no longer owned the companies they ran, the managers questioned whether simply trying to earn maximum profits for themselves and their stockholders could serve any longer as their sole or primary goal in business. Searching for new identities and for new sources of approval for their actions, many corporate managers began looking upon themselves as professionals.

The Meaning of Professionalism

When they called themselves professionals, business executives usually had several things in mind. They meant, first of all, that they possessed the technical expertise, the competence, to operate successfully the large, complex businesses that were replacing the simpler enterprises of earlier times. A study analyzing the family origins of 9,000 business leaders in 1932 lent some credence to this assertion. It found that 32 per cent were college graduates and that nearly 45 per cent had taken at least some college classes. The study showed, however, that only 7.3 per cent had received formal business training in college, and it concluded that little correlation existed between a college education and success in the business world. (The study also showed that over half the business leaders came from families with backgrounds in business or the professions. Rags-to-riches success stories remained the exceptions to the rule for advancement in American business.) A corollary of the belief by business leaders that they had the type of education and training needed to manage the businesses of their day was their contention that the general public, which did not have this education and training, should leave business and economic matters in their hands. In referring to themselves as professionals, business executives also meant that they were more than money-grubbing profit seekers. They intended, they said, to operate their businesses in ways beneficial to all Americans. Like other professionals—lawyers, doctors, and clergy—they would serve society.

For some, service meant simply making available to Americans products of good quality at reasonable prices. Henry Ford exemplified this type of business executive when he promised: "I will build a motor car for the great multitude. It will be large enough for the family but small enough for the individual to run and care for . . . it will be so low in price that no man making a good salary will be unable to own one." For a growing number, however, service meant more than providing good products at low prices. It meant, as well, mediating the conflicting desires of different interest groups in American society. Elbert Gary, the president of the United States Steel Corporation, took this point of view. In 1921, he defined corporate management as a "position of balance" between "investors, employees, employers, consumers, or customers, competitors, and all others who may be interested in, or affected by, the actions or attitudes of the managers." He went on to observe that "the management of the corporation . . . must have constantly and uppermost in mind the rights and interests of the general public."

Professional Education

Central to business leaders' identification of themselves as professionals was the possession of a professional education. Technical training in finance and business administration gave them, they claimed, the tools needed to manage the complex enterprises of their day. A professional education also, they asserted, broadened their outlook on life and helped them understand the connections between business and the rest of American society. Although, as we have seen, most business leaders remained self-educated in the 1920s and 1930s, they aspired to recognition as professionally educated men.

The University of Pennsylvania established the first collegiate school of business in the United States with the creation of the Wharton School of Finance and Economy in 1881. Other business schools soon appeared at the University of California (1898), the University of Chicago (1898), Dartmouth (1900), the University of Wisconsin (1900), Washington and Lee (1906), Harvard (1908), Northwestern (1908), and Columbia (1916). A tremendous explosion of collegiate education in business followed in the 1920s. By 1928, 89 universities and colleges enrolled 67,000 students in business courses. Growth in business education slowed during the Great Depression, but by 1940 some 110 business schools enrolled over 100,000 students.

These pioneers in business education were probably most successful in imparting technical skills—accounting, finance, and the like—to their students. Few succeeded in giving them a broad outlook on the place of business in society. Most courses were too narrowly conceived and presented. It is hard to imagine, for instance, that New York University's courses on "Principles of Dress," "Hosiery and Underwear," and "Window Display" did much to raise the consciousness of the students who took them.

Professional Ethics

Business executives also sought recognition as professionals by formulating codes of business ethics in which they promised they would act in a responsible manner toward each other and the American public. The most far-reaching of these was the "Principles of Business Conduct" issued by the United States Chamber of Commerce in 1924. Principle 13 of this code expressed the idea of business serving society: "The primary obligation of those who direct and manage a corporation is to its stockholders. . . . Notwithstanding this, they act in a responsible capacity, and in such a capacity owe obligations to others—employees, to the public which they serve, and even to their competitors." Within one year, over 750 business organizations with 300,000 members had approved these principles.

Business practices did not, however, change strikingly. It is true that cutthroat competition lessened as many industries matured and became oligopolistic. But, too often statements of business ethics, particularly those concerning relations between businesses and their customers, were simply hot air. Investigations into business practices undertaken by the federal government in the 1930s showed that the public had often been deceived in the 1920s. The codes were for cosmetic effect, nothing more. In fact, the development of public relations paralleled the rise of advertising in the 1920s, and both were designed to sell business and its products to the American public. Public relations firms deliberately presented business in a favorable light; their purpose was to convince Americans that their nation's businesses were serving society.

Community Affairs

As self-appointed trustees for society, business leaders and their companies became deeply involved in community affairs. It was in the Progressive Era and the 1920s that business service clubs such as the Rotary and the Kiwanis were formed and spread across the nation. Also in this period corporate giving to philanthropy began replacing donations by individual business people. Women formed the National Federation of Business and Professional Women's Clubs in 1919. In the 1920s local welfare federations, community chests, hospitals, and universities started depending heavily on organized corporate philanthropy for the first time. By 1929, some 350 cities possessed community chests to raise funds for philanthropic causes, and these organizations relied mainly on businesses for their support.

The spread of corporate philanthropy raised some questions still worth pondering today. For what purpose does a corporation exist—to make a profit, to serve society, or some combination of the two? Does management have the right to give corporate earnings away to charity rather than to reinvest them in capital improvements or to pay them out as dividends to stockholders? Might society not benefit more from the strong economy made possible by capital improvements than by business giving to charity? Could business giving insidiously influence American values and institutions, since businesses give only to those organizations whose ideals and work they approve? Finally, who decides the priorities of large, wealthy firms, now for the most part under the control of a separate class of professional managers?

The Public Image of Business

During the 1920s, the public generally did perceive business leaders as professionals. The seeming success of the assembly line in bringing material goods to a growing number of Americans won them a high degree of respect. As we have seen, Americans have generally admired business executives, but at no time has this admiration been greater than in the 1920s. One of the best-sellers of the decade was *The Man Nobody Knows*, written by Bruce Barton, a leading advertising executive. A biography of Jesus Christ, the book pictured Christ as a successful businessman who "picked up twelve men from the bottom ranks of business and forged them into an organization that conquered the world." As the public accepted business leaders as professionals, they replaced lawyers, doctors, and clergy on the boards of trustees of universities and on the vestry boards of churches across the United States.

With the coming of the Great Depression, however, this prestige eroded. Americans blamed business people for the hard times, especially when corporate philanthropy failed miserably to help those out of work. Then, too, federal investigations into business practices and ethics revealed that they were not as sound as business leaders claimed. Joseph Kennedy, the father of John, Robert, and Ted, summed up the prevailing mood. Placed in charge of the newly created Securities and Exchange Commission in 1934, he noted that "the belief that those in control of the corporate life of America were motivated by honesty and ideas of honorable conduct was completely shattered."

The prosperity of the war years of the 1940s largely redeemed American business people in the eyes of the public. Most businesses converted fairly smoothly to wartime production, and as unemployment disappeared, Americans became less critical of their nation's business leaders and business system. Business executives regained much of the prestige they had lost in the 1930s, but they would never again be held in the high esteem of the 1920s.

THE NEW MANAGEMENT OF AMERICAN BUSINESS

The 1920s, 1930s, and 1940s were pivotal years in the development of business management in the United States. As American companies diversified their products and markets, their systems of centralized management proved inadequate to handle the growing complexity of their operations. Led by Du Pont and General Motors, some corporations introduced decentralized management systems better suited to their shifting needs and developed further the systems of financial controls, especially cost accounting, first pioneered by railroads in the nineteenth century. As some of their markets matured, they came to depend on market segmentation and new forms of advertising to sell their goods. As management structures and methods changed, so did the nature of the men running America's big businesses. Management was divorced from ownership, and a growing number of business leaders came to think of themselves as professionals who had a duty to serve society.

The crises of these years, the two world wars, and the Great Depression brought changes not just to individual companies but also to government-business relations. Just as they sought rationality and predictability by redesigning their management structures and reworking their relationships with society, the companies also revamped their relationships with the federal government as part of this search for security. A new type of association between business and government emerged, one that has lasted, with some changes, to the present day.

Selected Readings

Alfred D. Chandler, Jr., has written extensively on the historical evolution of the diversified, decentralized company in the United States. His *Strategy and Structure* (Cambridge, Mass.: MIT Press, 1962) analyzes the adoption of decentralized management by General Motors, Du Pont, Standard Oil of New Jersey, and Sears, Roebuck. His *Pierre S. Du Pont and the Making of the Modern Corporation* (New York: Harper & Row, 1971), written with Stephen Salsbury, provides a detailed look at managerial change within the Du Pont Company. Arthur Kuhn, *GM Passes Ford, 1918–1938* (University Park, Pa.: Pennsylvania University Press, 1986), compares the development of management systems at Ford and General Motors. Alfred P. Sloan, Jr., *My Years with General Motors* (New York: Macfadden-Bartell, 1965), explains how and why General Motors adopted decentralized management. Mira Wilkins, *The Emergence of Multinational Enterprise: American Business Abroad from the Colonial Era to 1914* (Cambridge, Mass.: Harvard University Press, 1970) and *The Maturing of Multinational Enterprise: American Business Abroad from 1914 to 1970* (Cambridge, Mass.: Harvard University Press, 1974), are the standard histories of American multinationals.

Specific studies examine particular aspects of business enterprise. Allan Nevins and Frank Hill give a detailed business history of Ford Motors in their three-volume account: *Ford: The Times, The Man, The Company, 1865–1915* (New York: Scribners, 1954); *Ford: Expansion and Challenge, 1915–1933* (New York: Scribners, 1957); and *Ford: Decline and Rebirth, 1933–1962* (New York: Scribners, 1963). A shorter account is Roger Burlingame, *Henry Ford* (New York: Alfred Knopf, 1955). James Worthy, *Shaping an American Institution* (Urbana: University of Illinois Press, 1984), looks at Sears, Roebuck. David Mowery, "Firm Structure, Government Policy and the Organization of Industrial Research: Great Britain and the United States, 1900–1950," *Business History Review* 58 (Winter 1984): 504–531, is an excellent examination of research and development efforts.

Several good books examine the relationships between business and society. On the development of advertising see Roland Marchand, *Advertising the American Dream: Making Way for Modernity, 1920–1940* (Berkeley, Calif.: University of California Press, 1985). On public relations see Richard Tedlow, *Keeping the Corporate Image: Public Relations and Business, 1900–1950* (Greenwich, Conn.: JAI Press, 1979). Morrell Heald investigates the professionalization of business in *The Social Responsibilities of Business: Company and Community, 1900–1960* (Cleveland: The Press of Case Western Reserve University, 1970). Alexa Benson Henderson, "Herman E. Perry and Black Enterprise in Atlanta, 1908–1925," *Business History Review* 61 (Summer 1987): 216–242, examines the career of an important black business leader. Philip Burch, Jr., *The Managerial Revolution Reassessed: Family Control in America's Large Corporations* (Lexington, Mass.: D. C. Heath, 1972), argues that many big businesses continued to be family-controlled, even after World War II.

IMPORTANT EVENTS, 1918–1945

1918   The Armistice of November 11 ends World War I.

1919–1920 The steelworkers' strike is defeated.

1920   Congress returns railroads to private control.
The U.S. Supreme Court affirms the "rule of reason" allowing oligopoly.

1921   Herbert Hoover is appointed secretary of commerce.

1922   Protectionism reaches new heights under the Fordney-McCumber tariff.

1929   The Wall Street crash triggers the Great Depression.

1932   Congress establishes the Reconstruction Finance Corporation to provide relief to banks and railroads.

1933   Unemployment peaks; the banking system collapses; Franklin D. Roosevelt launches the New Deal with a "bank holiday."
The Glass-Steagall Act regulates banks.
The National Recovery Administration begins "codes of fair competition."
The Business Council is formed to advise the New Deal.

1934   The Securities and Exchange Commission is established.

1935   The National Labor Relations Act grants workers the right to organize and belong to unions.

1936   The Robinson-Patman Act protects small retailers.
John Maynard Keynes explains the causes of the Great Depression.

1937   Sit-down strikes sweep some industries.
The Supreme Court upholds the National Labor Relations Act and ends traditional restrictions on federal regulation of business.

1941   The nation again faces a war-mobilization crisis.

1942–1945 Both trade unions and businesses gain economic benefits from wartime mobilization policies.

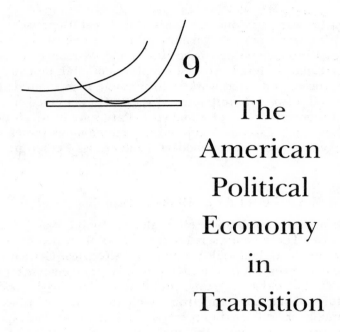

9 The American Political Economy in Transition

The crises of world war and severe economic depression affected America's political economy no less than the nation's business system, permanently changing the relationships between the federal government and business. When the United States entered World War I in 1917, the federal government had taken only the first steps toward regulating business. At the end of World War II in 1945, it had instituted a limited welfare state and recognized new responsibilities for promoting the material well-being not only of business firms but of other groups as well.

The steps of this transition were fraught with sharp ideological clashes regarding the proper role of government in controlling business firms. The steps included bitter and sometimes violent conflicts between industrial workers and their employers. The transition began and ended with the U.S. participation in World Wars I and II, crises in which the survival of the nation was at stake. Between the wars was another crisis: the Great Depression of the 1930s, the worst business calamity ever. The depression paralyzed industrial production, destroyed banks, and devastated the nation's workers who suffered from unemployment and despair. These crises aroused industrial workers to promote their interests (secure wages and jobs). The responses to these crises resulted in a more powerful government and a limited welfare state in which business firms and their executives enjoyed less autonomous power as U.S. public policy tried to accommodate the interests of other groups.

FROM WAR TO PEACE, 1918–1921

The American mobilization effort during World War I had been impressive. The military services had raised an armed force of 4.7 million men and deployed it in time to help defeat Germany. Business and government had devised effective arrangements for retooling industry and redirecting the flow of industrial goods and foodstuffs to the European front. With the return of peace, business and labor both tried to preserve the benefits of that experience in the postwar political economy, and some public officials suggested making permanent the wartime policies of government direction of economic affairs.

Labor and the Postwar Economy

The sudden U.S. declaration of war in 1917 created a crisis of industrial mobilization that presaged what many hoped might become a more powerful position for labor in the American economy. The federal government struck a new arrangement with trade unions: in return for a pledge to refrain from strikes and to cooperate in achieving full industrial production, the unions were to have the right to organize the workers in the nation's industrial plants. This arrangement triggered a chain of events in which workers tried to enlarge their power to influence wages and working conditions permanently. The culmination was a bitter strike in the steel industry, which ended in defeat for the union movement in 1920.

In 1917 and 1918, the federal government empowered the National War Labor Board (NWLB), a special agency set up for the emergency, to oversee this arrangement. The NWLB actively mediated disputes between employers and employees. It prevented employers from continuing their peacetime antiunion policies, and in firms that had a particularly hostile record toward unions, the board established "work councils" in an attempt to prevent disputes from disrupting production. All told, the NWLB mediated disputes in 1,100 plants affecting 711,500 employees during the war. In two well-publicized incidents, when Western Union, the country's largest telegraph firm, and Smith and Wesson, a Massachusetts gunmaker, balked at NWLB policies, the agency took them over, installing public officials to manage them for the duration of the emergency.

These wartime policies awakened hopes in the trade unions that the postwar political economy would include an "industrial democracy" in which workers, like businesses, would enjoy the rights of association and the ability to influence wage levels through the process of collective bargaining. To try to realize these hopes in the postwar economy leaders of the American Federation of Labor decided to concentrate their resources on the nation's steel industry. Under the leadership of Elbert H. Gary and the United States Steel Corporation, that industry had successfully eradicated the remaining vestiges of union influence during the prewar years. But the war crisis seemed to promise federal support, for the first time in history, for the union cause.

Union leaders realized that the steel industry was central to the industrial economy, and they thought that if they could establish a union in it, they could proceed to organize other basic mass-production industries that theretofore had also successfully resisted collective bargaining. So in the summer of 1918, encouraged by the policies of the NWLB, AF of L organizers began the slow process of signing up steelworkers for the cause. When the war ended in November, government encouragement ceased. Nonetheless, the union organizers decided to proceed, rallying members with a plea for the eight-hour day and forty-eight-hour workweek. (The twelve-hour day was the standard in the steel industry at the time.) The organizers met bitter, sometimes violent resistance from the steel companies and local government officials sympathetic to them, who equated unionization with Bolshevism. (Lenin's Bolshevik faction had seized power in Russia late in 1917, founding the USSR and threatening to spread the Russian Revolution elsewhere.) As was the case with almost all manufacturers, steel executives adamantly supported the open shop.

When the confrontation occurred in the steel industry, the workers were defeated, and the drive to unionize large industries was turned back for over a decade. In September 1919, a special steelworkers' organizing committee of the AF of L called a strike of the nation's leading steel firms. Steel management bitterly resisted the strikers, refusing to negotiate with them; on several occasions, the firms called on the police, who violently broke up the strikers' picket lines and meetings. The steel firms eventually hired strike-breakers to enter the mills under armed guard, and the firms managed to restore production by Christmas. Finally, on January 8, 1920, recognizing that its resources were exhausted and that the strike had failed, the union asked its supporters to return to work. This outcome ensured that labor-management relations in mass-production industries would remain much as before the war, with management still able to dictate the terms of employment to workers and conflict thus continuing between them. The strike revealed that the peacetime federal government was unwilling to perform a neutral role in industrial disputes or to grant labor the same privileges of associational activity enjoyed by business.

The drama of the steel strike overshadowed another development that threatened, as a result of wartime experiences, to upset the capitalist organization of the American economy. When the nation's railroad firms were unable adequately to coordinate service during the intense mobilization demands of 1917, the federal government had assumed control of the carriers, placing their management under the United States Railroad Administration (USRA). This temporary wartime agency fundamentally altered the economic relationships associated with that vital industry. Underlying federal operation was the theory that disinterested public servants might be better able than private owners to provide the nation's shippers and passengers with efficient, low-cost transportation service. In practice, the USRA, in order to achieve the cooperation of railroad workers, substantially raised wages and, by appointing union leaders to high posts, granted workers' representatives an active voice in determining personnel policies.

After the war, William G. McAdoo, who had served as director-general of the railroads in 1918, proposed that Congress continue government operation to see if the wartime efficiency could be extended to peacetime. The railroad unions countered by proposing the "Plumb Plan." This plan, developed by a union attorney, Glenn Plumb, suggested that a federal corporation, with equal representation from management, workers, and the public, operate the nation's carriers permanently. Supported by workers in other trades, the railroad unions agitated for the plan but were unable to obtain a sympathetic hearing in Congress. The Transportation Act of 1920 returned the railroads to private operation under ICC regulation. Congress also charged the commission with the task of developing a policy for the consolidation of rail firms so that they might operate more efficiently.

The political economy of the postwar decade did not undergo any of the fundamental changes the labor movement favored—not the operation of the railroads along socialist lines nor union recognition nor collective bargaining. The war years saw a rise in union membership that peaked in 1920 at over 5 million workers. But with the defeat of the steel strikers and the failure of the Plumb Plan, militant union activity receded, and membership declined in the 1920s, ebbing to a low of 3.4 million in 1930, or 6.8 per cent of the nonagricultural work force.

Welfare Capitalism

In the 1920s, most business leaders, as we have seen, rejected the idea of bargaining with the labor unions. Instead, under the leadership of the National Association of Manufacturers, they tried to break them with considerable success. Rather than accept unions, some businesses promoted the concept of welfare capitalism. By welfare capitalism they meant that the businesses, not independent trade unions, should look after the best interests of the workers.

As developed by leading businesses, welfare capitalism encompassed a broad range of activities: housing, educational, medical, religious, and recreational facilities for employees, profit-sharing plans, and retirement pensions. Welfare capitalism often also involved improvements in working conditions, higher wages, and the establishment of company unions. Although company unions were of some help in improving working conditions, they were not allowed to bargain collectively on behalf of workers with management on such fundamental issues as wages and hours of work. Company unions were effectively controlled by management, were limited to individual companies, and mainly provided avenues of communication between management and workers.

From the point of view of management, welfare capitalism was one way to make the business world predictable and rational. It kept workers loyal to their companies while only slightly raising labor costs. Most important, it kept independent unions, which most business executives saw as a disturbing element, at bay. Workers were less enthusiastic. They correctly viewed it as a very paternalistic system that left management in control of their lives. When

changes in federal law finally gave workers the chance to form independent unions of their own choice during the 1930s, they gladly
did so. In the 1930s, welfare capitalism faded away, as the federal
government and newly organized mass industrial unions—the
United Auto Workers, the United Steelworkers and the like—
assumed responsibility for the welfare of labor.

Business and the Postwar Economy

Just as labor had sought to preserve wartime changes that allowed a
larger role for associational activity and a greater ability to manage
economic uncertainties, so too did business firms and their organizations. The federal government had fostered trade associations
during the war; it had also suspended the antitrust laws in the interests of achieving rational, managerial coordination of the flow of
goods and capital in the business system. The War Industries Board
in particular had encouraged trade associations to form in industries where none had existed, so that officials in Washington would
have organizations of business firms to help them achieve economic
mobilization. The result was the evolution of a system of "open
prices" wherein trade associations fixed prices and thwarted competition in the interests of maximum efficiency.

Led by the Chamber of Commerce, American business leaders
worked to preserve those arrangements in the postwar world. The
War Industries Board lapsed with the coming of peace, but the
Chamber of Commerce led an effort to have its price-fixing functions shifted to a new Industrial Board within the Department of
Commerce. The president of the Chamber of Commerce observed
that it was a foregone conclusion that the regulation of business
was in the offing, a fact that deserved "cordial acceptance by organized business." Regulation, in his view, would involve a suspension
of the antitrust statutes and result in "agreements between businessmen in the public interest." The Chamber of Commerce
wanted a system of cartels, agreements among firms to cooperate
and administer prices.

The Chamber of Commerce was unsuccessful in realizing the
thoroughgoing cartelization of the American business system. Business leaders, however, were able to prevent a complete dismantling
of associational agencies and programs. Business associations
thrived in the postwar years even though they enjoyed no formal
rights of price administration. Trade association spokesmen adeptly
explained to the public and elected officials alike that they repre-

sented a "new individualism" of cooperative activity in the service of the public, exchanging information, eliminating waste, fostering labor-management harmony, enlarging the benefits of product standardization, and in general improving the efficiency of the business system and thereby the prosperity of the American people. In their view, cooperation, including price fixing, produced social benefits impossible to achieve under unbridled competition among firms.

This view of cooperation received a boost when the Supreme Court broadened its "rule of reason" doctrine in a 1920 case involving United States Steel. Refusing to break up the steel giant, the Court ruled that it was legitimate, under the law, for a firm to achieve dominance in its industry, so long as that firm did not prevent competition from occurring. In other words, a firm was allowed to remain an oligopoly if it allowed smaller firms to exist in the same industry. The net effect of this ruling was that the tendency toward merger remained largely unchecked in the American business system in the years to come.

HERBERT HOOVER AND THE ASSOCIATIVE STATE

One of the major supporters of business associations in the postwar years, and a significant figure in the American political economy, was Herbert Hoover. The son of a Quaker blacksmith in Iowa, Hoover was orphaned at the age of ten. Sent to live with an uncle in Oregon who later made a fortune in real-estate speculation, the young Hoover obtained a degree in geology at Stanford University in 1895. He then went on to make his own fortune in mining engineering projects around the world—earning fame as "the great engineer"—and his success convinced him that the key to uplifting and improving human society lay in the systematic application of rational principles to human affairs.

Hoover also became known as "the great humanitarian." The outbreak of World War I in August 1914 had found him in London wealthy but politically uninvolved. The horrors of the war prompted Hoover to organize relief measures for war-torn Europe, and when the United States entered the war in 1917, President Wilson pressed him into government service as his wartime food administrator. Hoover became enormously popular in the United States during the war because he exuded a traditional American faith in the value of every individual and a devotion to humanitarian causes. He was among the American leaders impressed by the accomplishments of the war effort; wartime mobilization taught him that individuals could, on their own accord, act in the public interest.

President Warren G. Harding appointed Hoover secretary of commerce after the 1920 election, and he proved to be an especially adept leader, building the Department of Commerce into a major federal agency and devoting his considerable energy and talent to promoting cooperation among businesses and between business and the government in the name of greater efficiency and prosperity. As commerce secretary, Hoover attempted to put into action his belief in communal cooperation and his commitment to the dignity of the free individual. This attempt confronted Hoover with a dilemma: how to reconcile and preserve the benefits of collective action, through trade associations, giant firms, or other bureaucracies, and guard the right of individual freedom. Hoover solved this problem in part through rhetoric, blending opposites like "cooperative competition" and referring to the "higher freedom." Aside from rhetoric, however, Hoover initiated programs intended to stabilize the economy while maintaining individual autonomy, a political economy that characterizes an "associative state." Hoover expected government officials and trade association leaders to clarify desirable objectives and expected individual Americans voluntarily to pursue them. In this vein, he worked actively with peripheral firms to have them cooperate in rationalizing their industries.

Hoover and Trade Associations

Trade associations were essential to this conception of a modern political economy; they were the institutions through which Hoover hoped to blend the benefits of collective action with the traditions of individual freedom and achieve the advantages of both worlds. Under Hoover's leadership, the Department of Commerce worked to restructure important features of the mobilization agencies while adapting them to the peacetime economy. Trade associations, especially those of peripheral firms, closely linked to government agencies were to become the bellwether institutions in the new "cooperative competition" that Hoover, other government leaders, and business spokesmen desired in the new political economy.

Hoover believed that the government should act as a source of up-to-date, scientifically derived business information and use that information to provide leadership for private business action. Under this direction, the Department of Commerce, as well as other economic agencies, developed information of all kinds—data on markets, supplies, production costs, and prices. The development and dissemination of such information was meant to help business conserve resources, eliminate waste, and standardize their products—all of which, when obtained, would result in an efficient business system.

As we have seen, one way in which business persons achieved these goals was through vertical integration and merger. Combinations among business firms thus were a common feature during the 1920s, as the United States experienced its second major merger movement. By the end of the decade, giant firms dominated important industries, and automobile, electrical, communications, and mass-distribution firms joined the list of integrated companies directing operations through managerial, as opposed to market, mechanisms.

Despite the growth of center firms in the American business system of the 1920s, important industries remained in which thousands of small firms interacted through the invisible hand of the market. Coal mining, textiles, clothing, and cement were examples of industries in which vertically integrated center firms did not prevail. Hoover looked to these peripheral firms to help build a new political economy as well. The Commerce Department generated information that individual business executives, in private associations with one another, were encouraged to use in practical ways to bring managerial order out of the chaos and inefficiencies of unbridled competition.

The cement industry illustrates Hoover's belief that it was possible to develop the benefits of cooperation while protecting the autonomy of the independent small firm. The manufacture of cement was geographically dispersed, and the relatively low level of capital investment required for a single cement plant allowed an ease of entry that forestalled domination by center firms. Under Hoover's leadership, the Department of Commerce worked closely with a trade association, the Cement Manufacturers' Protective Association, to analyze costs and set prices. The Supreme Court invoked the antitrust statutes to forbid outright price fixing, however, so the government disseminated cost and price information through the trade association. The system worked so well that when other agencies requested sealed bids for construction projects, the supposedly competing cement manufacturers submitted bids that were nearly identical.

Hoover's vision of new business arrangements was widely shared in the 1920s. State and local governments developed partnerships between executive agencies and private associations that permanently reshaped the political economy. The decade saw an expansion of governmental services, as well as government staffs and budgets, in the cities and states. Highway departments developed close relations with contractors, cities' service departments with real estate promoters, and so on. Especially noteworthy were state and local policies that institutionalized businesses like real estate, pharmacy, and medicine through licensing laws that set standards, restricted entry, and, among other matters, allowed a system of price controls for essential services.

Hoover and the Economy

In the 1920s, some Americans believed that the nation had developed a new "people's capitalism" capable of generating higher and higher plateaus of prosperity. Business, professional, and government leaders forged new partnerships that narrowed the areas in which unchecked market forces could govern business relationships, convinced as they did so that their actions still preserved the essential attributes of individualism, that they were reducing, if not eliminating, the human hardships that accompanied downturns in the business cycle while ensuring that prosperity would permanently advance.

Although from its inception the American economy had generated ever higher levels of material wealth, downturns in the business cycle were, as we have seen, inevitable if undesirable realities. Theoretically, government controls could be used to tame the business cycle, but such manipulation ran contrary to the American tradition of private action and individual freedom. Through associational activities, guided by government policies, Hoover and others thought they had found a desirable compromise mechanism for controlling the American economy.

A central idea of this approach was to control the overall fortunes of the American system by influencing individual business decisions. Hoover was confident that private organizations, especially the National Bureau of Economic Research founded in 1920, could show individual businessmen how decisions made with the public interest in mind could smooth the ups and downs of the volatile business cycle. While awaiting this enlightened state of affairs, the trade associations and individual firms should cooperate with social workers and philanthropically minded leaders to devise welfare programs to improve the lives of workers and their families and provide the means for softening the human impact of any business downturns that materialized. Businesses were encouraged to agree to maintain wage rates and share available markets among themselves and available jobs among their employees. Hoover and his advisers tried, unsuccessfully, to have trade associations develop reserve funds to invest in case of a business downturn, thereby stabilizing the business cycle. Governments likewise could invest in public facilities to ensure relatively even economic growth.

Even as the 1920s witnessed Hoover's innovations regarding the business cycle and the trade associations, however, his were not the only policies having an impact on business. Three other features of government-business relations were noteworthy. First, the tariff, traditionally such an important point of contention, reached new heights of protection under the 1922 Fordney-McCumber law. The return to traditional protectionism was mitigated to some extent by a widespread agreement that duties should be adjusted by administrative, not legislative, action. The tariff commission could recommend changes in duties of up to 50 per cent after investigating business needs and the nation's trade relations. Second, Secretary of the Treasury Andrew Mellon, one of the world's wealthiest men, worked to have federal taxes on business and personal income, taxes which had risen during World War I, substantially reduced. Mellon and his supporters believed that higher rates of investment and therefore greater prosperity would result. Finally, during the preceding decade would-be reformers had succeeded in enacting a constitutional amendment that forbade the manufacture and sale of alcoholic beverages. By declaring certain business activities—brewing and distilling were major industries—illegal, the reformers expected Americans, aided by enforcement and educational programs, to attain the public interest goal of an alcohol-free society. Prohibition during the 1920s was evidence of a popular willingness to place unprecedented restraints on business enterprise. Although alcohol consumption declined remarkably under the law, some business leaders, especially the Du Ponts of Delaware, who disliked the amendment, successfully obtained its repeal in 1933, arguing in part that prohibition was a dangerous antibusiness precedent.

THE GREAT DEPRESSION

The ideas and institutions of the associative state met their greatest test after the Wall Street crash of 1929, and failed. As the crash evolved into the Great Depression, President Hoover tried to apply his principles of voluntary cooperation. He called on experts from the government and private life to help him identify the public interest and then implored businesses to act accordingly. However, these efforts could not withstand the acute crisis that the crash caused in the American banking system. Banks that were unable to convert their assets to cash as a result of the collapse of stock values and real-estate prices went out of business, with customers losing their deposits. As private investment declined, so did employment, and the weaknesses in the American economy by 1931 contributed to similar crises in Europe. In the United States, people saw a lifetime of careful saving disappear behind the closed doors of banks, millions of workers lost their jobs, and business firms either went bankrupt or had to scramble frantically to readjust payrolls, inventories, and investments in order to survive. As the depression deepened, more Americans, including the very trade associations and business leaders with whom Hoover had been attempting to build a new political economy, repudiated the president's policies.

Shortly after the crash, Hoover called the nation's business leaders to the White House and informed them that the public interest required the maintenance of prices and wages. Although not all businesses were willing to cooperate, the Chamber of Commerce encouraged its members to follow the president. The construction industry, through its trade association, tried to obtain pledges for new or expanded construction projects, while federal agencies speeded up government building projects. But by the end of the year, despite a temporary upturn in business and continuing exhortation from the White House, business activity began diverging from the president's goal. Investments, inventories, and jobs fell off; the collapse of the securities markets and the failure of banks contracted the money supply. Desperate times seemed to call for new approaches.

One new approach was the establishment of the Reconstruction Finance Corporation (RFC) in 1932. Congress, responding to the urgings of the nation's bankers and realizing that large infusions of public capital might alleviate the situation, modeled the RFC on a wartime agency that had helped finance the production demands of mobilization. Congress authorized the RFC to lend up to $2 billion

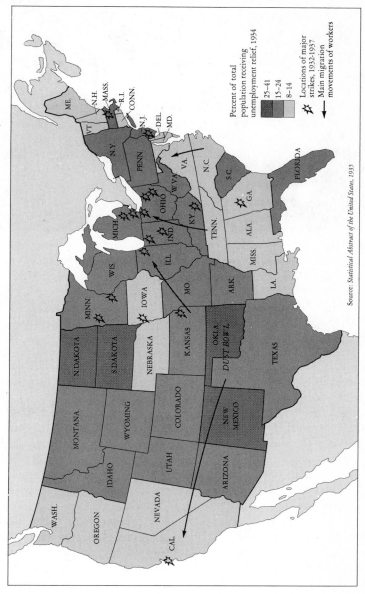

Map 9.1
The Great Depression
SOURCE: From John P. McKay et al. *A History of Western Society*, 3rd ed. Copyright © 1987 by Houghton Mifflin Company.

Percent of total population receiving unemployment relief, 1934

25–41
15–24
8–14

Locations of major strikes, 1932–1937

Main migration movements of workers

Source: *Statistical Abstract of the United States, 1935*

This is one of the best-known photographs of the 1930s. The billboard was erected by a business association trying to rehabilitate the reputation of American capitalism; the bread line ironically shows a failure of American capitalism in human terms. From this failure emerged the very New Deal programs that had such a significant impact on American business. (Margaret Bourke-White, LIFE Magazine, copyright 1937, Time Inc.)

to banks and other credit institutions and to the railroads. As the creditor of last resort, the federal government tried to provide desperately needed relief to American business.

The president agreed to the RFC, as well as other distress measures, but did so reluctantly, worrying that individual freedom might become permanently impaired. Moreover, his policies came under increasing attack. There were cries for a return to laissez-faire policies and government retrenchment from traditionally minded business executives and politicians who believed that the economy's natural business cycles had built-in, self-correcting mechanisms that, left to run their course, would eventually result in an upturn. On the other hand, some business groups, especially the Chamber of Commerce, called for a suspension of the antitrust statutes and a revival of the government-directed business planning of World War I. The Chamber of Commerce wanted business to decide on "codes of fair competition" that would allocate available markets, fix prices, and establish minimum wages—all under government supervision and enforcement. Hoover, however, rejected both approaches. The Chamber of Commerce's proposal went against his belief in voluntary action while resorting to unfettered market forces abrogated his responsibilities to act in the public interest.

Meanwhile, the Great Depression deepened. "I know there were students actually starving," remembered one survivor of undergraduate life in the 1930s at the University of Kansas. "There was a biological company that would pay a penny apiece for cockroaches," he recalled, "and some students went cockroach hunting every night." Like this man, most Americans who lived through the 1930s remembered the decade as a period of hard times, and with good reason. Between 1929 and 1932, 110,000 businesses failed in the United States, and industrial production fell by one-half. By the winter of 1932–1933, at least one-quarter of the work force was unemployed, some 14 million people, with many others employed only part-time. In the last weeks of the Hoover administration, the nation's banking system started to collapse when borrowers defaulted and frightened depositors suddenly tried to withdraw funds. In state after state, governors were forced to declare "bank holidays"—a suspension of banking transactions altogether—in a desperate attempt to stave off the complete collapse of public confidence and to help those banks that remained sound to solve their own problems.

THE NEW DEAL

Franklin D. Roosevelt

In the midst of economic crisis, the American electorate rejected Herbert Hoover in favor of Franklin D. Roosevelt in the presidential election of 1932. Roosevelt's background was sharply different from Hoover's. Roosevelt, like his distant cousin Theodore, came from a well-to-do family and was by profession a politician. He had served as a member of the New York legislature and as assistant secretary of the navy during World War I before running for vice president on the unsuccessful Democratic ticket in 1920. Roosevelt had, especially after being crippled by polio in the early 1920s, a warmth toward individuals who suffered and a conviction that democracy and capitalism must be made to work. Roosevelt

*On the way to his inauguration in 1933, Franklin
D. Roosevelt attempts conversation with a glum
President Herbert Hoover. Roosevelt's inauguration
marked a turning point in U.S. history, for the new
president was prepared not only to have the federal
government help nonbusiness groups of Americans
achieve a greater measure of economic security but
also sometimes to reject the political wishes of business leaders. (The Bettmann Archive)*

had been elected governor of New York in 1928, so he entered the
White House an experienced politician.

Roosevelt exuded warmth and charm, qualities that Hoover
lacked in public. Roosevelt was also flexible, willing to try new approaches to the nation's crisis. During the campaign of 1932, he
had promised the American people a "new deal" but had been
vague about what proposals would be forthcoming either for restoring prosperity or for a new political economy. With his inauguration in 1933, however, Roosevelt and the Democratic congressional
majorities unleashed bold new initiatives, and as the new public
policies that came to characterize the New Deal evolved in the
1930s, a substantial change occurred in the relationships among

business, commercial agriculture, labor, and the federal government. Federal programs eased the human suffering of unemployment, reduced the number of unemployed workers, and restored confidence that the American business system could once again provide for the material well-being of the American people.

Restoring Confidence in the Business System

In his inaugural address, the new president tried to instill hope. Roosevelt's message rang clearly: "The only thing we have to fear is fear itself." In his first action as president, Roosevelt ordered a national bank holiday. Next, working from plans developed by officials in Hoover's Treasury Department, the new administration presented Congress with emergency banking legislation to provide for federal inspectors to examine the closed banks and allow those that were sound to reopen. This action calmed nervous depositors and forestalled further runs to withdraw currency from the staggering banking system. Subsequently, the government instituted a system of federal deposit insurance to assure depositors that even if a bank failed, their personal accounts were secure. These actions were crucial to the effort to restore public confidence in the nation's business system. Now the banks, following federal regulations and supervised by Treasury Department auditors, could make investment capital available without fear of long lines of frightened depositors.

Efforts to restore the banking system meant a new program of federal regulation, which also extended to the securities industry. Widespread suspicion about the manipulation of stock and bond prices by securities dealers and speculators had long existed, suspicions that the Wall Street crash had only increased. An investigation of the banking and securities industries conducted by a Senate committee from 1932 to 1934 showed grounds for those suspicions. The committee's lawyer, a Sicilian immigrant named Ferdinand Pecora, uncovered widespread unethical practices among the nation's most prominent bankers and securities dealers. After the Wall Street crash, for instance, Charles E. Mitchell of the National City Bank secretly made available $2.4 million of bank funds to bank officers, without collateral or interest payments, to enable them to speculate in the market. In the course of this investigation, Congressman Sam Rayburn of Texas expressed the concern of many: "When a people's faith is shaken in a business the business becomes halting and lame. . . . Only one thing can follow in the wake of this destroyed confidence . . . the evils that attend socialism, bolshevism, and communism."

One result of the committee's revelations and the collapse of the banking system prior to Roosevelt's inauguration was the Glass-Steagall Banking Act of 1933. The law, which bankers generally favored, strictly regulated banks by requiring them to keep the Federal Reserve Board informed of the amount and nature of all their loans and investments. To prevent the competition that Congress believed had led banks toward insolvency, the law forbade the payment of interest on checking accounts, and it gave the Federal Reserve Board the power to set maximum interest rates on savings accounts. Commercial and investment banking were separated, and commercial banks were forbidden to underwrite or deal in securities other than those issued by state and local governments. Subsequently, the Banking Act of 1935 gave the Board of Governors of the Federal Reserve System central authority to control interest rates and the nation's money supply.

Other legislation in 1933 and 1934 restored popular faith in the paper instruments so essential to the conduct of the modern American business system. The Federal Securities Act required full disclosure of new securities issues offered to investors and the registration of those issues with the federal government. The Securities and Exchange Commission, set up in 1934, licensed stock exchanges, regulated trading, and prohibited price manipulation. The government began to control the margin rates (the amount of money a person could borrow to buy stocks) in an effort to contain the rapid changes in the prices of securities.

Although government officials, looking for practical means of making the banking and securities industries function effectively and achieve public favor during the worst crisis in their history, initiated the reforms, business leaders helped shape the laws. As the first chairman of the Securities and Exchange Commission, Roosevelt named Joseph P. Kennedy, a successful Boston speculator and father of a future president. Although there was occasional grumbling by business people who now had to confront a new set of regulations issued by a new federal bureaucracy, Kennedy was by and large successful in achieving compliance with both the spirit and the letter of the new regulatory system. "We of the SEC," Kennedy noted soon after his appointment, "do not regard ourselves as coroners sitting on the corpse of financial enterprise. On the contrary, we think of ourselves as the means of bringing new life into the body of the security [sic] business."

The National Recovery Administration

The new president and his supporters were willing to go much further than the changes in the banking and securities industries in trying to reform the American business system permanently. One of the first measures of the New Deal, albeit a temporary one, was the creation in 1933 of the National Recovery Administration (NRA). With the NRA, initially conceived as the centerpiece of Roosevelt's new program, the New Deal reformers hoped to reconstruct the government-business partnership that had mobilized the economy during the crisis of World War I and use it to solve the domestic crisis of depression.

This new government-business partnership involved codes of fair competition, a kind of planning. The goal of the NRA was to suspend the antitrust laws and have federal officials cooperate with business leaders from the trade associations to write rules that allocated available markets among firms, fixed prices, and ensured minimum wages and decent working conditions for labor. The so-called codes of fair competition replaced competition with price fixing according to rational plans enforced by government power. The intended result was to be a planned industrial system involving both center and peripheral firms (there were separate New Deal programs for agriculture).

After Congress established the NRA in 1933, Roosevelt appointed General Hugh Johnson, who had earlier served the War Industries Board, to head the agency. In flamboyant style, Johnson exhorted the various industries to draw up the fair competition codes. Calling for business's cooperation, Johnson explained that the codes would "eliminate eye-gouging and knee-groining and ear-chewing in business. Above the belt any man can be just as rugged and just as individual as he pleases." His call got results: 3,665 codes were proposed (Johnson cut the number to 981). There were codes for major industries dominated by center firms and codes that encompassed peripheral firms in lesser industries. Burlesque theater operators even wrote a code that limited the number of performances. All these codes were designed to prevent the overproduction of goods and services and the consequent pressures for price cutting that threatened to bankrupt firms and increase unemployment.

The NRA was an unprecedented intrusion of federal authority into the business system, at least in peacetime. Not only were the codes difficult to write, given the complex networks of economic relationships in the American business system, but the idea of having the government enforce them was questionable on constitutional grounds. So Johnson chose to use the force of public opinion, not police power, to encourage recalcitrant firms to sign codes. The NRA chose a blue eagle as its symbol. Merchants agreeing to a code were to display the eagle, and cooperating manufacturers to use it as a symbol on their goods. In parades and rallies the NRA encouraged Americans to purchase only items displaying the blue eagle and only from those merchants who showed it. Johnson wanted to arouse a patriotic fervor reminiscent of wartime to stimulate all Americans to a cooperative effort to rationalize and reform the business system so that the nation could recover from the hard times.

The entire NRA effort was soon stuck, however, in a quagmire of disputes that belied the agency's vision of cooperation in the public interest. Patriotic cooperation among business firms with competing interests was not forthcoming. Moreover, opposition arose from consumers, who soon came to view the NRA as a grand exercise in gouging and price fixing. Conflicts also arose between management and labor. The law creating the NRA had guaranteed rights of unionization and collective bargaining, which workers demanded and management resisted; a rash of strikes ensued. By 1934, business executives were beginning to complain about undue federal intervention in private affairs even though that intervention was intended to save the business system from its worst excesses. By the end of 1934, the NRA was all but dead, a victim of the mistaken belief that it was possible, in the absence of a visible enemy, to rally a diverse nation with a long tradition of individual freedom and managerial prerogative to cooperate in the name of the public good.

Searching for new measures to correct the flaws in the American political economy that had produced the depression, the federal government in 1935 launched a new measure, the National Labor Relations Act, that indelibly changed the relationships between the business community and industrial workers. Meanwhile, deciding on a suit brought by Schechter Poultry Company of Brooklyn, New York, the Supreme Court declared the NRA unconstitutional in 1935. The Court ruled, in part, that the NRA's poultry code could not apply to a local processor under the interstate commerce clause of the Constitution. In those industries where the business leaders involved saw code agreement as desirable—such as coal mining and oil production—separate legislation continued the arrangements begun under NRA auspices.

Labor and the Political Economy of the New Deal

The bargaining relationships between American management and labor began to shift fundamentally in the 1930s, partly because of the militancy of millions of men and women seeking to gain the control over their wages, hours, and working conditions that was possible only through collective action. These changes were also a result of the willingness of New Deal political leaders to respond to the unionization impulse positively. Never before in peacetime had there been an administration willing to place the authority of the federal government on the side of collective bargaining. Because the economic crisis was so deep and threatened to be permanent, politicians, led by Senator Robert Wagner of New York, sought to restore vigor to the business system by granting workers the means, through unions and collective bargaining, of increasing their share of the nation's wealth. In doing so, they would of course be purchasing the products of their own industrial handiwork and would, it was hoped, stimulate a permanent recovery.

In the broadest sense, the new labor relations that emerged in the 1930s resulted from the strong feelings of class consciousness that the depression experience aroused. America's material wealth had always been distributed unevenly, but now, with unemployment a fact and layoffs an ever-present threat, American industrial workers acted on the basis of the reality that their immediate economic interests were sometimes fundamentally at odds with the desire of management to control production costs through low wages and long hours.

One result of these new perceptions and attitudes was the National Labor Relations Act of 1935. This law granted workers the right to form unions of their own choice with leaders and treasuries independent of management, and it required business to agree to collective bargaining. The Wagner Act, as the law was popularly known, established procedures whereby a federal agency, the National Labor Relations Board, could assure workers of their rights and enforce the law against any firm that resisted. Due in large part to the actions of countless industrial workers and the dedication of their union leaders, it now was federal policy to allow workers the same advantages of association as those enjoyed by business.

Not surprisingly, the implementation of this new labor policy occurred only after a protracted struggle. Management resisted the Wagner Act in the courts, and, until the Supreme Court affirmed its constitutionality in 1937, argued that it violated the Constitution.

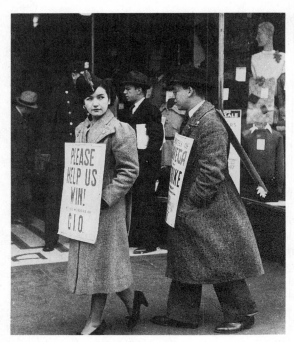

*These strikers, members of a union affiliated with
the CIO, were typical of American workers in 1937,
who were determined to win the collective bargaining rights allowed them by New Deal legislation. (Library of Congress)*

In the meantime, large-scale labor struggles broke out, especially in
the mass-production industries employing large numbers of unskilled and semiskilled men and women. In those struggles, management typically resisted the unions with every means at its
disposal, including the use of armed force in localities where local
officials were sympathetic. The most dramatic strikes occurred in
1937, before the Supreme Court's decision, in the automobile
industry. Workers there, seeking to have General Motors and
Chrysler obey the new Wagner law, occupied strategic factories in
sit-down strikes instead of leaving and setting up picket lines. Management could not dislodge the workers without risking the destruction of factories. Finally, in part because of fears of the public-
relations cost of further resistance, General Motors and Chrysler
signed collective bargaining agreements. Ford, on the other hand,

faced with the same worker militancy but without a sit-down strike, employed informers and armed guards to keep the union out, with violence if necessary. During 1937, over 400,000 industrial workers disrupted business by participating in over 450 sit-down strikes.

The movement to unionize mass-production industries remained unfinished by the end of the 1930s. Even where the unions succeeded in forcing management to sign a collective bargaining agreement, management invariably insisted on maintaining the principle of the open shop: contracts applied only to the men and women who had joined the union, and other workers were free to negotiate their own terms. Management hoped thus to weaken the unionization impulse by dividing workers from one another and to assure themselves of a supply of labor in the event of a strike. In spite of management resistance, however, workers established strong unions in virtually all of the nation's mass-production industries. On the eve of World War II, over 8.7 million American workers, or 15.8 per cent of the nonagricultural work force, belonged to unions. More than any other single factor, its labor policy earned the New Deal the animosity of business executives in every region and in every industry.

The New Deal and Small Business

Even though New Deal reformers witnessed the failure of business cooperation through government-inspired codes of fair competition and earned the hostility of employers with the National Labor Relations Act, they did not abandon policies intended to help particular segments of the business community and to restore prosperity. After 1934, the president and his advisers tried to find ways of restricting the power of large corporations within the business system as a means of reinvigorating the economy. While still willing to grant subsidies to important industries and to use the Reconstruction Finance Corporation to assist in the modernization of plants, the government began to focus its interest on helping smaller enterprises survive in a system that had increasingly come to be dominated by giant firms.

Two policies especially sought to help peripheral firms. The Robinson-Patman Act of 1936 took aim at the price discrimination that large retailers and chain stores could exercise against independent small merchants by forbidding manufacturers and wholesalers from giving preferential discounts to their biggest customers. Another law strengthened "fair-trade" measures by which manufacturers fixed prices on goods to protect the profits of small dealers. More threatening to corporate America, however, was the renewed vigor with which Roosevelt's administration began to apply the antitrust statutes in 1937. The Department of Justice began to pursue large oligopolistic center firms in the courts. In the end, however, few practical results were obtained before the mobilization demands of World War II called an effective halt to the new antitrust efforts.

Business Opposition to the New Deal

As the new political economy evolved in the 1930s, a growing chorus of complaint began to be heard from American business leaders and their organizations. Prior to the 1930s, business allegiance had been divided between the Democratic and Republican parties, but by the end of the decade, business rested solidly in the Republican camp. Some New Deal measures, especially the NRA, were initially popular among important elements of the business community, and others, such as the regulation of the securities industry, were clearly in the long-range interests of the business system. But because the New Deal responded favorably to the demands of other groups, especially industrial labor, it—and President Roosevelt—became increasingly unpopular among business executives by 1934 and 1935.

Policies supporting collective bargaining were not the only New Deal programs that affronted business. In 1933, the New Deal launched a major program to develop hydroelectric power in the Tennessee River Valley. The overseeing body, the Tennessee Valley Authority, was a public corporation, and it sparked bitter complaints from privately held utility firms that feared that federal investments in the generation and sale of electricity threatened traditional capitalism. The Roosevelt administration also devised large-scale programs of temporary public employment and work relief. And in 1935, Congress enacted the Social Security law to provide old-age pensions, unemployment compensation, and aid to the indigent and their children. Although these measures did not directly threaten business, the perceived beginning of a limited welfare state went contrary to the traditional beliefs in rugged individualism that many business leaders espoused. Moreover, in spite of Roosevelt's constant concern over unbalanced budgets, the New Deal programs increased federal deficits modestly and threatened business firms with higher tax levies.

Business leaders expressed their opposition to Roosevelt and the New Deal in speeches, editorials, resolutions, and campaign contributions. By the time of the 1936 election campaign, the Liberty League, a political group organized by executives from Du Pont and General Motors, was outspending even the Republican party in trying to unseat the president. In his campaign for reelection, Roosevelt responded mercilessly. The president railed against "economic royalists" who took "other people's money." At the close of the campaign, Roosevelt told a crowd of supporters roaring their approval that the wealthy business interests—"the forces of self-ishness and of lust for power"—had "met their match" in the Roosevelt White House. "I should like to have it said of my second administration that in it these forces met their master." For the first time in the nation's history, the sharp polarization over the political economy resulted in the reelection of a president (for Roosevelt won by a landslide in 1936) who owed few political debts to business firms and associations and who was in a political position that allowed the possibility of confrontation between the federal government and the nation's largest corporations.

Corporatism Survives

Such a confrontation never really materialized, although Roosevelt did use his power on occasion against business. There were significant exceptions in the general business opposition to Roosevelt, and business still exerted influence on federal economic policy. As vitriolic as some spokesmen for local chambers of commerce, the resolutions of trade associations, and the private comments of wealthy bankers and industrialists were, the tradition of corporatism survived and even expanded during the New Deal. Moreover, the Roosevelt administration felt that receiving the counsel of business leaders on economic policy was desirable. In 1933, the Department of Commerce formed the Business Council, a group of forty to sixty top executives who chose their own membership, to advise the federal government on the best ways of achieving permanent economic recovery. From this advisory relationship there gradually emerged by the middle of the 1940s mechanisms by which leaders of the nation's wealthiest banking and industrial corporations helped shape federal policy toward the economy.

The Business Council became the chief means by which corporate executives influenced policy in the 1930s. Although some executives quit the council in response to the government's new labor policies, others, led by men like W. Averell Harriman of the Union Pacific Railroad and Gerard Swope of General Electric, stayed on, forming committees to advise government officials on particular policies and providing a conduit to the White House. The council was especially influential in the framing of the Social Security Act of 1935. Business leaders helped to write a self-financing program of old-age pensions that were graduated according to the individual's earnings before retirement. The effects were to ensure that the retirement program did not redistribute income from wealthy to less wealthy Americans (as some reformers proposed) and to create a new social institution—retirement—that would remove older persons from the work force, in favor of creating job opportunities for younger, presumably more vigorous workers. Similarly, the unemployment compensation provisions of the new law, while requiring employers to pay insurance premiums, reduced those costs for firms that enjoyed relatively low layoff rates. Like old-age pensions, unemployment insurance was to be self-financing and thereby kept within strict limits.

Responses to Keynes's Economic Theory

One of the most important influences on attempts to understand and deal with the political economy in the 1930s and later had British roots. In 1936, the British economist John Maynard Keynes published *The General Theory of Employment, Interest, and Money,* a book that challenged widely held convictions about economics. Before Keynes expressed his ideas, classical economists argued that the business cycle contained its own self-correcting mechanisms. Investments produced prosperity as firms built new plants and purchased durable goods. When a downturn in the business cycle occurred, in this view, interest rates eventually dropped and stimulated new investments, returning the economy to prosperity.

Keynes showed that this idea was inaccurate. Investments of capital, he reminded his readers, relied on savings, and the Great Depression had exhausted savings. Without a pool of capital available for investment, and with low levels of consumer demand providing little incentive for investments in any case, it was possible for the business cycle to flatten at an undesirably low level. The only recourse was government intervention with policies aimed at stimulating investment, thereby putting men and women back to work, making it possible for them again to save and provide the private sector with capital. Employed men and women would demand goods and services, thereby providing incentives for businesses to invest.

Keynes outlined three courses of action that government could take. He thought of these actions in an ascending order of desirability. First, government should control interest rates. Once it had control over the cost of capital, government could adjust interest rates downward when the economy was slackening. If controlling interest rates proved insufficient, government should follow a second course of using taxes to redistribute income and enlarge the market for goods. Taxing the wealthy to benefit the poor would make it possible for more people to buy more goods. When businesses saw sales opportunities and realized that government was keeping the cost of capital low, firms would invest in new plants or operate their factories more fully, stimulating prosperity. Finally, Keynes argued, when interest-rate controls and income redistribution failed to stimulate desired investment levels, governments must augment private investments with public investments. In his eyes, traditional notions of balancing governmental budgets in a depression were misguided; government deficit spending was necessary to make up for insufficient levels of consumer demand and private investment.

Keynes's ideas about deliberate deficit government spending as a means of stimulating consumption and moving the economy out of depression provoked the most controversy. Americans had traditionally relied on private decisions regarding investment, confident that individuals trying to benefit themselves helped the general economy. In the 1920s, for example, recognizing the human problems associated with downturns in the business cycle in a society that was urban and industrial (where few citizens could be even close to self-sufficiency in sustaining their lives), Secretary of Commerce Hoover had encouraged businesses to increase their investments when prosperity faded into depression. Now, however, Keynes's ideas threatened both the faith in private decisions and the economic power of wealthy men and firms. Public investments for social purposes (dams, hospitals, housing for the poor, and the like) were seen by those advocating Keynes's point of view as both desirable in human terms and necessary for the nation to achieve and maintain prosperity. Keynes's ideas, in other words, could be, and were, interpreted to challenge the authority and power of American business, especially the bankers and managers responsible to the wealthiest corporations.

Disagreements over Keynes's ideas began in the first year of the New Deal. Observing the calamity of the worldwide depression and recognizing the importance of decisions in the United States to recovery, Keynes on his own initiative tried to influence American opinion and Roosevelt's policies. He published an open letter to the president, conferred with administration officials, and met with Roosevelt in 1934. The president's reaction was negative. "He left a whole rigamarole of figures," he told Secretary of Labor Frances Perkins. "He must be a mathematician rather than a political economist." Some of Roosevelt's advisers, however, were more receptive to Keynes's ideas. Business had partly revived under the New Deal, but when the economy dipped into a serious recession in 1937 and 1938, the advisers were able to persuade Roosevelt to accept a Keynesian strategy, less on the grounds of economic theory than on the proposition that government spending would help the unemployed Americans who had suffered for so long. By 1938, however, Roosevelt was having difficulties persuading Congress to follow his lead, and in the end the New Deal never adopted a recovery program modeled on Keynes's ideas. Instead, huge government investments in defense (and later for World War II) began in 1940 to moderate and eventually to end the depression. The issues raised by Keynes resurfaced, as we shall see in Chapter 11, toward the end of the war as American leaders worried about a peacetime return to depression.

The Supreme Court and the New Deal

The judicial branch of the federal government held much of the responsibility for the fundamental shift in government-business relations that occurred in the 1930s. As we saw in Chapter 6, the U.S. Supreme Court had ruled in 1895 that the federal government could not regulate manufacturing. The Court considered manufacturing by itself an intrastate affair and thus not subject to federal jurisdiction. Other Court decisions in the decades after 1895 also discouraged federal attempts to regulate business. In 1935, for instance, it ruled the NRA codes unconstitutional because they also regulated intrastate commerce.

Then in 1937 the Supreme Court dramatically reversed itself in a case testing the constitutionality of the Wagner Act. The Wagner Act provided for government-supervised elections within factories to determine whether or not workers wanted a union and, if so, which union they preferred. Management, resisting the trade union movement with every means at its disposal, challenged the law in the courts, claiming that such elections were entirely local affairs beyond the purview of Congress under the interstate commerce clause. The government lawyers defending the Wagner Act argued that although the elections were local, the affected firms were tied to the national and international economic system. The Wagner Act's defenders expressed the view that the modern American industrial economy was so intertwined that what occurred in one location had an impact in other locations. The strict distinction between intrastate and interstate commerce seemed not to fit modern industrial conditions. The majority of the justices agreed and upheld the Wagner Act. The court's decision meant that a decades-long struggle to define the meaning of the interstate commerce clause was over. After 1937, Court doctrine allowed Congress to pass legislation affecting every aspect of the conduct of business in the United States.

In a sense, thus, the most lasting impact of the New Deal on government-business relations was constitutional. As early as the Gilded Age, some Americans had argued that Congress must take steps to govern business in the industrial age. Important new areas of federal regulation were in fact developed, especially in the Progressive Era. But federal power had always been checked by judicial interpretations of the Constitution. After the New Deal court cases, however, Congress was free from the traditional strict interpretations of the Constitution and could choose to regulate nearly every aspect of business behavior. The range of public policy issues potentially affecting business was thereby widened by the end of the 1930s.

BUSINESS AND WORLD WAR II

World War II broke out in Europe on September 1, 1939. President Roosevelt immediately began seeking public support of policies to improve American defenses and ultimately to help defeat Nazi Germany. The United States did not declare war until after the Japanese attack on Pearl Harbor on December 7, 1941. In the meantime, the military services began to prepare for war, Congress began appropriating funds for war goods and enacted a draft law, and Roosevelt called a halt to reform initiatives in favor of gaining the full-fledged cooperation of industrial leaders. By 1942, enormous government expenditures for the war effort were promoting dramatic economic expansion and permanently affecting the structure of the American business system.

Mobilizing Industry

During this second wartime crisis of the twentieth century, the Roosevelt administration evolved a confusing array of executive agencies to coordinate mobilization policies and allocate production priorities. The president apparently preferred to have final decisions made in the White House, and he was unwilling to grant business firms and trade associations the same autonomy to fix prices and set priorities that they had enjoyed under the War Industries Board during World War I.

Nevertheless, the president recognized that the nation required the full cooperation and talents of business executives. Only persons possessing skills and experience in business would be able to arrange the production of materials required by modern warfare. Thus, as was the case in the earlier conflict, Washington was soon crowded with executives staffing new civilian and military agencies whose task it was to arrange a steady stream of supplies and sophisticated equipment for armed forces around the globe. In finding the needed executive talent and establishing the necessary administrative structure, Roosevelt relied heavily on the corporate executives loosely affiliated with Department of Commerce through the Business Council.

In order to gain the cooperation of business, the Roosevelt administration negotiated policies through the Business Council. This pattern, which started before Pearl Harbor, lasted for the entire period of the war. In these negotiations, business leaders insisted on four basic principles. First, the federal government was not to construct or operate industrial facilities that would compete with private firms. There were to be no wartime equivalents of the Tennessee Valley Authority. Second, and this demand was important only before the attack on Pearl Harbor, corporations wanted to be allowed to continue the production of civilian goods as they geared up for war production. Fearing a return to the depression should the war crisis abate, business leaders wanted to use existing plants; they worried that the costs of heavy capital expenditures for the production of war goods might prove a drain on profits in peacetime. Third, in cases where business did have to invest in new facilities, business leaders insisted that the tax laws allow for their rapid depreciation. In other words, the federal government had to

World War II not only provided vast opportunities for American business firms, but it also created labor shortages that were filled by women. In this photograph, women are assembling the nose section of U.S. warplanes. (National Archives/Records of the Office of War Information)

assure America's corporations of their profit margins. Last, in areas like aircraft manufacturing where civilian markets were small, the government must capitalize new production facilities for private firms to operate at nominal rentals. As Secretary of War Henry Stimson, a prominent Republican who had joined the president's cabinet, said, "If you are going to . . . go to war . . . in a capitalist country, you have to let business make money out of the process or business won't work."

Mobilization and the Structure of American Industry

The gargantuan, unprecedented mobilization effort of World War II had major effects on the structure of American industry. Military expenditures greatly accelerated the concentration of production in a few big firms. In 1939, before mobilization began, the largest one hundred American industrial firms controlled 30 per cent of the nation's manufacturing output. By 1943, the proportion was re-versed: the one hundred largest firms enjoyed a 70 per cent share of manufacturing output. This dramatic, sudden rise of giant indus-trial firms was a direct result of the procurement practices of the military services: the army and navy preferred to work with as few suppliers as possible to ensure a maximum flow of critically needed guns, munitions, and equipment; the benefits of the "visible hand" of large firms reassured the armed services, which were very con-cerned with the efficient dispatch of war supplies.

When small business owners and their congressional allies real-ized what was happening, their outcries produced an investigation conducted by Senator Harry S Truman of Missouri. Government policies were amended to mitigate to some extent the tremendous concentration of money and power in the hands of a few giant in-dustrial corporations. Congressional pressure helped secure large sums of federal capital for the aluminum industry, for instance, capital that went to the small Reynolds and Kaiser firms, allowing them to become rivals of the giant Aluminum Corporation of America. The Transportation Act of 1940 and decisions by the In-terstate Commerce Commission also brought about freight rates more favorable to small business firms struggling to develop indus-trial plants in the South and West. Wartime policies ensured that the South and West became important manufacturing regions.

Mobilization and Industrial Labor

The one significant area in which business was unable to negotiate favorable mobilization policies was labor relations. The labor sur-pluses of the depression had enabled management to maintain the principle of the open shop, even in the face of the militant and growing unionization of industrial workers. With the coming of the war, however, labor was suddenly in short supply, which gave its demands more clout. The unions had also gained political power, for workers and poorer Americans had provided Roosevelt with the margin necessary for reelection in 1940.

The unions believed that once they had won a collective bargain-ing contract, all of a firm's workers should be required to support and join the union that had won them gains, and that employers should hire only union members (the closed shop). This position seemed reasonable from the perspective of the men and women who had sacrificed to build a union, but it was anathema to busi-ness. First, the closed shop took away businesses' right to hire whomever they chose. Second, the closed shop eliminated the possibility that management might be able to play nonunion workers off against union workers and thereby break the power of the unions.

What emerged as government policy during the war was a compromise, called the union shop, which the unions liked more than business did. The government required firms with war contracts to sign "maintenance of membership" agreements with their unions. Under this form of the union shop, management could hire whomever it chose, but after a specified time each employee had to join the union or lose his or her job. The result of this federal labor policy, backed up by its power to require compliance as a requirement for getting contracts for war production, was the firm implantation of unions in American industry. By the end of the war, the number of workers who belonged to a union rose to over 14 million, or nearly 22 per cent of the nonagricultural work force.

TOWARD A LIMITED WELFARE STATE

The Great Depression and the two world wars profoundly reshaped the American political economy. The wars in particular forged new partnerships between business and government that indelibly affected attitudes and institutions as the exigencies of the times led to federal encouragement of long-standing business desires to control the market.

If war mobilization in the industrial age affected the political economy, so too did economic calamity, which augmented desires among all groups to improve their ability to control their economic circumstances—their security. The Great Depression was the greatest domestic crisis in the United States since the Civil War. Like the wars that preceded and followed it, the depression redefined the relationships between the federal government and its citizens. Roosevelt's programs failed to end the depression, but the temporary work relief and the Social Security Act created a limited welfare state that softened its effects. Whenever the business cycle turned down after the 1930s, federal programs that originated in the New Deal stood ready to cushion the worst effects of unemployment.

Even though the New Deal did not end the depression, its programs were important for the future security of the American business system. The banking system and the securities industry were able to service the needs of business again thanks to New Deal measures that salvaged them from the excesses that followed the Wall Street crash of 1929. The federal sanction of the trade union movement after 1935 was also important. Unionized workers received higher wages than workers had before the unions, and were able thereby more fully to participate in the American economic system as consumers. The entrance of millions of industrial workers in to the consuming American middle class was especially important for a business system that was more and more trying to market consumer durable goods.

The search for economic security involved much more than the bargaining relationships between business and labor, or the limited welfare state created by the New Deal, however. In the postwar years, federal policies also were developed to promote and maintain economic prosperity. In the 1930s and the 1940s, the federal government greatly broadened its involvement in the American business system. As in the Progressive Era, the government continued to regulate specific industries; in fact, the regulatory work of the federal government widened considerably under Franklin Roosevelt. But for the first time the federal government began assuming responsibility for the economic health of the nation as a whole—a concern that would become still more pronounced after World War II. As Americans continued their elusive search for economic security and the good life in the 1950s, 1960s, and 1970s, the federal government began to play ever-larger roles in their lives.

Selected Readings

A standard account of the 1920s that explains the importance of emerging consumer industries and the coming of the depression is William E. Leuchtenberg, *The Perils of Prosperity, 1914–1933* (Chicago: University of Chicago Press, 1958). Peter Fearon, *War, Prosperity and Depression: The U.S. Economy, 1917–1945* (Lawrence: University Press of Kansas, 1987), is a readable, up-to-date survey. Ellis W. Hawley, "Herbert Hoover, the Commerce Secretariat, and the Vision of an 'Associative State,'" *Journal of American History* 61 (June 1974): 116–140, is a perceptive analysis of Hoover's political economy. K. Austin Kerr, *Organized for Prohibition: A New History of the Anti-Saloon League* (New Haven: Yale University Press, 1985), explains Prohibition as a business control measure.

Labor historians have supplied much insight into union activity in this period. Two general works are by Irving Bernstein: *The Lean Years* (Boston: Houghton Mifflin, 1960) and *Turbulent Years* (Boston: Houghton Mifflin, 1970). Melvin Dubofsky and Warren Van Tine explore the life of a key labor leader in *John L. Lewis, A Biography* (New York: Quadrangle Books, 1977). David Brody, *Labor in Crisis: The Steel Strike of 1919* (Philadelphia: Lippincott, 1965), and Daniel Nelson, "The Company Union Movement, 1900–1937: A Reexamination," *Business History Review* 46 (Autumn 1982): 335–358, are also valuable.

For the New Deal years, William E. Leuchtenberg, *Franklin D. Roosevelt and the New Deal* (New York: Harper & Row, 1963), is a standard account. *The New Deal and the Problem of Monopoly* (Princeton: Princeton University Press, 1966) by Ellis Hawley is a classic. Robert M. Collins, *The Business Response to Keynes, 1929–1964* (New York: Columbia University Press, 1981), carries the story of corporate liberalism forward. A most interesting account of the World War II years in John Morton Blum, *V Was for Victory: Politics and American Culture During World War II* (New York: Harcourt Brace, 1976). Harold G. Vatter, *The U.S. Economy in World War II* (New York: Columbia University Press, 1985), is also valuable. Kim McQuaid, *Big Business and Presidential Power* (New York: William Morrow Co., 1982), explains how President Roosevelt and his successors interacted with the leaders of center firms.

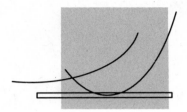

PART 5

Recent
Trends
in
American
Business

1946 to the Present

IMPORTANT EVENTS, 1950–1987

1950   The Celler-Kefauver Act limits vertical and horizontal integration.

1952   IBM enters the computer market.

1968   The conglomerate merger movement reaches a high point.

1970   Some 86 per cent of America's 500 largest industrial companies are diversified.

1974–1984 Small and medium-sized companies create most of the new jobs in the United States.

1984   Women compose 10 per cent of the managerial work force.

1985   Foreign trade rises to 20 per cent of the U.S. GNP.

1986   Ling-Temco-Vought, a leading conglomerate, fails.

1987   McDonald's operates 9,800 outlets in 46 countries.

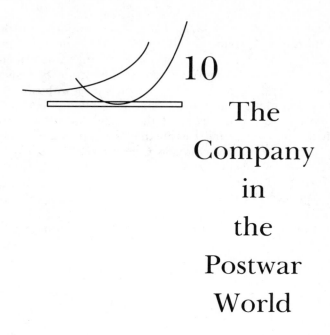

10
The Company in the Postwar World

Jerome Ottmar left his home in Massachusetts one day in 1964 to go on a typical business trip for his firm, the Textron Company. Within less than one week he visited Textron's chain-saw plant in Gastonia, North Carolina, its outboard-motor factory in Greer, South Carolina, its golf-cart plant in Augusta, Georgia, its marine-engine test station in Boynton Beach, Florida, and its machine-toolmaking facilities in Springfield, Vermont. He also took part in conferences in New York, Providence, Rhode Island, and Montreal. As late as the 1940s, the Textron Company operated only in the area of textiles. As Ottmar's wanderings suggest, however, Textron diversified in the 1950s and 1960s as its management sought new opportunities in America's rapidly expanding business system. By 1964, Ottmar was one of three executive vice presidents running Textron's 27 different divisions and 113 plants.

The years following World War II saw tremendous growth in the American business system, and Textron was only one of many companies participating in that expansion. With the American government backing free-trade policies, American products invaded the world market, and increasing numbers of American business executives began thinking in global terms. The domestic market also broadened as the consumerism of the 1920s and 1930s continued apace in the postwar years. Just as they had created a new type of business firm—the multidivisional, decentralized company—to take advantage of new business opportunities in the 1920s, so business leaders forged additional types of business structures to take advantage of opportunities in the postwar period. As these new forms of big business developed, the division between center and peripheral firms in America's business system widened, continuing a trend that had begun with the rise of big business in the nineteenth century.

THE POSTWAR ECONOMY

Economic Growth

"Growth" is the word that best characterizes the economy of the United States for the two decades after World War II. Many Americans feared a recession, or even a depression, after the end of the war, but such worries proved unwarranted. The American economy experienced rapid expansion into the 1970s, its growth interrupted by only a few short and mild recessions. Between 1945 and 1960, America's real GNP rose by 52 per cent, and its per capita GNP increased 19 per cent. Over the next decade the nation's real GNP soared an additional 46 per cent, and its per capita GNP rose by 29 per cent. Price stability accompanied and contributed to this economic growth. Consumer prices rose by only one-fourth between 1950 and 1962, in marked contrast to the rampant inflation soon to come. The traumatic experiences of the Great Depression began fading in people's memories as prosperity spread over their land. Prophetically, one of the most popular songs of 1945 was "Let the Good Times Roll."

The vibrant economy of the United States was the envy of the world during the 1950s and 1960s. America's share in the industrial output of the globe regained the level first attained in the 1920s, roughly 42 per cent of the world's total, and stayed there into the

1970s. In light of the economic prowess of their nation, it is not surprising that some Americans spoke glibly of the "American Century" or that a famous economist described the United States as the "affluent society."

Structural Changes in the Economy

Major alterations accompanied the growth in America's business system, opening opportunities for entrepreneurs in a variety of fields. Americans became more involved with foreign countries than before, and the American economy grew increasingly linked to the world or global economy. Within the United States, structural changes begun before World War II accelerated after the conflict, most notably the production of a vast array of consumer durables. Cars, television sets, and household appliances poured off assembly lines as America continued to develop a consumer society. Even more noticeable was the remarkable expansion in the nation's service industries.

The economic expansion that occurred in this period greatly enlarged the scope of the modern American consumer society, the outlines of which had become readily apparent in the 1920s. One indication was the continuing growth of the advertising industry. Spending on advertising had declined during the slump of the 1930s, and the decline had continued during World War II when mobilization commanded attention. In the five years after the end of the war, however, advertising expenditures soared from $2.9 billion in 1945 to $5.7 billion in 1950, or 2 per cent of GNP. In 1986, firms spent $102.1 billion on advertisements directed at American consumers, or 2.4 per cent of GNP. Although the proportion of advertising expenditures to the size of the economy did not grow very significantly, the total volume of advertising messages increased dramatically as expenditures kept pace with the nation's growth. This trend, combined with the ability in the decades after 1945 to exploit the new medium of television for commercial purposes, meant that advertising was more ubiquitous in Americans' lives. Businesses were more and more able to portray the consumption of goods and services as important values.

The economy of the United States became increasingly linked to that of other nations after the war as a series of international trade and monetary agreements promoted free trade. American leaders believed that free trade stimulated both economic growth at home and global economic development, from which they expected international political stability to spring. As we have seen throughout this book, foreign trade always played an important role in the economic growth of the United States, but as a large internal market developed in the nineteenth and early twentieth centuries, its significance lessened. The maturing of the national market combined with the advocacy of free trade by the United States after World War II reversed this trend. Foreign trade grew in volume and economic importance once again. American exports and imports, which together came to 10 per cent of the nation's GNP in 1965, equaled 20 per cent of the nation's GNP in 1985. World trade itself expanded by a factor of five between 1950 and 1970, and America participated in this expansion. As we shall see, American multinationals, in particular, greatly increased their involvement in the global economy during the 1950s and 1960s.

A major area of opportunity for American entrepreneurs in the postwar era lay in service industries, which have always been important in America's economic growth. In the nineteenth century, manufacturing and services developed together, reinforcing each other. Transportation improvements helped create the national market so necessary for large-scale industrialization, and investment banking houses marketed the securities of the nation's railroads. The pattern of complementary development continued in the early twentieth century. New advertising firms, for instance, allowed manufacturers to reach the growing market for consumer goods in the 1920s. The significance of service industries became increasingly pronounced after World War II.

The service sector, broadly defined to include trade, finance, transportation, and government, accounted for 68 per cent of America's GNP by 1970, and the proportion remained about the same in the 1980s. By way of contrast, the contributions of the extractive industries (agriculture and mining) and manufacturing declined. Of the 36 million new jobs created in the United States between 1957 and 1987, 90 per cent were in services, and of the 23 million women who found jobs in America during that period, 97 per cent became employed in service industries. While some of the service jobs were in low-paying, dead-end positions, others were in well-paying industries with good prospects for advancement. Exports of services—business consulting, telecommunications, and computer services were the most common—also improved the foreign trade picture of the United States. In 1980, the United States was the single greatest exporter of services, accounting for 12 per cent of the world's total exports.

IBM and the Data-processing Industry

The data-processing industry—dominated by International Business Machines (IBM)—illustrates the increasing importance of service industries in American daily life. The data-processing industry first developed to serve the needs of the federal government and America's growing number of big businesses. The managers of government and business bureaucracies depended on more and more data supplied at an ever-faster pace as the basis for their decisions. It was the availability of such data, for instance, that allowed decentralization to proceed at Du Pont and General Motors in the 1920s. This requirement of business and government created a market for new office machines, such as tabulators and calculators, before World War II and for computers in the postwar period. In the early and mid-1980s, the market for computers broadened, as new types became available for small and medium-sized businesses and found their way into household use. By the 1980s, computers had become a ubiquitous feature of the American scene.

The origins of the computer industry and of IBM stretched back to the founding of the Computer-Tabulating-Recording Company (CTR) in 1910. CTR made time clocks, scales, and—most important for the future—tabulating machines. The federal government used those tabulators in processing census returns, and some railroads employed them in handling their statistics. In 1914, Thomas Watson, who had begun his business career selling cash registers, joined CTR and a year later became the company's president.

Watson remade CTR in the 1920s and 1930s by focusing its resources on tabulators and other office machines. Renamed IBM in 1924, the firm offered electrically powered office machines that were among the most advanced in the United States. IBM based its growth not on technological prowess, however, but on sales and service. Before joining CTR, Watson had worked at National Cash Register, and his experiences there—first as a salesman and later as a corporate officer in the company's Dayton, Ohio, headquarters—molded his approach to business. National Cash Register stressed sales and service, and Watson took this emphasis with him to IBM. One of his favorite sayings was "We sell and deliver service." This salesmanship, backed up by service, made IBM a leader in the business-machine industry. With earnings of $9 million on revenues of $40 million in 1939, IBM was more profitable than any of its competitors—Burroughs, National Cash Register, Remington Rand, and Underwood—and trailed only Underwood in size.

The demands of the military began reshaping the data-processing industry during World War II. Fed by federal funds, some companies moved beyond the production of tabulators and calculators to the making of the world's first computers (unlike tabulators, computers have electronic memories that can retain mathematic rules and apply them to new sets of data automatically). IBM, generally more interested in sales than in pioneering new technologies, initially lagged behind Remington Rand and some other companies in developing computers. However, when Thomas Watson, Jr., took over as president from his father in 1952, IBM entered the computer market, and by the mid-1950s it had a line of mainframe computers that competed directly with Remington Rand's UNIVAC. (A mainframe computer is a large, high-capacity computer capable of handling all of an organization's data-processing needs. General Electric became the first private business to own a mainframe computer when it purchased a UNIVAC in 1954.) This first generation of computers was based on vacuum-tube technologies, and the resulting machines were large, bulky, and difficult to cool.

By the 1950s and early 1960s, the first generation of computers was being replaced by a second generation that utilized transistors and diodes rather than vacuum tubes. Smaller, more reliable, and cooler in their operations than their predecessors, these machines represented a major advance in computer technology. Sperry Rand (the Sperry Corporation and Remington Rand merged in 1955) led the industry in making this switch. Characteristically, IBM allowed others to blaze the trail with transistorized computers, only to seize the lead through superior salesmanship and service. "It doesn't do much good to build a better mousetrap," noted Louis Rader of Sperry Rand's UNIVAC division, "if the other guy selling mousetraps has five times as many salesmen." With gross revenues of nearly $2.5 billion and a net income of $333 million in 1965, IBM commanded 65 per cent of the market for computers in the United States. Sperry Rand, its closest rival, controlled only 12 per cent of the market. It was said that the computer industry was run by Snow White (IBM) and the Seven Dwarfs (its competitors).

As it grew in importance within the United States, IBM also expanded overseas. In 1949, Richard Watson (Thomas Jr.'s brother) became the head of the newly formed World Trade division. World Trade took charge of all of IBM's foreign operations, controlling production or sales subsidiaries in 130 countries around the globe. With revenues of almost $1.1 billion in 1965, IBM World Trade had become one of America's major multinationals.

In 1965, IBM introduced its first third-generation mainframe computer, the 360, in response to moves by several of its competitors, most notably Honeywell. (Using integrated circuits rather than transistors, third-generation computers are faster and less prone to breakdowns than their earlier counterparts.) In the 1960s and 1970s, IBM successfully withstood antitrust suits mounted against it by the federal government and by other computer companies. Under new leadership (Thomas Watson, Jr., retired in 1973), IBM boasted net earnings of $5.3 billion on gross revenues of $54 billion in 1987.

The computer industry entered a new stage of development in the mid-1980s with the invention of powerful microchips that allowed personal computers and minicomputers to handle many tasks once done only by mainframes. In 1984, revenues from the sale of microcomputers surpassed those from mainframes for the first time. This alteration in the nature of the computer industry brought realignments among the leading firms making computers. IBM continued to possess the lion's share of the world market for mainframes, 68 per cent in 1986. In 1981, IBM successfully entered the personal-computer field, but in 1986 IBM possessed only 34 per cent of the personal-computer market, and two years later a scant 23 per cent. IBM's failure to exploit fully the nonmainframe computer fields opened the way for a host of new companies— Apple, Compaq, Zenith, Amstrad, and Digital Equipment, among others—and made the computer industry more competitive than at any time since the mid-1950s. In an unprecedented move, nine makers of personal computers announced in 1988 that they would no longer follow IBM's lead in the development of a new electronic circuitry but would employ an alternate design of their own. By this time, too, some computer-makers, most notably Digital, were also challenging IBM for much of the mainframe business.

THE CONGLOMERATE COMMOTION

Diversification and Decentralization

As the example of IBM demonstrates, the expansion of the American economy opened new opportunities for business firms. Influenced by the earlier pioneering efforts of Du Pont and General Motors, an increasing number chose diversification as their growth strategy. As they diversified their products and markets to take advantage of growing consumer desires, these companies often adopted decentralized, multidivisional management systems similar to the one developed at General Motors by Alfred P. Sloan, Jr., in the 1920s. By 1970, some 86 per cent of the five hundred largest industrial companies in the United States were diversified to the extent that they possessed at least three different divisions. By this time, 73 of America's largest 100 industrial companies had adopted some form of decentralized management.

As it diversified its product lines and regional coverage, for instance, IBM decentralized its management structure. As we have noted, World Trade was set up as a division separate from domestic operations in 1949. Decentralization occurred within IBM's domestic operations in 1956 when Thomas Watson, Jr., separated the company into five major divisions. This reorganization took place at a three-day conference Watson convened for over a hundred IBM managers. "We went in a monolith," Watson later observed, "and we emerged three days later as a modern, reasonably decentralized organization with divisions with profit responsibility and clear lines of authority."

In the postwar years, business diversification took four routes in the United States. Some companies diversified through internal development, moving outward into new areas from a base in either a broad technology or a narrow specialty. Thus, internal research led Uniroyal, originally a maker of rubber products, into the related fields of chemicals, plastics, and fibers. Others diversified by purchasing companies to complement their existing technologies. White Consolidated Industries found itself in the mid-1950s in the unprofitable business of making sewing machines and moved into the general area of industrial equipment and consumer appliances as a defensive maneuver by acquiring other firms. By the same token, Continental Can, which started as a manufacturer of tin cans and crown caps, diversified after 1939 by purchasing companies making metal, glass, and paper containers, glass closures, bottle caps, and flexible packaging material. Still other businesses diversified by buying companies that sold products using the same or similar channels of distribution for similar markets. In 1966, for example, American Brands (formerly American Tobacco) entered the fields of prepackaged foods and alcoholic beverages. In each of these three types of diversification, fairly clear relationships existed between the old and new goods a company made and sold. Such clear relationships did not exist in the fourth type of diversification, conglomerate diversification.

The Coming of Conglomerates

Conglomerates became the hot news of the American business world in the 1960s. "The word 'conglomerate' lands on the business pages with monotonous regularity these days," observed a financial writer in 1967. "Indeed, a case might be made that conglomerates are the most important current trend in the universe of big business." A new phenomenon in the late 1950s and the 1960s, conglomerates were (and are) companies with many different divisions—usually eight or more—making and selling totally or almost totally unrelated products. (Thus, conglomerate businesses resemble the rocks from which they take their name: a conglomerate rock is composed of rounded fragments varying from small pebbles to large boulders, held together by a cementlike mixture such as hardened clay.)

Conglomerates became increasingly common in the 1960s as the United States experienced its third major merger movement of the century. Mergers of manufacturing and mining companies reached a peak in 1968 at 2,500, and 715 of these mergers were conglomerate-type mergers. Even so, conglomerates did not become the dominant form of big business in the United States. Even in 1966, at the height of the conglomerate movement, only 46 of the 500 largest industrial companies in America were conglomerates. There were many reasons for the formation of conglomerates, but several stand out.

First, some firms doing business in one field diversified into additional areas as a defensive strategy. Companies of this type sought more profitable investment opportunities for their funds. Textron diversified for this reason, moving capital out of its declining textile plants. So did the Borden Company. Worried about low profits in milk products, Borden's officers led their company into the production of chemicals, cosmetics, and fertilizers.

Second, some business executives formed conglomerates on the assumption that all businesses, no matter how diverse, could best be managed by a small group of executives in the head office. These executives, it was argued, could coordinate the accounting, planning, and financial services of the many divisions for the benefit of the entire company. And it was thought that expertise acquired in one area of operations could be transferred to other areas—again for the benefit of the whole company. Those believing in this approach to business called it synergy, and they often expressed the idea in shorthand as 2 + 2 = 5. Officers in these corporations

The Textron Corporation is a conglomerate with diversified products. One is the helicopter manufactured by Bell Helicopter Textron, which produces items for the U.S. Government, foreign governments, and civilian markets. Another part of the corporation is Speidel, which produces watches, watch attachments, bracelets, neckchains, and British Sterling men's toiletries. Other facets of the corporation include consumer finance operations, a commercial finance company, and insurance services. (Textron Corporation)

tended to be ambitious empire builders who viewed diversification as a natural part of growth. Those at Litton Industries were a good example of this type of business practitioner. They began expanding and diversifying without any real notion of where they were headed.

The gains that could be made from "paper entrepreneurialism" also contributed to the rise of conglomerates. Business managers found that they could often boost the earnings of their companies by acquiring other firms, even though no new assets were created. By rearranging the ownership of companies (the stock certificates), they could show a dramatic rise in profits. One method worked in the following way: if the stock market price of a company was less than its book value (the market value of its assets), another firm

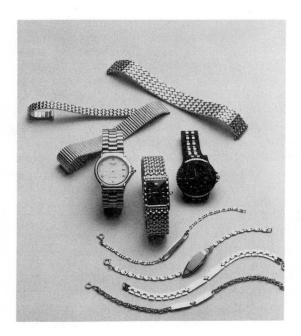

could increase its earnings by buying the undervalued company and combining the books of the two companies. If the purchased company had losses, this situation was an additional benefit, for the acquiring company could use those losses to lower its taxes.

Finally, government actions spurred the development of conglomerates. Although the Justice Department sometimes brought anti-trust actions against other forms of big business in the 1950s and 1960s—in 1957, for instance, it forced Du Pont to sell its stockholdings in General Motors—it took no actions against conglomerates. In fact, conglomerates were initially viewed as increasing competition in the American business world, because their many newly established divisions entered fields dominated by well-established firms. In 1950, Congress passed the Celler-Kefauver Act, which placed new limitations on horizontal and vertical integration as growth strategies for expanding businesses. As a result, business executives trying to increase their operations often did so by forming conglomerates, which were not affected by the Celler-Kefauver Act.

The Management of Conglomerates

In the 1960s, the officers of conglomerates often asserted that a new type of business executive was evolving: a young, ambitious manager with generalized management talents, a person who was versatile, adaptable enough to solve any problem in any business. Trained especially in the techniques of financial management, this new breed could, it was claimed, run a company well without knowing much about its products or production methods.

How successful were the managers cast in this mold? They did put together large companies. Gulf & Western, for instance, expanded its sales from $10 million in 1958 to $1.3 billion just ten years later. But most of the expansion of conglomerates was done through buying other companies—72 mergers in the case of Gulf & Western—not by internally generated growth. Earnings—that is, profits—provide a better measurement of the success of conglomerates. On the average, conglomerates performed no better than other types of big businesses in either the 1960s or the 1970s.

In fact, management problems limited the success of many conglomerates. Two major difficulties surfaced. Too often, executives in the head offices of conglomerates failed to supervise and coordinate the work of their company's many divisions. Conglomerates usually lacked the good information flow and statistical controls established at decentralized, multidivisional companies like Du Pont and General Motors. Sometimes, the head office did not know what the divisions were doing. In 1960 through 1962, General Dynamics lost $425 million because the corporate office located in New York failed adequately to supervise and place controls on sloppy work done by the Convair Division, which was making commercial jet airplanes in Los Angeles. Moreover, as time passed, it became apparent that more than generalized management talents, more than agility with numbers, was needed to run a corporation. Some knowledge of a corporation's production operations was also needed, but too often conglomerate managers did not possess this basic knowledge.

Ling-Temco-Vought: The Rise and Fall of a Conglomerate

In many respects a typical conglomerate, Ling-Temco-Vought (LTV) experienced many of the ups and downs that other conglomerates faced in the 1960s and 1970s. The company came to life, expanded rapidly, entered a period of decline, was reborn in a different form, and went into bankruptcy—all within a single generation.

LTV was started by Jimmy Ling. After serving in the navy during World War II, Ling settled in Dallas where he raised $2,000 to enter the electrical contracting business. His firm, the Ling Company, prospered in the postwar building boom. To raise additional money for expansion, Ling went public in 1954, selling common stock in his company to whoever would buy it. (A charismatic supersalesman, Ling hawked the stock from a concession stand at the Texas State Fair!) He used the funds acquired in this manner to buy additional electrical contracting companies, and by 1959, always more interested in growth than in profits, Ling was boasting that his company would soon appear on *Fortune* magazine's list of the five hundred largest industrial companies in the United States.

Ling began diversifying his operations in the early 1960s. In 1960, he bought the Temco Company, a producer of military aircraft and missiles. In the same year he moved after a still larger prize—the Chance Vought Corporation, a Dallas-based company that also made aircraft and aerospace products. Here Ling met his first opposition, for Chance Vought's management did not want to sell their company to him. Ling responded with a maneuver used many times by conglomerates desiring to acquire other companies: he attacked and conquered Chance Vought through a stock tender offer. Ling offered Chance Vought's stockholders more for their common stock than the stock's market value. Because Chance Vought's management did not own a controlling interest in the common stock of their company, they were helpless in the face of Ling's stratagem. As soon as Ling acquired a majority share of Chance Vought's stock, he voted his own candidates into office, and by the end of 1961 had melded the company into his growing corporate empire.

By 1963, Ling had completed his first efforts at expansion. LTV ranked well up on *Fortune*'s list and was making a reasonable profit. Although the company had grown a great deal, however, it was not yet a conglomerate. In 1964, LTV made 93 per cent of its sales in the related fields of military hardware and aerospace products. But Ling was not satisfied with simply administering his sizable company. He desired further expansion, and in the process of this growth LTV became a conglomerate.

Ling entered unknown waters with the acquisition of the Wilson Company in 1967. Wilson was itself a diversified business with three major divisions: the nation's third-largest meat-packing company, a large sporting goods firm, and a pharmaceuticals company. A year later LTV acquired the Greatamerica Corporation, another diversified business (insurance, car rentals, Braniff Airlines). Finally, in 1969, Ling gained control of Jones & Laughlin Steel, America's sixth-largest steelmaker, through a stock tender offer. In the late 1960s, this strategy of rapid diversification into unrelated fields seemed to work. The stock market responded favorably to Ling's moves, and the price of a share of common stock in LTV soared to a high of $169.

However, this situation was illusory and temporary. Problems resulting from LTV's rapid expansion soon led the company into a period of decline. The most basic difficulty was debt. Ling borrowed money for his acquisitions in the late 1960s, and LTV was burdened with $1.9 billion of debts by 1969. Two other related problems made this situation worse. In his eagerness to purchase companies, Ling paid much more than they were worth, which meant that now, as part of LTV, the companies could not earn enough income to pay off the debt LTV had incurred in buying them. Moreover, again because of the haste with which he pushed expansion, Ling acquired firms with dubious prospects. Jones & Laughlin was a sick company when Ling bought it, and nothing succeeded in breathing new life into it.

The results of Ling's careless, headlong expansion soon endangered LTV's very existence. In 1969, LTV needed to earn a minimum of $60 million to pay the interest on its debts. However, partly because of the onset of a nationwide recession, it made only $2 million. The consequence was perhaps inevitable. In mid-1970, Ling was forced out of the management of LTV. Paul Thayer, who had been the head of LTV's aerospace division, replaced him as the company's president.

Thayer sought to save LTV by making it less of a conglomerate. Working with creditors, he reduced and restructured the company's debts and sold profitable divisions to raise sorely needed cash. By the mid-1970s, LTV had restricted its operations to just three fields: aerospace, steel, and energy. Within these three areas Thayer expanded LTV in the late 1970s and early 1980s. In 1977, LTV purchased the Lykes Corporation, a steel company, and six years later Republic Steel, making LTV the nation's second-largest steelmaker. None of Thayer's efforts were able to rescue the company, however. Hurt especially by a decline in the steel market, LTV posted deficits of $1.4 billion in the four years after 1982 and declared bankruptcy in July 1986.

Conglomerates and American Business Since 1969

Darlings of the stock market and the American public during the 1960s, conglomerates fell into disrepute in the early 1970s, only to rise again during the late 1970s and 1980s.

Merger activity slowed in the early 1970s, particularly among conglomerates. The number of conglomerate-type mergers dropped from 715 in 1968 to only 301 in 1974 and to just 123 one year later. Most important in slowing merger activity was a recession that began in 1969 and lasted into the 1970s. Conglomerates had come of age with a boom in the stock market in the 1960s. In the early 1970s, the stock market collapsed, and so did many conglomerates. The earnings of conglomerates—often burdened by heavy debts incurred to finance expansion in the 1960s, as in the case of LTV—plummeted. So did their stock prices. After reaching the high of $169 per share in 1967, the price of LTV's stock dropped to $7 per share in 1973. The price of a share of stock in Litton Industries dropped from $104 to $4 and that of a share of Textron from $58 to $15 in the same period. By exposing the financial weaknesses of the conglomerate structure, the recession made them less attractive to investors.

In the late 1970s and the 1980s, merger activity once again increased. As shown in Table 10.1, 1,530 mergers (of companies worth at least $1 million) whose values totaled over $34 billion took place in 1979, 2,391 worth almost $53 billion occurred in 1983, and 4,381 worth almost $205 billion took place in 1986. Despite the drop in number of mergers in 1987, there were 30 acquisitions of firms worth at least $1 billion by other companies; the most active fields for merger activity that year were, in descending order, chemicals, retailing, banking, communications, machinery, mining, oil and gas, and petroleum refining. Although 1988's number of mergers fell farther—to 3,487—they were valued at almost $227 billion.

There were several causes for this revival in merger activity. America's political system permitted it. The federal government took few actions to try to prevent the mergers. Key appointees of President Ronald Reagan were reluctant to take actions interfering with the mergers. In 1983, the new head of the Antitrust Division of the Department of Justice was an attorney who previously had defended large corporations against antitrust suits. At the same time, state laws that aimed at restricting takeovers by preventing out-of-state companies from buying in-state companies were declared unconstitutional. The U.S. Supreme Court, under the interpretation of the commerce clause of the Constitution first enunciated in the 1937 decision upholding the National Labor Relations Act, struck down such state laws as illegally giving individual states the power to regulate trade crossing state lines, thus impinging upon what was seen as one of the exclusive powers of the federal government. Moreover, until the mid-1980s, stock markets were depressed. The prices of many common stocks were low relative to the actual values and earnings potentials of the firms, and this situation encouraged takeovers. Finally, companies or individuals were able to secure the financing required for the purchases; brokerage houses and banks, which earned giant commissions, were active participants in the merger frenzy, eagerly arranging financing for takeovers.

Issues Raised by Conglomerates and Mergers

The conglomerate activity of the 1960s and the renewed merger movement of the late 1970s and the 1980s raised significant ques-

Table 10.1

Mergers and Acquisitions in the United States, 1979–1988

Year	Number of transactions	Percentage of change	Value (in millions)	Percentage of change
1979	1,530	—	$ 34,197.2	—
1980	1,560	+2.0%	32,882.8	−3.8%
1981	2,329	+49.3	70,064.4	+113.1
1982	2,298	−1.3	60,697.8	−13.4
1983	2,391	+4.1	52,691.4	−13.1
1984	3,164	+32.3	126,073.7	+139.3
1985	3,437	+8.6	145,464.3	+15.4
1986	4,381	+27.5	204,894.6	+40.9
1987	3,920	−11.8	177,203.3	−13.5
1988	3,487	−11.1	226,642.6	+27.9

SOURCE: *Mergers & Acquisitions,* May/June, 1989, p. 53.

tions about the nature of the economy and society of the United States. Merger activity, its critics argued, was a misallocation of the nation's economic and financial resources. Companies spent too much time, effort, and money buying or trying to buy each other, without adding to the country's productive capacity. And in fact, by the late 1970s, acquiring companies typically had to pay 50 per cent more than the market price of a target company's stock to purchase it through a stock tender offer. To do so, the acquiring companies often went deeply in debt, a situation that, as in the case of LTV, could later hurt them severely. The merger movement may have injured the economy as a whole, as well as individual companies, by siphoning off into the acquisition game funds desperately needed to modernize factories. Also, the time and energy business executives spent in preparing for or trying to avoid mergers distracted them from the other aspects of running their companies. Those involved in the mergers argued that, to the contrary, the mergers strengthened the economy. Mergers, they claimed, created more efficient, more competitive companies—corporations better able to sell American products in the international market.

Social and political as well as economic issues surfaced. The matter of the concentration of power, first raised in the antitrust campaign following the rise of big business in the 1870s and 1880s, reappeared. As a result of mergers, for example, oil companies came to control about 35 per cent of the copper, 25 per cent of the uranium, and 25 per cent of the coal in the United States by 1978. While conceding that this situation might be efficient in technological and economic ways, critics complained that it placed too much power in the hands of a few large corporations.

MULTINATIONALS

Postwar Multinational Enterprise, 1945–1970

Just as the growth in the American economy opened up opportunities for the further diversification of business at home, the expansion of the global economy after World War II encouraged worldwide business diversification. U.S. multinational corporations were among those companies benefiting from this situation. As we saw in Chapter 8, U.S. companies began overseas operations well before World War II. But the return of prosperity after the war brought increased foreign activity. By 1970, at least 3,500 U.S. companies had direct foreign investments in some 15,000 enterprises. The total amount of direct foreign investments came to $78.2 billion in 1970 (in current dollars), an increase that more than kept pace with the expansion of the American economy. By 1970, the direct investments of U.S. companies overseas equaled 8 per cent of the GNP of the United States.

As it had since the 1920s, when it replaced mining in importance, manufacturing attracted the greatest share of the investment funds of U.S. multinationals. Also, as in times past, the types of manufacturers investing abroad remained the same: those with technological advantages or unique products (such as companies in the electrical, office equipment, and chemical industries) and those already well established overseas. As in earlier times, most of these businesses invested in foreign plants and factories to extend the markets for their products—something they discovered they could not do by simply increasing their exports from the United States. Language, cultural, and legal barriers often made it necessary for U.S. companies to set up manufacturing plants, not simply sales offices, overseas. Moreover, cheap foreign labor often made a move abroad very attractive.

As early as the 1920s, U.S. multinationals realized that they had to respect and adapt to the customs and regulations of the countries in which they did business. This concern took on a new urgency in the postwar world, as independence movements in Latin America, Africa, the Middle East, and Asia rearranged the social and political environments of those regions. Increasingly, U.S. companies had to enter into partnership agreements (often as the junior partner) with newly created nationalistic governments if they hoped to continue operating at all (the new governments sometimes confiscated foreign ventures). U.S. oil companies, which replaced British domination of the Middle East (and particularly Saudi Arabia) immediately after World War II, made such arrangements with many Middle Eastern governments in the late 1960s and the 1970s.

As they adapted to worldwide changes, U.S. multinationals altered their management structures. In the 1920s, some American corporations with investments in foreign manufacturing set up foreign companies that, in turn, evolved into international divisions within their parent corporations, and over the next three decades additional companies established international divisions. This arrangement, however, was not wholly satisfactory, for all too often these foreign divisions became isolated from the rest of the company. During the 1950s and 1960s, multinationals began moving away from structures with separate international divisions. Instead, they adopted "global," "worldwide," or "cosmopolitan" management structures. In some of these structures, the top operating management of the domestic products divisions took over the prime responsibility for the international business in their products (they were usually given advice by staff officers who were experts on specific countries or regions). In another type of new structure, multifunctional operating subsidiaries overseas (usually defined by region) were accorded equal status with operating divisions in the United States. In yet a third type of structure, divisions based on product and region were commingled. Most of these reorganizations, regardless of specific form, had one common result: the top management of the companies became more involved in worldwide operations than before. The isolation of the international division from the rest of its company ended.

International Telephone & Telegraph: The Life of a Multinational

By 1970, the International Telephone & Telegraph Corporation (ITT) had become one of the largest multinationals in the world. Composed of 331 subsidiaries and 708 subsidiaries of subsidiaries, the corporation possessed factories in twenty-seven countries and had operations in seventy. With over 400,000 employees around the world, ITT had sales of $5.5 billion, a sum larger than the revenues of many nations. In its history and operations ITT summed up for many people what multinationals were all about.

Sosthenes Behn founded ITT as a small telephone company in Puerto Rico and Cuba in 1920. From the first, Behn was determined to build up an international communications system rivaling the one American Telephone and Telegraph had established within the United States. In 1923, ITT won the right to provide telephone service in Spain, and two years later the company acquired the international holdings of the Western Electric Company. In the 1930s, ITT joined in cartels with its European competitors to operate the communications business of Europe and Latin America, emerging particularly strongly in Germany and Argentina. World War II disrupted many of ITT's operations, and the immediate postwar settlements left ITT in some disarray. Its operations in Spain and Argentina were nationalized, and its profits fell. In 1956, Behn left the company, and he died a year later.

ITT, a multinational corporation, is a successful operator of complex electronic equipment. This satellite earth station is sold by a subsidiary, Alcatel, with more than a thousand in operation worldwide. The managers of ITT and its many subsidiaries use this equipment to communicate with each other around the globe and sell the service to other firms. (Alcatel NV)

Harold Geneen, the executive vice president of Raytheon, took over as ITT's president in 1959. A powerful man (a joke at ITT asked whether the *g* in Geneen was pronounced soft as in "Jesus" or hard as in "God"), Geneen led the company in new directions. Worried about ITT's future in Europe, he diversified the corporation by purchasing American companies: Avis (1965), Apcoa (1966), Cleveland Motels (1967), Transportation Displays (1968), Levitt Company (1967), Pennsylvania Glass and Sand (1968), Rayonier (1968), Continental Baking (1968), and Sheraton Hotels (1968). At the same time, despite his initial anxieties, Geneen expanded the operations of ITT in Europe in the early 1970s. With some 200,000 employees, ITT Europe became the largest U.S. company on the Continent and the seventeenth largest company (when ranked by sales) in Europe.

Further growth raised political questions in the early and mid-1970s. ITT bought the Hartford Company, the fifth largest property and liability insurance company in the United States, in 1971. However, before the Justice Department (which had filed antitrust suits against ITT) allowed ITT to make this purchase, the company had to agree to divest itself of several earlier acquisitions. Then, in both 1971 and 1972, the company came under the suspicion (never conclusively proved) of having donated $400,000 to the Republican party in return for receiving the Justice Department's permission to purchase the Hartford Company. At about the same time, ITT was implicated for trying to stop the election of Salvadore Allende, a Marxist, as president of Chile and for working with the Central Intelligence Agency to disrupt the Chilean economy (again, these charges were not conclusively proved). The actions of ITT, and public perceptions of them, raised the question of who controlled corporations spanning national boundaries and led one critic of ITT to describe it as "the sovereign state of ITT."

ITT continued to expand under Geneen's guidance into the late 1970s, although at a somewhat slower rate than in the 1960s. By 1980, with revenues of $23.8 billion, ITT had become the world's largest conglomerate, as well as one of its leading multinationals. Running such a large and diverse company, however, was a difficult task. Profits dropped precipitously in the 1970s, and in 1979, Rand Araskog, who had been running the company's defense and aviation division, replaced Geneen as president. Araskog cut back and restructured his corporation's debts—debts incurred in making many of its acquisitions. Like Thayer at LTV, Araskog divested his company of many of its operations: ITT sold all or part of 100 subsidiaries between 1979 and 1987, reducing the number of employees at ITT from 348,000 to 123,000. ITT under Araskog became a somewhat leaner, more rationally structured business than it had been in the 1960s.

U.S. Multinationals in the 1970s

The changes taking place at ITT reflected events in the world of multinationals in general in the 1970s. U.S. multinationals continued to grow, but at a slower rate than in the 1950s and 1960s. This slower growth rate resulted partly from an increasing number of restrictions placed on the multinationals' activities by assertive national governments eager to tax them, alterations in accounting policies that made acquisitions less desirable, the countervailing power of the beginnings of multinational labor unions, and the increasing difficulties multinationals encountered in the protection of their patents. In part, too, U.S. multinationals were, like other U.S. businesses, losing their competitive edge in the international marketplace. A major indication of the slowing of the expansion of multinationals was that they sold many of their foreign subsidiaries in the 1970s. Between 1971 and 1975, they divested themselves of 1,359 foreign subsidiaries, nearly 10 per cent of the total. Most of these divestitures, one-third of which involved European subsidiaries, were made on a voluntary basis because of declining profits. They were not simply the result of pressures from the host country.

Issues Raised by Multinationals

Multinationals raised important questions about their effect on the American economy and their influence on the economies of foreign nations. Domestic critics argued that the operations of the multinational companies injured the economy of the United States in a number of ways. The capital outflow for direct investments abroad, they claimed, hurt America's balance of payments. By constructing plants overseas rather than at home, multinationals also reduced U.S. exports while increasing imports. The building of overseas factories cost Americans their jobs as lower-priced imports entered the market. Then, too, technically trained personnel and advanced technology needed at home ended up overseas instead. Critics of multinationals also focused on the issue of control. The United States, they pointed out, could not tax most profits earned by multinationals until (and unless) those profits were sent home. Even more disturbing was the possibility that the interests of U.S. multinationals might, at times, run contrary to those of the United States and that the companies might therefore act against the foreign policy of the nation. (In 1982 and 1983, Dresser Industries was caught in just such a controversy. Its French subsidiary, with the strong support of the French government, sought to sell pumps to the Soviet Union for a major oil and gas pipeline. The U.S. government, however, ordered Dresser's head office in the United States to have the French subsidiary stop the sale.)

Defenders of multinationals replied that the companies contributed in a positive way to the economic growth of the United States. They helped, it was said, ease the balance of payments problem by creating overseas markets for American goods. Moreover, it was pointed out, American subsidiaries abroad were large purchasers of goods made in the United States. Then, too, their defenders argued, multinationals gave the United States access to advanced foreign technology, thus making the U.S. economy more competitive. As for the question of control, the proponents of multinationals observed that the companies could act as instruments of U.S. foreign policy (the possible cooperation between ITT and the Central Intelligence Agency in trying to influence politics in Chile was an example of this) and that multinationals could serve United States foreign policy and defense needs by preventing others from securing monopolies over such key raw materials as oil, iron ore, copper, bauxite (aluminum ore), and uranium.

The expansion of direct investments abroad by multinationals also raised issues for foreign nations. Some recipient nations feared that U.S. investments would stunt their economic growth by taking large earnings out of the country, by destroying local business initiative, and by hurting their balance of payments. Yet, as defenders of multinationals observed, the corporations helped develop the economies of their host countries by providing capital, technology, and managerial skills that might otherwise not be available. Far from sapping local business initiative, they could stimulate it by showing people new ways of doing things.

THE MODERN CORPORATE BUSINESS SYSTEM

The Spread of Big Business and the Revival of Small Business

Conglomerates and multinationals were two variants of big business, and their development continued a trend begun in the mid-nineteenth century: a relatively small handful of big businesses dominated key segments of the U.S. economy, especially manufacturing. In 1962, the 5 largest industrial corporations accounted for over 12 per cent of all assets used in manufacturing, the 50 largest possessed over one-third of the nation's manufacturing assets, and the top 500 had over two-thirds. Some companies grew especially large and important. In 1965, three industrial giants—General Motors, Standard Oil of New Jersey (now Exxon), and Ford—had more gross income than all the farms in the United States. In 1963, the revenues of General Motors were eight times those of New York State, and nearly one-fifth those of the federal government.

However, the development of big business did not end the importance of small business to the American economy. Manufacturing, in which big businesses were especially important, became less significant in the economy of the United States in the postwar years. In 1982, small businesses accounted for 38 per cent of the nation's GNP. Small businesses helped the U.S. economy in several ways. They generated new jobs, an especially important factor when big businesses were laying off workers. Small businesses, particularly service companies, were especially important as employers of women and minorities. Small businesses also helped the economy by commercializing technological innovations. Big businesses continued to account for most of the private spending for basic research and development, but small firms nonetheless played an important role in bringing innovations to the marketplace.

The position of small businesses varied considerably in the different segments of the nation's business system. In the late 1970s and the 1980s, as throughout the twentieth century, opportunities for small business ventures in farming continued to decline. In numbers, small businesses dominated the service industries, a fast-growing field with promising prospects for the future. (Big companies were, however, becoming increasingly significant in services as time passed. In 1984, for example, large banks such as Citicorp and Bank of America possessed assets twice as large as those of such leading industrial firms as Exxon and General Motors.) Most of the remaining small firms were in sales, a field in which profits differed tremendously. Relatively few small businesses were found in manufacturing, but their prospects seemed to be improving. Small businesses seemed to benefit especially from the growth of a competitive global market, which called for smaller, more flexible factories. Reversing their century-old reliance on vertical integration, more and more big businesses in manufacturing turned instead to small companies to supply components for their finished products. Small companies came increasingly into demand as subcontractors because the larger firms—again responding to the demands of the fast-paced world market—sought flexibility in their operations.

Agribusiness

A trend toward concentration took place in farming as large farms, "agribusinesses," came more and more to dominate agriculture in the United States. The earlier division of farming into two segments—small family farms, often operating in the red, and large corporate farms, usually more efficient and profitable—continued in the postwar years. Many family farmers found their economic positions untenable and left farming for other occupations. Between 1945 and 1974, 4.2 million more Americans left farming than entered the field. By 1988, only 2.2 per cent of the nation's working population was engaged in agriculture, down from 27 per cent in 1920, 14 per cent in 1945, and 4.5 per cent in 1973; and many of these "farmers" worked at farming only part-time. In just one decade, the 1960s, some 900,000 independent farms disappeared, many swallowed up by large corporate farms. By 1964, the largest 10 per cent of America's farms were responsible for 48 per cent of all farm output in the nation, up from 24 per cent in 1948. By 1986, 10 per cent of the farms, those with annual gross receipts of over $250,000, accounted for 75 per cent of all farm income.

The main problem facing family farmers was the growing need for large amounts of capital. A scientific and technological revolution transformed farming in the postwar years; large tractors and other types of mechanized equipment, hybrid seeds for corn and other crops, and chemical fertilizers (whose use soared tenfold between 1940 and 1970) all cost money. By 1970, an Illinois farmer raising corn on 400 acres required a minimum capital investment of $250,000. Successful farming became capital-intensive, and the amounts of capital needed grew ever larger, as farm size (the average farm consisted of 200 acres in 1950, 450 by 1983) and equipment requirements rose.

Problems faced by Americans with small and medium-sized farms, already apparent by the 1960s and 1970s, deepened in the 1980s. Temporarily blessed by high prices for their crops, farmers purchased new farmland and equipment in the late 1970s, hoping that crop prices and land values would keep rising, and they did so with borrowed money: the debt of farmers increased from $54 billion in 1971 to $212 billion by 1985. However, the rosy future hoped for by farmers failed to materialize.

Foreign markets for U.S. farm products collapsed in the early 1980s because of the growing self-sufficiency in food production of many other nations, the rising value of the dollar (which raised the cost of farm exports), and an inept U.S. foreign policy regarding agricultural products. The loss of foreign markets proved catastrophic because, by the late 1970s, foreign sales had taken one-third of the production of U.S. farms: 47 per cent of the total annual sales of the wheat crop, 38 per cent of the soybean crop, and 20 per cent of the corn crop. As a result of lost sales, crop prices and land values plummeted; farmland values fell from $844 billion in 1981 to just $690 billion four years later. In Iowa, the average price for an acre of farmland dropped from $2,000 in 1981 to $841 in 1986; in Minnesota, the decline was from $1,281 to $609, and in California, from $1,900 to $1,571.

Many Americans with medium-sized family farms were forced to sell out because they could not pay the loans that they had used to buy land and equipment. Those with small farms often suffered the same fate but were sometimes able to hang onto their marginal farming operations—which they continued to view as a way of life as much as a way to make a living—by taking other jobs and farming only part-time. Large corporate farmers did better in this economic crisis; they possessed varied sources of capital that they could draw on to get through the hard times. Increasingly, their farms were part of large, vertically integrated farm-products business empires, such as Holly Farms and Cargill, which made profits not from growing food but from processing and marketing it. In fact, corporate farms often bought the family farms that failed. While the number of farms in the United States declined, the amount of land in production remained about the same, and the trend to larger farms continued.

Franchising

Although the distinction between big businesses and smaller concerns became pronounced in most fields as the twentieth century progressed, some blurring occurred in the form of business franchising. In franchising, a would-be entrepreneur (the franchisee) purchases the right to do business in a certain line of work from a company in that field (the franchiser). In return for this sum, and also usually for additional yearly payments based on the amount of sales made, the franchisee reaps benefits provided by the parent company. The franchiser usually provides national advertising (including a well-known trademark), advice and guidelines about conducting business (and often training in the business at its national headquarters), and the benefits of mass-purchasing discounts. Many Americans came to view franchising as an ideal combination of, or middle ground between, large and small businesses. Franchisees embraced franchising as a way to have the independence and entrepreneurial opportunities that they associated with small business without forsaking what they perceived to be the security of big business. For the franchiser, franchising offered the possibility of rapid business expansion at little cost, since the franchisee supplied most

An example of a successful franchise enterprise is Wendy's International, Inc. As Western culture becomes more pervasive worldwide, restaurants like Wendy's and McDonald's can be found in Tokyo, Paris, and London, as well as in Home Town, U.S.A. (Courtesy of Wendy's International, Inc.)

of the capital. And the various annual fees levied on the franchisees promised a prosperous future for any franchiser whose product caught on with the American public.

Franchising has had a long history in the United States. As we have seen, Cyrus McCormick used franchised dealers to sell his reapers in the nineteenth century. Building on McCormick's experiences, automobile manufacturers and petroleum companies began selling cars and gasoline through franchised dealers in the opening decades of the twentieth century. Soft-drink makers, led by Coca-Cola, sold their goods through franchised bottlers. Restaurant franchising began in the 1920s with A & W Root Beer and Howard Johnson establishments.

Franchising grew at a phenomenal rate after World War II. By the 1950s and 1960s, it seemed as if everything was being franchised: fast foods (McDonald's, Kentucky Fried Chicken), motels (Holiday Inn was one of many), coin-operated laundries, companies selling household pets, and businesses making security systems. By

1967, sales made by franchised businesses accounted for about 10 per cent of America's GNP.

This franchise boom slowed temporarily in the early 1970s. The economic recession that opened the decade exposed weaknesses in the financing and management of many franchised businesses, just as it had with the conglomerates. In addition, government investigations revealed fraud, shoddy business practices, and other problems. Some franchised businesses, it became clear, were simply pyramid schemes in which the only way the franchisee could hope to make money was to sell additional franchises to others. Above all, it became apparent that the franchisees often could not obtain independence or even financial stability in the franchise system. The parent company often profited at the expense of the franchisees. Despite these revelations, the franchise movement recovered momentum during the late 1970s and early 1980s. Americans continued to view franchising as a way to fulfill their dreams of becoming independent entrepreneurs, and franchising spread from lawn care to day-care for children. In 1980, some 442,000 franchise outlets generated $336 billion in sales in the United States.

McDonald's

In 1945, the United States possessed 3,500 fast-food outlets; thirty years later the number had swollen to 440,000, many of which were franchised businesses. With a net income of $549 million on revenues of $4.9 billion in 1987, McDonald's was one of the largest, with 36 per cent of the American fast-food market. As its golden arches rose over outlets around the world, McDonald's also became a substantial multinational enterprise.

McDonald's owed its rise to Ray Kroc and to the eagerness of aspiring entrepreneurs to purchase franchises from his company. Kroc, a salesman, first met the McDonald brothers, who were operating a hamburger stand in San Bernardino, California, in 1954. Then fifty-two years of age, Kroc was on a road trip selling milkshake makers. What he saw at the McDonald brothers' stand impressed him: speedy service, standardized production methods for hamburgers, a fast turnover of customers, and high profits. After making an initial agreement with them in 1954, Kroc bought out the McDonald brothers six years later, acquiring all aspects of their business, including the name, trademark, and recipes. From this beginning, Kroc hit the road to sell franchises. By 1965, McDonald's had 710 stands in 44 states. Twenty-two years later, the company possessed 9,800 outlets in 46 countries and was opening a new one every 17 hours.

Although most of the early McDonald's outlets were owned and run by franchisees, McDonald's soon discovered that it could earn larger profits by owning and operating its outlets directly. As a result, the company mounted a major effort to buy back its franchises in the 1970s. By 1983, McDonald's owned and ran 31 per cent of its hamburger outlets, and these company-owned stands generated three-quarters of McDonald's revenues in that year.

McDonald's continuing success resulted from several factors. The company made its profits on volume production. Through the standardization of production methods, McDonald's in effect turned the preparation of hamburgers into a factory operation. Far from being free agents, franchisees had to follow extremely precise and detailed instructions from corporate headquarters in every step of doing business. (The company's instruction manual for franchisees was 385 pages long.) The low wages McDonald's paid its mostly teenaged employees also enhanced its profits. McDonald's paid the minimum wage and even tried to have Congress approve a special subminimum wage for the fast-food industry. Finally, a successful mass advertising campaign—$789 million was budgeted for advertising and promotion in 1987—made McDonald's a household word across the United States and throughout much of the world.

THE BUSINESS EXECUTIVE

What types of people ran America's businesses in the postwar period? What were the characteristics of business leaders? What were their social and economic backgrounds? Answers to these questions reveal a great deal about the business system of the United States and its place in the economy of the world.

The Socioeconomic Background of Business Leaders

As in times past, most business leaders continued to come from the upper-income ranks in the United States. Rags-to-riches stories remained exceptions, not the rule, in American business. In 1976, some 85 per cent of the business leaders of the United States came from middle-class backgrounds. All but one were men, and none were from minority groups. Most were well educated. About 86 per cent had graduated from college, where 33 per cent had majored in business, 25 per cent in engineering, 23 per cent in economics, and 15 per cent in the humanities. Another 24 per cent had earned master's degrees, and 16 per cent had earned doctorates. Of those who professed a religion, 71 per cent were Protestant, 13 per cent Roman Catholic, and 7 per cent Jewish. An increasing number came from a background in finance. By 1979, one-third of the leaders of America's top one hundred companies had a background in finance, up from only 14 per cent thirty years earlier.

Women in Business Management

With the exception only of Katherine Graham of the *Washington Post,* no woman had reached a top managerial position in big business as late as 1984, and women remained underrepresented in the management of American business in general. Even though they composed 40 per cent of the labor force in 1976, women held only 19 per cent of the jobs in management (and of these women managers, 20 per cent were either self-employed or unpaid family workers). This situation, in part, reflected the generally low position of women workers in the American economy. In 1975, the median income of working women was only 57 per cent of that of men, and the average female college graduate earned less than the average male high school dropout. In 1984, even though women composed 69 per cent of the white-collar work force, only 10 per cent of all managers were women.

By the late 1970s and 1980s, however, a growing number of women were obtaining entry-level and middle-management positions in big businesses, heralding their later arrival in the top ranks of business. During this time women also came to compose an ever-larger proportion of the students in graduate business programs at colleges and universities. In the early 1970s, women typically made up about 5 per cent of the MBA classes at most institutions, but a decade later—by which time the MBA was fast becoming the required degree for entry-level management positions—women composed 30 per cent of such classes. Not all areas of American business were equally receptive to these women; they had more success in finance and the service industries than in basic manufacturing.

Women also advanced as entrepreneurs on their own. Women started businesses at twice the rate of men in the late 1970s and early 1980s, so that between 1977 and 1985 the number of businesses owned by women doubled, reaching a total of 3.7 million. Companies owned by women nonetheless generated less than 10 per cent of the sales made by U.S. businesses.

Juliette Moran was one of the women who succeeded in business. After receiving a B.S. in chemistry from Columbia in 1939, she went to work in Macy's book department at $17 a week, only to leave that company when turned down for a fifty-cent raise a year later. After a series of research jobs in government and business, Moran accepted a position as a chemist with General Aniline and Film (GAF). From research she moved quickly into the budgeting operations of the company—what she later called "the big change in my business life." Her talents were recognized by one of the company's top executives, Jesse Warner, and Moran became his assistant when Warner assumed the presidency of GAF in 1962. Five years later, she had risen to vice president in charge of marketing, personnel, and public relations; by 1978, she was earning $112,000.

Blacks in Business

On the evening of January 14, 1983, William Brock committed suicide by shooting himself in the head. As personnel manager, Brock had been the highest ranking black officer at Volkswagen of America's assembly plant in New Stanton, Pennsylvania. He found himself caught in the middle of a dispute between the firm and its black employees on the issue of job discrimination and, unable to resolve the conflict, killed himself. Brock's death highlighted a fundamental question for blacks beginning to move into management ranks in the postwar era: how to maintain a black identity while climbing the corporate ladder.

Advancement in America's predominantly white companies called for adjustments on the part of blacks. Fleming Golden, a thirty-four-year-old black executive, recalled the changes he had to make at IBM. "I was always a flashy dresser. I had lots of orange and green suits," he observed. "Then one day an older white guy took me áside and said, 'Hey, don't get offended, but it's about those suits you wear. They just don't blend in at IBM.'" He switched to wearing pinstriped suits: "My boss mentioned that he liked the suit I was wearing. I got the message." Golden also gave up playing basketball with his black friends after work in favor of golf with other IBM executives. For Golden these changes worked, and he got ahead. But, as the case of William Brock illustrated, the pressures of trying to remain black in the white corporate world were sometimes overwhelming.

Most blacks never enjoyed even the opportunity to try to succeed in white-owned businesses. In 1980, for instance, only 130 of McDonald's 5,554 domestic outlets were owned by blacks. While they made considerable gains during the 1970s, blacks nonetheless remained grossly underrepresented in U.S. management ranks at the close of that decade. In 1978, about 4 per cent of the managers and officers of major corporations were black (blacks composed about 12 per cent of the American work force). Moreover, of those few blacks in management, only a handful had made it into top management in big businesses.

Black capitalism—black ownership of businesses—offered some hope for blacks excluded from management in white businesses. As we have seen, black-owned businesses have long existed in the United States, some serving primarily black communities. In recent years, black-owned businesses have grown in importance. Between 1972 and 1981, the total sales of the one hundred largest black-owned businesses in the United States rose from $473 million to $1.9 billion, an 81 per cent increase when adjusted for inflation. Despite this progress, black enterprise remained small when compared with leading nonblack businesses. No black-owned business made *Fortune*'s list of the top five hundred industrials in 1983. Johnson Products, the largest black-owned business of any type, with assets of $30 million, trailed far behind Ametek, the five-hundredth largest industrial company, which had assets of $292 million. In fact, the combined sales of the top one hundred black businesses were less than the sales of Uniroyal, number 177 on *Fortune*'s list.

The Social Responsibility of Business

Prodded by the federal government, which greatly increased its regulatory powers over businesses, and by the desires of business executives to win social acceptance for themselves and their companies, U.S. corporate leaders espoused the doctrine of the "social responsibility" of business in the years after 1945. By this doctrine they meant that their companies would act responsibly toward the American public on such matters as truth in advertising, the hiring of women and minorities, and cleaning up the environment. Like their predecessors in the 1920s, business leaders asserted that their companies existed to serve society, not simply to make a profit. As did the business professionals of earlier years, the corporate leaders of the 1950s, 1960s, and 1970s accomplished less than they claimed, but some changes did occur. Under pressure from the federal government, more women and minorities were hired, advertising became somewhat more honest, and steps were taken to avoid air and water pollution. (See Chapter 11 for more details on legislation dealing with these topics.)

Measuring what was accomplished under the doctrine of the social responsibility of business is difficult; clearly, business deeds and business rhetoric did not coincide. For instance, at the same time that they were trying to project an image of corporate social responsibility, the officers of a number of leading oil companies acted in ways that hurt consumers and independent retailers of gasoline. In the 1960s, these officers conspired to prop up the retail price of gasoline in several states and cooperated to keep the price of the crude oil they purchased in California low. Another controversy involved the promotion of beer drinking on college campuses. Despite reports that implicated alcohol abuse as the cause for low grades, vandalism, and occasional student deaths, major brewers and distributors spent in the neighborhood of $20 million in 1984 to promote their beers on campuses across the nation.

Attracting the most public attention were scandals in 1986 and 1987 that besmirched the reputations of several of the nation's leading brokerage houses. Investigations by the Securities and Exchange Commission revealed that numerous members of brokerage firms had used knowledge gained from their work in arranging mergers and speculated in the stocks of the companies involved in the mergers. Called insider trading, this practice blatantly violated federal statutes and traditional ethical norms.

One item that can be measured is corporate giving to philanthropy. By 1980, corporations were donating $2.6 billion annually to philanthropic causes. In that year, Exxon gave $38 million, IBM $35 million, and Atlantic Richfield $34 million. Even companies reporting losses made contributions: General Motors $27 million, Ford $11 million, and Chrysler $2 million. Where did these funds go? About 40 per cent went to education, including universities, 30 per cent to health and welfare projects, 15 per cent to parks and civic improvement projects, and 10 per cent to art and culture. Generally speaking, while the largest corporations were the biggest donors in absolute terms, they did not give the highest proportions of their earnings to philanthropy. Medium-sized companies, especially those in retailing and wholesaling, gave a higher percentage—

probably because they had stronger ties to their local communities than big businesses with offices across the United States and the world.

As in the past, corporate giving raised questions about business goals. Should a company exist to make a profit for its stockholders or to serve society somehow? If a corporation does want to serve society, how best can this goal be accomplished? By making contributions to philanthropic causes? Or by reinvesting its profits in more modern plants and equipment, thus strengthening the nation's economy? Agreement has still not been reached on answers to these questions.

THE MODERN COMPANY

By the mid-1980s, big businesses in the United States had changed considerably from those of thirty or forty years earlier. Above all, they were more diversified. They produced and sold a broader range of products for a wider variety of consumer markets both at home and abroad. But big businesses did not squeeze smaller concerns out of the U.S. economy altogether. Small businesses remained significant, especially in sales and service. If the opportunities of the postwar world brought changes to the business firm, they also altered the nature of government-business relations in the United States. The growth of a consumer society, based on the outpouring of consumer products from U.S. factories, led the federal government into a much broader range of regulatory activities than ever before. And these activities, some critics argued, contributed to the economic decline of the United States to the extent that deregulation was necessary.

Selected Readings

Charles Gilbert, ed., *The Making of a Conglomerate* (Hempstead, N.Y.: Hofstra University Press, 1972), and the editors of *Fortune,* *The Conglomerate Commotion* (New York: Viking Press, 1970), offer solid introductions to the history of conglomerates. The history of diversified companies in general may be examined in Jon Didrichsen, "The Development of Diversified and Conglomerate Firms in the United States, 1920–1970," *Business History Review* 46 (Summer 1972): 202–219. Stanley Brown, *Ling* (New York: Bantam Books,

1972); Max Boas and Steve Chain, *Big Mac* (New York: New American Library, 1977); Anthony Sampson, *The Sovereign State of ITT* (Greenwich, Conn.: Fawcett, 1973); and Robert Sobel, *I.B.M.: Colossus in Transition* (New York: Bantam, 1983), examine specific companies.

The works of Mira Wilkins, cited at the end of Chapter 8, are the standard studies on the history of multinationals. Charles Cheape, *Family Firm to Modern Multinational* (Cambridge, Mass.: Harvard University Press, 1985), is a valuable case study. D. J. Storey, ed., *The Small Firm: An International Survey* (New York: St. Martin's Press, 1983), and Steven Soloman, *Small Business USA* (New York: Crown Publishers 1986), look at small businesses in the United States and abroad. For a case study on the history of one small business see Mansel Blackford, *Pioneering a Modern Small Business: Wakefield Seafoods and the Alaskan Frontier* (Greenwich, Conn.: JAI Press, 1979). Dorothy Riddle, *Service-Led Growth* (New York, Praeger, 1986), examines the importance of service-industry companies. John L. Shover, *First Majority—Last Minority* (DeKalb, Ill.: Northern Illinois University Press, 1976), and Jay Staten, *The Embattled Farmer* (Golden, Colo.: Fulcrum, 1987), look at changes occurring in farming.

On the nature of the American businessman and businesswoman in the postwar period see William Whyte, Jr., *The Organization Man* (New York: Simon and Schuster, 1956); Michael Maccoby, *The Gamesman: The New Corporate Leader* (New York: Simon and Schuster, 1976); and Margaret Hennig and Anne Jardim, *The Managerial Woman* (Garden City, N.Y.: Doubleday, 1977). George Davis and Glegg Watson, *Black Life in Corporate America* (Garden City, N.Y.: Doubleday, 1982), is a useful survey.

IMPORTANT EVENTS, 1946–1989

1946   Congress charters the Council of Economic Advisers in the Employment and Production Act.
General Motors wins a major strike, and union power begins to recede.

1947   The Taft-Hartley Act restricts union activities.

1956   Congress funds the Interstate Highway System.

1962   The Trade Expansion Act promotes overseas trade through negotiated tariff reductions.

1964   The Civil Rights Act requires fair employment for minorities and women.

1966   Congress creates the National Highway Traffic Safety Administration.

1970   The Penn-Central Railroad declares the largest-ever bankruptcy.
The Clean Air Act establishes environmental standards.
Congress creates the Occupational Safety and Health Administration.

1972   The Water Pollution Control Act orders a stop to the discharge of industrial pollutants.
Congress creates the Consumer Product Safety Commission.
The Business Roundtable forms to influence new regulations.

1977   Business wins eased environmental regulations.

1978   The Airline Deregulation Act is passed.

1980   The banking law changes, and deregulation begins.

1982   AT&T agrees to divest local telephone companies in an antitrust settlement.

1984   The Reagan administration rescues the bankrupt Continental Illinois Bank.

1988   Congress approves a trade bill designed to protect U.S. markets from foreign competition.

1989   The federal government commits billions of dollars to rescuing the savings and loan industry from massive failure.

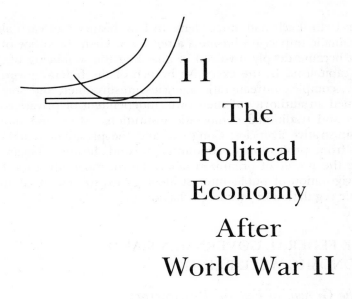

11

The
Political
Economy
After
World War II

The experiences of the Great Depression and wartime prosperity etched themselves deeply on Americans' consciousness. Those experiences meant that after 1945, government exerted more power over business affairs than ever before. Both the depression and World War II had fashioned a stronger federal government that sometimes responded to the wishes of trade unions or others whose interests differed from business's. The growth of rival sources of power threatened the ability of business executives to act independently, and as the U.S. political economy evolved in the postwar decades, business associations and corporations found it necessary to engage continually in political activities to influence public policies. In general, the political rivals of business were not antagonistic to the values of capitalism. The general American public, and often business leaders themselves, still turned to the federal government to guide economic prosperity and to provide a measure of security, and sometimes business executives discovered that their preferences had to give way to other concerns.

Three main trends appeared in the American political economy after 1945. Each had antecedents in U.S. history, but each also had a dramatic impact on business after 1945. First, the office of president became deeply involved in guarding the well-being of American capitalism. In the executive branch of the federal government, large, complex bureaucratic agencies mushroomed and sometimes claimed an authority of their own, independent of private corporations and traditional democratic institutions. More and more, the administrative agencies, Congress, and the president relied on advice from professional economists. Second, business began to reduce the power of organized labor. Third, especially after 1960, a reinvigoration of public-interest ideology led to new social and economic regulation of business behavior.

THE FEDERAL GOVERNMENT AND ECONOMIC WELL-BEING

The Growth of Federal Bureaucracy

Ever since the rise of big business in the nineteenth century, large-scale, impersonal organizations, which existed independently of the lives of the individuals who comprised them, increasingly characterized American society. The process of bureaucratization occurred not only in manufacturing, financial, and transportation enterprises but also in labor unions, social institutions (such as churches, school systems, and universities), trade associations, and political organizations of various kinds.

Nowhere was the growth of bureaucracy more apparent, however, than in government. Government—federal, state, and local—grew slowly but steadily throughout the first half of the twentieth century but expanded remarkably during the 1940s and thereafter. Government employment of civilians, including teachers, rose from 9.5 per cent of the labor force in 1940 to 16.8 per cent in 1986. The federal government alone employed 3.9 per cent of the labor force in 1970, up from 2.4 per cent in 1940. Clearly, the growth of the public sector reflected the increased activities conducted by governmental agencies.

The growth of government also meant an expansion of government involvement in the economy. That involvement took a large number of institutional forms, some of which had developed before World War II. In the years after the war, the federal government more than ever assumed responsibilities for the health of the econ-

President Harry S Truman's signing of the Employment Acy of 1946 was an important public event, symbolized by the number of souvenir pens he intended to distribute. (Wide World Photos, Inc.)

omy to ensure that the end of wartime mobilization would not bring a return of the Great Depression. During the postwar period, the views of professional economists became especially important in shaping fiscal and other policies.

The Employment and Production Act of 1946

On February 20, 1946, President Harry S Truman signed into law the Employment and Production Act. No other action better symbolized the growth of the government's economic authority resulting from the depression and wartime experiences. The law was a compromise between those Americans who wanted the government to assume responsibility for investment decisions in the economy and those who believed that private interests should determine investment decisions. The measure provided a kind of "economic constitution" of the federal government's responsibilities in managing the overall level of prosperity in the United States. The law chartered the Council of Economic Advisers, a new federal agency, to watch over the U.S. economy. The Council was to inform the president about business conditions, to recommend desirable policies, and to issue an annual report on the nation's economic health. To review the information and recommendations generated by the Council of Economic Advisers, the law set up a Joint Economic Committee in Congress. With the signing of the Employment Act, which received few dissenting votes in the House of Representatives and none in the Senate, ultimate authority for the nation's economic well-being shifted from the private arena of corporate boardrooms to the public arena of legislative and presidential politics.

The roots of the shift lay in the desire to prevent the recurrence of the Great Depression. The nation's prosperity due to wartime full employment seemed to confirm Keynes's theory that large public expenditures could create prosperity. Many experts believed that the U.S. industrial economy was "mature," meaning that given the existing inequitable distribution of wealth, there was little reason for business firms to invest in new productive facilities to satisfy already saturated markets. Encouraged by Keynesian economists, some political and labor leaders agreed that without massive and continual government intervention, the peacetime economy would remain stagnant with an undesirably high level of unemployment.

The Employment Act of 1946 thus represented the result of attempts to deal with these concerns. The Senate originally passed a bill with a number of innovations designed to correct the stagnation that had beset the business system during the 1930s. It stated that "all Americans able to work and seeking work have the right to useful remunerative, regular, and full-time employment." To assure such a sweeping right, the Senate bill proposed a planning mechanism, the National Production and Employment Budget. In this scheme the government would estimate the gross national product necessary to achieve full employment as well as the anticipated volume of investment and spending from the public and private sectors. Any deficiency would first be made up by encouraging private investment and spending and, if that proved insufficient to achieve full employment, by spending federal funds. Such federal spending, it was clear to all concerned, might include public works on the model of the Tennessee Valley Authority, not only for electrical power but for such broad social goals as health care and housing.

Business leaders sought a greater emphasis on a public-private partnership in postwar economic policy than the Senate's bill provided. They successfully lobbied the House of Representatives to re-write the legislation. Business leaders had a strong ally during this legislative struggle in the Committee for Economic Development formed during the war years. The Business Council, which advised New Deal officials, had foreseen the need for postwar economic planning. Shortly after the attack on Pearl Harbor, the group's chairman, R. R. Deupree of Procter and Gamble, had voiced his concern: "The challenge which business will face when this war is over cannot be met by a laissez-faire philosophy or by uncontrolled supply and demand. Intelligent planning . . . and courage will be needed to carry us through the reconstruction period." By September 1942, the Commerce Department and the Business Council had cooperated to form the Committee for Economic Development. Its purpose was to combine the talents of professional economists and corporate executives to influence federal policy.

The Committee for Economic Development tried to steer a middle course between older laissez-faire ideas and large-scale state intervention into the economy. The big business leaders and their economists rejected the notion that the American industrial system was mature and therefore stagnant. These executives believed that it was possible to determine the public interest objectively, that there was no necessary conflict between the public interest and the interests of the firms or trade associations for which they worked, and that a cooperative partnership between business and government was desirable and achievable. The Business Council and the Committee for Economic Development thus opposed the full employment bill because it went too far in removing decisions from the private sector and placing power in the hands of government officials.

If the Business Council and the Committee for Economic Development laid the groundwork, the U.S. Chamber of Commerce was the most directly influential group in lobbying Congress to enact the Employment and Production Act of 1946. Eric A. Johnston, the Chamber's national president during the war, led the Chamber away from its earlier opposition to federal intervention in the nation's economic affairs and pressured Congress to pass a law to the Chamber's liking. Gone was the provision to have public investments to guarantee full employment. Instead, the measure provided for technical expertise in guiding the federal government's promotion of private business initiatives for the expansion of economic activity and thereby of fuller, if not full, employment. The new law contained language intended to safeguard the nation from rampant inflation. It signaled greater acceptance by key business leaders that economic leadership ultimately resided in the policies of the federal government, that business and public officials had to act in concert if the nation was to prosper.

The Rise of Professional Economists in the Federal Government

Although economists had advised the government since the 1920s, their role became much larger after the passage of the Employment and Production Act of 1946. They began to have a significant effect on the conditions in which business executives made decisions in the private sector. Professional economists did not fully come into their own, however, until after John F. Kennedy became president in 1961. By the end of the 1950s, Democratic congressional leaders were voicing complaints about President Dwight D. Eisenhower's willingness to accept recessions in the business cycle and their attendant unemployment. Kennedy agreed with this view and as president sought to reduce the unemployment caused by business downturns, to launch social reform programs aimed at eliminating poverty, and to boost defense expenditures. A rapidly expanding economy, stimulated by the correct federal fiscal policy, would, Kennedy hoped, achieve these goals.

Kennedy found that the tradition of corporatism begun in the early twentieth century served him well in this regard. The president turned for professional advice to Walter Heller, Chairman of the Council of Economic Advisers. Following Heller's recommendations, Kennedy proposed reductions in federal taxes to stimulate private capital-goods spending and consumer purchases, while at the same time increasing expenditures for social reform, defense, and a new space program. His aim was to stimulate the economy by deficit spending, anticipating that inflation could be controlled and that eventually an expanded economy would produce greater tax revenues, thereby reducing the federal deficit. The president needed the support of business leaders who could command public attention and congressional backing in order to achieve these goals, but he feared that the nation's business executives would oppose such measures as imprudent. Kennedy's fears proved groundless, however. In fact, the essentials of his proposals agreed with views expressed by the Committee for Economic Development. Late in 1962, Kennedy addressed the Economic Club of New York, and its members received his ideas warmly. The president told Heller that the speech was "straight Keynes and Heller, and they loved it." Later, a National Association of Manufacturers official expressed support for tax reduction *"even in the face of* a current deficit which can only be partially moderated." Unfortunately, Kennedy's assassination prevented him from enjoying the fruits of his political initiative. After Congress enacted his fiscal program in 1964, the American economy boomed. Soon, however, the costs of the Vietnam War, combined with President Lyndon B. Johnson's reluctance to raise taxes, overheated the economy, and inflation rose out of control.

Nonetheless, the success of Kennedy's initiative had the effect of ensuring an influential role for technical economic analysis within the federal government. During the Kennedy-Johnson years, social scientists employed by the federal government were active as never before in providing indicators and guideposts with which the politicians could assess policy. These activities occurred, moreover, in the public sector, quite independent of decisions made in corporate boardrooms. President Johnson began a planning, programming, and budgeting system throughout the executive branch that required agencies to consider the costs and probable economic outcomes of their programs, and their reports were evaluated and programs coordinated by a planning staff. Later, in 1970, President Richard M. Nixon and Congress agreed to change the Bureau of the Budget into an Office of Management and Budget further to evaluate and forecast economic trends and events. Under Nixon, the federal government moved further toward a system of national planning. Nixon created the Domestic Council in an attempt to clarify objectives, explain alternative policies, make policy recommendations, and coordinate and evaluate programs. In 1974, Congress established its own Budget Office to provide the legislators with economic analyses independent of those developed in the executive branch.

GOVERNMENT AND THE FRAMEWORK FOR BUSINESS ACTIVITY

The federal government not only became deeply involved in assuring the economic well-being of the nation in the post–1945 period by seeking general prosperity and growth, but it also engaged in activities deliberately designed to shape the business environment.

Economic analyses were one aspect of these activities, as were varying political responses to the specific interests of particular industries or segments of the business community. By the later 1970s, some policymakers, most notably on the Federal Reserve Board, had moved beyond Keynesian economic theory to a different perception of the nation's general economic needs—namely, recognition of the need to regulate the total supply of money in the economy. Through the 1960s, American economic growth appeared to be on an upward trend, but after 1970, stung by the costs of the Vietnam War and shocked by sudden increases in energy prices, the business system encountered new problems of inflation, stagnation, and international competition, the solutions to which involved government action affecting the framework of business activity.

Tariff Policy

Like other aspects of federal economic policy, tariff policy became an ever more complex affair, depending, insofar as it affected particular industries, on technical analyses by professional economists of business conditions both here and abroad. Within the complexity, broad policies of trade liberalization emerged only to be countervailed by renewed political pressures for protection from foreign competition after the onset of stagflation (an unprecedented situation in which growth stagnated while inflation flamed) in the 1970s. On the whole, the general trend of the 1960s and 1970s was toward freer international trade. Pressures to protect Americans from foreign competitors mounted in the 1980s, however. Congress responded in 1988 with a new trade bill, which sought to strengthen the hand of federal officials in negotiating access to foreign markets for U.S. firms by threatening to withhold access to U.S. markets by European and Asian competitors.

Beginning in the mid-1930s, the executive branch of the federal government generally followed a policy of trade liberalization, grounded in the belief that if each nation pursued its own advantage independently of political barriers, all peoples would benefit. After World War II, American business and political leaders had such confidence in the strength of the economic system and the ability of U.S. firms to dominate key world markets that it seemed advantageous to liberalize foreign trade even more, so that U.S. firms might more readily import raw materials and export finished products, while American farmers disposed of food surpluses in

The flood of foreign compact cars affected the U.S. car industry in recent decades, not only by taking a sizable market share but also by making the American auto firms revise their designs and make smaller cars. This photograph taken in Japan around 1980 shows a cargo of Hondas being loaded for shipment overseas. (Courtesy of American Honda Motors)

hungry world markets. Multinational firms, especially, saw advantages in free-trade policies. Their executives moved capital around the world to take advantage of lower-priced raw material and lower labor costs in developing nations.

Trade liberalization proceeded further after passage of the Trade Expansion Act of 1962. Increased overseas trade was a central feature of President Kennedy's foreign policy, for he believed that the resulting stronger world economy would reduce the appeal of socialism. Through 1967, a so-called Kennedy round of international reciprocity negotiations occurred that effectively lowered many tariff barriers around the world and opened the American market further to foreign goods.

This tendency toward trade liberalization occurred in the face of counterpressures for protectionism emanating from business and labor organizations hurt by foreign competitors. The Trade Expansion Act of 1962 included provisions for federal assistance to business firms and workers hurt by foreign competition. Government agencies, advised by economists, tried to guard against unfair foreign competition. This modern protectionism, however, did not take the historic form of raising tariff duties. Instead, Americans injured by foreign competition proposed restraints on exports by foreign producers, and such restraints were imposed in the textile, shoe, steel, and automobile industries. The American automobile firms, for example, saw their position in the American market erode in the flood of Japanese imports in the later 1970s, and in 1981 they succeeded—in alliance with the auto workers' unions—in having the federal government negotiate an agreement by which the Japanese "voluntarily" restricted sales in the American market below prescribed limits.

Antitrust Policy

Antitrust litigation was another area in which government influenced business decisions in the decades after 1945. With the exception of a few spectacular cases, antitrust actions during this period attracted little public notice because most of the cases were very technical. The issues of firm size and price fixing among competitors that had once received the attention of presidents and their rivals seemed to have faded.

Actually, the volume of antitrust cases and the size of the government agencies dealing with antitrust issues expanded after World War II. The Antitrust Division of the Department of Justice grew to employ hundreds of attorneys and dozens of economists. Comparable development occurred in the Federal Trade Commission, which formed a separate Bureau of Competition to engage in antitrust activities. This trend in both agencies gave evidence of the growing bureaucratization of antitrust activity as more and more of it was placed in the hands of specialists who engaged in time-consuming court actions involving judicial rulings on arcane points of law.

The emergence of antitrust litigation as a mostly technical, bureaucratic enterprise did not mean that important policy changes went unconsidered. In fact, Congress provided an important modification of the existing antitrust statutes when it passed the Celler-Kefauver Act of 1950. This measure stated that the government could examine market share as evidence of anticompetitive, monopolistic practice. Earlier, in the Progressive Era, some politicians had unsuccessfully argued that a firm that controlled more than 25 per cent of the market in its industry should be declared in violation of the antitrust statutes. Although the Celler-Kefauver amendment did not specify a figure, its passage meant that in the future business executives would have to consider overall market share as a part of their fundamental strategy, lest they run afoul of government litigation. Such considerations, for instance, restrained General Motors from deliberately destroying smaller competitors.

Not all antitrust suits were technical and arcane. One spectacular antitrust decision involved the American Telephone and Telegraph Company. The nation's largest firm in terms of assets, AT&T provided 70 million customers with high-quality telephone service at low rates. It employed 1 million people, had 3.2 million shareholders, and borrowed more money than anyone but the federal government. Because of an antitrust suit begun in 1974, this giant had to divest itself of its local operating companies, an undertaking of staggering complexity.

The case against AT&T arose initially because of government accusations of anticompetitive practices, not from an upswell of public outrage. Earlier, the Justice Department had obtained an agreement that prevented AT&T from entering the computer industry, even though its Bell Laboratories had provided major technological innovations that made modern computers possible. This earlier agreement had protected firms in the computer industry, including IBM, from the enormous resources at AT&T's command, resources that the communications firm might have used to dominate the computer industry. After AT&T agreed to divest itself of its local companies, however, the government allowed it to enter the computer business. In 1984, the smaller but still sizable AT&T began marketing computers in competition with IBM and other firms.

Banks, Money, and Economic Theory

Just as long-standing concerns with trade and antitrust policy continued to involve the federal government during the postwar decades, so did banking and monetary issues. The once-vehement conflict over the metallic base for the nation's coinage had ended, and now, especially with the emergence of stagflation, the issues involved new ideas about the relationship between the supply of money and the nation's economic health.

The widespread worries about inflation were, in the long span of history, new. As the American society became more affluent, economists' concerns about scarcity began to recede and be replaced by concerns about inflation. Historically, inflation had accompanied wars, and prices had dropped in postwar recessions. But after World War II, when a deliberately contrived inflation was moderated by government controls, prices did not go down. In fact, the long-run trend of the U.S. economy in the twentieth century was toward inflation. Because inflation affected business investment decisions and the costs of labor and materials, it evolved as an area of lively political dispute and vitally affected federal policy.

During the 1960s, an economic theory called monetarism emerged as a powerful idea. Associated with Milton Friedman, an economics professor at the University of Chicago, the monetarists challenged the federal government to follow a new course regarding inflation. Friedman observed that inflation and the supply of money were historically closely related. From this viewpoint the government should carefully monitor and control the money supply in order to control inflation. Since the banking industry provided money to business firms and consumers, the Federal Reserve Board, which governed the banks, should become the principal agency in the fight against inflation.

Congress responded in 1975. A joint resolution charged the Federal Reserve System with watching and controlling the money supply in order to produce "maximum employment, stable prices, and moderate long-term interest rates." The Federal Reserve Board began reporting regularly on its policies of monetary growth. But the problems of stagflation continued into the 1980s. Keeping tight reins on the supply of money had the effect of raising interest rates, slowing business investment and consumer spending, and threatening depression levels of unemployment. Nevertheless, monetary policy was another significant area in which public action set the boundaries in which business executives arrived at investment, employment, and production decisions.

The Military-Industrial Complex

The federal government embarked on yet another significant new policy after 1945 that affected the American business system. Before World War II, the nation's peacetime military forces were kept at low levels. After 1945, however, U.S. leaders perceived a continuing threat to the very existence of capitalism around the world as a result of the growth of the power of the Soviet Union. These perceptions were heightened by the Communist revolution in China in 1949 and the war that broke out in Korea in 1950. In addition, sometimes other Asians, and Africans and Latin Americans as well, began to look to China and Russia as desirable socialist models for economic development and national independence. After 1945, in brief, U.S. leaders faced a continuing "cold war" between the two economic and political systems, punctuated by "limited" warfare in Korea and, later, Southeast Asia. These perceived dangers to the security and self-interest of the United States and its trading partners gave rise to a policy of partial but continual defense mobilization, a policy that reshaped the relationships among developers of technology, business corporations, and the military services. In 1961, President Eisenhower termed those new relationships the "military-industrial complex," and his phrase caught on because it summarized a new and seemingly permanent set of institutions. Because of the continuing cold war, the Department of Defense became one of the nation's major consumers. In 1977, for instance defense purchases of $92.8 billion took up 4.8 per cent of the American GNP, and those purchases rose to $277.6 billion and 6.6 per cent of the GNP in 1986. Clearly, defense had emerged as a major force in the American business system.

The market for weapons, the increasing technological complexity of weapons systems, and their maintenance involved corporate executives, scientists, and engineers as well as military personnel. During World War II, as we have seen, the military services preferred to arrange contracts with large industrial corporations, and the effect of these procurement policies was to speed up the concentration of assets into fewer and fewer big businesses. The emergence of the military-industrial complex reinforced that trend. One researcher found that "from 1940 to 1965 the fifty largest corporations in the country always received somewhat more than half of all prime military contracts, while small business never received as much as 20 percent."

Not only did a large market with only one customer develop in defense, but also arrangements were made in which there were sole suppliers for major weapons systems. Traditional practices of competitive bidding by private firms for government contracts simply were not economically feasible in this situation. The technological complexity of aircraft, missiles, ships, and other military goods grew enormously, so much so that private firms lacked the resources to develop them without assurances of their ultimate sales. The Defense Department therefore became a significant source of funds for scientific and engineering research. Between 1955 and 1965, federal spending for science grew from $3.3 billion to $14.8 billion,

Manufacture of aircraft for the United States Air Force is a mammoth, complex job, requiring close cooperation between business firms and the military. In the design, procurement, and production of military hardware, lines between civilian firms and the services blurred as U.S. leaders after 1945 felt compelled to maintain a strong national defense. The resulting phenomenon was what President Dwight D. Eisenhower dubbed the "military-industrial complex." (Peter Menzel/Stock, Boston)

most of which was defense-related. The Defense Department developed close relations with private firms (and, to a lesser extent, universities) for the development of new weapons. Then, typically, when a large firm received a contract for the design and production of a weapon, that firm subcontracted with other companies for assistance. The result was an elaborate network of funding, contracting, and subcontracting that extended across the nation and into a majority of the congressional districts (whose representatives voted the necessary appropriations). Moreover, the defense procurement system was susceptible to abuse. Firms sometimes allied with military officers to produce expensive weapons systems of questionable value, and the extraordinary defense contract profits enjoyed by the unscrupulous often became public scandals.

Eisenhower termed these arrangements the military-industrial complex because he was concerned about the "acquisition of unwarranted influence." Eisenhower believed in a "public interest" that transcended the self-interest of the military services and defense contractors who, he feared, were able to arrange decisions that were not always in the nation's best interests. Moreover, there were powerful forces within the business community and the military services to influence increased funding levels and to maintain cordial relations. In 1958, for instance, the Committee for Economic Development called for larger defense appropriations from which individual members' corporations clearly stood to benefit. Moreover, retired military officers, many of whom still had strong ties with the military, populated defense contractor offices. In 1969, some 2,072 retired colonels, captains, admirals, and generals were employed by defense suppliers.

In the years after Eisenhower's retirement, the issues he had raised caused continuing controversy. President Kennedy appointed Robert S. McNamara of the Ford Motor Company as secretary of defense, and McNamara and his associates used business management principles to try to control the logistics of the military services. Nevertheless, the goods and services of defense dwarfed the sales of even the nation's largest firm, and the problems of dealing with an enterprise of such magnitude remained. Moreover, although defense expenditures clearly benefited individual workers, communities, and firms, they retarded employment levels in the economy as a whole. Military spending deprived businesses of human and capital resources they otherwise could have used to compete more effectively in world markets. And many people resented such high levels of defense spending when tremendous social problems still existed. The nation's leaders, for the most part, favored these continuing and after 1980 substantially increasing peacetime defense expenditures, so the problems associated with the military-industrial complex remained unsolved.

FEDERAL AID TO BUSINESS

From its foundation in 1789, as we have seen, the federal government used its resources to aid business directly in the development of the nation's economy. This developmental activity continued in the middle of the twentieth century, but the new conditions of stagflation and worldwide business competition after 1970 created a new dimension: the federal government began serving as a banker of last resort to ailing corporations.

The cloverleaf highway intersection—this one in New Jersey—was but one of the highway design innovations for speeding the flow of traffic. After President Eisenhower signed the Interstate Highway Act in 1956, the federal interstate highway system utilized such designs across the nation. (Standard Oil of N.J. Collection, University of Louisville Photographic Archives)

Highways

In the nineteenth century, the federal government helped private entrepreneurs develop railroad facilities, especially when the network approached the trackless barriers of western plains, deserts, and mountains. In the twentieth century, the widespread popularity of automobiles and trucks led the federal government to become heavily involved in the financing of improved roads, once a largely local concern.

After World War II, as the popularity of automobiles and trucks continued to grow, motorists and shippers encountered serious problems. Traffic simply did not move freely across the country, and congestion, especially in and around cities, added considerably to the cost of moving goods. The solution seemed to be expressways, divided highways specifically designed for fast travel. City planners liked the concept, because they envisioned expressways as devices to shape urban environments in socially desirable ways, and economists concerned about the business cycle saw road construction as a public-works project with the potential for stimulating employment during recessions.

In response, Congress authorized in 1956 the funding of a 41,000-mile National System of Interstate and Defense Highways. The bill created a highway "trust fund" that housed special tax revenues collected from fuel, tires, and other equipment. All motorists would pay for the roads, and all were free to use them, but the main purpose of the construction was to satisfy the requirements of the business firms seeking a more efficient trucking industry. By 1960, some 7,570 miles of expressways were open to traffic, with the remainder under construction or being planned. The federal government had launched a major public-works program in which the public provided capital facilities of use to countless American business firms.

Rescuing Corporations

If the financing of express highways was a significant event in the tradition of federal aid to business, the use of federal resources to rescue ailing corporations was a new departure. As economic growth faltered and stagflation set in after 1970, some major corporations fell into deep trouble. One response to failure was to invoke the bankruptcy laws and allow private investors, under court supervision, to reorganize the firm's assets. Another response was to use federal resources to refinance the failing firm, and government leaders followed this latter course when the failed firms were among the largest in the American business system, even though the policy flew in the face of traditional rhetoric regarding competition, risk taking, and free enterprise.

The bankruptcy of the Penn Central Railroad in 1970, the largest such failure in American history, prompted the federal government to begin making large investments in the nation's northeastern railroads. The Penn Central was born of a 1966 merger between the New York Central and Pennsylvania railroads, lines that had been among the nation's most important transportation firms for generations. By the 1960s, the railroad industry in general and northeastern railroads in particular faced serious troubles. Interstate Commerce Commission regulations required the carriers to maintain service on 21,000 miles of track for which operating costs exceeded revenues. Public financing of roads for the trucking industry had cost the railroads important freight traffic, while inept regulation prevented their integrating rail and truck transportation. The formation of the Penn Central had been a response to these conditions, with the promoters of the new railroad convinced that merger would produce operating efficiencies, improved service, and, in turn, profitability. This proved not to be the case, however, for the new railroad's management failed fully to integrate operations and to take advantage of the opportunities provided by the merger. As the Penn Central's service declined, freight shippers turned to competitors, and the railroad was forced into bankruptcy. Concurrently, other railroads in the region were also in bankruptcy, threatening to liquidate their assets and end service altogether.

Federal officials saw the certain deterioration of northeastern railroad service and the threatened termination as clearly contrary to the public interest; the industrial prosperity of the Northeast and Midwest depended on railroad service. Early in 1974, President Nixon signed the Regional Rail Reorganization Act to revitalize railroads in the Northeast. The law authorized the Consolidated Rail Corporation to form from the remains of seven bankrupt railroads, guaranteeing loans to it and compensating former creditors. The Penn Central was the heart of the new Conrail, as the firm was called, 85 per cent of which the federal government owned (with the remainder of the stock in the hands of the carrier's employees). Over the next several years, the government pumped in about $3.28 billion of capital to restore facilities. The employees granted significant wage concessions, and Conrail, under able management and regulatory relief granted by Congress, was able to close down unprofitable lines. By 1983, Conrail was reporting profits and increases in its working capital, and the government was looking for buyers for its share of the railroad's assets.

In two other spectacular cases during the 1970s, the federal government used its resources to prevent bankruptcies of major industrial firms. In 1971, the Lockheed Corporation, America's largest defense contractor, teetered on the edge of bankruptcy because of problems with civilian aircraft. To save the firm, the Nixon administration arranged a $750 million loan package, $250 million of which was guaranteed by the federal government. This arrangement allowed Lockheed to escape bankruptcy. Then in 1979, during the administration of President Jimmy Carter, the nation's tenth-largest industrial firm, Chrysler, which had been losing money in its automobile business, informed the nation that without

Chrysler Chairman Lee Iacocca and President Jimmy Carter shake hands to con-
clude the federal "bail-out" of the ailing giant auto firm. The Michigan congressmen
present were also clearly pleased with the pact. Federal aid to Chrysler turned out to
be a success story, and Iacocca became a prominent public figure and author of an
autobiography, reckoned to be the best-selling business book ever published.
(Wide World Photos, Inc.)

additional credit it would fail. The federal government agreed to a
guarantee of $1.5 billion of credit to rescue the ailing corporation.
The arrangement included substantial wage concessions from the
members of the United Auto Workers in exchange for placing a
union representative on Chrysler's board of directors. The package
and the subsequent performance of the firm were monitored by a
special Loan Guarantee Review Board headed by the secretary of
the treasury. Government officials were willing to make such a large
commitment in hopes of saving the firm and maintaining employment. Finally, after several years of operating on the brink of de-
fault, Chrysler was able to reestablish itself, earn profits, and repay
its loans in 1984.

Nor was the federal rescue of ailing corporations confined to industrial firms. When an economic downturn in the early 1980s produced the nation's worst recession since the 1930s, the results
produced insolvency in some important banks. The New Deal banking reforms had included federal depositor's insurance. When insol-

vency loomed, the usual government policy was to arrange a merger of the insolvent bank with a solvent bank as a less costly way of protecting deposits. However, in the case of the insolvency of the Continental Illinois National Bank and Trust in the summer of 1984, officials of the Reagan administration decided to provide government-guaranteed loans to Continental Illinois, forcing management changes as a condition; Continental Illinois's liabilities were simply too large to force a merger with a healthy bank.

THE NEW REGULATION

As it had from the early 1800s, the federal government continued to shape the political environment within which American businesses operated and to aid them through developmental economic policies. Along with this aid came federal regulation, and in the decades after 1960, the federal government became involved in a new burst of regulatory activity. Earlier forms of regulation had been political responses to the advent of the new center firms that were reordering business activities in the industrializing economy; the burst of new regulation that occurred after 1960 involved the creation of new government agencies to deal with the broad human, social, and environmental effects of a mature industrial system.

Ralph Nader and the Origins of the New Regulation

On November 29, 1965, an event occurred that more than any other symbolized the appearance of new impulses for the regulation of business behavior: the publication of *Unsafe at Any Speed: The Designed-in Dangers of the American Automobile* by Ralph Nader. The son of Lebanese immigrants, Nader was a brilliant young attorney and free-lance journalist who attacked the nation's largest industrial company, General Motors, for designing and marketing a defective automobile, the Chevrolet Corvair, in which unwitting consumers were maimed and killed. Worst of all, Nader revealed that General Motors had sold the vehicle knowing that its suspension system was inadequate for certain driving conditions. The company had decided to proceed with the manufacture and sale of the faulty Corvair without regard to the public safety, Nader charged, to protect its investment.

For Nader, the point of attacking General Motors was not simply to question the motives of its executives but to call attention to a larger issue. "A great problem of contemporary life," he observed, "is how to control the power of economic interests which ignore the harmful effects of their applied science and technology." General Motors and the Corvair's problems were thus symbolic, a point of departure for a revival of the idea that the public interest must prevail over the profit motive of powerful corporations. Business executives, as we have seen, sometimes boasted of their social responsibility; Nader demonstrated that their behavior sometimes ran contrary to their rhetoric. The problem was worsened by the ever-growing complexity of the consumer products spewing from modern factories.

The publication of *Unsafe at Any Speed* might not have been a memorable event by itself, but Nader graphically expressed a growing concern among the consuming public. The automobile was not only an integral part of the American business system but was central as well to the lifestyles of the vast majority of Americans. Nader's revelations struck a raw nerve in American culture, because people realized that they could not automatically trust manufacturers to provide reasonably sound products. Nader's concerns got even greater publicity when a congressional committee revealed unsavory behavior on the part of General Motors executives who apparently intended to discredit the author. James P. Roche, the president of GM, apologized to Nader in testimony before the committee.

Two important events followed the revelations of GM's behavior. One was the creation in 1966 of a new regulatory agency, the National Highway Traffic Safety Administration, to govern the design of automobiles sold in the United States. Although Nader was acutely disappointed by the agency's subsequent performance, a new regulatory agency was nevertheless born. Furthermore, riding the crest of his nationwide publicity, Nader established the Center for Study of Responsive Law in 1968 (later, in 1970, he founded the Public Interest Research Group with funds won in a court suit against GM for the firm's invasion of his privacy). Vigorously promoting the use of the law as an agent of social change, "Nader's Raiders," as the press dubbed the men and women associated with Ralph Nader, soon initiated a spate of reports critical of business behavior and the failure of government adequately to regulate that behavior.

Sources of the New Regulation

Before Ralph Nader drew attention to the problems of the Corvair, questions of the public interest had typically arisen from concerns over fairness in apportioning material benefits and entrepreneurial opportunities among business firms, between management and labor, and toward commercial farmers. During the 1960s, the traditional forms of regulation that had begun with the creation of the Interstate Commerce Commission in 1887 continued. However, Nader was able to awaken and mobilize reform impulses arising from an entirely different kind of society, a consumer society concerned about issues arising from material abundance rather than scarcity.

The new regulation that began in the 1960s was in large part a product of the success of the business system. The success of industrialists in organizing the mass production of consumer goods, first so evident in the consumer-durables industries in the 1920s and later apparent in the fantastic production achievements of World War II, had created unprecedented material abundance. The confidence of economists, politicians, and business executives in their abilities to foster fiscal policies conducive to permanent plateaus of prosperity contributed to a national mood of complacency. In short, a large segment of the American population came to take for granted not only consumer goods, such as automobiles and electrical appliances, but amenities, items that increased pleasures as well. They assumed as their birthright a good life of material plenty, comfort, safety, and security.

Signs of the consumer-amenity society abounded by the 1950s. The executives of industrial firms, as we have seen, increasingly based their strategies on marketing considerations rather than the more traditional production orientations. Business entrepreneurs developed new technologies to make products more appealing to consumers. Automobile manufacturers promoted automatic transmissions and air conditioning, as well as attractive colors and design details like tailfins, to ease driving and improve passenger comfort. Color film and television replaced black and white images in popular favor, while recorded sound became available in high-fidelity stereo. By the end of the 1950s, historian David Potter described material abundance as a distinguishing characteristic of American civilization, and economist John Kenneth Galbraith, while decrying the continuation of poverty, analyzed what he termed the "affluent society."

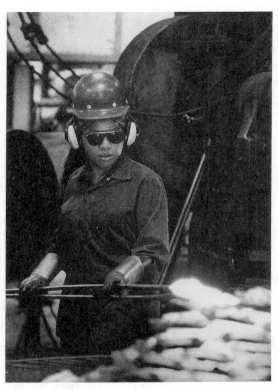

*During World Wars I and II, women entered the
U.S. industrial work force in increasing numbers.
Although women experienced intense pressure from
men to leave their higher paying jobs after both
wars ended, eventually employment opportunities for
women in business dramatically enlarged, thanks in
part to the federal civil rights legislation of the
1960s. (Robert V. Eckert/The Picture Cube)*

The quest for the amenities of life extended far beyond the development of consumer goods and the marketing strategies of large
corporations. After 1960, vocal and powerful groups of affluent
Americans began to question the side effects of the headlong drive
for material abundance. Some who had moved to the suburbs, for
instance, in search of green spaces and fresh air disliked the decisions of business developers seeking further growth. Environmental
pollution became an emotional issue. Other Americans—the con-
servationists—opposed corporate and governmental development of

scenic lands, forests, and rivers. Union leaders and workers expressed the belief that successful corporations should ensure safe and healthful workplaces. Consumer activists like Ralph Nader asserted that marketing strategies must not result in products that unnecessarily endangered human lives. A general concern about the quality of life in the present and the future arose. This concern, in turn, led to political demands for new forms of government regulation to guard the public interest, to protect the quality of life. By the end of the 1960s, many of these groups coalesced into an environmental movement that sought a changed relationship between business and government in which experts guarded the quality of life.

Quite apart from the issues arising from the apparent conquest of the age-old problem of economic scarcity came still further demands for changes in public policy. The continuation of racial injustice in a nation that officially expressed the ideal of equality produced a powerful civil rights movement in postwar America. The civil rights reformers called upon the nation's institutions to treat all citizens equally. Black leaders demanded fair employment practices in the private as well as the public sector. By the early 1960s, black demands had helped fuel the feminist movement, which maintained that the public interest required equality of treatment between genders as well as between races. Promoters of equal rights for women and blacks sought enhanced government regulation of the employment and personnel policies of business, as well as other institutions.

Civil Rights Regulation

Black Americans had long sought federal help in achieving a greater measure of racial justice in American institutions, including business. Black Americans as a group had historically received a disproportionately small share of wealth. One problem was inadequate access to higher-paying and secure jobs. In 1940, as the nation was mobilizing its resources for war, a black union leader, A. Phillip Randolph, successfully pressured President Roosevelt to issue an executive order banning racial discrimination in firms enjoying defense contracts. As the civil rights movement grew more powerful after World War II, it demanded new federal legislation to bring an end to racial discrimination.

The major result of the civil rights movement, the Civil Rights Act of 1964, contained a provision that had a new regulatory impact on American business. One of the law's provisions outlawed racial and gender discrimination in employment. An Equal Employment Opportunities Commission was established to gather information and emphasize conciliation as a way of ending discriminatory personnel practices. Under the new law, when an individual believed he or she was being treated unfairly by an employer or a union, he or she could institute a court suit to end the practice. The Department of Justice could participate in the suit when it observed "a pattern of practice . . . of general public importance." Under this measure neither employers nor unions would any longer be free to practice racial discrimination in hiring, promotion, or job-security policies. Business, in effect, faced a new round of regulation in its personnel policies.

New Regulatory Measures

Many other public-interest demands were met by legislation enacted after 1960. After the laws governing equal rights for citizens came measures intended to safeguard recreational and wilderness water and land in perpetuity, as well as laws that regulated the automobile industry. Between 1965 and 1972, a federal policy evolved regarding the protection of the environment. At first the main concern was "ecology," the interrelationships among natural environments and living organisms. By the 1970s, however, public concern had broadened so that the human health issues related to the adverse effects of industrial production predominated.

From the long list of new regulatory measures regarding the environment three actions deserve special notice. In 1967, Congress enacted the Air Quality Act to establish a system by which the federal and state governments could cooperate in efforts to lessen automobile and industrial air pollution. A complex measure that expressed the new concern with environmental quality, it did not seem to be effective. Congress tried to improve matters with the Clean Air Act of 1970, which required government agencies to establish and businesses to reach clean-air standards by 1975. The criteria to be used were based on health considerations, not technological feasibility or economic costs. Then in 1972, again using health criteria, in the Federal Water Pollution Control Act Congress mandated an end to the discharge of industrial pollutants by 1985. In both cases the legislation set clear regulatory goals and a timetable for their achievement. In the meantime, President Nixon consolidated various environmental regulatory functions into the

The public's worry about damage to the environment by industrial waste and accidents reached a peak with the massive oil spill in Alaska's Prince William Sound by the Exxon tanker Valdez *in March 1989. The environmental disaster (above and opposite) not only brought tightened safety regulations for shipping in the area but also affected decisions about future oil-development policies. (Alaska Department of Environmental Conservation)*

Environmental Protection Agency (EPA) by which means, he said, the government could treat the environment "as a single inter-related system." State governments followed suit, creating environmental agencies to cooperate in solving the problems of air and water pollution at the local level.

Behind all these regulations lay a political commitment to protect the health and welfare of future generations of Americans and a recognition by congressional majorities that the private decisions of business executives did not necessarily conform to that public interest. It had become clear that the criteria of regulation should be scientifically derived by experts not beholden to any particular corporate interest. The legislation, in short, embodied a realization that much more than the factors of production were appropriate considerations in public policy. The regulators assumed that the material abundance of American society was sufficient to justify such health and welfare concerns, and that a "people of plenty" should apply scientific knowledge in maintaining the resources used by all peoples.

Enactment of this new environmental legislation provoked a hailstorm of criticism from business executives and their trade associations. The problem with the new regulations, in their view, lay in the health and welfare criteria that the government wanted to apply to production and marketing decisions. Regulations, business executives complained, must take into account the costs to the firms being regulated (and thereby the costs to society as a whole) and the technological feasibility of achieving clean air and water. Moreover, the complexity of achieving the mandated goals soon mired the EPA and the affected business firms in a morass of bureaucracy that, from the point of view of production- and profit-minded executives, unnecessarily diverted attention from normal entrepreneurial goals. In brief, business complained that the new regulation was impractical.

Business criticisms led to significant amendments to the environmental laws in 1977 as Congress accepted the complaints of industrialists concerning the economic and technological feasibility of achieving regulatory goals. Congress changed or extended the deadlines it had imposed earlier for achieving significant reductions in air and water pollution. After 1977, regulators tried to account for the views of industrialists as well as environmentalists and to weigh the costs as well as the benefits of specific regulatory policies. In the 1980s the measurement of costs and benefits by economic analysis became the standard policy of the Reagan administration.

New Regulation of the Workplace

Closely related to the concerns expressed in the 1960s over the state of the natural environment were matters of health and safety in the workplace. Unrest among workers complaining about health and safety conditions rose during the decade, and seeing the chance to solidify their support among workers, both Presidents Johnson and Nixon favored legislation intended to improve and safeguard working conditions. In 1970 Congress created the Occupational Safety and Health Administration (OSHA) in the Department of Labor to sponsor research on desirable occupational safety and health standards and to prescribe regulations to achieve them. At the time, in addition to workplace accidents that killed thousands of workers and caused millions of disabling injuries each year, government officials estimated that occupational diseases and illnesses annually killed 100,000 Americans and afflicted 390,000 more.

Business associations were adamant in their opposition to the creation of OSHA and its subsequent regulations. One complaint concerned the costs of meeting the law's requirements. The Chamber of Commerce claimed in 1981 that business already had spent about $48 billion in capital expenses to meet the new requirements, $5 billion in that one year alone. (On the other hand, occupational illnesses were costing the Social Security system and other welfare agencies $3 billion annually during the same period.) Nor were the costs encountered by business the only reason for its opposition. The creation of OSHA enabled workers to complain formally of working conditions to sympathetic federal officials and thereby to gain a greater measure of control over the terms of their employment. Business executives bitterly resisted relinquishing their traditional prerogative of control over working conditions. They complained about federal safety inspectors wasting their time, imposing unreasonable rules, and in general creating confusion and senseless intrusion in factories, workshops, stores, and offices.

New Consumer Regulation

One result of the gradual emergence of an affluent society more and more concerned with the quality of life was direct federal involvement in the affairs of consumers. As producers of goods, business people, farmers, and workers had learned techniques of organization and political action to protect their interests. Consumers, however, remained amorphous and for the most part unorganized. Yet the right of consumers to have safe products of high quality available at fair prices seemed indisputable, and the political appeal of consumer issues was powerful, as Ralph Nader had demonstrated. Traditionally, Americans had left the safeguarding of consumer interests largely to the collective power of purchasing decisions. In an age in which producer interests were well financed and politically powerful, however, the marketplace did not always protect consumers. Moreover, as products became technologically more complex, it was difficult for individual consumers to make rational purchasing decisions.

The new consumer regulation began in 1966 with the formation of the National Highway Traffic Safety Administration. Acting on behalf of its policyholders, the insurance industry aided Nader's cause in order to promote improved safety standards in the design of vehicles. The consumer movement broadened in the 1970s. In 1972, the Supreme Court allowed the Federal Trade Commission wider powers to investigate business practices on behalf of consumers, and Congress created the Consumer Product Safety Commission to set and enforce safety standards for thousands of schools, household, and recreational goods. Three years later, Congress passed the Warranty Act of 1975, which required businesses to disclose warranty information to consumers in clear language, to establish meaningful procedures to handle consumer complaints, and to declare the limits of their warranty obligations.

The changes in government regulation of business on behalf of consumers also included the courts. Traditionally, judges had applied the legal doctrine of *caveat emptor,* "let the buyer beware," when consumers complained about the purchase of an inferior product. Consumers could recover from manufacturers of defective products only if they proved negligence. The legal barriers protecting manufacturers crumbled in 1960, however, when the New Jersey Supreme Court ruled that the driver of a new Chrysler automobile whose steering mechanism suddenly failed, demolishing the car and painfully injuring the occupant, did not have to prove that the manufacturer was negligent. In effect, the court ruled that consumers enjoyed an implied warranty from manufacturers. That year there were fewer than 50,000 product-liability cases before American courts, but by 1963 the figure had jumped to 250,000; in

1970 it had climbed to 500,000. After 1960, manufacturers felt that the nation's legal doctrine had become *caveat venditor,* "let the seller beware."

Business Response to the New Regulation

The new regulations of the 1960s and 1970s and their agencies had one unifying theme. Unlike earlier federal regulatory activity, which for the most part was directed at specific industries, the new regulation cut across traditional boundaries between industries to affect virtually all American businesses. For instance, while Congress in 1887 had directed the activities of the Interstate Commerce Commission toward the railroad industry, the Clean Air Act of 1970 was directed to all firms whose processes discharged pollutants into the air. Moreover, the older forms of regulation had left most business executives with very large areas of private discretion. Business executives had faced antitrust policies, and the Securities and Exchange Commission had governed the issuing of securities after 1934; but apart from the important areas of labor relations, governed by the National Labor Relations Board and the wages and hours laws of the New Deal, most manufacturing firms encountered little federal regulation. That situation was dramatically changed by the 1960s.

Business people complained vociferously about the impact of the new political environment. Traditional trade associations tried to protect the interests of their members, while the more widely based groups (the National Association of Manufacturers and the Chamber of Commerce, for example) tended to oppose all regulation as unwarranted intervention in the American system of private enterprise. Neither general opposition to regulation nor traditional means of political influence to protect particular interests seemed effective enough to executives of some of the nation's largest industrial firms, so they formed a new business political organization, the Business Roundtable, in 1972. Meeting quietly, and keeping full membership lists secret, the Business Roundtable practiced practical politics. Its strategy usually was to accept the goals of the new regulation but to argue that realism demanded substantial modifications of policy. Using a small lobbying force of the top executives of the largest industrial firms, the Roundtable became especially effective in the late 1970s. Business leaders helped Congress amend the air and water pollution laws, and the Roundtable successfully prevented the establishment of a consumer protection agency that reformers wanted as a further expansion of regulation. Members of the Roundtable also helped influence fiscal policy during the Carter administration, although they were unsuccessful in restraining budget deficits under President Reagan.

Deregulation

While new regulations stemming from concerns within the consumer-amenity society were appearing, there was a simultaneous movement to remove some of the more traditional forms of regulation that had begun in 1887. Beginning with the push for railroad regulation in the nineteenth century, some business firms and trade associations actively sought government assistance in reducing the potential destructiveness of competition and in adjudicating differences arising from firm size or regional location. To a considerable extent the movement for the regulation of business had been sparked by businesses themselves. The movement for deregulation, however, stemmed largely from the technical and theoretical concerns of the Council of Economic Advisers, expressed in their required annual report.

By the 1970s, social scientists were voicing discontent with existing regulatory practices. Basically, economists observed that regulatory agencies had institutionalized a "command-and-control" view of business activity in which expert bureaucrats determined the public interest and issued rules to control the behavior of corporations. Meanwhile, political scientists argued that regulatory agencies experienced a life cycle in which they may have begun as watchdogs of the public interest but soon were "captured" by the industries they sought to govern. Empirical observation of the regulation of transportation industries, and later of energy, communications, and financial industries, seemed to indicate that regulation failed to realize the public interest and instead resulted in a bureaucratic tangle that entwined private corporate interests, legislators, and the regulatory agencies in self-serving ways. To both the economists and the political scientists some system of decentralized decision making seemed desirable. They believed that government responsibility should be limited to establishing appropriate frameworks within which business executives, observing market opportunities, could make decisions on how best to serve the public most efficiently and at the lowest cost.

The views of the social scientists were intellectually, but not politically, powerful. However, when they were combined with policy needs as defined by elected officials, including the president and influential congressional leaders, a potent movement for deregulation developed. At first deregulation emerged as a body of ideas that seemed appropriate for certain ailing industries. President Richard Nixon and his successor, Gerald Ford, echoed the complaints of business that federal regulation imposed higher costs and therefore unwarranted burdens on consumers. Both presidents therefore sometimes resisted imposing new regulations on business. By the end of the 1970s, the control of inflation had become the first priority in the nation's economy policy. Seeking to slow inflation substantially without providing intolerably high levels of unemployment, President Carter turned to deregulation as a policy that would decrease business costs, restore the pressures of price competition on some firms, and thereby cut into the inflationary spiral.

Deregulating Transportation Industries

Transportation industries were the first to experience the full force of deregulation in the 1970s. The Airline Deregulation Act of 1978 led the way, soon followed in 1980 by the Rail Act and the Motor Carrier Act. Sometimes opposed by the business firms most directly affected, since such firms generally preferred the security that regulation offered, each of the laws tried to restore price competition and thereby lower costs to consumers. They allowed regulated industries more flexibility to adapt to changing market conditions and technologies, thus producing in the long run more efficient transportation services within the American economy.

The federal government, through the Civil Aeronautics Board (CAB), had regulated the airline industry since the 1930s. The CAB controlled both the fares that carriers could charge and the routes the airlines could fly. The original purpose of those restraints on competition was to encourage investors to develop the airline industry. By the 1970s, that objective seemed no longer valid. Instead, regulation appeared to provide an environment of safe capital investments, little managerial initiative, high wages for airline employees, and, of course, high costs for travelers. The growth of successful, low-cost intrastate carriers in California and Texas, operating outside of CAB rules, gave evidence that the American airline industry was inefficient and costly.

The reform of the airline industry began in 1976, when the CAB started to ease restrictions on routes and fares. Under the leadership of Alfred Kahn, an economics professor appointed chairman of the Civil Aeronautics Board in 1977, deregulation moved forward steadily. The airline companies, fearful that losses in route monopolies would endanger profits, and the airline unions, believing that deregulation would result in enormous pressures to reduce wages, resisted. Under Kahn's leadership, however, the CAB allowed more and more fare discounting and granted carriers entry into new markets. When the results of increased competition appeared to be better service at lower costs, while the airline companies continued to enjoy profits thanks to higher passenger traffic, Congress was won over. The Airline Deregulation Act of 1978 called for the dissolution of the CAB over a six-year period, with free entry of airline companies into routes of their choosing at fares to be determined by competition. The first major victory of deregulation had been won. Subsequently, competition forced rapid change in the airline industry's business structure. By 1988, six firms controlled 90 per cent of U.S. domestic air travel, and fares were rising.

After deregulating the airlines, Congress turned to trucks and railroads in 1980. Economists had complained that the regulation of the trucking industry since 1935 by the Interstate Commerce Commission had resulted in gross inefficiencies. The ICC had allowed the truckers to establish regional rate bureaus to fix prices, and the commission's regulations sometimes necessitated circuitous routing or required carriers to drive empty trucks on return trips. Regulations also prevented new firms from entering the business. Not only did prices to shippers seem to be high as a result, but regulations were costing the nation valuable fuel resources. In 1980, Congress responded to those arguments, presented by the Council of Economic Advisers and representatives of President Carter, by making it easier to enter the trucking business and allowing competitive forces to determine rates. After deregulation, some large trucking firms went bankrupt, while others, applying capital resources and managerial skills, captured the less-than-full-truckload business. The larger trucking firms increased their share of the industry's business under deregulation, and thousands of independently owned operators entered the field.

Similarly, the Rail Act of 1980 allowed rail executives much greater flexibility in charting the course of their firms. The railroads could now make separate contracts with individual shippers. They were allowed to adapt more fully to new technologies by loading containers or trailers on flatcars. Congress instructed the ICC to show more leniency in allowing mergers between rail firms, especially mergers that would improve operating efficiency, and between railroads, barge lines, and trucking companies. After passage of the new law, some of the largest railroads began to combine in an effort to provide more traffic sources that could now move over longer routes. Once, fear of the industry being dominated by a few huge firms had prevented mergers, but with trucking providing a competing mode of transportation, those fears now seemed unimportant.

Deregulation of Banking

The deregulation movement of the 1970s also profoundly affected the banking industry. Some economic experts and politicians became concerned in the 1970s about the rate at which capital was accumulating to meet the nation's business needs. In 1970, President Nixon expressed his worry over the low rate of "national savings" and their effective utilization, and he appointed a special presidential commission to recommend new policies. In 1973, it called for more competition in the banking industry in order to improve the efficiency by which savings were accumulated and capital transferred to borrowers. Then, as the inflation rate worsened during the decade, economists voiced concerns that banks were no longer able to attract savings under existing rules.

Before the 1970s, Congress had enacted legislation to encourage stability in the banking industry while at the same time preventing monopolies from forming. Some regulations of the 1930s, which had been a response to problems associated with the banks and the depression, were lifted. In the 1970s, with the advent of extraordinarily high inflation and new electronic technologies applicable to financial firms, pressures for change mounted. As securities firms began offering accounts paying savers high rates of interest, huge sums of capital flowed to them out of banks, thrifts, and insurance companies, all of which were hurt in their ability to make loans for new homes, factories, and machinery.

The Depository Institutions Deregulation and Monetary Control Act of 1980 reversed the earlier policy. With the new law, the federal government created a framework in which the three types of institutions could compete with one another for deposits and loans. Thrift institutions (savings-and-loan banks) could write loans on more than real-estate mortgages, and both they and the banks could raise interest rates paid to depositors. Banks began entering the securities business by offering brokerage services. Banking service charges for small depositors grew substantially under deregulation as banks tried to attract depositors with larger savings. The banking industry began a wave of mergers as larger institutions sought to do business with depositors as well as borrowers on a national basis.

Deregulation combined with economic circumstances to bring about unexpected and unwanted changes in the nation's savings-and-loan industry. Laws passed in 1980 and 1982 allowed the thrift institutions, which had traditionally made long-term loans to homeowners, to enter new fields. Seeking higher returns on their loans than could be obtained in the residential housing field, the savings-and-loan banks made real-estate development and construction loans, which carried a high degree of risk. Inexperienced in these fields, and sometimes engaging in fraudulent activities, savings-and-loan executives often found themselves overextended. The failure of federal government agencies to monitor the activities of the thrift institutions adequately made the problem worse. Cutbacks in regulatory staffs meant that no one was watching what the officers of the savings-and-loan institutions were doing. As a result, by 1989 some 500 of the nation's 3,000 savings-and-loan banks were insolvent, and Americans faced a bill of over $150 billion to bail them out.

Deregulating Communications

The deregulation of communications industries began in the 1980s, again under the belief that competition would ultimately result in greater efficiencies and lower costs for the consumer. In 1980, the Federal Communications Commission allowed the nation's largest firm, the American Telephone and Telegraph Company, to begin selling (as opposed to leasing) communications equipment to its customers. In 1981, the same agency began removing restraints on the operation of commercial radio stations, while Congress extended the life of television broadcast licenses from three to five years and reduced government surveillance of the broadcasters.

The 1982 antitrust agreement with AT&T, while technically not a deregulation, conformed to its general spirit. The antitrust tradition also involved a commitment to price competition among firms, exactly the situation deregulation was intended to obtain. The shakedown of the telecommunications industry following the breakup of AT&T saw it encountering competition from new rivals harnessing satellite and computer technologies. Meanwhile, as we have seen, AT&T was allowed to enter the computer business and began marketing those machines and linking them with telecommunications.

PUBLIC POLICY AND LABOR RELATIONS

Significant political events not only altered government-business relations after 1945, but they also changed relationships between labor unions and business corporations. Legislation passed in the1930s had granted workers the rights of collective bargaining. The National Labor Relations Act of 1935 combined with worker militancy to produce an industrial union movement that pressed management to make concessions in its traditional prerogatives of wages, hours, and work rules. By producing labor shortages and intense patriotic pressures for full production, World War II furthered the labor movement and made it a factor with which industrial managers had to deal, however grudgingly.

The Right to Manage

American business executives and their trade associations presented a united front on very few issues. New Deal labor policy was one such issue. The impact of the Wagner Act and of the militant upsurge of union sentiment that swept through factories in the 1930s cut across divisions of industry, firm size, and region that otherwise separated business executives. The union movement not only called into question the prevailing distribution of wealth in American society but threatened managerial prerogatives of the governance of firms according to business executives' definitions of self-interest.

The labor movement and its supporters in the federal government represented a pluralist vision of industrial democracy. Workers wanted more than higher wages. They sought a significant voice in determining the rules and pace of work. Especially during the full employment years of World War II, workers engaged in "wildcat" strikes that interrupted production schedules in order to affect industrial decisions in factories. On occasion, labor leaders even expressed an alternative vision of a socialist industrial system in which democratic processes determined basic managerial decisions, wealth was distributed more equally, and investment decisions were based on social goals rather than profit considerations. Although most national union leaders and government officials during the war cooperated to restrain worker radicalism, government agencies responsible for maintaining full war production sometimes enforced regulations on business that in effect partially removed management's exclusive privilege of operating its plants.

All of these trends affronted management's conception of its role in the industrial system. Most industrial executives thought that

416

they should be responsible for investment decisions, price and cost controls, production schedules, and work rules. When workers accepted employment in a factory, in management's view they agreed to abide by management's decisions, including the hours of work, the speeds at which machines and assembly lines operated, and the wages the firm paid.

In the eyes of corporate executives there were thus many problems with the federal government's labor policy as it developed after 1935. Although managers had succeeded in preserving their prerogative to employ whomever they chose by accepting the "maintenance of membership," or union-shop provisions of wartime labor policy, they still saw the unions as far too powerful and intrusive. Events immediately after the war reinforced their view. During 1945 and 1946, a time of reconversion to civilian production, the nation witnessed a record number of strikes involving more workers than ever before. A coal miner's strike threatened the country with cold homes and closed factories, while in the spring of 1946 the railroad workers threatened a general strike of that industry. The government's only recourse to protect the public interest was temporary nationalization of the vital industry. The railroad strike was settled while President Truman was in the process of asking Congress for authorization to draft the workers into the army so that he could order them to their jobs.

The strike during the reconversion period that most threatened corporate executives' right to manage occurred against General Motors. Led by Walter Reuther, the United Auto Workers asked for much more than wage concessions. Faced with the lifting of wartime price controls and the prospect of less than full production, the union sought to protect and augment workers' earnings in case of a recession. Reuther demanded a 30 per cent wage increase without compensatory automobile price increases. He demanded the right to inspect the corporation's books to demonstrate that it could pay higher wages from its profits and insisted on a contract that protected union security and improved workers' abilities to control their jobs. Reuther anticipated a victory over the world's largest industrial firm, believing that management would not wish to face a shutdown while its competitors were beginning to satisfy the pent-up demand for consumer goods.

General Motors won the strike, however, which involved almost 300,000 workers and lasted 113 days. The company resisted sharing corporate financial information with the union and insisted that "wages, hours of employment and other conditions of employment are the only matters which are subject to collective bargaining." Management claimed "sole responsibility" for the firm's affairs, including provisions for disciplining workers who violated their contract with General Motors. The company successfully confined the conflict with the union to strictly economic matters, granting wage increases well below Reuther's original demand and resisting public disclosure of the firm's decisions about prices and wages. After this victory, business executives in general sought to solidify the principle of managerial prerogatives with a general revision of the prevailing labor law, the National Labor Relations Act of 1935.

The Taft-Hartley Act of 1947

The National Association of Manufacturers, joined by the Business Council, the Chamber of Commerce, and many other trade associations, sparked an effort to revise the National Labor Relations Act of 1935. In so doing, business leaders adopted what they believed was a realistic position. The NAM and its supporting groups recognized that however undesirable unions and collective bargaining might be in principle, they had become deeply entrenched in American industrial society. The best course to follow thus seemed not the union-busting campaigns that had followed World War I but a reshaping of law to restrict union activities to the narrowest possible economic considerations while retarding future union growth.

In preparing the agenda for labor-law reform, the business associations emphasized the importance of the public interest in industrial disputes. The law, they insisted, should place management and labor or an equal footing; in their view, the Wagner Act and wartime government policies had tilted the law in favor of the workers. Industrial relations should take place in an orderly framework in which workers were bound to abide by contracts until they expired. Employers should not have to face jurisdictional disputes in which one union competed with another for workers. Finally, bargaining should never be conducted on an industry-wide basis, but only on a plant-by-plant or individual-firm basis unless employers agreed otherwise.

When Congress wrote the Taft-Hartley Act in 1947, it responded to the spirit, if not the specifics, of the business associations' agenda. This lengthy and complex law required union leaders to swear that they were not members of the Communist party, to account for their organization's finances, and to refrain from making political contributions. The law prohibited the closed shop but allowed the union shop, thereby preserving management's rights to hire whomever it chose. Unions had to provide a sixty-day notice before launching a strike, and the federal government, when it deemed that disputes were adversely affecting the public interest, could order striking workers to return to their jobs for eighty days while bargaining continued. To retard the further growth of unions, the new law allowed states to require the open shop with so-called right-to-work laws. Employers now enjoyed the right to use their resources to try to persuade workers not to participate in unions.

Because Congress had responded favorably to the desires of business to restrict union activity, business leaders generally applauded the Taft-Hartley Act. Union leaders, on the other hand, wanting a system of industrial relations in which workers could participate in shaping corporate policies directly affecting them, sought its repeal. John L. Lewis of the United Mine Workers even called the Taft-Hartley Act "the first ugly, savage thrust of Fascism in America."

Labor Relations After 1947

The passage of the Taft-Hartley Act had important political reverberations for business and labor alike. No longer did a common antilabor stance unite American business executives and their trade associations. Some large industrial firms withdrew from active participation in the National Association of Manufacturers as the business community split along lines of size, function, and region. For the unions the failure to win broader rights during the reconversion period combined with the effects of the new federal law to produce a situation of stagnation. In general, union membership began a period of long-term decline, falling from a peak of almost 36 per cent of the nonagricultural work force in 1945 to slightly more than 25 per cent in 1980. As industrial jobs relatively declined in number with changing economic trends, the government's labor policy made it difficult to establish unions in areas where they were not already powerful in 1947.

In the great manufacturing industries that had arisen with the Industrial Revolution, there were, of course, still many serious and bitter disputes between management and labor after 1947. A few firms were intransigent in resisting collective bargaining. But the general pattern of management behavior in dealing with labor was one of aggressive realism. Industrial executives accepted the power of unions but continued to be aggressive about restricting issues to workers' concerns about economic security. And as long as the economy was experiencing long-term growth, management was willing to concede higher wages, which firms could accommodate with automation and productivity growth or pass along to consumers through higher prices. In 1956, Ford Motors agreed to begin a supplemental unemployment-benefits program to soften the blow for laid-off workers during depressed business cycles, a policy that the unions extended to other firms in contract negotiations. Unions, meanwhile, found that to comply with federal regulations they had to employ specialized experts and improve systems of disciplining local leaders and rank-and-file members, practices that augmented tendencies toward bureaucratization.

PREPARING FOR THE FUTURE

In the forty years following World War II, significant changes occurred in the American political economy. Much that was traditional in federal policy toward business remained, but some long-standing attitudes toward regulation took on new forms. Government did little to affect the permanence of big businesses as institutions dominating the production of industrial wealth, even as those institutions themselves were changing with the emergence of multinational and conglomerate forms of organization. Even though big business remained a major feature of the American economic system, other organizations sometimes acted to counteract its power. The union movement, although it never achieved the stature envisioned by some of its founders, remained a significant force. Moreover, responding to newly expressed political impulses, the federal government began enacting the new regulations of the 1960s and 1970s and injected new complexities into the politics of business, the effects of which cannot yet be assessed. Nor was this the end of the matter, for the federal government also engaged in a policy of deregulation. Always complex, government-business relations became still more complicated, as developmental, regulatory, and deregulatory policies overlapped.

Selected Readings

Historians have only begun to explore the inner workings of the American political economy after 1945. No general treatments of either business history or political history focus on the main themes of their interaction during the period. There are, however, a number of significant if more limited studies.

For the relationships between business and federal fiscal policy, two studies stand out: Robert M. Collins, *The Business Response to Keynes, 1929–1964* (New York: Columbia University Press, 1981), and Kim McQuaid, *Big Business and Presidential Power, from FDR to Reagan* (New York: Morrow, 1982). The latter volume focuses on the Business Council, while the former includes much discussion of the Chamber of Commerce and the National Association of Manufacturers. Otis L. Graham, Jr., *Toward a Planned Society: From Roosevelt to Nixon* (New York: Oxford University Press, 1976), is a fascinating introduction to an important subject affecting the political economy.

For labor relations and federal policy, see Howell John Harris, *The Right to Manage: Industrial Relations Policies of American Business in the 1940s* (Madison, Wisc.: University of Wisconsin Press, 1982). Mark H. Rose, *Interstate: Express Highway Politics, 1941–1956* (Lawrence, Kans.: University Press of Kansas, 1979), provides a good analysis of a subject that directly affects everyone. Paul A. C. Koistinen, *The Military-Industrial Complex: A Historical Perspective* (New York: Praeger, 1980), is a collection of important essays. Robert Griffith, "Dwight D. Eisenhower and the Corporate Commonwealth," *American Historical Review* 87 (February 1982): 87–122, is an important addition to the literature of the political economy. For antitrust policy, Richard Hofstader, "What Happened to the Antitrust Movement?" in Earl F. Cheit, ed., *The Business Establishment* (New York: John Wiley & Sons, 1964), remains insightful.

For the environmental movement, Samuel P. Hays, *Beauty, Health, and Permanence: Environmental Politics in the United States, 1955–1985* (New York: Cambridge University Press, 1987), is encyclopedic. Peter Temin and Louis Galambos, *The Fall of the Bell System* (New York: Cambridge University Press, 1987), is a model study in recent history that explains the importance of ideology for understanding deregulation. Robert Reich and John Donahue, *New Deals: The Chrysler Revival and the American System* (New York: Times Books, 1985), is also revealing. Pietro S. Nivola, "The New Protectionism: U.S. Trade Policy in Historical Perspective," *Political Science Quarterly* 101, no. 4 (1986): 577–600, provides a good overview.

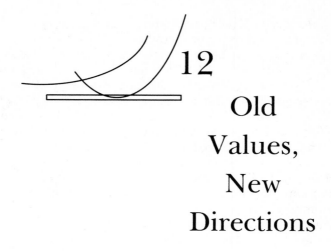

12
Old
Values,
New
Directions

By the last part of the twentieth century, American society and the American business system had changed remarkably from Francis J. Grund's time. America remained a civilization in which business values predominated, although the nation's business institutions and the complex web of entrepreneurial interactions that comprised its business system had fundamentally changed with new technologies and new opportunities. Some of the features of American civilization that the German immigrant had observed with so much approval—the entrepreneurial spirit, the profit motive, the orientation toward the future—remained, but many others had vanished. One hundred and fifty years after Grund published his remarks, there was less reason for optimism. Earlier generations had either built or enjoyed the world's highest standard of living; by the 1970s, the United States was no longer first in the world in per capita income.

The founders of the United States had agreed with Adam Smith that the purposes of political economy and the objectives of the business system were to provide wealth for the nation's citizens. On that basic point there was consensus, but heated disputes about the structure of that political economy and business system wracked the nation from its beginning into its third century. Those disputes continued in the 1980s as American leaders realized that their business system was not, in comparison with that of some other nations, providing goods and services as well as it could. The orientation of Americans may have shifted in the twentieth century from a producer outlook to a consumer-amenity outlook, but that shift did not mean that concerns with providing material plenty disappeared. If anything, they increased.

As the nation entered its third century, the concern about political economy revolved around two key propositions. One was that the federal government should become less involved in directing the behavior of business entrepreneurs and firms. The second was that federal officials should recall the nation's developmental tradition and embark on new policies of a considered, coordinated approach to the American political economy aimed at revitalizing firms and industries that were failing relative to their counterparts in other nations, and at stimulating new sorts of entrepreneurial activities.

BUSINESS VALUES AND AMERICAN SOCIETY

American leaders who sought new directions for the business system and the political economy seldom if ever questioned the business values that Grund and other observers had admired, although they recognized that both business institutions and the political economy had dramatically changed since the 1830s. "Free enterprise" and "market economy" remained catchwords in American rhetoric, even as the growth in the size of the firm and the concentration of capital in fewer and fewer hands lessened the impact of market forces on the production and distribution of goods and services and reduced the proportion of the citizenry that could hope to control directly the strategic and operational decisions of the giant firms. Despite these changes, American values remained staunchly capitalistic.

With the advent of the managerial revolution and the rise of big business, however, Americans developed a suspicion of business to accompany their admiration. In the love-hate relationship that began in the late nineteenth century and evolved thereafter, business remained at "the very soul of an American" insofar as the broader culture was concerned. Arguments for the determined and systematic use of government power to replace capitalism with some other system or to move investment decisions away from profit goals and toward broad social goals were, for the most part, not sustained and politically weak. Americans admired successful giant firms, and leaders in other walks of life sought to adapt business techniques to the control of other institutions. But some American leaders—and many citizens—also worried that individual business opportunities were diminishing and that the power of giant firms reduced the chances of the individual achieving autonomy, thereby endangering liberty and democracy itself. Such fears prompted the antitrust movement, among other matters.

Suspicions of Big Business

At the root of American suspicion of big business was the concern with individualism that advocates of democracy in the nineteenth century so highly prized. In that century, the entrepreneurs of the specialized firms interacted with one another through the invisible hand of the market. Those market forces were impersonal and un-affected by special privileges arising from either great wealth or old deferential, feudal customs, so it was thought; the market respected the autonomous individual and was therefore impartial and demo-cratic. However, with the managerial revolution and the efforts of business leaders to control the market through both illegal cartels and legal mergers, a concern arose that a private, self-selected elite of bankers and managers might unfairly and undemocratically dominate American life.

Those concerns led some politicians to seek to restore market forces through the antitrust laws. They also led to a rash of critical examinations of particular business firms and even of entire indus-tries in the early twentieth century, at the same time as the manage-rial revolution and the giant "trusts" were beginning to mature. The investigations were manifold, and some, most notably the ex-posé of the meat-packing business by Upton Sinclair, arose from a desire to persuade Americans to adopt socialism. Theodore Roosevelt, in fact, labeled the investigators muckrakers and admon-ished them to moderate their inquiries lest their stories promote the development of American radicalism and the rejection of capi-talism. Other investigations, however, arose from different con-cerns. One writer, Ida Tarbell, attacked the Standard Oil Company as an undesirable trust because she believed that a restoration of competition in the oil industry would better serve the nation. Other muckrakers revealed that big businesses enjoyed marketing powers that left individual consumers with little bargaining power, while the giant firms victimized the small merchants that were once a fixture in the American community. Dramatic examples of unscrupulous business practices titillated readers. Most damaging were accounts of the ways in which a few business people bribed public officials and manipulated political affairs contrary to American democratic ideals.

Muckraking as a cultural phenomenon flourished in the first years of the twentieth century only to die down by World War I. But some of the suspicions that muckrakers aroused remained, and many politicians supported significant regulatory measures as a result. A few consumer cooperatives emerged as well, in an effort to countervail the marketing power of the huge firms and to provide members with comparative information about complex products upon which they could make rational purchasing decisions. Moreover, investigative reporters continued from time to time to reveal unsavory business practices.

Public Relations and Business Values

Partly in reaction to the muckrakers' stories, American business developed new tools of public relations to promote and entrench business values during the twentieth century. Eventually, public relations developed as a business itself, closely tied to the advertising industry, or as an important part of corporation hierarchies, explaining the views of top executives and providing them with advice about the public image of their firms.

The emergence of public relations was directly related to the growth in size of the corporation. Executives at the head of large firms became removed from the scene of daily operations and could not give their personal attention to every aspect of the business. They turned to others to help them develop favorable attitudes toward their firms. Modern public relations began in the turn-of-the-century railroad industry, which as the nation's first big business was the first to face the problems of impersonal, bureaucratic management and of potentially hostile government regulation.

Public relations spread from the railroads to other firms. A principal function of public relations was to persuade Americans to accept the big business system of the twentieth century and thereby to ensure that business values continued to predominate in society. This persuasion took two main directions. One direction, fostered especially by the National Association of Manufacturers, was to "sell the American way of life to the American people." In the depths of the Great Depression of the 1930s, the greatest failure ever of the business system to provide wealth to the American people, some business leaders feared that Americans might turn to socialism. Those fears had a basis in fact, for voters supported political leaders, including President Franklin D. Roosevelt, who were willing to try alternatives to private investments in order to return the people to prosperity. Partly to avoid such an eventuality, business turned to public relations.

The production miracles of World War II did much to restore public faith in the business system, but the fact that the executives of the large corporations were a self-selected elite whose powers and privileges lay hidden from view accounted for the second main direction of public relations: to impress upon the public the notion that the large corporations were socially responsible. General Electric, for instance, used a slogan, "Progress is our most important product," and hired a Hollywood actor, Ronald Reagan, to promote the virtues of American capitalism. By the middle of the century, business was producing a great deal of public relations rhetoric praising the blessings of the material wealth while explaining that the corporations acted in the best interests of all Americans. Perhaps Charles E. Wilson, head of General Motors, best expressed this viewpoint to a congressional committee in 1952 when he said, "What is good for the country is good for General Motors, and what's good for General Motors is good for the country."

The public-relations campaigns undoubtedly contributed to the growing popular acceptance of the large corporations and helped make the anonymous executives who operated their bureaucracies more appealing figures. Big business required individuals to fit into the complex maze of organization charts, and big-business executives wielded power through committees and other group activities. The large-scale organization did not seem to reward the individualism Americans traditionally admired, but public-relations efforts helped the public adjust to the institutional realities of big business. Public-relations campaigns were, in part, efforts to sanction the power of the small numbers of men, relative to the general population, who controlled a growing share of manufacturing and other capital assets.

Still the very existence of public relations gave evidence of a tension between business and a democratic governmental system. In the early years of the Republic, American leaders had viewed the independent entrepreneur, whether in control of a farm or a small

Charles E. Wilson (left), the former head of General Motors, was the secretary of defense under President Dwight D. Eisenhower (right) in the 1950s. In a public statement, Wilson equated the prosperity of General Motors with progress for the American people. Wilson's view was prevalent among many U.S. business leaders in the post–World War II period. (UPI/Bettmann Newsphotos)

specialized firm, as the bastion of liberty. As the individual entrepreneur declined in importance in the nation's business system after 1850, however, the link between democracy and capitalism broke down as it became apparent that government had to play some role in business.

PROBLEMS IN THE AMERICAN BUSINESS SYSTEM

Sustained threats to big business and the private elite that controlled the corporations never materialized in the United States. Unlike every other advanced industrial society, America did not have a socialist movement that ever approached achieving national political power. Instead, the growth of wealth, however unevenly divided among the population, meant that growing numbers of Americans, except in times of depression, were able to enjoy abundance. Along with the business values so widely held among Americans, the effectiveness of the business system in providing employment and consumer goods forestalled radical threats. Potential problems loomed, however, when abundance began to shrink slightly in the 1970s and investment decisions no longer appeared to augment the wealth of Americans as much as in the past. Americans retained their business values and were persuaded to accept big business, but they also began to experience important changes, mostly relating to a new international business environment.

In the latter part of the twentieth century, the business system faced problems that some executives, politicians, and economists worried were endemic, presenting the nation with long-term adjustments. In the 1940s, publicists glibly spoke of the "American century," but by the 1970s, U.S. firms no longer led the world in many important fields. Economic growth slowed, and per capita income actually declined slightly, just as Americans experienced high rates of inflation. In 1970, no European nation had a personal income higher than that in the United States, but by 1979, nine European nations, and by 1986 Japan, had surpassed the United States. In many industries, foreign firms—especially Japanese—captured important markets.

The New International Business Environment

The success of Japanese and other foreign firms in the 1970s indicated that American business had entered a new phase of its history. In the eighteenth century, entrepreneurs found their most lucrative opportunities in overseas commerce. Not until the domestic market developed in the nineteenth century did their focus turn inward. By the end of the nineteenth century, the success of American enterprise made the United States the wealthiest nation in the world. After World War II, foreign trade once again began accounting for a significant share of American wealth. By 1985, exports and imports comprised a sum equal to 20 per cent of the GNP.

American business executives and government leaders had deliberately fostered this postwar international business environment. Government leaders sought economic development abroad as part

The Talbots chain of women's clothing stores was purchased in 1988 by a Japanese firm, JUSCO, making it another in the lengthening list of U.S. firms owned by foreign companies. (Talbots)

of a long-range strategy of persuading the peoples of other nations to reject alliances with the Soviet Union. Business executives, eager to seize profitable opportunities wherever they found them, developed a worldwide outlook and used American capital to construct multinational firms. U.S. leaders expected to dominate this developing interdependent worldwide business system.

The new international business environment began to haunt Americans after 1970, however, and expectations of U.S. leadership in the world's business affairs began to fade. Two trends seemed especially important in this regard. First, as the Industrial Revolution spread into Asia and Latin America, American-led multinational firms exported capital abroad to take advantage of cheaper foreign raw materials and wages. By the 1980s, for instance, clothing was being cut in China, sewn in Indonesia, and sold in U.S. stores, while American textile mills lay idle and some American clothing workers were either unemployed or reduced to poverty-level wages. Second, foreign entrepreneurs were able to take advantage of the international business environment and to penetrate the American business system. Foreign-based multinational firms were seizing positions in domestic U.S. manufacturing and retailing, a process that at the end of the 1980s was abetted by the relatively low value of the U.S. dollar and the need of the federal government to borrow unprecedented sums of money. In 1988 alone, a Canadian firm purchased American department stores and became the third-largest retailer in the United States, and a Japanese firm purchased the venerable Firestone firm to assume second place in the U.S. tire industry. Such actions worried some Americans, who feared that the nation was losing control over its economic destiny.

Finally, the dream of the "American century" faded in part because some foreign entrepreneurs proved more adept than their American competitors. Japanese business, which had embarked on a vigorous rebuilding program after the devastation of World War II, led the way. The Japanese realized that the economic health of their small island-nation depended on its being able to produce exports competitive in world markets. After 1950, Japanese firms began to gain world leadership in field after field. The success of Japanese business made Japan the third-wealthiest nation by the 1970s, even though it had to import virtually all its raw materials. Other nations experienced similar business successes, and by 1988, the trade deficit—the gap between imports and exports—of the United States was $137 billion. In contrast, Japan reported a trade surplus with the United States alone of over $50 billion.

Steel: A Case Study of a Changing International Business

The steel industry exemplifies the new international business environment faced by Americans in the latter part of the twentieth century. Ironmaking had been an important business in America since colonial times, and steel became the symbol of the nineteenth-century Industrial Revolution. By pioneering the managerial revolution in industrial production, Andrew Carnegie built the world's largest, most profitable steel firm by the end of the nineteenth century, and U.S. firms continued to dominate the world's steel industry well into the twentieth century. American producers paid the highest wages, had the lowest costs, and were the largest exporters in world markets. After 1950, however, American steel companies lost their leading role. By 1979, these firms produced only 16 per cent of the world's steel, and foreign producers were successfully marketing large amounts of steel in the United States. By the end of the 1970s, leading Japanese steel mills enjoyed a 30 to 35 per cent cost advantage over their American competitors in the production of flat-rolled steel products; and in 1984, as the American economy recovered from a deep recession, foreign firms captured 26 per cent of America's domestic steel market. The decline of American steel production seemed to symbolize the decline in the industrial prowess of U.S. firms in general.

The Japanese advantage in steel resulted from their shrewd investment decisions and focus on gaining export business. Japanese steelmakers initially enjoyed advantageous labor costs, although by 1979 Japanese labor costs were about 70 per cent of their American competitors'. Far more important to the industry were the Japanese advantages in plants. Japanese entrepreneurs invested in new large-scale facilities that took advantage of the most advanced technologies. By 1978, Japan had fourteen of the world's largest modern blast furnaces, whereas the United States had none. Located at seaports, the Japanese blast furnaces were able to receive high-quality, low-cost ore and coal carried cheaply in ships. All these advantages allowed the Japanese to export 40 million metric tons of steel in 1978, including 7.5 million metric tons to the United States. In the same year American firms exported only 3 million metric tons altogether.

Apparently, American steel executives had lost sight of the principles that had originally made their industry the world's leader. Carnegie had succeeded by giving unremitting attention to reducing costs. He had insisted on introducing the latest technology, whatever the capital costs. Carnegie was always willing to incur capital expenses that seemed to promise long-term gains. For instance, he expended large sums of capital to shift from the Bessemer to the open-hearth process in the late nineteenth century. He had also recognized the economies of scale, that the "hard driving" (high-volume production) of large efficient blast furnaces and finishing mills resulted in the lowest costs. Carnegie also kept track of the changing market for steel and of his rival firms. Steel executives of the 1950s through the 1970s, in contrast, invested in only one completely new plant, Bethlehem Steel's facility at Burns Harbor, Indiana. All other investments were to add onto existing facilities or were intended to provide quick returns by reducing bottlenecks in the mills rather than providing entirely new efficient facilities. In the long run, some investments were self-defeating, because they left entire plants uncompetitive.

American business executives were more interested in short-term profits than their Japanese competitors. They realized that if they

The steel industry's decline, symbolized here by a nearly inactive mill, hit certain communities especially hard. The Pittsburgh area, once the center of basic steel manufacture, had lost most of its mills by the end of the 1980s. (Thomas Craig/The Picture Cube)

kept their firms' capitalization relatively low, earnings would appear to be a more impressive percentage of assets than if larger sums went into modern, efficient plants. The Japanese steel industry increased its assets over 23 per cent a year between 1966 and 1972, while its American competitors increased their assets 4 per cent annually in the same period. The five largest Japanese firms averaged a 1.8 per cent return on assets while the eight largest U.S. companies showed a 3.8 per cent return. In the long term, the Japanese executives gained superior facilities as a result of their patience. American steel executives in the 1970s spoke confidently of their firms' health, while they failed to be fully informed of what was happening in rival firms in foreign countries.

American steel executives made different investment decisions than their Japanese counterparts in part because they expected the market for steel products to enable them to increase profits, even with relatively antiquated plants. In 1973, the International Iron and Steel Institute forecast a worldwide demand in 1980 for over 1 billion tons of steel. This large market, it was predicted, would make even the inefficient American plants profitable. The forecast, however, was wrong; by the early 1980s, in the depths of the worst downturn in the business cycle since the Great Depression, there was a glut of steel on the world market. (In 1979, Americans purchased 113 million tons of steel, but in 1982 they bought only 78 million tons.) Japanese and other foreign producers captured larger shares of the shrunken market because their furnaces and mills were efficient. The American steel industry fell into deep trouble.

Steel executives used mixed strategies to respond to the decline of their industry. Firms closed older and less efficient factories and laid off workers permanently. The American steel industry slashed its capacity from 160 million tons in 1977 to just over 120 million tons in 1986. United States Steel, which lost $1.5 billion in 1982 and 1983, cut the number of its steelworkers from 93,000 in 1981 to 49,000 in 1983. Steel executives also sought mergers of the large firms to allow the sharing of efficient facilities and to enable them to obtain a firmer hold on special parts of the market for finished steel goods. In 1984, LTV consummated its merger strategy by adding Republic Steel to its other holdings, thereby becoming the second largest steelmaker in the United States. Japanese firms also pursued their own merger strategies, purchasing significant interests in U.S. firms. A 1984 deal between National Steel and Nippon Kokan gave the American firm a fresh infusion of capital and access to the latest technology and gave the Japanese company a firm foothold in the U.S. market. Other American steel executives hoped for similar arrangements that would allow them to take advantage of foreign resources in supplying the American market for steel. Even United States Steel negotiated to import slab steel from foreign producers to finish in its rolling mills.

While American steel companies were pursuing these survival strategies of joint ventures, mergers, and internal reductions, steel executives also looked to diversification to improve their firms' profits. David M. Roderick, the chairman of United States Steel, aggressively turned his firm into a diversified conglomerate. In 1982, United States Steel purchased the Marathon Oil Company for $6.5 billion and began to earn large profits in the oil and gas business. Under Roderick's leadership, United States Steel began investing in other manufacturing, production, and real-estate ventures. By 1983, only 25 per cent of United States Steel's assets lay in steelmaking, which generated only 31 per cent of the firm's sales; 53 per cent of its sales were in oil and gas. In 1986, the firm reflected its status as a diversified holding company by changing its name to USX. United States Steel's diversification strategy, maintained by USX, resulted from an awareness that as the American economy grew spectacularly after 1950, the relative importance of steel declined steadily, partly for technological reasons. Manufacturers purchased less steel, using other metals, plastics, ceramics, and concrete. Meanwhile, in 1986, diversification into steel forced LTV, second only to USX in the industry, into the largest industrial bankruptcy in the nation's history.

By the 1980s, the most successful steel firms in the United States were the so-called mini-mills. These mini-mills were smaller firms with low management and capital costs that usually produced steel only for a regional market. For example, Raritan River Steel in New Jersey began in 1980 to produce wire steel rods, which it sold to manufacturers of spark plugs, springs, fences, and even coat hangers. Raritan Steel profitably sold its product for about $300 per ton, while the large integrated firms like United States Steel faced costs of about $450 per ton. In fact, in 1984 United States Steel decided to abandon the wire rod market to its smaller mini-mill competitors, which by then had captured over 20 per cent of the domestic steel market. Executives of the large integrated steel firms tried to shift their resources into the production of higher-valued specialty steels as one strategy of restoring profits to their firms.

The Political Economy of Steel

As the steel executives tried different business tactics in hopes of finding new entrepreneurial opportunities, they also sought assistance from the government in protecting them from foreign competition. The industry—along with its trade association, the American Iron and Steel Institute, and the United Steelworkers union—engaged in a public-relations campaign, explaining that the ills that beset it were caused by unfair foreign actions. The industry tried to persuade federal officials to impose new restrictions, either quotas or tariffs, on the importation of foreign steel.

This protectionist campaign was, to a considerable extent, successful. In 1984, when foreign producers had captured 26 per cent of the American steel market, U.S. officials reached agreements with foreign producers for voluntary restrictions on their exports to the United States—in an attempt to cut the foreign share of the American market to 20 per cent. Helped by the falling value of the dollar, which, together with efficiency gains in U.S. mills, made American steel more competitive in world markets, in 1987 foreign steel fell to a 21 per cent share of the U.S. market. In 1988, with the dollar still a depressed currency, U.S. steel planned to revive its export trade.

INTO THE FUTURE

The steel industry's quest for protection from foreign competition was symptomatic of problems that beset American business in general in the latter decades of the twentieth century. On the one hand, protecting U.S. steel producers from foreign competition preserved jobs for American workers. On the other hand, the higher costs of American-made steel raised price levels for the manufacturing firms that consumed steel, especially for automobiles and appliances. Protecting the U.S. steel industry had the effect of hurting the international and domestic competitiveness of other important American industries. This dilemma, so clear in the case of steel, was also true in other areas. The problem led to considerable discussion among U.S. leaders about the need for a revitalization of American business.

As the nation entered the last decade of the twentieth century, Americans expressed considerable consensus favoring a new direction in political economy—that policies must rest on the business values of capitalism, allowing individuals to seek and grasp entrepreneurial opportunities. There was little agreement about particulars, however. Echoes of older debates reverberated. Two centuries after the acrimony between Hamilton and Jefferson, there were still cries for protecting American businesses and their workers from foreign competition (as shown in the case of steel), and still open questions about the extent to which federal policy should foster domestic manufacturing. Opponents of protection argued, in language more modern than Hamilton's, that the best future lay in the international trade that protectionism would only dampen. Some business and political leaders believed that deregulation would foster desirable opportunities and allow Americans to adapt to changing economic conditions, less fettered by traditional policies consciously guarding the commonweal. Other Americans were less certain, fearful that deregulation had placed some people and firms at the mercy of large suppliers or customers and that it had even endangered lives by allowing—because of competitive pressures—reductions in expenditures for important safety and service considerations.

In the 1990s, it is clear that another generation of Americans faces the uncertainties of historical change. Businessmen, businesswomen, workers, consumers, government officials—indeed, all Americans—face new challenges as the twentieth century comes to a close. The nation and its business system are entering a still-

This scene might have made Henry Ford stare in amazement, and then again, perhaps not. As manufacturing becomes more and more automated with the use of robots and requires fewer workers, service industries are becoming a larger part of American business enterprise. (General Motors Corporation)

unnamed postindustrial era, and fundamental changes are occurring all around us. Most employment opportunities are now found in service, not manufacturing, industries. Manufacturing industries remain important to the overall health of the economy, but the production of goods in many cases requires a less intensive use of labor. Robots are replacing humans in repetitive factory jobs in some key industries.

Just as the changes wrought by the Industrial Revolution were unclear to the entrepreneurs who initiated it, the government officials who encouraged it, and the business managers who consolidated it, so too are the changes in the business system and the larger society being wrought by postindustrial conditions not fully clear. What is clear, however, is that Americans still have faith in their business system and still venerate the successful entrepreneur, whether he or she gains that success in new venturesome small firms or in large-scale corporations. As they try to reach ever-higher levels of material abundance for themselves and their children,

Americans demonstrate again that they have not forsaken their tradition of valuing the individual, the entrepreneur, and the profit motive.

Selected Readings

For an understanding of how management, labor, and government officials interacted regarding the steel industry in the twentieth century, Paul A. Tiffany, *The Decline of American Steel* (New York: Oxford University Press, 1988), and John P. Hoerr, *And the Wolf Finally Came: The Decline of the American Steel Industry* (Pittsburgh: University of Pittsburgh Press, 1988), are valuable.

Index